Table of Contents

Introduction

There could be any number of reasons that you picked up this book. Maybe you've become curious about genealogy after watching a television show. Perhaps you've always been interested, but you didn't have the time to pursue it until now. Possibly, you're a student with a project to complete on your family history. No matter what the reason, you probably need some help getting started, and we're here to help!

The amount of available family history resources has skyrocketed in the 19 years since we wrote the first edition of this book (boy, are we getting old!). This is an exciting time because scanned images of key records are coming online at an unprecedented rate. Also, technologies such as DNA testing have been refined and are now invaluable tools that complement evidence from paper records.

Although the technology and amount of material available has changed over the years, you still need a solid foundation for your research. We've written *Genealogy For Dummies* to give you the necessary resources and advice to balance online sources and DNA evidence with traditional research to ensure you are successful every step of the way.

If you're a repeat reader of *Genealogy For Dummies* (previous editions were known as *Genealogy Online For Dummies*), we think you'll be pleased to find all sorts of new and updated information, including how to use social networking for family history purposes and expanded coverage of DNA testing methods. And, if you're brand new to genealogy, we think you'll be equally pleased with the easy-to-understand directions and information about the resources that await you.

At this point, we feel obligated to give you a couple of warnings or reminders. First, genealogy is an addictive pursuit and a long journey. You might find yourself staying up all hours of the night chasing down that elusive ancestor. Please don't blame us if you start falling asleep at work due to your genealogical research routine. Also, on a more serious note, keep in mind that online research and DNA testing are merely two tools among others for finding information about your family. To thoroughly research your genealogy, you must use a number of tools — many of which we talk about throughout this book.

Now that the disclaimers are out of the way, put the kids to bed, let your pets out, and boot up that computer. Your ancestors are just waiting to be found!

About This Book

If you type in the word *genealogy* into a popular search engine like Google, you'll see millions upon millions of pages that mention the subject. In fact, at the time we wrote this, such a search returned 151,000,000 results. With so many choices, it's impossible to know where to start without a map. That's what this book is all about. Although we don't cover every available resource, we do point you toward the sites and technologies that give you the best chance for researching many different family lines.

You're probably asking yourself how this book differs from the many other genealogy books on the shelf. Some books tell you only the traditional methods of genealogical research that have you traveling hundreds of miles to visit courthouses and archives in other states. Unfortunately, these books neglect the many opportunities that online research and new technologies provide. Other books that do cover online genealogy tend to group resources by how users access them (all link-based sites are listed together, all subscription sites are listed together, and so on), rather than telling you how you can integrate the many online resources to achieve your genealogical goal. As genealogists, we understand that researchers don't conduct searches by trying all the link sites, then all the subscription sites. We search by looking for people or places anywhere we can find.

Web addresses (or URLs) throughout the book are in a `different font` to set them apart from regular text. This way, you can easily see the sites we recommend that you visit to try something or read more online. Additionally, to make it easier for you to follow a set of specific instructions, when you should type something, **bold type** indicates what to type.

Foolish Assumptions

In writing and revising this book, we made a few assumptions. If you fit one of these assumptions, this book is for you:

>> You're psyched up and ready to jump into researching your family history with both feet.

>> You have at least a little computer experience, are now interested in pursuing your family tree, and want to know where and how to start.

>> You have a little experience in genealogy and some experience with computers, but you want to find out how to put them together.

>> You're an experienced genealogist or family historian and you're looking for ways to make your research more efficient.

You can have a lot of computer experience and be a novice to genealogy or online genealogy and still benefit from this book. In this case, you may want to dive right into the chapters about strategies for finding online resources.

Icons Used in This Book

To help you get the most out of this book, we created some icons that tell you at a glance whether a section or paragraph has important information of a particular kind.

REMEMBER

The Remember icon marks important genealogical stuff, so don't forget it.

TIP

When you see the Tip icon, you know we're offering advice or shortcuts to make researching easier.

WARNING

Look out! The Warning icon indicates something tricky or unusual to watch for.

Beyond the Book

In addition to what you're reading right now, this product also comes with a free access-anywhere Cheat Sheet that includes a description of how to use Helm's Genealogy Toolbox as well as discussions of genealogy myths, charts, and forms, among other things. To get this Cheat Sheet, simply go to www.dummies.com and enter **Genealogy For Dummies Cheat Sheet** in the Search box.

Where to Go from Here

Depending on where you're reading this introduction, your next step is one of the following:

>> You need to go to the front of the bookstore and pay for this book so that you can take it home and use it.

>> If you've already bought the book and you're at home (or wherever), you can go ahead and start reading in depth, following the steps for the online activities in the book as they come along.

We don't expect you to read this book from cover to cover, in the order we wrote it. It definitely doesn't hurt our feelings knowing you may skip through the sections looking for only the information that you're interested in at a particular moment! Each section in each chapter can stand alone. If we think something relevant in another section can supplement your knowledge on a specific topic, we provide a note or reference telling you the other place(s) we think you should look. However, we tried hard to do this referencing in a manner that isn't obnoxious to those of you who choose to read the book from cover to cover. We hope we've succeeded in addressing both types of readers!

Now that we've explained a bit about the book, are you ready to get started and to become an official genealogist? You might be asking yourself, "What are the requirements for becoming an official genealogist?" You simply need an interest in your ancestry and a willingness to devote time to pursuing information and documents. It's time to dive in and start collecting the puzzle pieces of your family history and remember to have fun!

1
Getting Started with Genealogy

IN THIS PART . . .

Learn how to use information that you know about yourself to create a timeline of your life.

Discover how items around the house can jump-start your genealogical journey.

Locate large collections of records that you can use to find details on the lives of your ancestors.

Learn how census records can be used to track the movements of your ancestors every ten years.

Discover how you can use primary sources to find the details of your ancestors' lives.

Chapter **1**

Beginning Your Ancestral Journey

R eady to dive into your family history? We certainly hope so! The best way to learn how to research is to jump right into it. We help you find the resources you need to be successful along the way.

If you're new to genealogy, we strongly suggest that you begin your journey with this chapter. (That's why we made it Chapter 1.) In this chapter, we walk you through the basics of recording genealogical data by starting with a very familiar person — you! We explore different methods of recording your research so you can see which way is best for you. Also, throughout the chapter, we provide some tried-and-true advice to keep you out of genealogical "hot water" in the future.

It's About Time(line)

TIP

Late one night, you decide to start looking for information on your great-great-grandfather Absalom Looney. After booting up your computer and connecting to the Internet, you put good old Absalom's name into your favorite search engine. Within a couple of seconds, a page appears telling you there are more than 51,000 results for Absalom Looney. How can you possibly sift through all the Absaloms onscreen and find the one you're looking for? Well, before you go any further, we should let you in on a little secret: Instead of starting your journey with Absalom, it's better to begin with the information you have about someone you know better — yourself.

Regardless of what your spouse thinks, we're convinced that you know you best! You know your birth date, place of birth, parents' names, and where you've lived. (We recognize that not everyone knows all this information; adoptions or other circumstances may require you to do the best you can with what you know until you can discover additional information about yourself.) Knowing some things about yourself, it's time to start recording the events of your life and to start learning the good research skills that help you delve into the lives of others. An easy way to see your life at a glance is with a *timeline*. A timeline is a simple way to show the events of your life chronologically.

When working on your timeline, we recommend beginning with current events and working back through your life. This is the method you'll likely use when researching an ancestor. First, note the basics: the dates you were married, started a job, or moved to your current house or apartment. Then move back to your last residence, occupation, and so on until you arrive at your birth date. Make sure you include milestones such as children's birth dates, marriage dates, military service dates, educational experience, religious events, participation in organizations and sports, and other significant events in your life. If you prefer, you can cover your life by beginning with your birth and working forward to the present. Either way is fine, as long as you list all the important events.

You have several ways to store your timeline. Some people prefer to start with index cards, placing one event on each card. If you want to use a digital tool, you can store notes in a product such as Evernote (www.evernote.com) or Microsoft's OneNote (www.onenote.com). Of course, there are products specifically designed to help you create a timeline. If you are somewhat computer savvy and like to keep your timeline on your computer, you can use products such as Timeline Maker Pro (www.timelinemaker.com) or Tiki-Toki (www.tiki-toki.com/desktopapp). In the next section, we walk you through the use of an online timeline resource made specifically for genealogists.

REMEMBER

The timeline that you create now becomes an important research tool for your descendants who decide to conduct research about you in the future. So, when you have the time, turn that timeline into a full-blown autobiography. This way, your descendants not only know the facts about your life, but also gain some insight as to why you chose the paths you did throughout your life.

Crafting an online timeline

If you're looking for an online way to create a family history timeline, then Twile (https://twile.com) may be the answer. Twile allows you to put events and photographs on a timeline, including the details that might give context to the event, such as the location of the event, who was present, and so on. You can share your timeline with other members of the family and view a growing collection of historical timelines to see what events were going on at the same time as the events in your life (or your ancestors' lives).

Twile permits you to add unlimited milestones and photos and allows you to import information from a GEDCOM file (see Chapter 14 for more on GEDCOM) and from the FamilySearch website (we talk more about FamilySearch later in this chapter). Also, it allows you to share your timeline with the family. When you are a member of Twile, you will receive emails asking questions that prompt you to add other memories to your timeline.

To begin your free timeline on Twile, follow these steps:

1. **Point your browser to** https://twile.com/.

2. **Click the green Get Started button in the center of the resulting page, *or* click the green Register button in the top-right corner.**

   Either path allows you to register for free.

3. **Fill out the personal information form, including your first and last name, email address, and password.**

   You can sign in using your Facebook account, if you have one and if you prefer to have the two applications linked. Also, make sure you read the terms and privacy policy so you know how your information will be used.

4. **Click the Sign Up button.**

   A page appears asking how you would like to start your timeline.

5. **Select Create a New Timeline.**

   A page appears to walk you through adding your first milestone — your birth.

6. **Select your birth day, month, and year from the drop-down boxes. Check the appropriate box for your gender. You can optionally add your maiden name (if you select the female gender) and a photo of yourself. When finished, click the green Next button.**

   A new page appears with questions about your father.

7. **Fill in your father's name and birthdate, and indicate whether he is deceased. Then click the green Next button.**

If you click on the Deceased? box, the date of death information appears. Also, if you prefer not to enter information on your father, you can click the Skip for Now link at the bottom of the page.

You guessed it: After submitting this page, you are taken to a page about your mother.

8. **Fill in your mother's name, birthdate, and maiden name, and indicate whether she is deceased (and enter date of death, if applicable). Then click the green Next button.**

You can also choose not to enter this information by clicking the Skip for Now link. A new page appears asking about the wedding of your parents.

9. **Enter the date of your parent's wedding using the drop-down boxes and click the green Finish button.**

If you don't know the date or prefer not to enter it, simply click the Skip for Now link. You are taken to the timeline page displaying the milestones that you just entered, with a pop-up window asking whether you'd like to take a look at the milestones you've entered so far.

10. **Click on the green Take a Look button to view your timeline.**

The timeline looks similar to the example in Figure 1-1. You may also see a message under the Add button prompting you to click it to add more milestones.

11. **Click the Add button and select to Add a Milestone.**

Twile walks you through the process of adding a milestone. For example, you might wish you add a significant birthday, your marriage information, or emigration information.

12. **Click on the green Next button.**

Twile updates your timeline.

Within a milestone, Twile gives you the ability to add extra information, such as location, photographs, and documents related to the milestone. For example, for the marriage milestone you can add information on the reception venue, best men, bridesmaids, and ushers. Be sure to use the words and documents features to provide evidence of the event and to cite your sources. To reach these features, try the following:

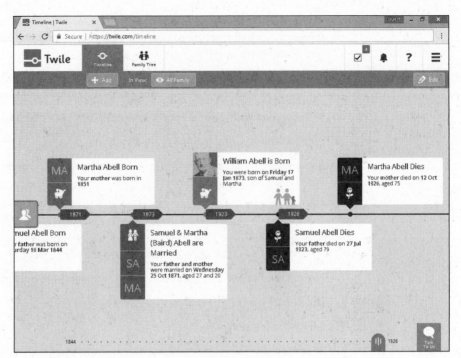

FIGURE 1-1:
The Twile
timeline.

1. **From the Timeline view, click on a milestone.**

   If you are not already on the Timeline view, click the Timeline button in the upper-left corner of the screen. On the Timeline page, the milestones appear above and below the timeline. For example, if you entered your birthdate, a milestone titled [Your Name] Born should appear. Grab your birth certificate and click anywhere on the milestone to see the pop-up box with further information.

   Before going any further — if you are concerned about privacy, please take a quick look at the last paragraph of this section — or use the information from the birth certificate of a relative who is deceased.

2. **Select Add Birth Weight from the Extra Information section.**

   The Extra Information section is located on the left side of the screen. A pop-up box with pounds and ounces fields appears. The birth certificate probably contains your birth weight, so feel free to enter it.

3. **Enter your birth weight in the two fields and click on the green Save button.**

   The weight now appears in the Extra Information section.

4. **If you have a baby picture of yourself that you want to include, click on the Photos button.**

   The Photos button appears on the right side of the screen under the title Add Something. After clicking on the Photos button, a dialog box appears.

5. **Select a photo on your computer to upload and click the Open button.**

   When it has uploaded, the photo appears on the screen.

6. **If you would like to add anecdotal information about your birth, click the Words button.**

   The Words button appears on the right side of the screen under the title Add Something. A pop-up box appears asking you to add a memory or comment. You might want to add a story your mother told you about the day you were born, or provide information on historical events from that day.

7. **Enter a memory or comment and click the green Save button.**

   The memory or comment appears on the page.

8. **Select the Document button.**

   To add a copy of the birth certificate as evidence of the event, click the Document button. A dialog box appears.

9. **Select a document on your computer to upload and click the Open button.**

   When it has uploaded, the document appears on the screen.

10. **Click the Add a Location button.**

    The Add a Location button appears on the right side of the screen under the Add Something box. After you click it, a pop-up box appears.

11. **Type a location into the box and click on a location match.**

    As you begin typing, Twile tries to match a location to the text you're typing. When a match appears, click on it. A map of the location then appears on the page. An example of a completed page appears in Figure 1-2.

You can choose to share milestones from Twile on Facebook. There are a lot of other features within Twile. We encourage you to experiment with adding and editing milestones to learn them.

WARNING

Please keep in mind that the information you are entering is being stored online in another location. Although Twile does its best to secure all the information uploaded on its site, it's still a good idea to carefully read the Privacy Policy. If you are concerned about privacy, consider only posting information that you wouldn't mind other people seeing if it were inadvertently disclosed.

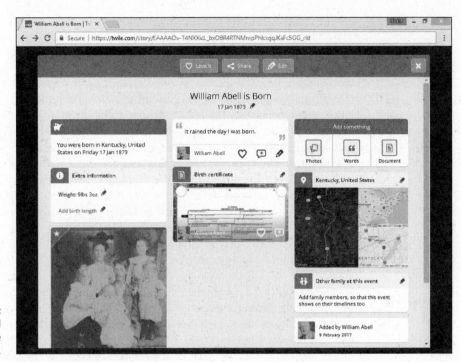

FIGURE 1-2:
A completed
milestone
information page.

Learning about Sources

As we just talked about using your birth certificate as evidence in the last section, now is a good time to talk about using sources in your family history research.

If you're like most people, you think you know a lot about yourself. If we ask you what your birthday is, you can tell us without batting an eye. But how do you know the birth date? You were obviously there, but you weren't in a condition to be a reliable witness, given that you were a newborn and most likely not fully aware of what was going on. This is where primary sources come in handy. Most likely, witnesses were present who helped create a record of the event.

Primary sources are documents, oral accounts — if the account is made soon after the actual event and witnessed by the person who created the account — photographs, or any other items created at the time of an event. Some primary sources include birth and marriage certificates, deeds, leases, diplomas or certificates of degree, military records, and tax records.

For example, a primary source for your birth date is your birth certificate. Typically, a birth certificate is prepared within a few days of the actual event and is signed by one or more witnesses to the birth.

The timeliness and involvement of direct witnesses makes the information contained on the record (such as the time, date, and parents' names) a reliable first-hand account of the event. It's important to recognize that just because a record was prepared near the time of an event doesn't mean that every fact on the record is correct. Typographical errors can occur or incorrect information can be provided to the creator of the record. Often, these errors are not caught when the record is created. For example, in the case of a birth certificate, new parents are preoccupied with things other than government paperwork during their stay at the hospital. When our youngest child was born, the birth certificate application was created and presented to us for signature. After reading it, we discovered three pieces of incorrect data. Fortunately, we were able to correct the birth certificate before it was submitted to the county clerk — even though the hospital clerk wasn't too happy about re-creating the document multiple times. So, it's always a good idea to try to find other primary records that can corroborate the information found in any record.

Secondary sources are documents, oral accounts, and records that are created some length of time after the event or for which information is supplied by someone who wasn't an eyewitness to the event. A secondary source can also be a person who was an eyewitness to the event but recalls it after significant time passes. You might encounter records such as a Delayed Report of Birth or an affidavit that contain a birth date that is based upon a person's recollection of when a birth occurred. Some of these records may have a witness who testifies that a birth occurred thirty years earlier.

Some records may be considered both primary and secondary sources. For example, a death certificate contains both primary and secondary source information. The primary source information includes the death date and cause of death. These facts are primary because the certificate was prepared around the time of death, and the information is usually provided by the medical professional who pronounced the person dead. The secondary source includes the birth date and place of birth of the deceased individual. These details are secondary because the certificate was issued at a time significantly later than the birth (assuming that the birth and death dates are at least a few years apart).

Secondary sources don't have the degree of reliability of primary sources. Often, secondary source information, such as birth data found on death certificates, is provided by an individual's children or descendants who may or may not know the exact date or place of birth and who may be providing information during a stressful situation. Given the lesser reliability of secondary sources, we recommend corroborating your secondary sources with reliable primary sources whenever possible.

REMEMBER

Although secondary sources are not as reliable as primary sources, that doesn't mean secondary sources are always wrong or aren't useful. A good deal of the time, the information is correct, and such records provide valuable clues to locating primary source information. For example, in the case of a birth date and birthplace on a death certificate, the information provides a place and approximate timeframe you can use as a starting point when you search for a birth record.

You can familiarize yourself with using primary sources by collecting some records that document the milestones that you created in Twile in the previous section. Try to match primary sources for each event in your timeline. If you can't locate primary source documents for each event in your life, don't fret! If you remember an event and provide details about it on the timeline, it can serve as a primary source document — because you write it about yourself.

For additional information on primary sources, see Using Primary Sources at the Library of Congress website for teachers at www.loc.gov/teachers/usingprimarysources.

We should also mention *tertiary sources*. Tertiary sources are compilations of primary and secondary sources, such as articles found online or in encyclopedias or almanacs.

For comparisons of primary, secondary, and tertiary sources, and examples of each, see James Cook University's overview of primary, secondary, and tertiary sources at http://libguides.jcu.edu.au/scholarlysources.

Or check out William Madison Randall Library's guide for identifying primary, secondary, and tertiary sources at https://library.uncw.edu/guides/primary_secondary_and_tertiary_sources.

For strategies on using primary sources online, see the Reference and User Services Association (of the American Library Association) page at www.ala.org/rusa/sections/history/resources/primarysources.

Using Genealogical Applications

You can use an online timeline to document your life (as described in the It's About Time(line) section earlier in this chapter), but a full-featured option is to use a tool of the genealogy trade from the beginning — a genealogical application. Over time, you'll collect a lot of information on your ancestors. You need something to help you keep everything straight and make sense of it all. Not only can a genealogical application keep track of the names, dates, and places of your ancestors, but it can also show you the gaps in your research and point you where to go next.

Nowadays, you encounter two different flavors of genealogical applications — those installed on your personal computer and those available on online family trees. Each type of application has pros and cons, so over the course of the rest of the chapter, we look at both types to illustrate them. Of course, you don't have to pick one or the other — you could be like us and use both kinds at the same time!

Both types of applications can store and manipulate your genealogical information. They typically have some standard features in common. For instance, most serve as containers for family facts and stories, have some reporting functions to see the data contained within them, and have export capabilities so that you can share your data with other family historians (or with another application). Each application may have a few unique features that make it stand out from the others. For example, one might have the capability to take information out of the application and generate online reports at the click of a button or integrate with data stored on subscription genealogical websites. Here's a list of some simple features to look for when evaluating applications:

>> **How easy to use is the application?** Is it reasonably intuitive how and where to enter particular facts about an ancestor?

>> **Does the application generate a view of its data so that you can take the next step in your research?** For instance, if you're partial to Family Group Sheets, does this application display information in that style?

>> **Does the application allow you to export and import a GEDCOM file? What other formats does it export to?** *GEDCOM* is a file format that's widely used for genealogical research. For more info about GEDCOM, see the sidebar in Chapter 14 titled "GEDCOM: The Genealogist's Standard."

>> **What are the limitations of the application?** Make sure the application can hold an adequate number of names, documents, and photographs (and accompanying data) to accommodate all the ancestors about whom you have information.

Keep in mind that your genealogy continues to grow over time.

REMEMBER

>> **Can your current computer system support this application?** If the requirements of the application cause your computer to crash every time you use it, you won't get very far in your genealogical research.

>> **Does this application provide fields for citing your sources and keeping notes?** Including information about the sources you use to gather your data — with the actual facts, if possible — is an important and a sound genealogical practice. Take a look at the section "Learning about Sources," earlier in this chapter, for more information about the importance of citing sources and understanding how to do so.

>> **Does this application have features that warn you of incorrect or incomplete data?** For example, some applications check the place-name that you enter against a database of locations and suggest a standard way of spelling the location.

>> **Does the application integrate with genealogical websites?** Integrating content between websites and genealogical software is an easy way to build your genealogical database, as well as to share your findings with others.

WARNING

When importing information from genealogical websites directly into your application, keep in mind that you need to take the extra step to verify the information and attach sources to the imported information. Some sites do not attempt to verify the information they contain, and without proper vetting you may download incorrect data.

Entering Information into RootsMagic Essentials

To help you get a better idea of how genealogical software installed on your personal computer can help you organize your records and research, and to help you figure out what features to look for in particular software packages, this section examines how to use RootsMagic, a popular genealogy program.

You can download a free trial version of RootsMagic Essentials software and install it on your computer:

1. Open your web browser and go to the RootsMagic site at www.
rootsmagic.com/Products.

2. Scroll down to the RootsMagic Essentials section and click the Free Download button.

3. Complete the information fields, including your name and email address. Enter your email address again in the Verify E-mail field shown in Figure 1-3.

4. Select the checkbox if you want to receive emails from RootsMagic.

5. Click Download.

The instructions for downloading the product appear. Be sure to click on the correct version for your computer's operating system. There are two versions — one for Windows and the other for Mac.

FIGURE 1-3:
Information fields
for the Roots-
Magic install.

6. **Click the RootsMagic Essentials Installer link.**

The software downloads to a directory on your computer.

7. **To begin the installation, double-click the downloaded file.**

When we installed it, the filename was RM7Setup.exe. The RootsMagic Setup
wizard pops up with a license agreement.

8. **Read through the licensing agreement. If you agree to its terms, click the
I Accept the Agreement option and then click Next.**

In the window that appears, choose where to have the RootsMagic Essentials
software stored on your computer.

9. **Identify where to store the application and then click Next.**

The Select Start Menu Folder field appears. This enables you to identify where
to put shortcuts for the program. The default location is a folder called
RootsMagic 7.

10. **If you want the shortcuts listed in RootsMagic 7, leave the default
location in the field. If you prefer to have shortcuts in another folder,
browse and select the folder or enter the location.**

11. **Click Next.**

The Select Additional Tasks window opens. If you want to set up any additional tasks (such as creating a desktop icon for the program or downloading a place database for geocoding and gazetteer components), select the appropriate checkbox.

12. **Click Next.**

The final information for the installation appears.

13. **Review the installation information and, if everything looks correct, click Install.**

When the software has finished installing, the Completing the RootsMagic Setup Wizard box appears.

14. **If you want to open RootsMagic now, select the Launch RootsMagic checkbox and click the Finish button.**

A window opens welcoming you to the software and asking you to identify which version of the product you're opening.

15. **Click the RootsMagic Essentials — Free Version link.**

Now that you have the RootsMagic Essentials software installed on your computer, let's get down to the nitty-gritty and start entering data. When you open the application for the very first time, you get a RootsMagic News window containing links to various announcements and stories of interest to RootsMagic users. If you want to read any of these, you can click the links; otherwise, just click Close.

When the RootsMagic News box closes, you see a Welcome to RootsMagic screen. To begin your family tree, follow these steps:

1. **Click Create a New File.**

A box appears, enabling you to do several things:

- Identify the new filename.

- Determine the location for the file.

- Set options, including the date format for the file, whether to display a number after a name, whether to display surnames in all capital letters, and whether to set up and support some additional fields for the Latter-day Saints and FamilySearch family tree support.

- Choose whether to start a file from scratch or import data from another program.

2. Enter the new filename in the New File Name box, set any of the optional formatting items, and identify whether you're starting a new file or importing an existing one; then click OK.

In our case, we're starting a family tree for the Abell family, so we entered **Abell** as the filename. We set the date format and selected the option for starting a new file.

3. Click OK.

The database is created and the Pedigree view opens, as shown in Figure 1-4.

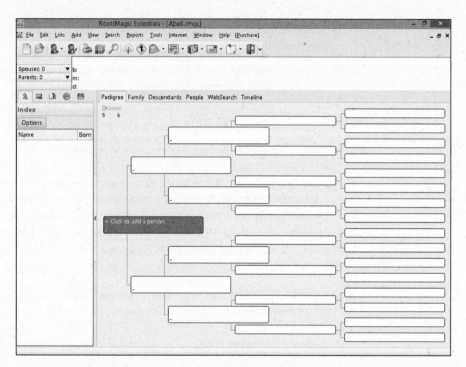

FIGURE 1-4:
The Pedigree tab.

You can start entering information about yourself in the Pedigree page (presuming that you choose to start with yourself). Then you can add information for four additional generations.

Completing the Pedigree Page

Usually, it's easiest to enter information about yourself, your spouse, and your children, and then work backward through your parents, grandparents, great-grandparents, and so on. After you complete your direct lines back as far as you can, enter information about each of your siblings, nieces and nephews, cousins, and other relatives. Always enter as much information as you can in each of the fields in the Add Person dialog boxes. Follow these steps to fill in the Pedigree page:

1. **Select the Click to Add a Person box in the Pedigree page.**

   The Add New Person dialog box appears, and then you can fill in details about yourself or an ancestor.

2. **Complete the Add New Person box and click OK.**

   Type the first and middle names in the Given Name(s) field and the last name in the Surname field. Then complete the remaining fields to the extent that you know the biographical facts about that person. Remember to use your maiden name if you're female — regardless of your marital status. Of course, we want to set a good example in this book when it comes to privacy for living relatives, so rather than typing information about one of us, we type in Matthew's great-grandfather, William Henry Abell.

   After you click OK, the Edit Person dialog box appears.

3. **Complete the Edit Person dialog box and click Save.**

   You can add more facts about yourself or an ancestor by clicking these buttons in the Edit window — Notes, Sources, Media, and Address. You can also add or delete facts by clicking the appropriate button and then following the prompts in the Fact Types box that appears. After you finish adding the details, click Save.

REMEMBER

   Make sure that you use the four-digit year when you enter dates in RootsMagic. If you inadvertently use only two numerals for the year, the software accepts the year as is, leaving it ambiguous for anyone who references your database in the future.

4. **Click Close.**

After you've entered your first person, you can click the next person box you want to complete or click the Add People to the Database icon on the toolbar and enter information for people related to the individual, such as spouse, children, and parents. You can keep track of family units by clicking the Family tab. We add more people to RootsMagic and discuss how to source information in Chapter 2.

Creating the Virtual You

If you're going to be researching using a variety of computers, you may prefer to use an online family tree rather than an application stored on one computer. Several companies have created online family tree applications, including Ancestry.com (http://trees.ancestry.com), My Heritage (www.myheritage.com), and Find-mypast (https://www.findmypast.com/family-tree). To give you a taste of what online family trees can offer, we look here at one full-featured application at Ancestry.com. In this application, not only can you enter genealogical information, but you can also upload media files and integrate your data with the content found on the Ancestry.com subscription site through the Hints function.

To get started, try the following:

1. **Point your web browser to** http://trees.ancestry.com/.

   The Ancestry.com online family tree page appears.

2. **Near the top of the page, enter your first name and last name, select your gender, age and a person to search for (father or mother), and click Start Your Tree.**

   A new page appears labeled Father's Information.

3. **Type in as much information as you know and click on the Search for Records button.**

   The searchable information includes first and last name, birth year and place, and the names of his father and mother. You can choose to enter additional information by selecting grandparent information from the drop-down box. When you click the Search for Records button, a pop-up box appears asking you to provide your email address to register.

4. **Enter your email address and click on the Save & View button.**

   The searchable information includes first and last name, birth year and place, and the names of his father and mother. The resulting page shows the search results for your father, as well as notifies you that your family tree has been saved and login information emailed to you. Certain items are marked with Preview buttons indicating that a subscription is required. Other items have a View button showing that it is free content.

5. **Click Trees in the black menu bar.**

   The menu bar is located at the top of the page next to the Ancestry logo.

6. **Click on the [Your Name] Family Tree.**

   The resulting page shows a three-generation ancestor view with you as the first person at the bottom; see Figure 1-5.

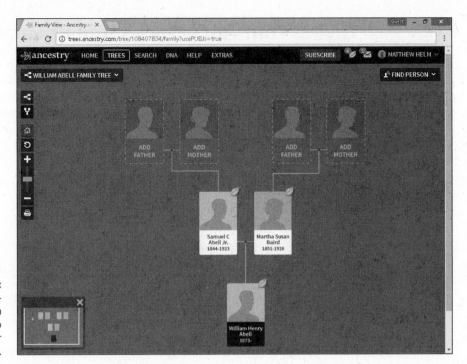

FIGURE 1-5:
A three-generation ancestor view to fill in with your ancestors.

7. Add the name of a family member to the tree by clicking the Add Father link or the Add Mother link.

In the pop-over box that appears, enter the first and middle names, maiden (or last) name, gender, birth date, birthplace, and, if applicable, death date and death place. A *pop-over box* is similar to a dialog box except that you must complete its fields and click a button to make it disappear. When you begin to enter a location in the Birthplace field, a list of potential matching locations appears beneath the field. You can select from the list to enter the information more quickly. You can also use this list to standardize the location that makes searches easier in the Ancestry.com database.

8. Click Save.

The new individual now appears on the family tree. If there is information on the individual in the Ancestry.com database, a shaky leaf will appear.

9. Click the leaf symbol to see the hint. When you finish reading the hint, click the gray Return to Tree box.

TIP

After clicking the leaf symbol, click on the Ancestry hints button in the upper-right corner of the pop-over box (next to the large leaf). Not every individual triggers a hint, so don't be concerned if you don't see one. If you follow a hint that leads to part of the paid subscription database, the site prompts you to subscribe to the Ancestry.com site.

Giving Your Ancestors Some Privacy

WARNING

Now that you have started your family tree, you might consider privatizing it — at least until you are comfortable with opening it up to the public. Keep in mind that by default the online family tree on Ancestry.com is set to be viewed by the public. This means that unless you make it private, the content you place there can be searched and read by anyone. To make your online family tree private (meaning that no one can view your tree without your permission), walk through these steps:

1. **Click on the Trees menu item on the Ancestry.com page.**

A drop-down box appears with the name of your online family tree and the option to Create & Manage Trees. You can find the Trees link in the black navigation bar at the top of the page.

2. **Select the Create & Manage Trees option from the drop-down box.**

A page appears with a list of online family trees associated with your account.

3. **Click the Manage Tree link under the name of your online family tree.**

The Tree Settings page opens.

4. **Choose Privacy Settings from the menu.**

The menu options are located just under the Tree Settings heading. You will find Privacy Settings between the Tree Info and Sharing menu options.

5. **Click on the Private Tree radio button and then the Save Changes button.**

You also have the option to prevent your tree from being found in searches. That means that no one will know to contact you to request access to see your online family tree.

Beefing Up Your Profile

Just like your ancestors' lives, your life is a lot more than just names and dates. To get a better picture of you, or your ancestor's life, you need to include details about important events such as marriages, buying a house, starting a new job, moving to a new town, and so on. To add some facts, try the following:

1. **If your family tree isn't onscreen, place the mouse cursor over the Trees menu item at the top of the Ancestry.com home page. A secondary menu drops down showing the family tree you created. Click the family tree name to display your family tree.**

Your family tree is displayed with the Pedigree page.

2. **Place the mouse cursor over the name of a person on your family tree and click on the box.**

A pop-over box appears with more information about the person on your family tree.

3. **Select Profile.**

You may encounter a pop-over box with more information about the Facts view. You can click on the Next and Explore Your Family Story buttons if you are interested in reading the hints, otherwise click on the "x" button in the top right corner of the pop-over box. Several tabs are available on the Facts screen: Lifestory, Facts, Gallery, and Hints. The Facts tab, shown in Figure 1-6, shows a summary of facts, sources, and family members associated with the person. The Facts page contains some basic facts that you already entered, such as birth and death.

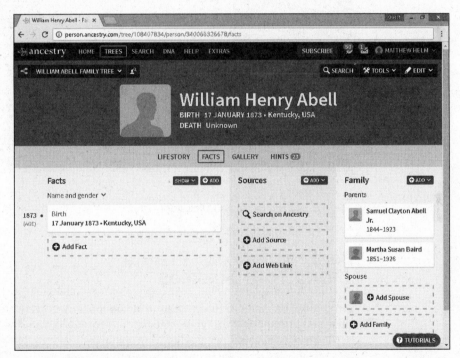

FIGURE 1-6:
The Facts tab.

4. **Click the Add a Fact link in the dotted box in the left column of the screen (under the Facts column).**

The Add a New Fact or Event pop-over box appears.

5. **Select the event type from the drop-down box, as shown in Figure 1-7.**

One or more fields appear on the page depending on the event that you selected.

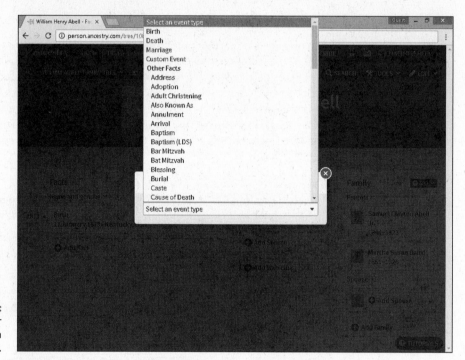

FIGURE 1-7:
The Add Fact or Event drop-down box.

6. **Fill out the fields and click Add.**

The information that you entered now appears in the Facts column.

Citing Your Sources

A *source* is any material (book, document, record, or periodical, for example) that provides information for your research — for more information on sources see Learning about Sources earlier in this chapter. We strongly encourage you to cite the sources of all facts and information that you enter into profiles on your family tree.

TIP

Keeping track of sources helps you remember where you discovered the information and helps other researchers retrace your steps. If you find conflicting information later, returning to the source can help you sort out the reliability of your information.

Follow these steps to cite a source for a fact you've added to your tree:

1. **Display the profile page for the person you want to cite a source for.**

Follow Steps 1 through 3 in the earlier section "Beefing Up Your Profile."

2. **Click the Add Source link.**

The link is located in the dotted box in the middle column under Sources. The Create Source Citation Information page appears, as shown in Figure 1-8.

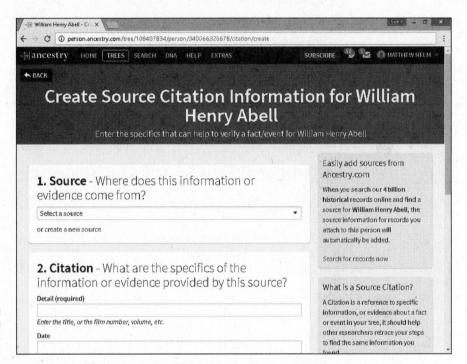

FIGURE 1-8:
Create Source
Citation
Information page.

3. **Click the Create a New Source link under Step 1 onscreen.**

The link appears just below the Select a Source drop-down box. The Create a New Source page appears.

4. **Fill out fields for the source of the information.**

You don't have to fill out all fields. The only required field is Title.

5. **Near the bottom of the page, click the Create a New Repository link.**

A *repository* is a place that holds the source you're citing, such as a library or a person's house, in the case of the location of family photos. The Create a New Repository page appears.

6. **Fill out the fields to describe the repository. When you're finished, click the Save Repository button to save the repository and return to the Create a New Source page.**

Note that after you've created a repository once, it's then available for you to use in future citations.

7. **Click the Save Source button.**

The source title is now reflected in the drop-down box under Step 1 on the Create Source Citation Information page.

8. **Complete the fields under the Citation portion of the source (Step 2 on the Create Source Citation Information page).**

The Detail field is the only required field in this section.

9. **Under Step 3 on the Create Source Citation Information page, select the box next to the fact or event that you want the source to document.**

10. **Click the Submit button.**

Getting the Full Media Experience

To provide a rich experience for your sources, consider adding media. For example, you can scan a birth record of an ancestor and add the image of the actual record as part of your source citation.

Follow these steps to add media to your Ancestry.com family tree:

1. **Display your family tree and open the personal profile to which you want to add media.**

2. **Click the Gallery tab.**

3. **Click the Upload Media image in the middle of the screen.**

The Upload Media page appears.

4. **Click the Content Submission Agreement link.**

We think it is always a good idea to read the submission agreement so that you know the terms and limitations of posting content to the Ancestry.com site. Click the back arrow on your web browser to return to the Upload Media screen.

5. **Drag the photo that you want to upload onto the dotted box labeled Drag or click here to upload.**

Alternatively, you can click on the green Choose Files button that launches a dialog box and select a file. While the files are uploading, the progress bar appears on your screen. After the upload is complete, the photo appears, along with some fields to fill out including Title and Details.

TIP

To select multiple files to upload at the same time, hold down the Ctrl key in Windows or the Command key on a Mac.

6. **Replace the title of the image in the Title field.**

The Title field must be filled in. The default title is the filename of the imported image. The filename isn't always a descriptive title, so feel free to make the name more meaningful.

7. **Change the media type in the drop-down box (under Details).**

8. **Fill in the Date, Place, and Description fields if you have this information.**

9. **If you want to attach media to additional people in your family tree, click the Add link and enter the person's name in the box that appears.**

For example, if you want to attach a photo of a family to each of the people in the photo who are included in your family tree, attach the photo to the names of the appropriate individuals.

TIP

When you begin typing, the name begins to fill in based on the people in your family tree.

10. **Click the Done button.**

The photo shows up as a thumbnail image in the Gallery.

TIP

You can add the photo to a Fact entry by clicking the Facts link in the menu bar, selecting the fact, and clicking on the Edit link in the upper-right corner of the fact box. Then select the Media link in the left column of the pop-over box. Click the plus button next to the photo to add it to the fact.

Reaching Out to Others

At some point, you might decide to make your research results available to the public. To clarify some information that you put into the database, you might want to create a comment about a particular ancestor.

It's important to know that comments placed on records of living individuals will not be viewable to the public unless you specifically give permission for others to see living individuals in your tree.

To post a comment:

1. **Display your family tree in Pedigree page, and then open the personal profile to which you want to add a comment.**

2. **Select the Tools drop-down box in the upper-right corner of the screen (between the Search and Edit boxes).**

3. **Click View Comments.**

4. **Type your comment in the box and click the Submit button.**

Hinting Around about Your Ancestors

A special function in the online family tree is the Ancestry Hint. Ancestry Hints are designed to search through the names that you enter and match them to records available on the Ancestry.com website. Even if you don't have an Ancestry.com subscription, you can use the Hints to point you to record sets that you may be able to find in other repositories.

To see what Hints might offer for an ancestor, follow these steps:

1. **Display your family tree and then open the personal profile for which you want to review Hints.**

2. **Click the Hints tab.**

   The Hints page shown in Figure 1-9 appears, listing record sources that contain a potential match with your ancestor:

   • The first column is the name of the record source.

   • The second column contains information about the particular record containing your ancestor's name. Note that this column doesn't provide all the information that might be contained within the record; however, it gives you an idea of the type of information that matched the record with your ancestor.

3. **Click the Review Hint button to take a closer look at the record.**

   If you have a subscription to Ancestry.com, you see more information about the record. If you don't have a subscription, you see a splash page that advertises membership and explains how to start a free, two-week trial.

4. **If the Hint isn't valid for your ancestor, click the Ignore Hint link.**

TIP

Ignoring the Hint doesn't delete it from the profile. The Hint is moved to the Ignored Hints page, where you can review it again by clicking the Ignored Hints link.

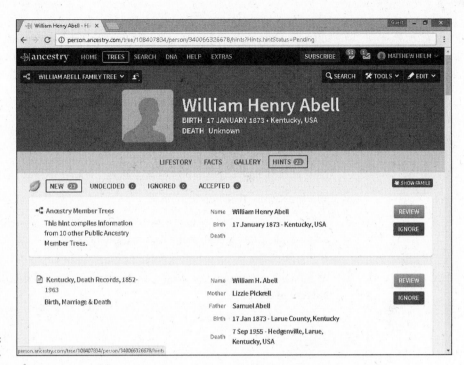

FIGURE 1-9:
The Hints page.

Giving Your Ancestors Some Mobility

If you're one of those people who are always on the go, and always need to access your family history, perhaps a good solution for you is a genealogy app. *App* is short for *application*, and typically can run on your smartphone or tablet. Apps on the market generally come in three flavors — free companions to genealogical software packages such as RootsMagic, apps that view online family trees, and apps that you enter data into through the app itself.

With the free Family Tree app from FamilySearch, you can build a new family tree directly in the app or you can link to an online family tree that you've already started on the FamilySearch website.

WARNING

When entering information and attaching memories in the Family Tree app, keep in mind that you are contributing to a public database — a database that can be seen by millions of people and that will be preserved in the FamilySearch vaults "forever."

The Family Tree app is available on the Apple App Store and Google Play.

The following steps show how to use the Family Tree app to add information to your family tree in an iPad. Although these steps apply specifically to an iPad, using the app on another type of device is similar.

1. **Turn on your iPad and locate the Family Tree app icon.**

   The icon has a white background with FamilySearch logo (a tree with leaves in the shape of boxes). If you haven't downloaded and installed the app on your iPad before, use the instructions that came with the device to find and download the app from the iTunes App Store.

2. **Tap the Family Tree app icon once.**

   A page appears explaining that information added in the app is contributing to a single public family tree, that hints are used for finding records, and you can save memories.

3. **After swiping through the three introduction pages, tap Done at the bottom of the page.**

   A What Is New box appears.

4. **Tap OK.**

   A login screen appears.

5. **Tap Create Account.**

   Type in your first and last name, username, and password (twice).

6. **Tap Continue.**

   Enter an email address or a mobile number to recover the account, should you forget your username or password.

7. **Tap Continue.**

   Type a contact name (that everyone will see), gender, country, birth date, and whether you are a member of the Church of Jesus Christ of Latter-day Saints. Enter the letters in the picture (to ensure you are not a computer filling out the form) and check the box agreeing to the terms and privacy policy (after reading them).

8. **Tap Create an Account.**

   A box appears requesting a verification code. If you put in an email address, check your email. If you typed a cell phone number, check your phone for the code.

9. **Enter the verification code and tap Verify.**

   If the code was correct, you see a new button marked OK, I'm Done.

10. Tap the OK, I'm Done button.

A sign-in page appears.

11. Close out the window and return to the Family Tree app.

Type in the username and password you just created.

12. Tap Sign In button.

The Pedigree page appears with a box containing your name and two boxes above it representing your parents. (See Figure 1-10.)

13. Tap the box with your name on it.

The person page appears with the information that you have already entered when you registered. You can elect to enter information on your spouse and parents by clicking on the appropriate menu item.

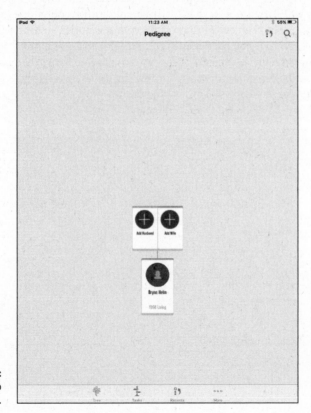

Telling Your Story

Family historians can be very good at telling the stories of their ancestors. If you have ever been to a family reunion and were "trapped" by one, you know what we mean. However, sometimes they forget to document their own lives — leaving a hole for their descendants. For example, not long after Matthew's mother passed away, Matthew was sorting through her papers and discovered elaborate time-lines of events from the lives of his mother's parents and siblings, but nothing on herself. Although he could piece together some items from the other timelines, there was still a significant void because she didn't tell her own story.

Now you might think that your story is boring and no one would want to hear it. But family historians sometimes wonder why a person made a certain decision or are interested in first-hand accounts of events that happened in the past. There are some applications for your computer, such as Personal Historian (www.rootsmagic. com/Personal-Historian), that assist you in writing your story. You can also find apps for your phone or tablet that record your memories — for example, Memories by FamilySearch. If you need some prompting to write your story, why not partici-pate in the #52Stories project (https://familysearch.org/blog/en/52stories). The goal of the project is for you to write a story every week for a year, so that at the end of the year you have 52 stories of your life.

Chapter **2**

Hunting for Your Ancestral Treasures

t's likely that one of the reasons you are reading this book is to learn how to record the history of your ancestors. In Chapter 1, we gave you some practical experience in documenting your life. This chapter presents skills for documenting the lives of your ancestors.

A Brief Message about Research Steps

We know you are eager to find the juicy details of your ancestors' lives and we don't want to slow you down. However, it is important to understand a little about how to research before jumping in head first. To help, we introduce a few ideas here, and then, in your spare time, you can read Chapter 13 for more information on the research cycle.

To ensure you are getting the most out of your research and you don't have to backtrack and research things again, it is a good idea to follow a research plan. We've come up with the Helm Online Family Tree Research Cycle to help you along the path. The Cycle contains six basic steps — planning, collecting, researching, consolidating, validating, and distilling. We cover each of these areas over the course of the book. In this chapter, we focus on the areas of planning and collecting.

Selecting a Person to Begin Your Search

Before you can get very far in your research, you need to take the first crucial step in planning — selecting a person to research. Selecting a person sounds easy, doesn't it? Just choose your great-great-grandfather's name, and you're off to the races. But what if your great-great-grandfather's name was John Smith? You may encounter millions of sites with information on John Smith — unless you know some facts about the John Smith you're looking for, we can guarantee you'll have a frustrating time online.

Trying a semi-unique name

The first time you research online, start with a person whose name is, for lack of a better term, semi-unique. By this we mean a person with a name that doesn't take up ten pages in your local phone book but is still common enough that you can find some information on it the first time you conduct a search. If you're really brave, you can begin with someone with a common surname such as Smith or Jones, but you'll have to do a lot more groundwork upfront before you can determine whether any of your findings relate to your ancestor.

Also, consider variations in spelling that your ancestor's name may have. Often, you can find more information on the mainstream spelling of his or her surname than on one of its rarer variants. For example, if you research someone with the surname Helme, you may have better luck finding information under the spellings *Helm* or *Helms.* If your family members immigrated to the United States in the last two centuries, they may have *Americanized* their surname. Families often Americanized their names so they would be more easily pronounced in English; sometimes the surname was simply misspelled and subsequently adopted by the family.

TIP

For more information on name variations, check out the Name Variations in the United States Indexes and Records page at FamilySearch:

https://familysearch.org/wiki/en/Name_Variations_in_United_States_Indexes_and_Records

Narrowing your starting point

If you aren't sure how popular a name is, try visiting a site with surname distribution maps. The Forebears website has a database for the meaning and distribution of 11 million surnames. Here's what to do:

1. **Open your browser and go to Forebears search site** (`http://forebears.co.uk/surnames`).

   The site appears with a search form at the top.

2. **Type the surname you're researching in the Enter a Surname field.**

   As you type, the site will suggest surnames. You can click on the drop-down list after you find a match for the surname you are using.

3. **Click Search.**

   The color surname distribution map appears as in Figure 2-1. The surname is more frequent in areas colored in deep blue. The tables at the bottom of the page provide more details on the surname.

FIGURE 2-1:
A distribution map for the surname Helm.

4. **To get a closer look at a particular area, click the country on the map. The regional level appears (for selected countries).**

   Figure 2-2 shows the frequency of the Helm surname in the United States in 2014. For some countries, you can change the date on the map through the date drop-down box located just above the map.

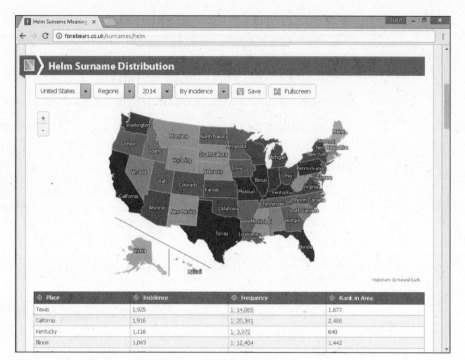

Place	Incidence	Frequency	Rank in Area
Texas	1,925	1: 14,065	1,877
California	1,916	1: 20,341	2,466
Kentucky	1,116	1: 3,972	640
Illinois	1,043	1: 12,404	1,442

FIGURE 2-2:
The regional view of the Helm surname.

TIP

A good reason to check out distribution maps is that you can use them to identify potential geographic areas where you can look for your family during the years covered by the site. If we hit a wall and can't find additional information online about a specific individual or the surname, we know we can start looking at records in these areas to find more clues about families with the name. We hope that by doing so, we'll find our branch. For a list of surname distribution sites by country see the Surname Distribution Maps article at https://familysearch.org/wiki/en/Surname_Distribution_Maps.

Choosing someone you know about

In addition to choosing a person you're likely to have success researching, you want to use a person you already know something about. The more details that you know about a person, the more successful your initial search is likely to be.

For example, Matthew used his great-grandfather William Abell because he knew more about that side of his family. His grandmother once mentioned that her father was born in LaRue County, Kentucky, in 1876. This gives him a point of reference for judging whether a site has any relevant information on his family. A site is relevant if it contains any information on Abells who were located in or near LaRue County, Kentucky, before or around the year 1876. Try to use the same technique with your ancestor. For more information on how to extract genealogical information from your family to use in your research, see the section, "Getting the 4-1-1 from Your Kinfolk," later in this chapter.

Selecting a grandparent's name

Having trouble selecting a name? Why not try one of your grandparent's names? Using a grandparent's name can have several benefits. If you find some information on an individual but you aren't sure whether it's relevant to your family, you can check with relatives to see whether they know any additional information that can help you. This may also spur interest in genealogy in other family members who can then assist you with some of your research burden or produce some family documents that you never knew existed.

REMEMBER

With a name in hand, you're ready to see how much information is currently available about that individual. Because this is just one step in a long journey to discover your family history, you want to begin slowly. *Don't try to examine every resource right from the start.* You're more likely to become overloaded with information if you try to find too many resources too quickly. Your best approach is to begin searching a few sites until you get the hang of how to find information about your ancestors online. And keep in mind that you can always bookmark sites in your web browser, or record the URL in a spreadsheet or your genealogical application, so that you can easily return to them later, when you're ready for more in-depth research.

REMEMBER

For the purposes of this chapter, we'll research Matthew's great-grandfather, William Henry Abell — although, feel free to use the following steps on a person that is your research interest.

Beginning to Put the Puzzle Together

We've talked a bit about planning your research in the previous sections. We hope that you have selected a person or group of people to research. Before turning to the computer, we suggest that you move to the second research phase and collect some information that will help you evaluate the information that you find online, in a library, or in an archive. As you will see, there may be a lot of resources that you haven't thought of that can propel your research.

REMEMBER

When collecting information about William Henry Abell, we actually started with information that his daughter, Edna Abell, could provide — both in person and through documents about Edna. As we go through the following sections, we note the items that we learned from Edna that eventually help our research effort.

TIP

GOOD INTERVIEW QUESTIONS

Before you conduct a family interview, pull together a set of questions to guide the discussion. A little planning on your part makes the difference between an interview in which the family member stays focused, and a question-and-answer session that invites bouncing from one unrelated topic to another. Here are examples of some questions that you may want to ask:

- What is your full name, and do you know why you were named that?

- Where were you born and when? Do you remember any stories that your parents told you about your birth?

- What do you remember about your childhood? Where did you go to school? Did you finish school? If not, why? (Remember to ask about all levels of schooling.)

- What were your brothers and sisters like?

- Where and when were your parents born? What did they look like? What were their occupations? How did your parents meet?

- Do you remember your grandparents? Do you recall any stories about them? What did they look like? Did you hear any stories about your great-grandparents? Did you ever meet your great-grandparents?

- When you were a child, who was the oldest person in your family?

- Did any relatives (other than your immediate family) live with you?

- Do you remember who your neighbors were when you were a child?

- Did your family have any traditions or celebrate any special holidays?

- Do you have any items (stories, traditions, or physical items) that have been handed down through several generations of the family?

- When did you leave home? Where did you live?

- Did you join the military? If so, what branch of service were you in? What units were you a part of? Did you serve overseas?

- What occupations have you had? Did you have any special training?

- How did you meet your spouse? When and where did you get married? Did you go on a honeymoon? Where?

- When were your children born? Do you have any stories about their births?

- Do you know who in the family originally immigrated to this country? Where did they come from? Why did they leave their native land?

You can probably think of more questions that are likely to draw responses from your family. If you need additional questions, take a look at a couple of online resources: 20 Questions for Interviewing Relatives (www.familytreemagazine.com/article/20-questions) or Family History Sample Outline and Questions (http://oralhistory.library.ucla.edu/familyhistory.html).

Getting the 4-1-1 from Your Kinfolk

It's likely that you have some valuable but overlooked sources of genealogical gold. You may be looking right through them as they hover around the dessert table at the family reunion, reminding you about every embarrassing moment from your childhood and overstaying their welcome in your home. Yes, they are your relatives.

Interviewing your relatives is an important step in the research process. Relatives can provide family records and photographs, give you the proverbial dirty laundry on family members, and identify other people who might be beneficial to talk to about the family history. When talking with relatives, you want to collect the same type of information that you provided about yourself when you created your timeline in Chapter 1.

Your parents, brothers, sisters, grandparents, aunts, uncles, and cousins are all good candidates for information about your family's most recent generations. Talking to relatives provides you with leads that you can use to find primary sources. (For more information on primary sources, see Chapter 1.) You can complete family interviews in person or through a questionnaire. We strongly recommend that you conduct these interviews in person; it's a lot easier to ask additional questions and follow up on leads! However, if meeting your relatives in person is not feasible, by all means, drop them an email, open a Skype session, or write an old-fashioned letter.

Skype is a software and service that you can use for voice and video calls. The video-calling feature allows you to talk face-to-face over the Internet. For more information on Skype, check out their website (https://www.skype.com/en/). Another option is to use the video call feature in Google Hangouts (https://hangouts.google.com).

TIP

There's no easy way to say this, so please excuse us for being blunt — you may want to begin interviewing some of your older relatives as soon as possible, depending on their ages and health. If a family member passes on before you have the chance to interview him or her, you may miss the opportunity of a lifetime to find out more about his or her personal experiences and knowledge of previous generations.

Here are a few tips to remember as you plan a family interview:

>> **Prepare a list of questions.** Knowing what you want to achieve during the discussion helps you get started and keeps your interview focused. (See the nearby sidebar "Good interview questions" for some ideas.) However, you also need to be flexible enough to allow the interviewee to take the conversation where he or she wants to go. Often, some of the best information comes from memories that occur while the interviewee is talking — rather than being generated strictly in response to a set of questions.

>> **Bring a recorder to the interview.** Use a recorder of your choice, whether it's your phone, tablet, computer, a voice recorder, or a video camera. Make sure that you get permission from each participant before you start recording. If the interviewee is agreeable and you have the equipment, we recommend you video-record the session. That way, you can see the expressions on his or her face as he or she talks.

>> **Use photographs and documents to help your family members recall events.** Often, photographs can have a dramatic effect on the stories that the interviewee remembers. If you have a lull in the interview, pulling out a photo album is an excellent way to nudge things along.

>> **Try to limit your interviews to two hours or less.** You don't want to be overwhelmed with information, and you don't want the interviewee to get worn out by your visit. Within two hours, you can collect a lot of information to guide your research. And remember, you can always do another interview if you want more information from the family member. Actually, we strongly encourage you to do subsequent interviews — often the first interview stimulates memories for the individual that you can cover during a later interview. Who knows? It might lead to a regularly scheduled lunch or tea time with a relative whom you genuinely enjoy visiting.

>> **Be grateful and respectful.** Remember that these are people who have agreed to give you time and answers. Treat them with respect by listening attentively and speaking politely to them. And by all means, be sure to thank them when you've completed the interview.

To accomplish two objectives at the same time, you might consider scanning documents and photographs while you are conducting the interview. Products such as the Flip-Pal scanner (http://flip-pal.com/) include software that can attach recordings to the images that you scan. Not only do you get a scan of a photo or object, but you can also get a verbal account of its history.

REMEMBER

A few years before Matthew's grandmother, Edna Abell, passed away, he had the opportunity to interview her using questions similar to those mentioned earlier in this chapter. During the course of the interview, Matthew asked about her parents. Edna stated that her father's name was William Henry Abell and mother's name was Lizzie Pickerell, and that the family lived in DeWitt County, Illinois, where she was born in 1901. Although Matthew learned much more from the interview, these items give us a place to begin our research for William. We'll be looking for William and Lizzie Abell in DeWitt County, Illinois around 1901.

Dusting off old photo albums

A picture is worth a thousand words — so the saying goes. That's certainly true in genealogy. Photographs are among the most treasured documents for genealogists. Pictures show how your ancestors looked and what conditions they lived in. Sometimes the flip side of the photo is more important than the picture itself. On the back, you may find crucial information such as names, dates, and descriptions of places.

Photographs are also useful as memory-joggers for family members. Pictures can help others recollect the past and bring up long-forgotten memories. Just be forewarned — sometimes the memories are good, and sometimes they're not so good. Although you may stimulate thoughts of some great moments long ago, you may also open a can of worms when you ask Grandma about a particular person in a picture. On the plus side, she may give you the lowdown on not only that person, but also every single individual in the family who has ever made her angry — this can provide lots of genealogical leads.

You may run into several types of photographs in your research. Knowing when certain kinds of photographs were produced can help you associate a time frame with a picture. Here are some examples:

» **Daguerreotypes:** Daguerreotype photos were taken from 1839 to 1860. They required a long exposure time and were taken on silver-plated copper. The photographic image appears to change from a positive to a negative when tilted.

» **Ambrotypes:** Ambrotypes used a much shorter exposure time and were produced from 1858 to 1866. The image was made on thin glass and usually had a black backing.

» **Tintypes:** Tintypes were produced from 1858 to 1910. They were made on a metal sheet, and the image was often coated with a varnish. You can usually find them in a paper cover.

- » **Cartes-de-visite:** Cartes-de-visite were small paper prints mounted on a card. They were often bound together into a photo album. They were produced between 1858 and 1891.

- » **Cabinet cards:** Cabinet cards were larger versions of cartes-de-visite. They sometimes included dates on the borders of the cards. The pictures themselves were usually mounted on cardboard. They were manufactured primarily between 1865 and 1906.

- » **Albumen prints:** These prints were produced on thin pieces of paper that were coated with albumen and silver nitrate. They were usually mounted on cardboard. Albumen prints were used between 1858 and 1910 and were the type of photographs found in cartes-de-visite and cabinet cards.

- » **Stereographic cards:** Stereographic cards were paired photographs that rendered a three-dimensional effect when used with a stereographic viewer. They were prevalent from 1850 to 1925.

- » **Platinum prints:** Platinum prints have a matte surface that appears embedded in the paper. The images were often highlighted with artistic chalk. They were produced mainly between 1880 and 1930.

- » **Glass-plate negatives:** Glass-plate negatives were used between 1848 and 1930. They were made from light-sensitive silver bromide immersed in gelatin.

When you deal with photographs, keep in mind that too much light or humidity can easily destroy them. Oil from your fingerprints isn't the greatest for old photos either, so you might want to keep a pair of light gloves in your research bag to use when handling these treasures. Also, some online resources can help you identify types of pictures. See the City Gallery website at `www.city-gallery.com/learning` for information about 19th-century photography, and visit the Identifying Photograph Types page at `www.phototree.com/identify.htm` for descriptions of several types of photographs.

REMEMBER

During the Interview with Edna Abell, Matthew asked to see a picture of William Henry Abell. Edna produced a family picture showing a man, woman, and four small children (see Figure 2-3). Edna said that the man was William Henry Abell, the woman Lizzie Pickerell, the daughter standing in the back was Leona, the daughter sitting next to the father was Edna, the daughter standing next to the father was Lillian, and the baby held by the father was William. This photo helped garner names for three other people to research.

FIGURE 2-3:
Family photo of William and Lizzie Abell.

Striking it rich in closets, in basements, and under beds

Are you a pack rat? A hoarder of sorts? You know what we mean: someone who keeps every little scrap of paper that he or she touches. If you are, you may be well suited for genealogy. In fact, if you're lucky, you descended from a whole family of pack rats who saved all those scraps from the past in their attics or basements. You may be able to share in their treasures — digging to find things that can further your genealogical research. For example, pay a visit to Grandma's attic, and you may discover an old suitcase or cigar box full of documents such as report cards, wartime ration cards, and letters. Eureka for the genealogist! These items may contain information that you can use to reconstruct part of your ancestor's past or to enhance it.

When you go through old family treasures, look for things that can serve as primary sources for facts that you want to verify. For more information on primary sources, refer to Chapter 1. Here's a list (although not an exhaustive one) of some specific things to look for:

>> Family Bibles

>> Property-related legal documents (such as mortgages, titles, and deeds)

- » Insurance policies

- » Wills

- » Family letters

- » Obituaries and newspaper articles

- » Diaries

- » Naturalization records

- » Baptismal certificates and other church records

- » Copies of vital records (such as birth, marriage, and death certificates, and divorce decrees)

- » Report cards and other administrative papers from school

- » Occupational or personnel records

- » Membership cards or identification cards with photos

These gems that you find buried around the house contain all sorts of information: names and vital statistics of ancestors, names and addresses of friends of the family and neighbors, military units, religious affiliations, medical conditions and names of doctors or hospitals, work histories, and so many other things that can add color to your family history as well as give you place names and time frames to guide you in your subsequent research.

REMEMBER

When talking with Matthew's grandmother, Edna Abell, he asked to see any documents she might have pertaining to her father. She produced a copy of an obituary for William H. Abell that appeared in the local newspaper on 8 September 1955 (see Figure 2-4). Information gleaned from the obituary included: William passed away the previous Wednesday at 6:30 am in Hodgenville, Kentucky at the age of 82. He left behind his wife, Betty; and children Leona Helm and Edna Helm in Decatur; Lillian Laiser in Clinton; William Abell in Wapella; and Harland in East Chicago, Indiana. William Henry Abell also had brothers Peter Abell in Wapella; James Abell in Hopedale; and sisters Lanie Chaudoin in Wapella; and Minnie Simms in Brownstown. His body was transported from Kentucky to Clinton for the funeral.

As you can tell, the obituary contained a treasure trove of information. This included death date and place, approximate birth date, his wife's name (it wasn't Lizzie, so we'll have to figure out what happened to her), his children's names and where they lived and his sibling's names and where they lived. That's six more people to research — that we didn't already know about.

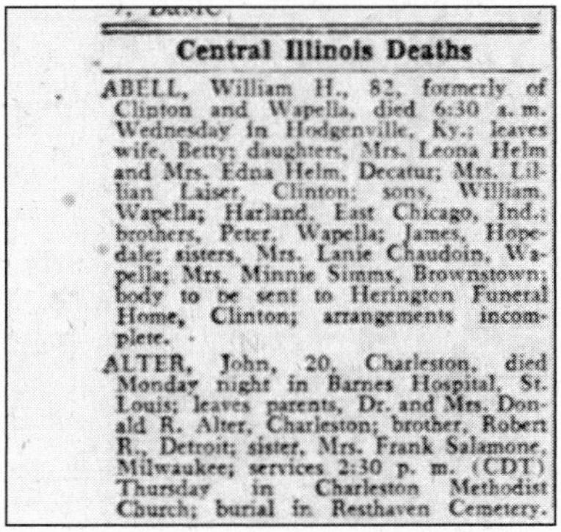

Central Illinois Deaths

ABELL, William H., 82, formerly of Clinton and Wapella, died 6:30 a. m. Wednesday in Hodgenville, Ky.; leaves wife, Betty; daughters, Mrs. Leona Helm and Mrs. Edna Helm, Decatur; Mrs. Lillian Laiser, Clinton; sons, William, Wapella; Harland, East Chicago, Ind.; brothers, Peter, Wapella; James, Hopedale; sisters, Mrs. Lanie Chaudoin, Wapella; Mrs. Minnie Simms, Brownstown; body to be sent to Herington Funeral Home, Clinton; arrangements incomplete.

ALTER, John, 20, Charleston, died Monday night in Barnes Hospital, St. Louis; leaves parents, Dr. and Mrs. Donald R. Alter, Charleston; brother, Robert R., Detroit; sister, Mrs. Frank Salamone, Milwaukee; services 2:30 p. m. (CDT) Thursday in Charleston Methodist Church; burial in Resthaven Cemetery.

FIGURE 2-4:
Obituary of William H. Abell.

Adding Your Ancestors One by One

Earlier in this chapter, we covered resources that you can arm yourself with as you launch into your research. Now that you have some of those resources collected, we can move into the third phase — researching.

REMEMBER

We always like to begin a search with one piece of proof in hand. To do this, we took a quick trip to an archive that holds Dewitt County, Illinois, records and was able to locate a copy of Edna Abell's birth record (see Figure 2-5) with the help of a friendly archivist. The birth record states that Edna Ella Abell, a white female, second child of the mother, was born on 23 March 1901 in Wapella, Illinois. Her father was Wm. H. Abell, of American nationality, born in Kentucky, a blacksmith who was 27 years old at the time of the birth. Her mother was Lizzy F. Abell, maiden name Pickerell, of American nationality, born in Kentucky and living in Wapella, Illinois. The medical attendant was G. M. Robertson, MD, of Wapella, Illinois.

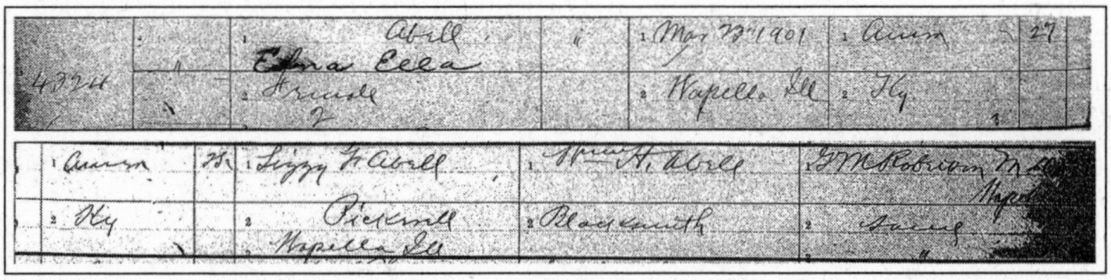

FIGURE 2-5:
Copy of Edna Abell's birth record.

From the interviews, photos, and documents that we collected (and discussed in the previous sections), we can assemble the following information useful in evaluating sources that we find online:

>> **Research target:** William Henry Abell, born around 1873 in Kentucky and died on 7 September 1955. We derived the birth date based upon the obituary stating that he was 82 when he died. The birth place was from Edna's birth record.

>> **Wives:** Lizzie Pickerell and Betty (we don't yet know her last name). The source for these were Edna's birth record and William's obituary.

>> **Children:** Five children, Leona, Edna, Lillian, William, and Harland. The source for the children came from the interview with Edna, photograph, and William's obituary.

>> **Siblings:** Peter, James, Lanie, and Minnie. The source for this came from William's obituary.

>> **Locations:** Wapella, Dewitt County, Illinois around 1901 and Hodgenville, LaRue County, Kentucky around 1955. The source for this was Edna's birth record and William's obituary.

>> **Research goals:** Find William's birth date, locations where he lived from 1873 to 1955, and marriage dates for both wives.

Using a bit of (Roots)Magic to keep track of your family

Although all of the information we received from the interview and documents is good, we want to research to get more primary sources to prove what these sources, especially the obituary (from the previous section) mentioned. The information is enough to get a good start in finding the records that we need. To make sure that we don't lose anything, we put this information into RootsMagic. Here's how:

1. **Open the RootsMagic Essentials application on your computer.**

   RootsMagic opens to the pedigree view. If you haven't used RootsMagic Essentials yet, please refer to Chapter 1.

2. **Double-click on the person in the Pedigree chart to enter information.**

   In our case, we clicked on William Henry Abell. The Edit Person page launches in a new window.

3. Click on the Add a Fact button.

The Add a Fact button (the button has a green plus sign) appears on the left side of the button bar on the Edit Person page. The Fact Types box appears.

4. Select a fact type from the list and click the Select button.

In our case, we clicked on Death, as we have William's death date from the obituary. After you click on a fact, you are returned to the Edit Person page with the fact information located on the right side of the screen.

5. Fill in the information that you know about the fact on the right side of the screen and click on the Save button.

We entered the following information on William: The date of his death was 7 September 1955 and place of death was Hodgenville, LaRue, Kentucky, USA (that is, we entered the town, county, state, and country). After you click the Save button, the fact appears on the left side of the page (see Figure 2-6).

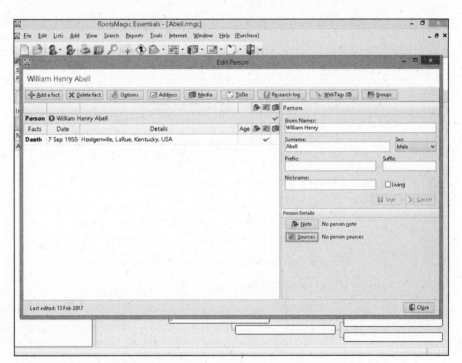

FIGURE 2-6:
A fact entered into the Edit Person screen.

6. Click the Sources button in the lower-right side of the box.

The Citation Manager opens for the fact.

7. Select Add New Source.

The Select Source Type box appears, as shown in Figure 2-7.

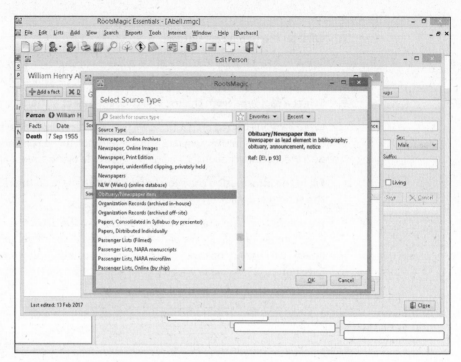

FIGURE 2-7:
The Select Source
Type box.

8. **Select from the list of source types.**

In our case, we searched for the source type Obituary/Newspaper item. If you can't find an existing source type to fit your need, select Free Form and enter your own source type.

9. **Click OK.**

The Edit Source box appears. Enter details about the source of your information. You should complete as many of the fields as you can for every source. Note that the fields have gray text in them with helpful tips.

10. **Click on the Media tab in the Edit Source page.**

11. **Click on Add New Media.**

The Add Media Item box appears. Choose the Media type from the drop-down box and then click on the Disk or Scan button (depending upon whether you already have an image of the source). We have an image of the source, so we chose Image for the Media type and clicked on the Disk button.

12. **Locate the image on your hard drive, select it, and click Open.**

The Media Properties box appears. You can enter a caption, description, date, reference number, and tags to the image.

13. **Click Okay.**

The image of the source appears in the Edit Source window.

14. **Select the Quality tab.**

You see three boxes that help you assess the quality of the source. Answer the questions in each box, and RootsMagic assigns a Quality score. In our case, we answered that the source is in its first recorded form, that it is secondary (we chose this because the death happened in Kentucky and there is a good possibility that the obituary was written by someone in Illinois who did not witness the death), and indirect evidence (we need to find another primary source, such as a death record to substantiate the obituary).

15. **Click Repository and then Edit Address.**

Enter information about the repository location. If it is held privately, then use the person's address.

16. **Click OK.**

A pop-over box appears asking for a Master Source Name. We tried to be as descriptive as possible by calling it "USA-Illinois-Decatur-Decatur Daily Review."

17. **Click OK.**

The source now appears in the Citation Manager.

18. **Click Close.**

You are returned to the Edit Person screen. Notice there is now a green check mark in the source column of the fact.

You may have already noticed another way to get to the Source Manager. Choose Lists ➪ Source List, click the Add a New Source button, and follow the preceding steps. This enables you to add a source that's not necessarily tied to one specific event in that person's life. If your ancestor kept a diary or memoirs of sorts, you might prefer to use this method of citing sources. Similarly, you have functionality to add sources that pertain to more than one person (called Family Sources in the drop-down list accessible from the Sources icon).

Because we also know the spouses of William, we put them in RootsMagic, too. Try the following:

1. **From the Pedigree view, click the Add a Person button.**

The Add a Person button is located in the top-left side of the button bar at the top of the page. It is in the shape of a little person with a plus sign. A drop-down box appears.

2. **Select Spouse from the drop-down box.**

Alternately, you can select an individual, parents, or child. The Add a Person box appears.

3. **Select Add New person.**

The Add Person box appears.

4. **Fill in the fields and click OK.**

Complete as many of the fields as you can. In our case, we filled in the name Lizzie Pickerell. We put *Lizzie*, even though we suspect the name is *Elizabeth*, because our sources thus far spell it this way. We can always change it later and add Lizzie as a nickname, if we find primary sources with Elizabeth.

Figure 2-8 shows the Family view of William Henry Abell with the items entered that we know about him (from the previous sections).

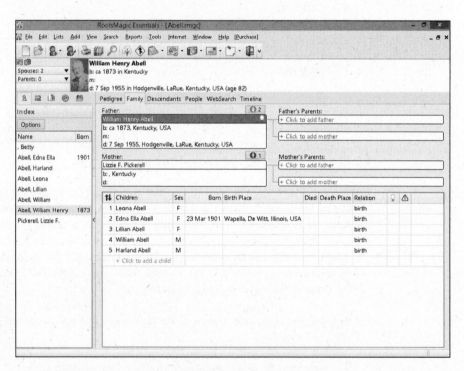

FIGURE 2-8: Family view of William Henry Abell.

After you've used RootsMagic Essentials for a while, you may find that you need more features such as the To Do list and Research Log. You can compare the features between RootsMagic and RootsMagic Essentials at www.rootsmagic.com/ RootsMagic/Features.aspx to determine whether you need an upgrade.

Logging your data into Ancestry Family Tree

We want to show you one additional way to keep track of the information that you've gathered thus far. We take you through the process of adding a person in the Ancestry Family Tree. If you need to add additional information on someone already in the Family Tree or need to add sources, refer to Chapter 1. Try the following:

1. **Point your web browser to** `http://trees.ancestry.com/`.

   The Ancestry.com online family tree page appears.

2. **Click Trees in the black menu bar.**

   The menu bar is located at the top of the page next to the Ancestry logo.

3. **Click on the [Your Name] Family Tree.**

   The resulting page shows the Pedigree view.

4. **Click on a person in the Pedigree view.**

   A box appears with the person's name and a menu bar with four buttons.

5. **Click the far-right button with the tool shapes on it.**

   A drop-down box appears with two options — Add Relative or Delete This Person.

6. **Select Add Relative and click on the type of relative to add.**

   A box appears with four choices — Father, Mother, Spouse, Child. We clicked on Spouse. Enter the individual's first and middle names, maiden name, suffix, gender, birth date, birthplace, death date, and death place.

7. **Click Save.**

   You are returned to the Pedigree view with the new person on the view.

For William Henry Abell, we added the information from the obituary, including approximate birth date, death date, and place, and details on his wives and children. Figure 2-9 shows the Facts view of William Henry Abell based on the information we gathered in previous sections.

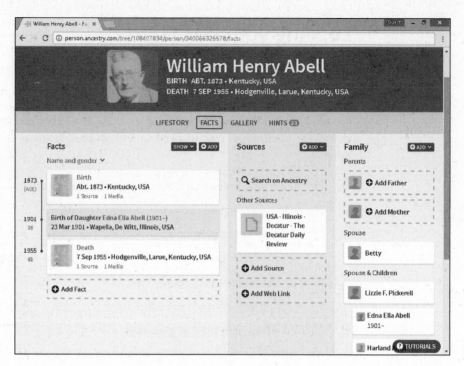

FIGURE 2-9:
Facts view of William Henry Abell.

Chapter 3

Searching Primary Resource Sites

Before the age of the Internet, searching for primary sources was like trying to find a needle in a haystack. A typical research session would begin in a crowded room containing paper indexes of census records. After searching through rows and rows of information, you would jot down some names that looked familiar along with a record's page number. Then you'd grab a roll of microfilm and scroll your way through it until you found the page number. Sometimes your potential ancestor wouldn't be on that page, requiring you to search line by line before and after the targeted page. If you still couldn't find the name for your search, you might have to read line by line through an entire county. Needless to say, it could take hours to find the individual, only to discover that it wasn't really your ancestor after all.

Fast-forward to the age of the Internet. Now you can find digitized versions of the census microfilm online; even better, most of them have indexes that link directly to the image. Although indexers still make mistakes, it takes a fraction of the time to search. Another bonus is that some sites provide links to other record sets that your ancestor may be in, which gives you even more evidence to substantiate your research. Finding primary sources is what online genealogy is all about. You can see the representation of the original record and draw your own conclusions as to what the record really indicates.

Millions of records are now available online. This chapter focuses on introducing some of the larger collections and gives you guidance on how to search for records using these sites. The searches that we conduct in this chapter are more general; for searches that focus on particular types of records, see Chapters 4 and 5.

If you need help in selecting a person to search for and in gathering information to help you in your search, take a quick look at Chapter 2.

WARNING

There is a lot of duplication of record sets on subscription sites. Make sure that you carefully look at the collections on each site before making a decision regarding a subscription. Sometimes there are special collections that are unique to a site. If you won't be using the collection often, you might consider a short term subscription just to get the records that you need. You can always check back later when new records are added and re-subscribe.

Touring Ancestry.com

A commercial site that has perhaps the most varied collection of genealogical resources is Ancestry.com. Over time, Ancestry.com has amassed its collection by acquiring several websites, genealogical software, and other data and print resources. The company, which started as a publisher of genealogical research books, now includes the Ancestry.com, Ancestry24 (a site with South African records), Ancestry Academy, Genealogy.com, FindAGrave.com, RootsWeb.com, Fold3.com, and Newspapers.com websites. It also owns the research company ProGenealogists. Although the majority of the Ancestry.com websites require a subscription, a great deal of resources are available to use for free. This section provides an overview of the resources and shows how to use the general search function. We refer to Ancestry.com in other portions of this book as well, when we talk about specific types of online sources.

Trying Ancestry.com for free

If you don't have a subscription to Ancestry.com, perhaps the first thing to do is register for a free two-week trial. Using the free trial, you can experience all the areas of the site that we cover in this book. It will also give you a chance to see if the site will fulfill your immediate research needs. To begin the free trial, do the following:

1. **Point your web browser to** www.ancestry.com.

   In the upper-right corner of the home page is a Free Trial link.

2. **Click the Free Trial link.**

The resulting page contains a table with three subscription options, as shown in Figure 3-1.

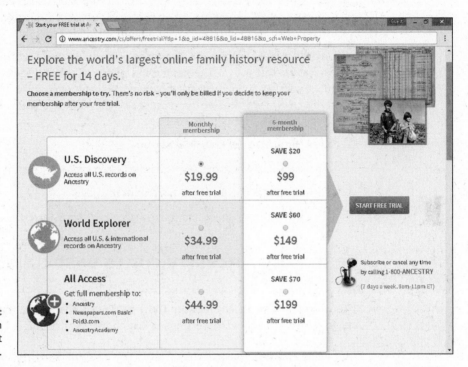

3. **In the Monthly Membership column, click a radio button corresponding to the collection that interests you.**

TIP

We suggest that you select the monthly membership option because Ancestry.com bills you after the free trial ends if you don't cancel in time (by the last day of your membership). The six-month membership is billed in a single payment, so the least amount of risk is in the monthly membership. As we will cover other Ancestry.com sites later in this book, you might consider the All Access free trial.

4. **Click the Start Free Trial button to continue.**

The Start Free Trial button is located just to the right of the membership options. The Create Your Account or Enter You Payment Details page appears (depending upon whether you are already logged into an account).

5. **If you haven't registered previously, enter your first name, last name, and email address, create a password, and click the Continue button.**

If you're already registered, simply click the Sign In link at the top of the page just under the Create Your Account heading.

The payment details screen appears. Fill in the account information, including your street address, city, state or province, zip or postal code, country, and phone number. Also, fill in future payment information, including the card type, card number, expiration date, and security code fields.

TIP

In the right column, note the description of the 14-day free trial cancellation process so that you can use it at the end of the trial period if you decide you don't want to continue with a subscription. Print this page and put the expiration date of the free trial on your calendar so that you remember when to cancel, if you choose to do so.

6. **Click the Start Your Free Trial button.**

   A page entitled What's the Key to Making Discoveries at Ancestry appears.

7. **Click the Begin button at the bottom of the page.**

   The Search page appears, and you can start using Ancestry.com.

Searching Ancestry.com's vast collection

The most efficient way to search Ancestry.com is by using the main search form. This allows you to receive results from all collections rather than from only a single record set. Follow these steps to search for an ancestor:

1. **Point your web browser to www.ancestry.com, the Ancestry.com home page, and click the Search button in the toolbar at the top of the page.**

   A drop-down menu appears where you can select the type of collection that you wish to search.

2. **Select the collection.**

   If you are not sure what you are looking for, just select All Collections.

3. **In the Search section at the top of the page, type a name into the First & Middle Name(s) and Last Name fields.**

   We entered the name William Henry and Abell in these fields.

4. **Type a place where your ancestor lived in the field labeled A Place Your Ancestor May Have Lived.**

   Because the field is a type-ahead field, it suggests locations as you type letters into the field. To select a location, scroll down to the location and click it to enter it into the field. Based on the information that we collected in Chapter 2, we put De Witt, Illinois into this field (it populated the field with De Witt County,

Illinois, USA). In the Birth Year field, we put 1873 (the date we estimated based on his obituary).

5. **If the name you're searching for is common, you may want to add optional information to distinguish one person from another. You can add life events (such as births, marriages, and deaths) by clicking the Show More Options link.**

A new line is created when you click the link, as shown in Figure 3-2.

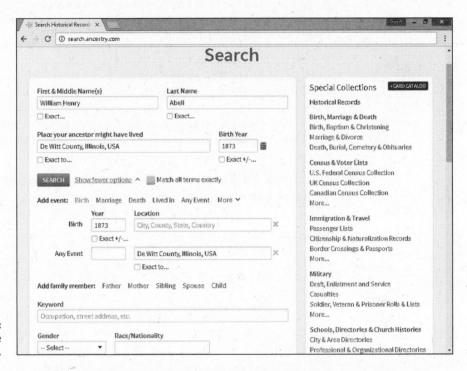

FIGURE 3-2:
An additional life event for birth.

6. **Click on a link next to the Add event label that you know more information about (the events include Birth, Marriage, Death, Lived In, and Any Event — there are additional types under the More drop-down). Enter the year and location of the event.**

You can add additional events by clicking the appropriate event link. For example, clicking Marriage adds a line for marriage information. We added a line for Lived In and set the date to 1901 and place to Wapella, De Witt, Illinois USA (this was what the birth record for Edna Abell reflected that we located in Chapter 2). To make sure that we get some records from Kentucky, we added a Death field with his death date and place from the obituary.

7. If you know family members who can be found via your ancestor (such as a parent or spouse), click the optional link next to the label titled Add Family Members.

We clicked on Spouse and added Lizzie Pickerell. Then, we clicked on Child and added Edna.

8. To add more search criteria, fill in the other optional fields available on the form.

9. If you'd like, you can limit search results to the exact spelling of the name by selecting the Match All Terms Exactly checkbox that is located on the same row as the Search button.

TIP

Use the Match All Terms Exactly option when you know that your ancestor's name is spelled a certain way. For example, the name of Matthew's ancestor Herschel is spelled Heruhel in one record set. To find this record quickly, Matthew would use the Match All Terms Exactly option. You can also use this functionality when you're researching a name that's spelled multiple ways and you want to find records with only one spelling. For example, you might want to find only records spelled Smythe and not Smith.

10. Click the Exact link under the First & Middle Name(s) and Last Name fields if you want to configure more search options.

The options described in these lists restrict the search on the name (see Figure 3-3):

- *Sounds like:* The Ancestry.com search engine contains phonetic algorithms that determine whether a name sounds like the name you entered into the field.

- *Similar:* This option is helpful when you search for common first names that are often shortened. For example, Richard is often shortened to Rich, Rick, or Dick.

- *Initials:* (This option isn't shown in Figure 3-3; it's under the First & Middle Name(s) Exact link.) Use this handy option when you search for people who are often referred to by their initials in records, such as W.H. rather than the full name.

- *Soundex:* The Last Name field has an additional choice to restrict the result to Soundex matches — for a way of coding names according to the way their consonants sound. If we search for Abell with this checkbox selected, we receive matches for names with the Soundex code of A140, including Abel, Able, Appel, and Apple, for example.

Another feature you can use is a wildcard symbol. You can use the asterisk (*) symbol to match any number of characters. For example, if we didn't know whether a record for William was under Abel or Abell, we could search for

"Abel*". The question mark (?) wildcard is used to replace just one character. For example, a search for "Ab?ll" would bring back results for Aball and Abell. You can use the wildcards together and anywhere in your search. However, your search must contain at least three letters.

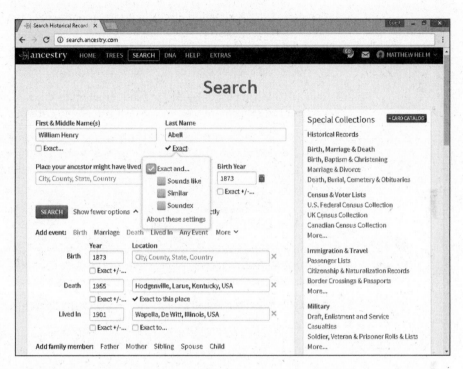

FIGURE 3-3:
Options under the Exact link.

11. **Click the Exact link under the Location field if you'd like to restrict the search to only the location you entered.**

   This option is helpful when you're searching for a common name and you know the location where your ancestor lived. The search then focuses on that person in the context of the location, greatly reducing the number of results.

TIP

   When you type a place-name in the field, additional choices appear, including limiting your search to the county, county/adjacent counties, state, state/adjacent states, or country. Using adjacent counties is particularly helpful when you're searching counties that were later divided into other counties. The adjacent-counties search picks up the new counties if they're adjacent to the old county.

12. **Enter a term into the Keyword field, should you want to limit your search to a specific criterion.**

   You can use a keyword to search specific items not covered in the other fields. For example, if you know that your ancestor lived near a specific post office or served in a specific regiment, you can enter that term into the field.

13. **Click the down arrow in the Gender field and select the appropriate gender, if restricting the search this way is beneficial to you.**

Choosing the gender is useful when you're searching for an ancestor who has a name that can be either male or female, such as Kelly.

14. **Complete the Race/Nationality field if race or nationality is a helpful factor for your ancestor.**

This field is helpful when you search census records in which, depending on the census year, either race or nationality was recorded.

15. **Set the Collection Focus by clicking the arrow on its drop-down menu if you want to set preferences for some of the search criteria.**

The Collection Focus menu tells the search engine to give preference in the results to records from a particular country or ethnic group. You can use this option when an ancestor immigrated to a particular country and you want to focus the search on the new country.

16. **Use the checkboxes under Collection Focus to limit searches to only certain resource types if you desire.**

TIP

We often use the functionality to limit searches to only historical records. This way, the results contain only records that we can use as evidence — rather than to someone's interpretation of a record in a family tree.

17. **After you finish setting all search options, click the Search button.**

The search results page appears, as shown in Figure 3-4.

Sifting through the results

Executing the search is only half the battle. When we search for William Henry Abell with the criteria mentioned in the previous section, we received 80,079 results. Of course, only a small percentage of these pertain to the William Abell we are interested in. The next part is going through the search results to find useful information on your particular ancestor. The search results page contains several sections, including

>> **Search Filters:** This section is located in the left column and lists the search criteria you used, along with sliders that you can use to adjust the filters.

>> **All Categories:** This section contains categories for displaying results. For example, you can select Census & Voter Lists to limit the results to those types of records.

>> **Results:** The Results section lists the number of matches and how they're sorted along the top of the right column.

FIGURE 3-4:
Search results
from Ancestry.
com.

It's important to be able to manage the results in order to avoid spending a lot of time going through records that aren't pertinent to your research. Here are some ways to navigate and view the results:

1. **On the search results screen, take a look at the results in the right column.**

If your search term matches a person in a family tree, that result appears first in the list. For example, in Figure 3-4, you see that a William Henry Abell with a close birth date and a spouse with a similar name as our search is found in a family tree. In addition to the information similar to our search, you can also see additional details pulled from the family tree (if available), such as marriage date and place, death date and place, and parent names. Along with family tree results, you can see matching records from other sources, including public member photos and scanned documents.

If additional family trees contain information similar to your search, click the See More Like This link on the right side of the Matching Person heading.

TIP

2. **Hover the cursor over the link containing the result name.**

If the result is an Ancestry.com record, the Preview box appears. The Preview box shows key elements of the record and, possibly, a thumbnail of the record, if it's digitized. This is a real timesaver, in that you can immediately judge whether the record pertains to your person without additional clicks.

3. **Sort search results by clicking the Categories tab in the upper-right corner.**

   This view contains the general record categories followed by the top five sources within these categories, as shown in Figure 3-5.

   TIP

   To see all results for sources in a particular category, click the See All Results link at the bottom of the category.

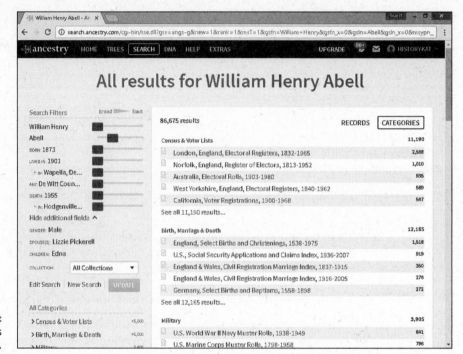

FIGURE 3-5:
The Categories
view.

4. **To restrict search results to a particular type of record, click a category in the All Categories section in the left column of the page.**

   This view contains the general record categories followed by the top five sources within these categories, as shown in Figure 3-5.

   TIP

   For example, if you select the Census & Voter Lists category, the results screen is filtered to include only the matches to the search that fit that category. Notice there's a list of subcategories of the census listed by year beneath the category.

5. **Click a record group in the right column that might contain records on your ancestor.**

   In our case, we clicked the 1940 United States Federal Census. A new page appears with names fitting the search criteria that are located in the record group. For example, Figure 3-6 shows a record for Wm H Abell indexed in the

1850 census. The record appears as the third one in the list. The record is indexed with a spouse named Betty and is located in Larue, Kentucky — consistent with the information that we collected on William in Chapter 2.

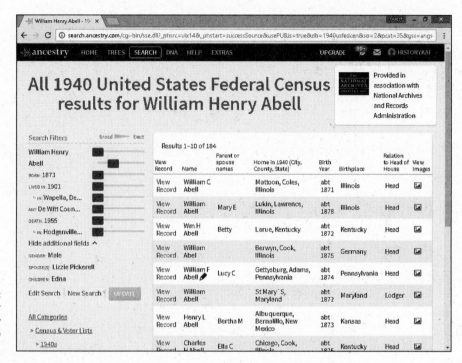

FIGURE 3-6:
The results for William Henry Abell in the 1940 census.

6. **Click View Record.**

   If there are other details about the record, you can see them on the Record view. In our case, the record for William includes the names and ages of household members, shown in Figure 3-7.

   TIP

   Note the box in the right column containing links to suggested records. These are records in other groups that meet the search criteria. This can be a shortcut to finding several records for the same individual without executing another search.

7. **If the Record view contains a thumbnail image with a View button, click the thumbnail.**

   The resulting page launches a viewer to show the digitized image of the primary source. Figure 3-8 shows the 1940 census record for William Henry Abell; notice that we've zoomed in on the record, so you can see the name better.

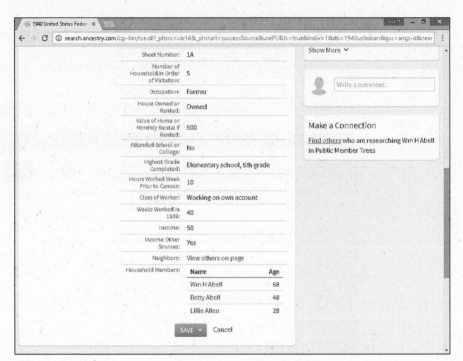

FIGURE 3-7:
The Record view on Ancestry.com.

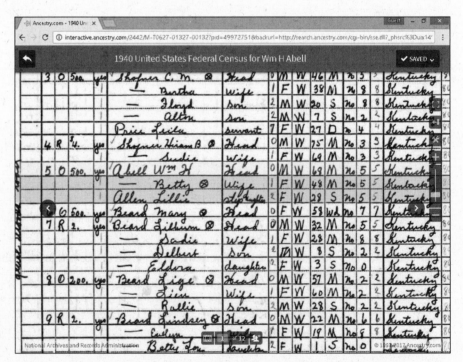

FIGURE 3-8:
The digitized census record for William Henry Abell.

8. **Click the Tools menu to control the image.**

If you need to rotate, flip, or invert the color of the image, you can use the Tools menu. The Tools menu is accessed by clicking on the Tools button — the third button down along the right side of the image.

TIP

If the handwriting is hard to read due to faded or smeared ink, sometimes you can read it easier by inverting the color of the image.

9. **To print this image, click the Tools button and then select Print.**

TIP

The Print Options page appears. Click Continue to send the image to your printer. It's a good idea to check the box Also print index and source data — that way you have the source information along with the image. Note that just above the Continue button is a box suggesting the best page orientation to print the record.

10. **To share the image, click Tools button, click the Share drop-down, button then the Facebook, Google+, Twitter, or email link.**

Clicking any link launches a new pop-over box with further instructions.

11. **If you have an online family tree, click the Save button in the upper-right corner of the screen to add the image to your tree.**

In the dialog box that opens, select the Save to Person in Your Tree option. (See Chapter 1 for details on creating an online family tree at Ancestry.com.) The Save to Person in Your Tree pop-over box appears.

12. **Select the tree name in the Tree drop-down box and type the name in the Person in Tree field.**

As you type, the name may prepopulate, if a match already exists in the family tree. If the person is not in the tree, click the Add to a New Person link.

13. **Click the Save button.**

The Add New Information to Your Tree page appears with two columns, as shown in Figure 3-9. The left column contains information from the census record, and the right contains information from your family tree.

14. **Select the checkboxes with the information you would like to import into your online family tree and click the Save to Your Tree button.**

The page for the individual to which you attached the record is displayed. You can click the Facts and Sources tab to see the information added from the record.

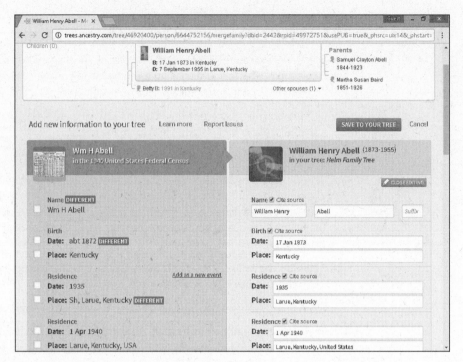

FIGURE 3-9:
The Add New
Information to
Your Tree page.

RootsWeb.com at a Glance

RootsWeb.com is a well-established online community for genealogists. It's been around for a long time and has gone through various renditions. Several years ago, it became part of the Ancestry.com family and has remained closely associated with Ancestry. Whereas Ancestry.com relies heavily on subscriptions to keep its collection growing, RootsWeb.com relies heavily on the generosity of its users to give their time, energy, and personal resources to make free genealogical data available for all to use.

Users can contribute to RootsWeb.com by submitting transcriptions of books and records, sharing their family trees in the WorldConnect Project (a database of family trees that now has more than 640 million names in it), participating in the Roots-Web Surname List, or RSL (a registry of surnames being researched worldwide and how to contact those researching the names), and posting messages and responses to the message boards and mailing lists hosted by RootsWeb.com. RootsWeb.com also offers web hosting, where you can build your own genealogy website.

To experience RootsWeb.com, point your browser to `http://home.rootsweb.ancestry.com/`. The directory on the home page gives you a quick and comprehensive look at what RootsWeb.com has to offer. Click any of the links to discover how you can contribute to the various RootsWeb.com projects.

Investigating FamilySearch

FamilySearch is the largest nonprofit genealogical website. It's sponsored by The Church of Jesus Christ of Latter-day Saints, but you don't have to be a member of the church to use it. The free resources available on the site include a photo collection area, an online family tree, and a collection of records containing more than four billion names.

Creating a free account

To make sure that you can use all the functionality of FamilySearch, it's a good idea to create a free account. To do so, follow these easy steps:

1. **Set your web browser to `www.familysearch.org`.**

   The FamilySearch home page appears.

2. **In the upper-right corner of the screen, click the Sign In link.**

   The Sign In page appears.

3. **Click the Free Account button in the upper-right corner of the page.**

   The Account Information page appears. Type in your first and last name, username and password (twice).

4. **Click Continue.**

   Enter an email address or a mobile number to recover the account, should you forget your username or password.

5. **Click Continue.**

   Type a contact name (that everyone will see), gender, country, birth date, and whether you are a member of the Church of Jesus Christ of Latter-day Saints. Enter the letters in the picture (to ensure you are not a computer filling out the form) and check the box agreeing to the terms and privacy policy (after reading them).

6. **Click Create an Account.**

   A box appears requesting a verification code. If you put in an email address check your email. If you typed a cell phone number, check your phone for the code.

7. **Enter the verification code and click Verify.**

   If the code was correct, you see a new button marked OK, I'm Done.

8. **Click the OK, I'm Done button.**

   A sign in page appears.

FamilySearching records

Here's how you search in FamilySearch:

1. **Sign into the FamilySearch site.**

   You can use the same username and password that you created in the previous section.

2. **Click the Search link at the top of the page.**

   The Search page appears as shown in Figure 3-10. To search for records on the site, fill in the First Names and Last Names fields. Note the checkboxes next to the First Names and Last Name fields. When you select the checkboxes, the search results match the name exactly. We entered William Henry Abell.

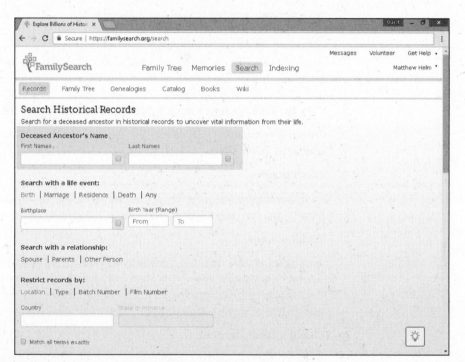

FIGURE 3-10:
The FamilySearch
Search page.

3. **Enter information in the Life Event fields.**

   As you click the links to each of these filters, the field appears onscreen. You can choose to enter information on birth, marriage, residence, death, or any place that your ancestor might be associated with. Note that you can put in a date range for the event.

TIP

Consider using date ranges anytime that you conduct a search on FamilySearch. For example, if you know the birth date was 1873, put a date range between 1870 and 1875, just in case the date of birth or age calculation for a particular record is incorrect. That way you won't miss any records. We entered the estimated birth date, added a residence in De Witt County, Illinois between 1895 and 1905 (based on the birth date of Edna in 1901), and put in William's death date and place.

4. **Enter names related to your ancestor if you want the search to restrict results by associated names.**

   As you click the links to each of these filters under the heading Search with a Relationship, the field appears onscreen. You can choose to enter names for spouse, parents, or another person associated with your ancestor. We entered Lizzie Pickerell from the information that we gathered in Chapter 2.

5. **Enter optional information in the Location, Type, Batch Number, and Film Number fields.**

   As you click the links to each of these filters, the field appears onscreen. The Batch Number and Film Number fields are for advanced searches and are useful when you have seen a reference to a particular data set on a website or in a book. Because we are expecting records from both Illinois and Kentucky, we did not restrict the location.

6. **Select the checkbox to make the search match all terms exactly, if you need to limit the count in the results.**

   We suggest you use this only if you try the search and receive too many results that aren't relevant to your ancestor.

7. **Click the Search button.**

   The search results page appears, as shown in Figure 3-11.

Using FamilySearch results

Although you may not receive as many results in FamilySearch as in Ancestry.com, it's still important that you know how to navigate the results to save you time. The search results page is divided into two columns. The left column contains filters that you can use to limit the search results. The right column lists the results. The most relevant results appear near the top. Other records that might have relevance appear under the blue box titled "The following results don't strongly match what you searched for, but may be of interest."

Each search result is divided into four columns: Name, Events, Relationships, and View. The Name column includes the Name of the person and the name of the collection where the person is found. A camera icon in the View column indicates that the collection includes images.

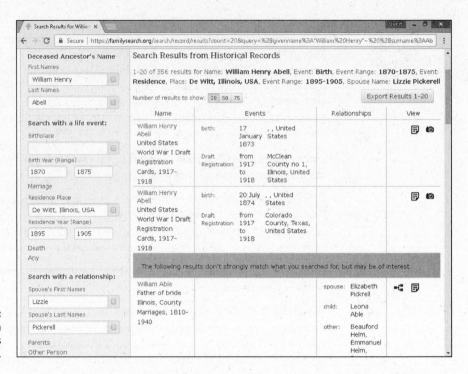

FIGURE 3-11:
The FamilySearch search results page.

If your search in the previous section generated some promising leads, follow these steps to explore the results:

1. **Click the name of the individual in the Name column.**

   A row appears below the record with more information, as shown in Figure 3-12. In our case, additional information is shown about William Henry Abell including his residence and birth date.

2. **To sort your search results by record category, click the Collections tab.**

   The Collections view appears as shown in Figure 3-13. The top five collections are displayed under each category. You can filter multiple categories by selecting the checkbox to the left of each collection. The maximum number of collections that you can select is 25.

3. **You can filter the results on the Records tab at the bottom of the first column, if you desire.**

   The filters include collections, birthplace, birth year, marriage place, marriage year, residence place, residence year, death place, death year, other place, other year, and gender.

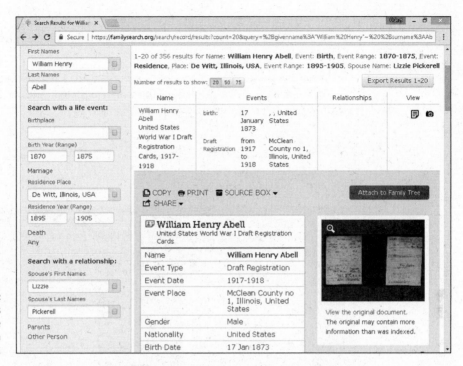

FIGURE 3-12:
The name is selected in the FamilySearch results.

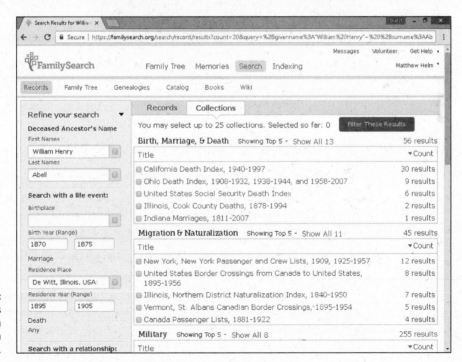

FIGURE 3-13:
The Collections view in FamilySearch results.

4. **If an image is available (as noted in the right column), click the Image link.**

   The image viewer is launched, as shown in Figure 3-14. You can use the floating toolbar on the right side of the screen to zoom in and out, rotate, invert the color, save, and print the image.

FIGURE 3-14: A draft registration card on FamilySearch.

5. **Click the Print icon in the floating toolbar.**

   The web browser print window appears, allowing you to select options for printing.

6. **Close the browser window to return to the record view. Click on the "X" in the upper-right corner to return to the search screen.**

7. **If you have an online family tree at FamilySearch, click the Attach to Family Tree button.**

   Note that this is a different online family tree than the one we created at the Ancestry.com site in Chapter 1.

Other FamilySearch search functions

A few other search pages on FamilySearch are well worth mentioning. These include Genealogies, Catalog, and Books. You can reach each of these by clicking their tabs at the top of the Search page; refer back to Figure 3-10.

The Genealogies search page searches the entries submitted by users to the Ancestral File and Pedigree Resource File. These are not primary sources; rather, they contain information submitted by other genealogists. The information contained within them has not been vetted, and you should take extra steps to verify all information. The two files are useful in providing hints on areas to investigate and can help jump-start your research.

You can explore the catalog of genealogical materials held by the Family History Library using the Catalog search. The resources referenced in the catalog have not necessarily been digitized, but several of them have been microfilmed and can be loaned to local Family History.

The third search function is the Books search. Here you can search a focused collection of 325,000 family history publications. Note that some of the publications contained within this collection are also found on websites such as the Internet Archive (www.archive.org).

Giving Back through FamilySearch Indexing

FamilySearch Indexing is a project through which volunteers help transcribe records from all over the world and submit them for posting on the website so that others can access them for free. It's a simple process. FamilySearch obtains the records and digitizes them. You download copies of the digital images to your personal computer. Then, using special online software, you index the data in the digital records. The result — a searchable index — is made available to the public free of charge. So far, more than one billion records have been indexed by more than 70,000 volunteers.

For more information about the FamilySearch Indexing project, go to https://familysearch.org/indexing/.

Saluting Fold3

Fold3 was originally named Footnote.com but was renamed shortly after being acquired by Ancestry.com. Fold3 is still run as a separate website and contains some content not found on Ancestry.com. Fold3 focuses primarily on military records, but also contains other records found on National Archives and Records Administration microfilm. In fact, the name of the site comes from the traditional flag-folding ceremony in which the third fold of the flag symbolizes the remembrance of veterans who have served in defense of the country. In addition to military records, the site has homestead records, city directories, passport applications, and census records.

Creating a trial account

Follow these steps to sign up at Fold3 (if you signed up for an all access account to Ancestry.com you may already have a Fold3 account):

1. **Set your web browser to** `https://www.fold3.com/.`

   The Fold3 home page appears.

2. **Click the Join Now link in the upper-right corner of the page.**

   The Membership choices page appears.

3. **Click the Start Free Trial button in the left column.**

   The registration page appears.

4. **Fill out the email address and password fields. Then click the Continue button.**

   TIP

   Be sure to click the Terms & Conditions link and read the Fold3 Terms of Use page so that you understand what you can and cannot do with the material on the Fold3 site. The page specifies what Fold3 does with information you provide as you use the site.

5. **Complete the payment information, including cardholder name, card number, expiration date, billing zip code, country, and phone number. Select the I Have Read and Agree to the Fold3 Terms & Conditions checkbox.**

   TIP

   Fold3 requires credit card information to initiate the seven-day free trial, but you aren't billed until the trial periods ends. If you don't want to be billed for a subscription, don't forget to cancel the account before the seven days have passed.

6. **After all fields are complete, click the Start Free Trial button.**

The Welcome to Your Fold3 Free Trial page appears.

7. **To continue using the Fold3 site, select the Start Searching Fold3 button.**

The Search Fold3 page opens.

Searching at Fold3

You can search for military and other government records at Fold3 using the following steps:

1. **Go to www.fold3.com and sign in.**

The Fold3 home page appears.

2. **Click the Advanced link (a box with a plus sign in it) located to the right of the Search form near the top of the page.**

The advanced search form appears, as shown in Figure 3-15.

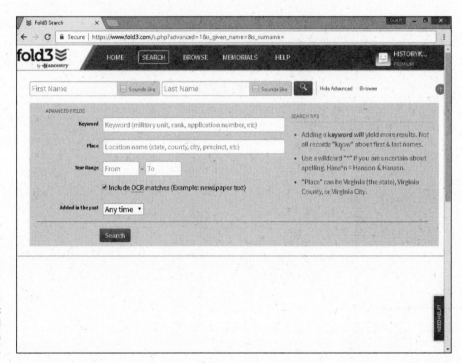

FIGURE 3-15:
The advanced search page on Fold3.

3. **Type the first name and last name of the person you're researching into the appropriate fields.**

We entered William Henry Abell.

4. **Enter a keyword or place if you want to limit your results. You can also search in specific year range or limit results to material added to the site during a particular time frame.**

Every piece of information you add to the search reduces the number of results you receive. If you execute a search and receive few or no results, omit optional search criteria to try to improve your search results. We typed Illinois in the Place field, and set the date range from 1873 to 1955 to reflect the information that we collected on William in Chapter 2.

5. **Click the Search button.**

The search results page appears, as shown in Figure 3-16. The far left column shows the number of results that appear in each record category. The center column provides filters to limit your search. The far right column shows the actual results based on the filters.

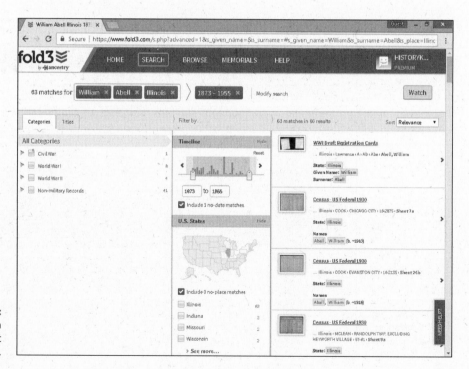

FIGURE 3-16:
The search results page at Fold3.

6. **To change the date range, move the sliders left or right, under the timeline section, depending on your preferred date range and then click the Update button.**

Note that the date changes in the fields as you move the sliders. You can omit records without dates by deselecting the Include No-Date Matches checkbox.

7. **Select a state, under the heading U.S. States, if you wish to limit the results by location.**

You can select a state by clicking the map or by selecting the checkbox next to the state name. The search results automatically update when you add a state filter.

8. **Select a result type or select an Added in the Past radio button.**

The search results update as you enable filters.

9. **Click a record title.**

The image viewer slides in from the right of the screen, displaying the digitized record, as shown in Figure 3-17.

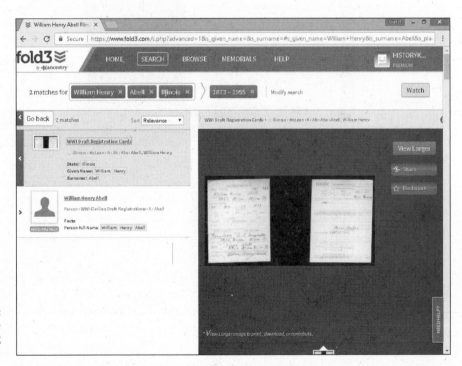

FIGURE 3-17:
The Fold3 image viewer displaying a record.

10. **Click the View Larger button.**

This enlarges the image viewer to full screen, as shown in Figure 3-18. The first time you access the viewer, you may encounter a pop-over box with a tutorial. You can run through the tutorial quickly to learn about the functionality of the viewer.

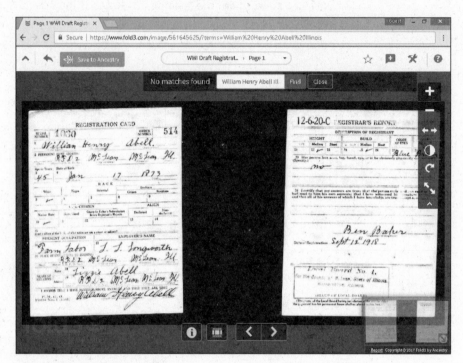

FIGURE 3-18: Full-screen window in the image viewer.

11. **Click the buttons on the toolbar on the right of the image to change the view of the image.**

- *Zoom In/Zoom Out:* To see the image more closely (to zoom in), click the plus sign (+) on the vertical bar on the left side of the image. Click the minus sign (–) to zoom out.

TIP

To see the full context of the information you're viewing, zoom out of the image when you first open it. Then zoom in closer to see elements more clearly. If the image is too high or too low onscreen when you zoom in and out of it, click the scroll bar on the far right side of the screen to reposition the image.

- *Fit to Window:* See the document at its full width onscreen.

- *Rotate:* Move the image 90 degrees clockwise. This button shows a curved arrow next to a tilted rectangle.

- *Brightness and Contrast:* Change the brightness and contrast of the image. You can also invert the color of the image by selecting the Invert checkbox. The button is a shining sun icon.

- *Fullscreen:* View the image at its maximum size onscreen. Press the Esc key on your keyboard or click the Full Screen button again to exit Full Screen mode.

12. **Move to another image in the collection.**

There are two methods to do this:

- *Click the arrow* at the bottom of the image to move to the next image in the collection.

- *Click the Show/Hide Filmstrip button* at the bottom of the page to open a window showing the few images on either side of the image you're looking at; see Figure 3-19. Click any thumbnail image to view the full image. To see more images in either direction, click the arrow on either side of the filmstrip.

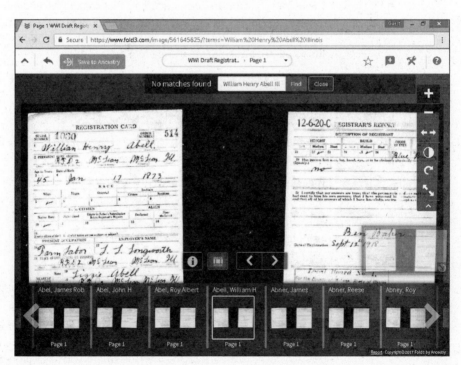

FIGURE 3-19:
The Filmstrip view
in Fold3.

Finding Your Past

Findmypast.com is one of a few sites owned by Brightsolid Online Publishing. It focuses on records from the United States, United Kingdom, Ireland, Australia, and New Zealand. You can find census records, census substitutes, vital records, newspapers, military records, and some passenger lists. A recent collection includes millions of Catholic Church records as part of the Catholic Heritage Archive. Some of the record sets are just textual, and others are a digitized image. There is also an online family tree application on the site.

You can get a 14-day free trial by following these steps:

1. **Set your web browser to** `https://www.findmypast.com/pay?isfreetrialrequest=true.`

   The findmypast.com free trial page appears.

2. **Click the Start Free Trial button.**

   The button is located in the two columns that contain the one-month and twelve-month subscription periods. We suggest that you select the one-month column to limit the amount of charges, should you forget to cancel the subscription during the free-trial period.

3. **Fill out the registration form and click the Register to Start Free Trial button.**

   The Payment Details page appears.

4. **Complete the payment details fields and then click the Start your free trial button.**

   The Free Trial Successfully Started Page appears. Click on the Start searching link located in the third column near the bottom of the Discover Your Ancestors box. The search form appears.

5. **Complete the First Name and Last Name fields.**

   We typed in William Henry Abell.

6. **If you want to limit the results based on time and location, complete the When and Where fields.**

   The When field has a drop-down menu that contains Born, Died, and Other event choices. You can also add a date range from the field next to the year field. It defaults to the –/+ 2yrs setting. The Where field has a drop-down menu in which you can choose one of four countries, or you can broaden your search and choose the World. To further refine your results, you can type in a location. We typed in 1873 for the birth year and 1955 for the death year, and we selected United States & Canada from the drop-down and typed Illinois in the field.

7. **Click the Search United States & Canada button.**

Your button may say something different if you selected a different collection. The search results page appears as seen in Figure 3-20. The left column contains filters that you can use to focus the results. The right column lists the search results.

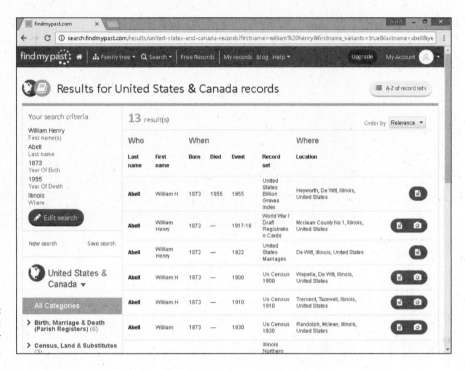

FIGURE 3-20:
The search
results page for
findmypast.com.

8. **To filter the results, click a category (or categories) in the left column.**

Details about the specific record appear in the search result.

9. **Click the Transcription icon (paper icon) or the Image icon (camera icon).**

If you click the Transcription icon, the transcription page containing textual information taken from the record displays.

If you click the Image icon, the image viewer appears, as shown in Figure 3-21. For our example, we click the Image icon.

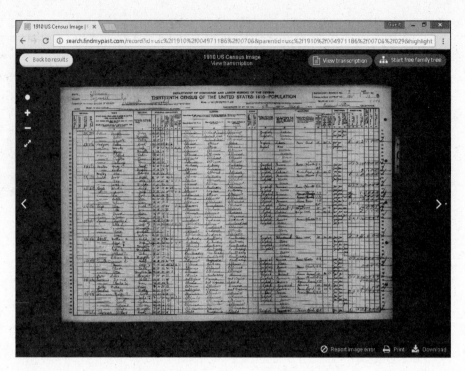

FIGURE 3-21:
The image viewer on findmypast. com.

10. **Click the Download button.**

Your web browser downloads the image as a .jpg file.

Exploring MyHeritage

MyHeritage offers access to over 7 billion historical records and over 35 million family trees. Also, the company also offers DNA research services, an online family tree, and desktop and mobile applications to organize your research.

MyHeritage prefers new users create an online family tree or buy a DNA test. However, you can get a 14-day free trial to search their records by following these steps:

1. **Point your web browser to** `https://www.myheritage.com/research`.

The MyHeritage SuperSearch page appears.

2. **Click the Advanced search link on the right side of the search box just below the picture of a magnifying glass.**

More search options appear in the box.

3. Type your ancestor's name into the name boxes, and select a gender.

We typed William Henry Abell and selected male. Note that there are drop-down boxes under both name fields where you can control how the search will treat the names that you enter.

4. Optionally, enter an event and relatives.

We typed selected birth from the drop-down box and entered 1873 for the year and Kentucky for the place. There are drop-down boxes with options to fine tune your search under each the date and place fields. We also entered death information and residence information from 1901 (that we learned when gathering information in Chapter 2). We also added Lizzie Pickerell as a spouse.

5. Click Search.

The results page appears (see Figure 3-22). Similar to other subscription sites, the results appear in the right column and filters appear in the left.

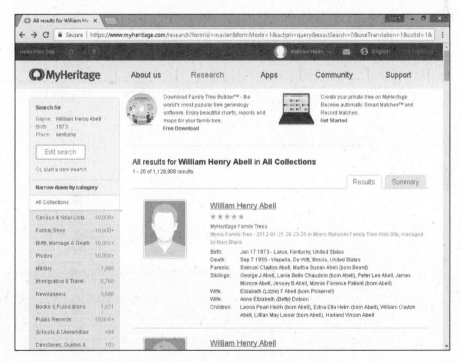

FIGURE 3-22:
The MyHeritage search results page.

6. Optionally, filter the list of results by selecting a category from the left column.

The page refreshes with filtered results.

7. **Click on a name to see more about the tree or record.**

   A Start Your Free 14-Day Trial pop-over box appears.

8. **Enter your first and last name and email address and click the Continue button.**

   The Payment page appears.

9. **Enter your first and last name and email address and click the Continue button.**

   The Payment page appears.

10. **Complete payment information and click the Begin Free Trial button.**

   The final confirmation page appears.

11. **Fill out the area code and phone number and click the Call Me Now button.**

   An automated service calls your phone with a confirmation number.

12. **Enter the confirmation code and click Next.**

   The record or family tree entry appears as in Figure 3-23.

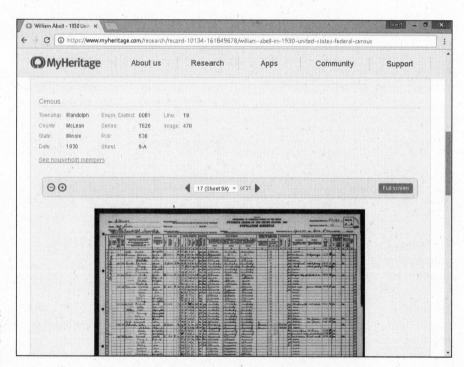

FIGURE 3-23:
The MyHeritage search results page.

Chapter **4**

Using All of Your Censuses

Although some people believe that the census is a nuisance every ten years, genealogists and family historians believe it's one of the most important sources of information. Censuses give us periodic snapshots of the composition of a household and are valuable for filling in the gaps in the lives of our ancestors. For example, if you look at the birth and death places for William Henry Abell (see Chapter 2 for the information that we gathered on him), you would think he lived all his life in Kentucky. By reviewing census records, we discover that he lived a number of places in Kentucky and Illinois.

Not so many years ago, only bits and pieces of transcribed censuses were online. Now, most comprehensive subscription sites contain digitized and indexed census records for the United States. Also, sites are making strides in placing census records for other countries online.

In this chapter, we show you what census records are currently available and describe some of the major projects that you can use as keys for unlocking government treasure chests of genealogical information.

Coming to Your Census

We like to think of researching an ancestor through census records like tracking a submarine. Every so often the submarine emerges, submerges, and then resurfaces. You don't really know the direct path the submarine took between the two points, but at least you can guess the general direction it's moving based on where it started and where it ended. Census records are similar in that you can use one census record as a starting point and a second census record (in a different year) as an ending point. Then you can look at common migration paths to predict the path your ancestor might have taken to get to his or her final destination.

To effectively use census records, it's important to understand what information they include and why they were created. *Census records* are periodic counts of a population by a government or organization. These counts can be conducted at regular intervals (such as every ten years) or special one-time counts made for a specific reason.

Detailed population census records are valuable for tying a person to a place and for discovering relationships between individuals. For example, let's take our William Henry Abell. We're not sure who his father was, but we do know that he was born in Kentucky. By using a census index, you may be able to find a William Henry Abell listed in a Kentucky census index as a member of someone's household. If the information about William in that record (age, location, and siblings' names) fits what you know from a family interview, you may have found one or more generations to add to your genealogy. You can use the name of the head of household and his or her spouse as a lead to investigate in identifying William's parents.

Often a census includes information such as a person's age, sex, occupation, birthplace, and relationship to the head of the household. Sometimes the *enumerators* — the people who conduct the census — add comments to the census record (such as a comment on the physical condition of an individual or an indication of the person's wealth) that may give you further insight into the person's life.

United States census schedules

Federal census records in the United States have been around since 1790. Within the United States, censuses are conducted every ten years to count the population for a couple of reasons — to correctly divide the number of seats in the U.S. House of Representatives and to assess federal taxes. Although census collections are still performed, privacy restrictions prevent the release of any detailed census information on individuals for 72 years. Currently, you can find federal census data on individuals for the census years 1790 to 1940. However, practically all of the 1890 census was destroyed due to actions taken after a fire in the Commerce Building in 1921 — for more on this, see "First in the Path of the Firemen," The Fate of the 1890 Population Census, at

```
https://www.archives.gov/publications/prologue/1996/spring/1890-
    census-1.html.
```

Federal census records are valuable because you can use them to take historical snapshots of your ancestors in ten-year increments. These snapshots enable you to track your ancestors as they moved from county to county or state to state, and to identify the names of parents and siblings of your ancestors who you may not have previously known. Also, by paying attention to neighbors listed in the census or by individuals who cohabitated with your ancestors, you may be able to determine families that later intermarried with your ancestor's family or discover why a family member was given a particular first name. For example, a child's first name might have been named after a close neighbor's last name.

REMEMBER

Each census year contains a different amount of information, with more modern census returns (also called *schedules*) containing the most information. Schedules from 1790 to 1840 list only the head of household for each family, along with the number of people living in the household broken down by age classifications. Schedules from 1850 on have the names and ages of all members of the household, and each subsequent census year's schedules contain additional information on members of the household.

AMERICAN SOUNDEX

You may run across the term Soundex — especially if you are working with the U.S. census, if you live in a state that uses Soundex as part of your driver's license number, or if you're just a nut for indexing systems. However, you might not realize that more than one Soundex system exists. The American Soundex, which is the one used for the U.S. census and the one most widely recognized, is not the only one, nor was it the first system developed.

The American Soundex system is an indexing method that groups names pronounced in a similar way but spelled differently. This indexing procedure allows you to find ancestors who may have changed the spelling of their names over the years. For example, you find names such as Helm, Helme, Holm, and Holme grouped in the American Soundex code H450.

(continued)

(continued)

The Russell Soundex system: Robert C. Russell patented the first Soundex system in 1918. The Russell Soundex system categorizes the alphabet phonetically and assigns numbers to the categories. You find eight categories and four other rules to follow. The odd-looking terms that refer to parts of the mouth are technical descriptions of how to make the sounds; just try making the sounds of the letters shown with each one, and you'll get the idea. Here's what they look (and sound) like:

Categories:

1. Vowels or oral resonants: *a, e, i, o, u, y*

2. Labials and labio-dentals: *b, f, p, v*

3. Gutturals and sibilants: *c, g, k, s, x, z*

4. Dental-mutes: *d, t*

5. Palatal-fricative: *l*

6. Labio-nasal: *m*

7. Dento- or lingua-nasal: *n*

8. Dental-fricative: *r*

Other rules:

- The code always begins with the first letter of the word.

- If you have two letters in a row that are the same, they are represented in the code as one letter (for example, *rr* is represented as *r*).

- If the word ends in *gh, s,* or *z,* those letters are ignored.

- Vowels are considered only the first time they appear.

The American Soundex system: The American Soundex system modified the Russell Soundex system. The changes include these:

- The code disregards vowels altogether, unless the first letter of the word is a vowel.

- The letters *m* and *n* are categorized together and represented by the same number.

- Words ending in *gh, s,* and *z* are treated the same as other words, and those letters are assigned values.

The American Soundex code begins with the first letter of the word and has three numbers following. Zeros are added to the code to ensure that it has three numbers.

The Daitch-Mokotoff Soundex system: The Daitch-Mokotoff Soundex system builds on the Russell and American Soundex systems and addresses difficulties in categorizing many Germanic and Slavic names that the other two systems encounter. The major points of this system are as follows:

- The code is made up of six numbers.

- The first letter of the word is also represented by a number. If the first letter is a vowel, it has the code 0.

- Some double-letter combinations that sound like single letters are coded as single.

- If a letter or letter combination can have two sounds, it is coded twice.

If you want more detailed information about the various Soundex systems, take a gander at the Soundexing and Genealogy website at www.avotaynu.com/soundex.html.

The Beider-Morse Phonetic Matching system: A problem with the various Soundex systems is that they often match names that are not really closely related. The goal of Phonetic Matching is to remove the irrelevant name matches, while not losing matches that are closely related. The features of the system include the following:

- Because the pronunciation of a name depends on the language that the name comes from, the system includes pronunciation tables for several languages, including Catalan, Czech, Dutch, English, French, German, Greek, Hebrew, Hungarian, Italian, Polish, Portuguese, Romanian, Russian, Spanish, and Turkish.

- After the language of the name is known, the name is converted to a sequence of phonetic tokens that are compared with other names that have been converted to tokens.

- Some double-letter combinations that sound like single letters are coded as single.

You can find more details on phonetic matching on the Phonetic Matching: A Better Soundex page at http://stevemorse.org/phonetics/bmpm2.htm.

And if you want to run some names through the American Soundex, Daitch-Mokotoff Soundex, and Beider-Morse Phonetic Matching systems at the same time, visit the Generating Soundex Codes and Phonetic Tokens in One Step converter at http://stevemorse.org/census/soundex.html.

Population schedules were not the only product of the federal censuses. Special schedules include census returns for slaves, mortality, agriculture, manufacturing, and veterans. Each type of special schedule contains information pertaining to a specific group or occupation. In the case of slave schedules (used in the 1850 and 1860 censuses), slaves were listed under the names of the slave owner, and information was provided on the age, gender, and race of the slave. If the slave was more than 100 years old, his or her name was listed on the schedule. Note, though, that enumerators may have included names for other slaves if he or she felt inclined to list them. Although the slave schedules do not contain a lot of information, they can be used as a starting point for further research. Figure 4-1 shows an example of a slave schedule from the 1850 census.

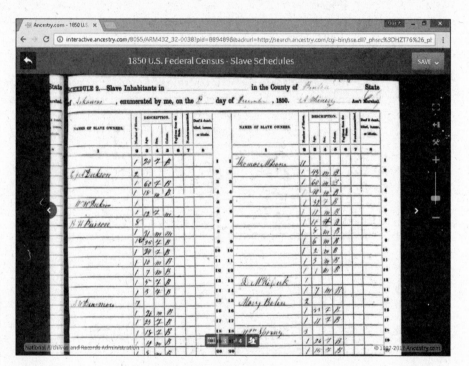

FIGURE 4-1:
1850 slave
schedule for
Benton County,
Arkansas.

Mortality schedules (used in 1850, 1860, 1870, and 1880) include information on people who died in the 12 months previous to the start of the census. For example, the 1860 schedule contains details such as name, age, sex, color, free or slave, married or widowed, place of birth, month of death, profession, cause of death, and number of days ill. Figure 4-2 shows a page from the 1860 schedule.

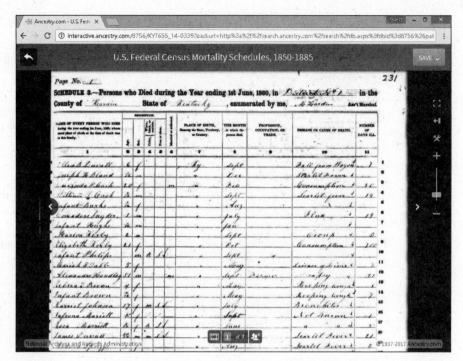

FIGURE 4-2:
1860 mortality schedule for Hardin County, Kentucky.

Agricultural schedules were used between 1840 and 1910. However, only the schedules from 1840 to 1880 survive. They contain detailed demographic and financial information on farm owners. Information contained on the schedules includes name of owner or manager of the farm, acres of land, cash value of the farm, value of implements and machinery, number and value of livestock, value of produce, and value of animals slaughtered; see Figure 4-3.

Manufacturing and industry schedules (taken infrequently between 1810 and 1880) contain information on business owners and their business interests. Details included on the 1850 schedule included the name of the company, product manufactured, capital invested, raw material used, kind of power used, average number of people employed, wages paid, and annual product produced; see Figure 4-4.

Veteran schedules include the Revolutionary War pensioner census, which was taken as part of the 1840 census, and the special census for Union veterans and their widows (taken in 1890). Information found on the 1890 special census includes rank, company, regiment or vessel, date of enlistment, date of discharge, and length of service. The remarks section includes information on disability and other comments the enumerator felt compelled to make. Figure 4-5 contains an example of the 1890 special schedule, including surviving soldiers, sailors, marines, and widows.

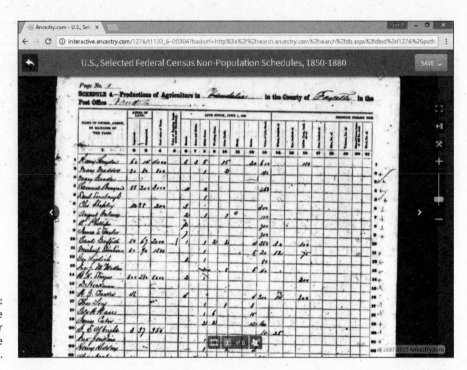

FIGURE 4-3:
1860 agriculture schedule for Vandalia, Fayette County, Illinois.

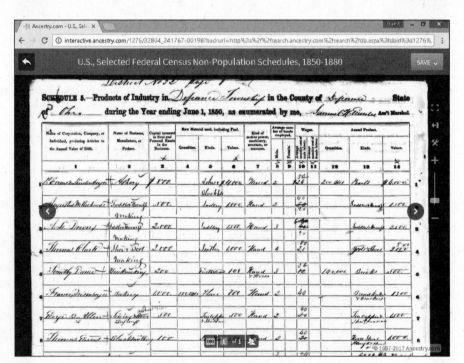

FIGURE 4-4:
1850 industry schedule for Defiance County, Ohio.

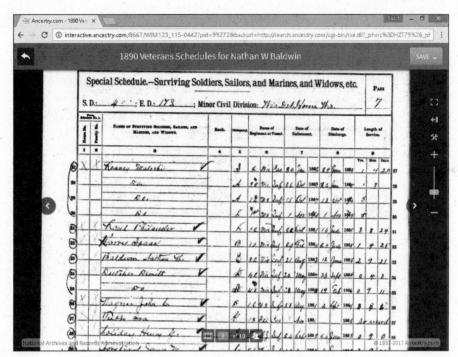

FIGURE 4-5:
1890 veteran special schedule.

State, territorial, and other census records

Federal census records are not the only population enumerations you can find for ancestors in the United States. You may also find census records at the state, territorial, and local level for certain areas of the United States.

Several state and territorial censuses have become available online. Ancestry.com (www.ancestry.com) has, within its subscription collection, state and territorial censuses for Alabama (1820–1866), California (1852), Colorado (1885), Florida (1867–1945), Illinois (1825–1865), Iowa (1836–1925), Kansas (1855–1925), Michigan (1894); Minnesota (1849–1905), Mississippi (1792–1866), Missouri (1844–1881), Nebraska (1860–1885), Nevada (1875), New Jersey (1895), New York (1880, 1892, 1905), North Carolina (1784–1787), North Dakota (1915, 1925), Oklahoma (1890, 1907), Rhode Island (1865–1935), South Dakota (1895), Washington (1857–1892), and Wisconsin (1895, 1905), as well as a host of other census records, including images of the U.S. Indian census schedules from 1885 to 1940.

Another source for state and territorial census images is at the free site HistoryKat (www.historykat.com). HistoryKat has images of Illinois (1810–1820). Figure 4-6 shows an image from the 1820 Illinois state census for Franklin County.

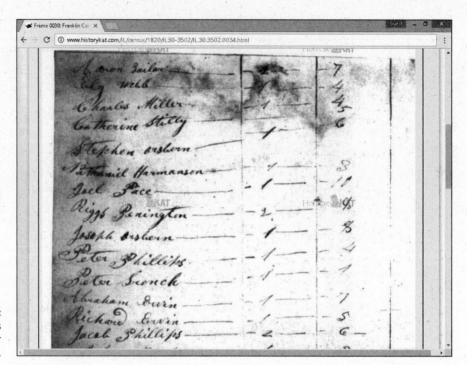

FIGURE 4-6:
The 1820 Illinois state census for Franklin County.

Indexes and some images for state and territorial censuses are also found at no charge on FamilySearch (www.familysearch.org). Locations available on the site include Alabama (1855, 1866), California (1852), Colorado (1885), Florida (1885, 1935, 1945), Illinois (1855, 1865), Iowa (1885, 1895, 1905), Massachusetts (1855, 1865), Michigan (1894), Minnesota (1865–1905), New Jersey (1855, 1865, 1885, 1895, 1905, and 1915), New York (1855–1925), Rhode Island (1885–1935), and South Dakota 1905–1945).

Special census records can often help you piece together your ancestors' migration patterns, account for ancestors who may not have been enumerated in the federal censuses, or provide greater details on ancestors who were members of a specific population. Some examples of special censuses available at Ancestry.com (www.ancestry.com) include

» **Census of merchant seamen, 1930:** Enumerates the name of each person on board, sex, race, age, marital status, ability to read/write, place of birth, citizenship status, ability to speak English, occupation, whether the person was a veteran mobilized for war/expedition, and address of next of kin

» **New York census of inmates in almshouses and poorhouses, 1830–1920:** Contains name, age, date of admission and discharge, habits, education, names and addresses of relatives and friends, questions on extended family, and questions on tendency toward self-sufficiency or dependence

>> **Puerto Rico, special censuses, agricultural schedules, 1935:** Lists the names of owners and managers of farms, acreage, farm value, machinery, livestock, and amount of staples produced on the farm

>> **U.S. special census on deaf family marriages and hearing relatives, 1888–1895:** Contains information on how the person became deaf and other relatives that might also be deaf

>> **U.S. special census of Indians, 1880:** Includes Indian name, English translation of the name, whether a chief, whether full-blooded, number of years on the reservation, and health information

>> **U.S. Indian census rolls, 1885-1940:** A collection of several censuses performed on Indian reservations; see Figure 4-7

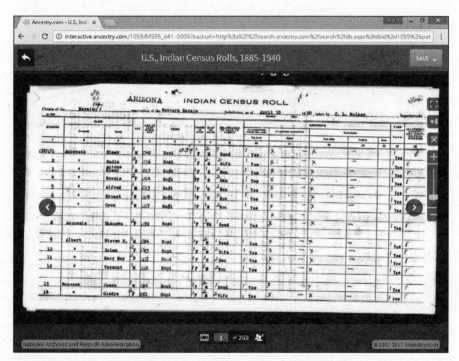

FIGURE 4-7:
The 1880 special census of Indians.

Finding Your Ancestors in U.S. Census Records

Imagine that you're ready to look for your ancestors in census records. You hop in the car and drive to the nearest library, archives, or Family History Center. On arrival, you find the microfilm roll for the area where you believe your ancestors lived. You then go into a dimly lit room, insert the microfilm into the reader, and begin your search. After a few hours of rolling the microfilm, the back pain begins to set in, cramping in your hands becomes more severe, and the handwritten census documents become blurry as your eyes strain from reading each entry line by line. You come to the end of the roll and still haven't found your elusive ancestor. At this point, you begin to wonder if a better way exists.

Fortunately, a better way *does* exist for finding and accessing U.S. census records. The easiest way, if you have the financial means, is to subscribe to a site that has indexed census records that link to images of the census microfilm. These sites include Ancestry.com (`www.ancestry.com`), findmypast.com (`www.findmypast.com`), and MyHeritage (`www.myheritage.com`). The free site, FamilySearch (`www.familysearch.org`) also has indexed census records. You can normally access the census records through the standard search mechanism on the site. If you need a refresher on searching these sites, see Chapter 3.

WARNING

Be careful when using these census indexes. Not all indexes include every person in the census. Some are merely head-of-household indexes. It's a good idea to read the description that comes with the index to see how complete it is. Also, the same quality control may not be there for every census year, even within the same index-producing company. If you do not find your ancestor in one of these indexes, don't automatically assume that he or she is not in the census. Also remember that many indexes were created outside the United States by people who were not native English speakers and who were under time constraints. It's quite possible that the indexer was incorrect in indexing a particular entry — possibly the person you're searching for.

Sifting through census record results

REMEMBER

As you might recall from Chapter 2, William Henry Abell was born around 1873 in Kentucky, was located in Wapella, De Witt County, Illinois, in 1901, and died in Hodgenville, Kentucky, on 07 September 1955. There are a lot of gaps between 1873, 1901, and 1955 that can be narrowed with census records. In this section, we walk you through the process of evaluating the census records found on the Ancestry.com website. We use the same search steps outlined in Chapter 3, so we won't repeat them here.

Figure 4-8 shows some of the results from Ancestry.com. A total of 3,818 results came back and only a very few will pertain to William. After all, during his lifetime there were only eight censuses — 1880, 1890, 1900, 1910, 1920, 1930, 1940, and 1950. The 1890 census is unavailable due to the actions taken after the fire in the Commerce Building in 1921 and the 1950 census is not available to the public until 2022 (due to privacy restrictions). This leaves six census years for research — a very manageable number.

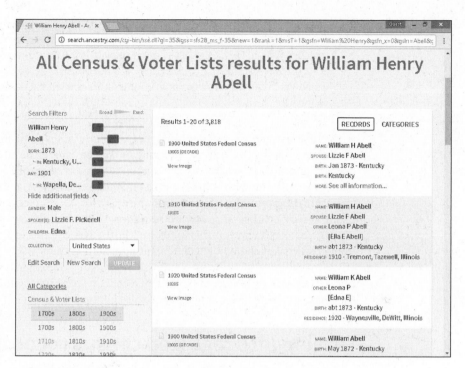

FIGURE 4-8:
Census search results from Ancestry.com.

Here is a quick evaluation of the search results:

>> **Search result 1:** The result is from the 1900 census. The search record matches the following elements that we assembled in Chapter 2: William H Abell, Lizzie F Abell, and birthdate of January 1873.

>> **Search result 2:** The result is from the 1910 census. The search record matches: William H Abell, Lizzie F Abell, Leona P Abell, [Ella E Abell], birth about 1873 in Kentucky.

>> **Search result 3:** The result is from the 1920 census. The search record matches William K Abell, Leona P, Edna E, birth around 1873 in Kentucky. The middle initial error is not uncommon in indexing — sometimes it is hard to read the handwriting of the census enumerator.

>> **Search result 4:** The result is from the 1900 census. The search record matches William Abell, but no other element except a birth in Kentucky. The birthdate is close — 1872, but we already have a better match for the 1900 census in the first search result.

>> **Search result 5:** The result is from the 1930 census. The search record matches William Abell, Betty Abell, birth around 1873 in Kentucky. Keep in mind that William was married to a Betty at the time of his death, according to his obituary.

>> **Search result 6:** The result is from the 1880 census. The search record matches William H, but the last name is spelled Abl. The birth date and place are a match — about 1873 in Kentucky. It is not unusual to see name spelling variations in census records. Some enumerators spelled the name like it sounded.

In the first six search results, we had pretty good luck. Five census records match our target ancestor. Of course, you may be asking where the 1940 census is. It doesn't appear until search result number 36. This is probably because the first name is abbreviated Wm H Abell with a birth date of about 1872. The abbreviation and conflicting year of birth prompted the entry for the 1940 census to drop down in the search results. Of course, if you knew you were missing one census year (1940), you could click on the 1940s link in the left column to filter the results. Doing that makes the Wm H Abell result number 2 on the list.

Our next step is to look at the digitized records to confirm the information from the index and to see what other nuggets are in the record.

Digging into digitized census records

We think that the best part of family history research is when you are able to see the actual record that is evidence of the existence of your ancestor. You never know what surprising information you may encounter.

WARNING

Before jumping into looking at census records, it is a good idea to understand more about how the record was created so you have the context of the information presented on the image. Census enumerators conducted the census by going from house to house within a pre-defined enumeration district. They would ask occupants a standard set of questions and record the answers. If the occupants were not home, the enumerators were authorized to get answers to the questions from the nearest available person with knowledge of the household. This means you will find incorrect information in census schedules, and that is a reason to always corroborate information with other records. In some census years, multiple copies of the census records were made. As they were handwritten records, mistakes were also made in recopying the schedules. Enumerators were provided instructions on how to complete the census returns. The 1940 instructions can be found at http://1940census.archives.gov/downloads/instructions-to-enumerators.pdf.

TIP

As far as a strategy for using digitized records is concerned, we like to begin with the newest record and work our way back in time. That way we can build on the information from record to record and triangulate any new information. In our case, we start with the search result for the 1940 census. Clicking on the result brings us to the record page (see Figure 4-9). This page is a transcription of the key elements of the census record. The transcription can be very handy if part of the record is hard to read — it is almost like having a second set of eyes to help you interpret the record. However, keep in mind that indexers do make mistakes, so it is okay if you don't agree with their interpretation of the record. Also, note that at the bottom of the page is a source citation for the record. The citation is something that you will want to use when putting the record's contents into your genealogical application.

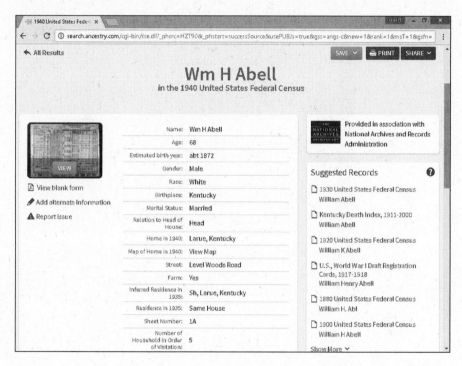

FIGURE 4-9:
The record page for the 1940 census.

If you click on the View button on the thumbnail of the census record, you are taken to the image viewer (see Figure 4-10). To make it easy to find your ancestor, the information matching the search result is highlighted on the page. In the next few paragraphs, we go through the schedule so that you know where to look for all the relevant information provided by the record.

The first important element of a census enumeration is at the top of the page. Starting on the left side, the schedule states that the record is from Larue County, Kentucky. In particular, the page was enumerated in the Magisterial District Number 3, Buffalo. This provides us with a geographical landmark for the schedule. The Supervisor's District (Number 4) and Enumeration District (Number 62-7) numbers are found in the upper right corner of the schedule. These can also be used to locate where the enumerator was when the record was created. These can be very handy in rural areas where addresses were not always used. The final piece of critical evidence is the date of the enumeration — 23–24 April 1940. You have the actual date that the enumerator asked the questions. This date can help explain why an individual may not be listed in the census (for example, they were born in 1940, but after the enumeration date).

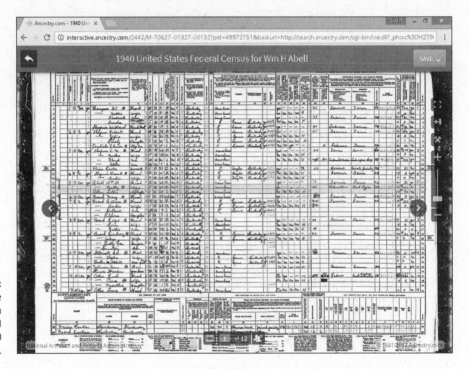

The image of the enumeration page for Wm H Abell in the 1940 census.

Armed with the enumeration district number, we can find a digitized map of the 1940 enumeration districts at the National Archives Web or Ancestry.com websites. An easy way to find the map is to use Steve Morse and Joel Weintraub's Viewing 1940 Enumeration District Maps in One Step web page. Try this:

1. **Point your browser to** `http://stevemorse.org/census/arc1940-1950edmaps.html?year=1940`.

   The page appears with drop-down boxes for the state, county, and city.

2. **Set the drop-down boxes to your desired location and click the Get ED Map Images button.**

   We set the state to Kentucky and county to Larue County. A new page appears with links to the National Archives viewer (preferred if you don't have an Ancestry.com subscription), the image files on the National Archives site, and the Ancestry.com viewer.

3. Click a link to view the enumeration district map.

We clicked on the Ancestry.com viewer, so we could link the map to William Henry Abell's record on our online family tree. The map appears in a separate browser window as seen in Figure 4-11.

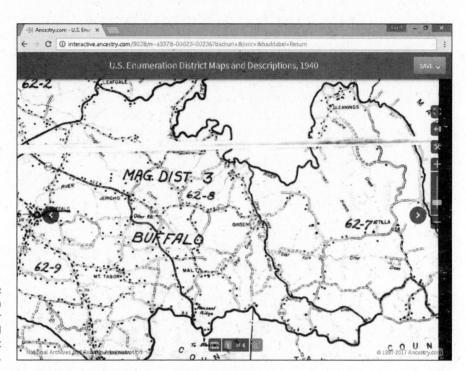

FIGURE 4-11:
The Enumeration District map for Magisterial District Number 3.

REMEMBER

Back to the census schedule, we scrolled down to the entry for Wm H Abell. His household begins on line 17. Starting with the left side of the entry, we can see that the house was located on Levelwoods Road, and it was the fifth residence visited by the enumerator. The property was a farm owned by William valued at $500. The value of the farm was consistent with neighboring properties. William was the head of a three-person household, a white male aged 68, born in Kentucky. The highest grade of school he completed was fifth grade. On 1 April 1935, William lived at the same residence. He was self-employed for 10 hours a week as a farmer and had worked 40 weeks during 1939. His annual income was $50. The record also indicated that William was listed on Farm Schedule 5. As for his wife Betty, she was a 48-year-old white female, born in Kentucky. She was the respondent to the census enumerator (as indicated by the circle with an "X" symbol). She also had a fifth-grade education and worked as the postmistress at the Post Office, earning a salary of $242. She worked 52 weeks in 1939. Also, living in the household was Lillie Allen, a step-daughter to William. She was a single, 28-year-old white female with a fifth-grade education. She was not listed as employed, but had made $30 over the past year, working 10 weeks in 1939.

Consolidating your discoveries

As you can see, we learned a lot about William and his family from the record that we covered in the last section. We can compare his information to his neighbors to get a sense of the community that he lived within. Up to now we've engaged in the planning phase and researching phase. Now, it's time to move into the consolidation phase and store our information. As we have confirmed that the information in the census record is consistent with what we knew about William, we can save the information to our Ancestry.com online family tree (even if you don't have an Ancestry.com family tree, you can save the record to your computer). Here is how:

1. **Click the green Save button.**

The button is located in the upper-right corner of the viewer. A drop-down box appears with choices on where to save the record.

2. **Choose a location to save the record.**

We chose to save it to William Henry Abell online family tree record. A new page appears comparing information from the record to the current information stored in William's online family tree record (see Figure 4-12).

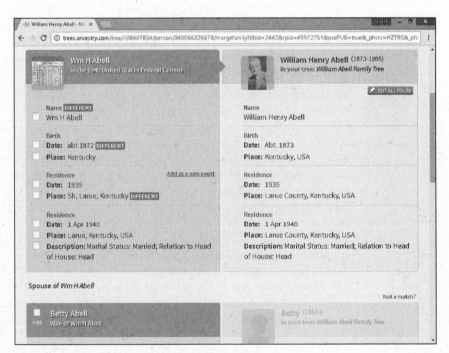

FIGURE 4-12: The Add New Information to Your Tree page.

3. Select the information that you wish saved to the online family tree.

Use the checkboxes to select the information. Note that the box specifies information that is different from the record in the online family tree, as well as, those items that are new. If the person's box is grayed out, click on the checkbox next to their name.

4. Optionally, edit any information that needs clarification by clicking on the Edit All Fields button located in the right column. Click the Close Editing button when the edits are complete.

In our example, the residence entry for 1935 shows the place as Sh, Larue, Kentucky. "Sh" isn't really a place — it is a code from the census meaning "Same House." So, we edited the field to say "Larue County, Kentucky, USA."

5. Click the Save to Your Tree button.

The facts page appears for the person to whom you saved the record.

Figure 4-13 shows the updated facts page for William Henry Abell. Notice that the 1940 United States Federal Census box was added to the Sources column and is linked to three facts (the purple lines drawn from the source to the fact shows the link). Also, see that a new entry shows under Web Links — to the 1940 Enumeration District Map. Notice that Lillie Allen has been added as a child under Betty. Because Lillie was a step-daughter, we edit the entry to show that William was not the biological father.

FIGURE 4-13:
William Henry Abell's facts page with new information.

1. **Click on the box of the person you want to edit.**

   We clicked on the Lillie Allen box under the Spouse & Children section of the Family Column. The facts page for the person appears.

2. **Click on the Edit drop-down button.**

   The button is located in the upper-right corner of the screen (a pencil icon is on the button). A drop-down menu appears.

3. **Select Edit Relationships and change the relationship information.**

   A pop-over box appears. You can choose to add an alternative father or mother or change the relationship of the current parent. We don't know Lillie's father, so we change William Henry Abell's drop-down from Biological to Step. If we discover the identity of Lillie's father in the future, we can associate her with him later.

4. **Click the "X" button in the upper-right corner to dismiss the pop-over box.**

   The facts page appears.

Using census records to tell a story

Family history is more than collecting the names and birth/death dates of people who lived in the past. It is about telling the story of their lives. Your ancestor was more than a line number on a census schedule within a particular county and state. They had jobs, possessed land, were educated at a certain level, and had relationships with the community around them.

As a final step in the consolidation phase, we should write up the results of our research on the census record and put it into our genealogy application. In our case, we add it to the Ancestry.com online family tree LifeStory page. Here's how:

1. **From the Pedigree view, click your ancestor's box and select the Profile button.**

   We selected William Henry Abell's box and clicked on the Profile button. The facts page appears.

2. **Click on the LifeStory link.**

   The LifeStory link is located in the menu just under the name of the ancestor. The LifeStory timeline appears with facts, maps, and historical articles, as seen in Figure 4-14.

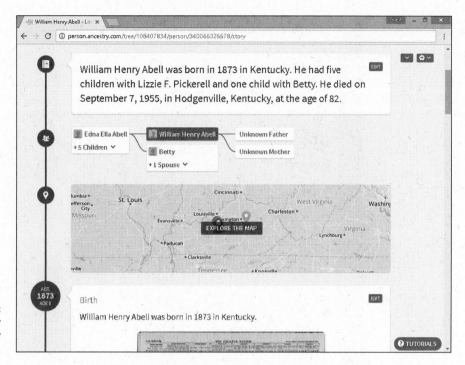

FIGURE 4-14:
William Henry
Abell's LifeStory
page.

3. **Edit a fact to provide additional details from the census record.**

   We scrolled down to the fact dated 1 April 1940 — marked "Residence, William Henry Abell lived in Larue, Kentucky, on April 1, 1940."

4. **Click the Edit button.**

   The Edit button is located in the upper-right corner of the fact. The fields in the fact become editable. Type or cut and paste information into the fields. We put our discoveries into the third field and adjusted the date to be the actual date on the census schedule.

5. **Click the Save button.**

   The text saves in the field.

To complete the research on census records, we would repeat the process for each census year. To triangulate information, compare the results from each census year. Table 4-1 shows an abstract of the information that we discovered in each census year.

TABLE 4-1

Information from Census Years

Census	1940	1930	1920	1910	1900	1880
Name	Abell, Wm H	Abell, William	Abell, William K.	Abell, William H.	Abell, William H.	Abl, William H.
Location	Kentucky – Larue County	Illinois – McLean County	Illinois – De Witt County	Illinois – Tazewell County	Illinois – De Witt County	Kentucky – Larue County
Age	68	57	47	37	27	7
Birthplace	Kentucky	Kentucky	Kentucky	Kentucky	Kentucky	Kentucky
Owned/Rented	Owned	Rented	Rented	Rented	Rented	
Value of Home	500	215				
Occupation	Farmer	Blacksmith	Farmer	Blacksmith	Farm Laborer	
Spouse	Betty	Betty	N/A	Lizzie F.	Lizzie F.	
Other Members of Household	Allen, Lillie	Allen, Lillie Allen, Nancy Allen, Evelyn Allen, Howard Abell, Harland	Abell, Leona P. Abell, Edna E. Abell, William C. Abell, Lillian M. Abell, Harland V.	Abell, Leona P. Abell, Ella E. Abell, William C. Abell, Lillian M.	Abell, Neona P.	Abl, Samuel C. Abl, Martha S. Abl George I. Abl, Lena B. Abl, Peter L.
Date	23-24 April 1940	29 April 1930	15-16 January 1920	04 May 1910	06 June 1900	01 June 1880

After looking through the six censuses, we pieced together the following new information about William Henry Abell. William lived in four counties in two states — starting and ending in Larue County (Kentucky), with stops in De Witt County (Illinois), Tazewell County (Illinois), and McLean County (Illinois). He was first married to Lizzie F. Pickerell around 1899 (1900 census) and married Betty between 1920 and 1930 (1930 census). We also have the approximate birth dates and states of Lizzie and Betty, five children, four step-children, and four siblings. Finally, we have the names and birth dates and states for William's parents (1880 census). By looking at six records we expanded the number of facts on William's online family tree page from three to eighteen (see Figure 4-15).

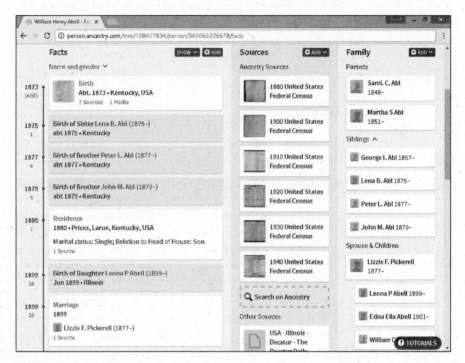

FIGURE 4-15: William Henry Abell's facts page after census research.

Census Records from Afar

Of course, the U.S. isn't the only country to carry out census enumerations. Several countries around the world have taken periodic snapshots of the population. The frequency of these enumerations wasn't always every ten years and wasn't always for the same purposes as in the U.S. Details on censuses are found as follows. We indicated whether there are online sources for the records.

Africa

>> **Ghana:** FamilySearch has added images of census records from 1984.

Asia

>> **Japan:** FamilySearch.org hosts census records from Ehime-ken from 1661-1875 at `https://familysearch.org/search/collection/2313184`.

>> **Philippines:** Censuses were taken by the United States for military personnel in 1900, 1910, and 1920 and are available on Ancestry.com. A census was also conducted in 1903 and is available on the Internet Archive at `https://archive.org/details/censusphilippin01ganngoog`.

Europe

>> **Albania:** FamilySearch.org has unindexed images of the 1930 census available online.

>> **Austria:** Some general information is available on the content of the Galicia censuses and is contained in two articles on the Federation of East European Family History Societies site: Austrian Census Returns from 1869 to 1890 (`http://feefhs.org/region/galicia-census-returns`) and Austrian Census for Galicia (`http://feefhs.org/region/galicia-austrian-census`). FamilySearch.org has posted census records for Wels, Upper Austria, citizen rolls for Linz 1658-1937, and Vienna population cards 1850-1896.

>> **Czech Republic:** The South Bohemian Census 1857–1921 contains digitized images from the 1857, 1869, 1880, 1890, 1900, 1910, and 1921 censuses. You can find the images at `http://digi.ceskearchivy.cz/DA?lang=en&menu=0&doctree=1t&id=5`. FamilySearch has placed more than 4.9 million images of census records and registers from 1800-1990 at `https://familysearch.org/search/collection/1930345`.

>> **Denmark:** The Danish Archives has census returns for the years 1787, 1801, 1834, 1840, 1845, 1850, 1855, 1860, 1870, 1880, 1890, 1901, 1906, 1911, 1916, 1921, 1925, 1930, and 1940. You can find information from these censuses at the Statens Arkiver site (`https://www.sa.dk/ao-soegesider/da/collection/theme/2`) and the Dansk Demografisk Database (`http://ddd.dda.dk/kiplink_en.htm`). The Dansk Demografisk Database also includes censuses and lists of emigrants and immigrants for Denmark. FamilySearch.org hosts the 1911 and 1916 censuses. MyHeritage (`www.myheritage.com`) has the 1901, 1906, 1911, 1916, 1921, 1925, and 1930

censuses online. Police Registers from Copenhagen 1890-1923 are available at http://www.politietsregisterblade.dk./index.php. Censuses for the county of Aarhus are online at www.folketimidten.dk.

>> **Estonia:** FamilySearch has placed over 600,000 images of population registers from Estonia. Years covered include 1918 through 1944.

>> **Finland:** MyHeritage (www.myheritage.com) has church census and pre-confirmation books dated 1657-1915 available online.

>> **France:** FamilySearch.org has indexes and images for the 1856 and 1876 censuses for Dordogne, France; and the 1830-1831, 1872, 1886, and 1891 censuses for Haute-Garonne, Toulouse, France. The English census of Pondichéry is available on the Internet Archive Wayback Machine at http://web.archive.org/web/20051018170723/http://pondichery.ifrance.com/index.html.

>> **Germany:** The collection at Ancestry.com contains the Mecklenburg-Schwerin censuses of 1819, 1867, 1890, 1900, and 1919; the Lübeck census of 1807, 1812, 1815, 1831, 1845, 1851, 1857, 1862, 1871, 1875, and 1880. FamilySearch (https://familysearch.org) and MyHeritage (www.myheritage.com) has also posted the Mecklenburg-Schwerin censuses of 1867, 1890, and 1900.

>> **Hungary:** Ancestry.com has the 1869 All Citizen Census, assorted census records from 1781-1850, Jewish Census of 1848, and Jewish names in property tax census of 1828. The National Archives of Hungary collection (http://mnl.gov.hu) includes the 1623, 1631, 1691, 1715,1775, 1787, and 1828 Urbarial Census; Jewish Census of 1848; 1857 Census, and 1877 Census.

>> **Iceland:** The National Archives of Iceland Census database (http://www.manntal.is/?lang=en) includes records from the censuses of 1703, 1816, 1835, 1840, 1845, 1850, 1855, 1860, 1870, 1880, 1890, 1901, 1910, and 1920. Ancestry.com hosts the censuses from 1870, 1880, and 1890.

>> **Ireland:** The 1901 and 1911 censuses, along with fragments and substitutes from 1821-1851 are available online at www.census.nationalarchives.ie. The following records are available at Ancestry.com — 1766 Religious Census, Census Abstracts 1841-1851, 1901 Census, and 1911 Census. Findmypast (www.findmypast.com) hosts records from the 1821–1851 census, 1901 and 1911 censuses, 1922 Army Census, and Census of Elphin of 1749. FamilySearch.org has the 1821, 1831, 1841, and 1851 censuses. MyHeritage (www.myheritage.com) has the 1901 and 1911 censuses and the 1851 Dublin city census.

>> **Italy:** FamilySearch.org contains census records from 1750–1900 for Mantova.

>> **Moldova:** FamilySearch.org has image only collections of Poll Tax Census (Revision Lists) and Census Lists 1796–1917. Ancestry.com has the Bessarabia, Revision Lists, 1837–1952.

- » **Luxembourg:** FamilySearch has uploaded 1.1 million images of census records from 1843 to 1900 at `https://familysearch.org/search/collection/2037957`.

- » **Netherlands:** FamilySearch houses census and population registers from 1574 to 1940 and Noord-Brabant Province population registers from 1820 to 1930. Ancestry.com has the Population Registers Index, 1850–Present and Census and Population Registers, 1645–1940 collections.

- » **Norway:** The National Archives of Norway (`https://media.digitalarkivet.no/en/ft/browse`) maintains online the censuses of 1663-1666, 1701, 1769, 1801, 1815, 1825, 1835, 1845, 1855, 1865, 1870, 1875, 1885, 1891, 1900, and 1910. FamilySearch.org, MyHeritage, and Ancestry.com have the 1875 Census.

- » **Poland:** Ancestry.com has the Będzin Jewish Census, 1939.

- » **Romania:** Ancestry.com hosts the Jewish Census, 1942.

- » **Russia:** FamilySearch contains Tver Confession Lists 1728–1913 and Tartarstan Confession Lists 1775–1932. Ancestry.com has the Jewish Families in Russian Empire Census, 1897.

- » **Slovakia:** FamilySearch.org hosts images from the 1869 Census.

- » **Spain:** FamilySearch houses the Catastro de Ensenada, 1749–1756.

- » **Sweden:** The National Archives houses a database of the 1860, 1870, 1880, 1890, 1900, 1910, and 1930 censuses at `https://sok.riksarkivet.se/folkrakningar`. The Research Archives, Umeå University Library houses the 1890 Census at `http://www2.foark.umu.se/census/Index.htm`.

- » **Switzerland:** FamilySearch.org contains census enumerations from Fribourg for the years 1811, 1818, 1831, 1834, 1836, 1839, 1842, 1845, 1850, 1860, 1870, and 1880.

- » **Ukraine:** FamilySearch.org has the Odessa Census Records 1897.

- » **United Kingdom:** For general information on census records, see the National Archives Census page at `www.nationalarchives.gov.uk/records/looking-for-person/recordscensus.htm`. Images of the 1841 through 1911 censuses are available at Ancestry.com, FindMyPast.com (`www.findmypast.co.uk`), Genes Reunited (`www.genesreunited.co.uk`), and MyHeritage. Transcriptions are sporadic for the 1841 through 1891 censuses at the FreeCEN site (`http://www.freecen.org.uk`) and TheGenealogist.co.uk (`www.thegenealogist.co.uk`).

North America

» **Canada:** Library and Archives Canada maintains information on the 1825, 1831, 1842, 1851, 1861, 1870, 1871, 1881, 1891, 1901, 1906, 1911, and 1916 censuses online at www.bac-lac.gc.ca/eng/census/Pages/census.aspx. Ancestry.ca (www.ancestry.ca) has the 1825, 1842, 1851, 1861, 1871, 1881, 1891, 1901, 1906, 1911, 1916, and 1921 censuses. MyHeritage (www.myheritage.com) hosts the 1825, 1842, 1861, 1871, 1881, 1891, 1901, and 1911 censuses. FamilySearch.org has the 1901 and 1916 censuses.

» **Guatemala:** FamilySearch.org, Ancestry.com and MyHeritage contain the Cuidad de Guatemala Census of 1877.

» **Mexico:** FamilySearch.org and Ancestry.com have the 1930 Census.

Oceania

» **Australia:** Individual state censuses date 1788. The first country-wide census was conducted in 1881. Most returns were destroyed, in accordance with law. You can substitute other records for census returns in the form of convict returns and musters and post office directories. These returns are available for some states for the years 1788, 1792, 1796, 1800, 1801, 1805, 1806, 1811, 1814, 1816, 1817–1823, 1825, 1826, and 1837. FamilySearch.org offers the New South Wales 1828, 1841, and 1891 censuses and Ancestry.com has the 1901 census for New South Wales online. A portion of the 1913 census is available at http://www.hotkey.net.au/~jwilliams4/act1913.htm. For more information on locating census returns, see the Census in Australia page at www.jaunay.com/auscensus.html.

South America

» **Argentina:** The first two national censuses were conducted in 1869 and 1895, and a census was conducted in 1855 for Buenos Aires. These censuses are available online at FamilySearch.org, MyHeritage and Ancestry.com. The 1914 national census is only available at the Archivo General de la Nación.

» **Peru:** FamilySearch.org hosts the Municipal Census, 1831–1866.

2 Bringing Your Ancestor to Life

IN THIS PART . . .

Discover effective ways to search for your ancestor using search engines.

Learn the power of geographic resources to provide context to the life of your ancestors.

Locate online resources for locations outside of the United States, as well as ethnic-specific sites.

Chapter **5**

Digging Deeper into Your Ancestors' Lives

As we all know, governments love paper. Sometimes it seems that government workers can't do anything without a form. Luckily for genealogists, governments have been this way for many years — otherwise, it might be next to impossible to conduct family history research. In fact, the number of useful government records available online has exploded in the past decade. Not only have government entities been placing records and indexes online, but private companies have put great effort into digitizing and indexing government records for online use.

In this chapter, we show you what kinds of records are available and describe some of the major projects that you can use as keys for unlocking government treasure chests of genealogical information.

These Records Are Vital

It seems that some kind of government record accompanies every major event in our lives. One is generated when we are born, another when we get married (as well as get divorced), another when we have a child, and still another when we pass on. *Vital records* is the collective name for records of these events. Traditionally, these records have been kept at the local level — in the county, parish, or in some cases, the town where the event occurred. However, over time, some state-level government agencies began making an effort to collect and centralize the holdings of vital records.

Reading vital records

Vital records are among the first sets of primary sources typically used by genealogists (for more on primary sources, see Chapter 1). These records contain key and usually reliable information because they were produced near the time that the event occurred, and a witness to the event provided the information. (Outside the United States, vital records are often called *civil registrations*.) Four common types of vital records are birth records, marriage records, divorce records, and death records.

Birth records

Birth records are good primary sources for verifying the date of birth, birthplace, and names of an individual's parents. Depending on the information requirements for a particular birth certificate, you may also discover the birthplace of the parents, their ages, occupations, addresses at the time of the birth, whether the mother had given birth previously, date of marriage of the parents, and the names and ages of any previous children.

REMEMBER

Sometimes, instead of a birth certificate, you may find another record in the family's possession that verifies the existence of the birth record. For example, instead of having a certified copy of a birth certificate, Matthew's grandmother had a Certificate of Record of Birth. This certificate attests to the fact that the county has a birth record and notes its location. These certificates were used primarily before photocopiers became commonplace, and it became easier to get a certified copy of the original record. If you encounter a Certificate of Record of Birth, be sure to do further research and find the actual birth record. Sometimes the information on the Certificate of Record of Birth was copied incorrectly or there may be further information in the birth record that is not reflected on the Certificate.

TIP

Birth records were less formal in earlier times. Before modern record-keeping, a simple handwritten entry in a book sufficed as an official record of an individual's birth. For an example of this type of birth record see Figure 2-5 in Chapter 2. Be very specific when citing a birth record in your genealogical notes. Include any numbers you find in the record and where the record is located (including not only the physical location of the building, but the book number and page number of the information too, and even the record number if one is present).

Marriage records

Marriage records come in several forms. Early marriage records may include the following:

>> **Marriage bonds:** Financial guarantees that a marriage was going to take place

>> **Marriage banns:** Proclamations of the intent to marry someone in front of a church congregation

>> **Marriage licenses:** Documents granting permission to marry

>> **Marriage records or certificates:** Documents certifying the union of two people

These records usually contain the groom's name, the bride's name, and the location of the ceremony. They may also contain occupation information, birthplaces of the bride and groom, parents' names and birthplaces, names of witnesses, and information on previous marriages.

REMEMBER

When using marriage records, don't confuse the date of the marriage with the date of the marriage bond, bann, or license. The latter records were often filed anywhere from a few days to several weeks *before* the actual marriage date. Also, don't assume that because you found a bond, bann, or license, a marriage took place. Some people got cold feet then (as they do today) and backed out of the marriage at the last minute.

TIP

If you have trouble finding a marriage record in the area where your ancestors lived, try looking in surrounding counties or parishes or possibly even states. Like today, destination weddings did occur! Lucky for those of us researching in the twenty-first century — most of our ancestors' destinations were nearby towns instead of exotic, far-off places. Typically, the reason some ancestors traveled to another location was to have the wedding at a relative's house or church. So if the record isn't in the location you expect, be sure to look in the areas where the parents of the ancestors lived.

Divorce records

One type of vital record that may be easy to overlook is a divorce decree. Later generations may not be aware that an early ancestor was divorced, and the records recounting the event can be difficult to find. However, divorce records can be valuable. They contain many important facts, including the age of the petitioners, birthplace, address, occupations, names and ages of children, property, and the grounds for the divorce.

Death records

Death records are excellent resources for verifying the date of death but are less reliable for other data elements such as birth date and birthplace because people who were not witnesses to the birth often supply that information. However, information on the death record can point you in the right direction for records to verify other events. More recent death records include the name of the individual, place of death, residence, parents' names, spouse's name, occupation, and cause of death. Early death records may contain only the date of death, cause, and residence.

Gauging vitals online

Historically, researchers were required to contact the county, parish, or town clerk to receive a copy of a vital record. This meant either traveling to the location where the record was housed or ordering the record through the mail. With the advent of online research, most sites covering vital records are geared toward providing addresses of repositories, rather than information on the vital records of particular individuals. The reason for this is the traditional sensitivity of vital records — and the reluctance of repositories to place vital records online due to identity theft and privacy concerns.

A few years ago, the number of resources containing information about specific vital records, including indexes and digitized records, began to greatly increase. Today, the vast majority of resources are indexes to vital records, but digitized records are starting to appear more frequently.

To get a better idea of how to search for vital records, we will try to locate records to fill in the missing information on William Henry Abell that we began researching in Chapter 2.

The best source to verify your research is a copy of the actual vital record. Digitization of vital records has boomed over the past few years. Initially, archives that house vital records were reluctant to digitize them due to privacy concerns. However, as more and more requests came in for vital records, these archives have allowed companies to place those records that fall outside the provisions of the privacy act online. If you can't find a copy of the vital record online, then the next best thing is an index that can point you to where the record is located. Then you can request a copy of the record.

There are a few strategies for finding vital record information online. You can use a search engine, a comprehensive genealogical index, or a Wiki page with links to online vital records resources.

We know from our research in Chapter 2 that William Henry Abell's obituary stated that he died on 7 September 1955 in Hodgenville, Kentucky at the age of 82. To prove that the information in the obituary is true, we want to locate his death certificate — that might also provide more information than what was in the obituary.

We start with a quick trip to a search engine.

1. **Go to the search engine Google (`www.google.com`) and type the search term** Kentucky death records **and click the Google Search button.**

   You might prefer to use a different state name, depending on whether your ancestor was from Kentucky or somewhere else. The results page appears with links to several vital records sites.

2. **Click the Kentucky, Death Records, 1852–1963 — Ancestry.com link.**

   We chose this link because William's death was in 1955 and the description of the site indicated original records. The resulting screen includes a search form requesting information.

3. **Type** William Henry **in the First & Middle Name(s) field and** Abell **in the Last Name field, enter** 7 Sep 1955 **and** Hodgenville, Kentucky **in the Death field, and then click the Search button; see Figure 5-1.**

   Again, you might want to substitute your own ancestors' names. If so, your results will vary a bit. A table containing three search results is displayed. The top result contains a record for William H. Abell with a birth dated of 17 January 1873 and a death date of 07 September 1955 in Larue, Kentucky.

4. **Click the icon on the far right of the row in the View Images column.**

   A page appears with subscription information. If you already have a subscription, you can log in to your account at the upper-right corner of the screen. If not, you have to follow the prompts to get a free 14-day trial. We fill in the login information and click the Sign In button. After the login, the page displays the image of the death record.

5. **After the image pops up, click the Zoom In button to see the image more clearly.**

   Figure 5-2 shows the image of the death record.

REMEMBER

From the death certificate we learn that William died in Hodgenville, Kentucky, on 7 September 1955 at 7:30 am of coronary occlusion that occurred two hours before his death. Contributing factors to his death included coronary arteriosclerosis and diabetes mellitus. He was a white male, worked as a blacksmith, and had the social security number 401-22-77?4 (the next-to-last digit is illegible). His body was sent to Clinton, Illinois, for burial. The physician was John Bradbury, and the informant was Mrs. William Abell. All of this information would be considered reliable as the death certificate is a primary source. However, the birthdate of 17 January 1873 and the parent names Samuel Abell and Lizzie Pickrell may not be as reliable as the birth occurred 82 years prior to the record, and Mrs. Abell was not present at the birth. But this information does point us in the right direction for discovering more about William's birth. The information on the death certificate confirms that contained in the obituary.

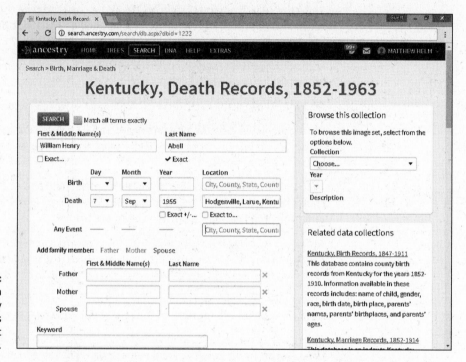

FIGURE 5-1:
The search form for the Kentucky Death Records collection at Ancestry.com.

You can find a number of vital records and civil registration resources at the Ancestry.com and MyHeritage (www.myheritage.com) subscription sites. The free site FamilySearch.org also contains several collections.

If you've had only a little luck finding a digitized vital record or index (or you need a record that falls within the range of the privacy act), your next step might be to visit a general information site. If you're looking for information on how to order vital records in the U.S., you can choose among a few sites. Several commercial sites have addresses for vital records repositories. Unfortunately, some of them are full of advertisements for subscription sites, making it difficult to determine which links will lead you to useful information and what is going to lead you to a third-party site that wants to make a sale.

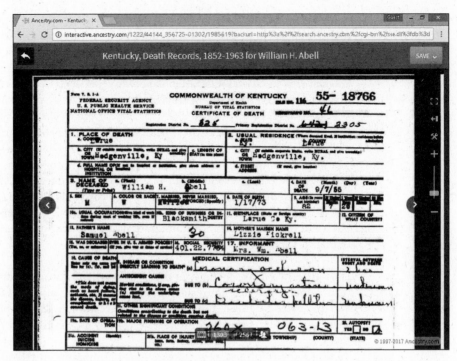

FIGURE 5-2:
Image recording
the death of
William Henry
Abell.

One site that contains useful information without the advertisements is the Where to Write for Vital Records page on the Centers for Disease Control and Prevention site (`www.cdc.gov/nchs/w2w.htm`). To locate information, simply click a state and you see a table listing details on how to order records from state-level repositories.

Investigating Immigration and Naturalization Records

You may have heard the old stories about your great-great-grandparents who left their homeland in search of a more prosperous life. Some of these stories may include details about where they were born and how they arrived at their new home. Although these are interesting and often entertaining stories, as a family historian, you want to verify this information with documentation.

Often the document you're looking for is an immigration or naturalization record. *Immigration records* are documents that show when a person moved to a particular country to reside. They include passenger lists and port-entry records for ships, and border-crossing papers for land entry into a country. *Naturalization records* are documents showing that a person became a citizen of a country without being born in that country. Sometimes an immigrant will reside in a country without becoming a naturalized citizen, and you can find paperwork on him or her, too. You can look for alien registration paperwork and visas. A *visa* is a document permitting a noncitizen to live or travel in a country.

Immigration and naturalization documents can prove challenging to find, especially if you don't know where to begin looking. Unless you have some evidence in your attic or have a reliable family account of the immigration, you may need a record or something else to point you in the right direction. Census records are useful. (For more information about census records, see Chapter 4.) Depending on the year your ancestors immigrated, census records may contain the location of birth and tell you the year of immigration and the year of naturalization of your immigrant ancestor.

Emigration records — documents that reflect when a person moved out of a particular country to take up residence elsewhere — are also useful to researchers. You find these records in the country your ancestor left. They can often help when you can't find immigration or naturalization records in the new country.

TIP

To find more information on research using immigration records in the U.S., we recommend taking a look at the National Archives: Immigration Records site at www.archives.gov/research/immigration/index.html. This site provides general information on using immigration records and also identifies the types of immigration records held by the National Archives. You can also check out Chapter 9: "Immigration Records," written by Loretto Dennis Szucs, Kory L. Meyerink, and Marian L. Smith, in *The Source: A Guidebook to American Genealogy,* Third Edition, edited by Szucs and Sandra Hargreaves Luebking (https://www.ancestry.com/wiki/index.php?title=Overview_of_Immigration_Research).

Although locating immigration, emigration, and naturalization records online has been challenging in the past, it's a growing field and more is available than ever. Common types of records that genealogists use to locate immigrants — passenger lists, immigration papers, and emigration records — have increased in availability on the Internet over the past decade and will likely continue to increase in numbers. A good starting point for determining an ancestor's homeland is to look at census records. (Again, for more information about census records, see Chapter 4.) Because a great deal of early immigration and naturalization processing occurred at the local level, census records may give you an indication of where to look for immigration records.

Some examples of online records, indexes, and databases include the following:

>> **McLean County Circuit Clerk:** McLean County, Illinois, Immigration Records (www.mcleancountyil.gov/index.aspx?NID=161)

» **MayflowerHistory.com:** Mayflower Passenger List (`http://mayflowerhistory.com/mayflower-passenger-list/`)

» **Iron Range Research Center:** 1918 Minnesota Alien Registration Records (`www.ironrangeresearchcenter.org`)

Although the number of websites offering immigration and naturalization records has grown substantially, it's still kind of hit and miss whether you'll find an independent site that has what you need. You're more likely to have success at one of the major subscription sites, like Ancestry.com or MyHeritage.

Ancestry.com's Immigration and Travel records include over 500 collections sorted into passenger lists, crew lists, border crossings and passports, citizenship and naturalization, immigration and emigration books, and ship pictures and descriptions.

MyHeritage (`www.myheritage.com`) also hosts records under their Immigration and Travel collection. These include passenger lists, citizenship and naturalization, immigration and emigration, and immigration documents. You can find the search form for this collection at `https://www.myheritage.com/research/category-4000/immigration-travel?formId=immigration-norels&formMode=&action=showForm`.

FamilySearch.org contains over 190 databases within their Migration and Naturalization collection. These include both domestic and foreign immigration record sets. For a list of available databases, see `https://familysearch.org/search/collection/list/?page=1&recordType=Migration`.

Passenger lists

One type of immigration record that you can find on the Web is passenger lists. Passenger lists are manifests of who traveled on a particular ship. You can use passenger lists not only to see who immigrated on a particular ship, but you can also see citizens of the U.S. who were merely traveling by ship (perhaps coming back from vacation in Europe).

A source for passenger lists is the Immigrant Ships Transcribers Guild passenger-list transcription project (`www.immigrantships.net`). Currently, the guild has transcribed more than 17,000 passenger manifests. The passenger lists are organized by date, ship's name, port of departure, port of arrival, passenger's surname, and captain's name. You can also search the site to find the person or ship that interests you. Other pages containing links to passenger lists include:

» **Rootsweb.com Passenger Lists:** `http://userdb.rootsweb.ancestry.com/passenger/`

» **Castle Garden (the precursor to Ellis Island):** `www.castlegarden.org`

- **Famine Irish Passenger Record Data File:** `http://aad.archives.gov/aad/fielded-search.jsp?dt=180&tf=F&cat=SB302&bc=sb,sl`

- **Ship Passenger List Index for New Netherland:** `www.rootsweb.ancestry.com/~nycoloni/nnimmdex.html`

- **Boston Passenger Manifests (1848–1891):** `www.sec.state.ma.us/arc/arcsrch/PassengerManifestSearchContents.html`

- **Maine Passenger Lists:** `www.mainegenealogy.net/passenger_search.asp`

- **Partial Transcription of Inward Slave Manifests:** `www.afrigeneas.com/slavedata/manifests.html`

- **Maritime Heritage Project: San Francisco:** `www.maritimeheritage.org/passengers/index.html`

- **Galveston Immigration Database:** `www.galvestonhistory.org/attractions/maritime-heritage/galveston-immigration-database`

If you know (or even suspect) that your family came through Ellis Island, one of your first stops should be the Ellis Island Foundation site. The site contains a collection of 25 million passengers, along with ship manifests and images of certain ships.

To illustrate how the Ellis Island Foundation site works, look for Harry Houdini, who passed through the port a few times. Use these steps to search for Harry Houdini and see the results:

1. Go to the Ellis Island site at `www.libertyellisfoundation.org`.

The search box is located just under the main header.

2. Type the passenger's name in the search boxes and click Find Passenger.

You should see a results box with the name of the passenger, residence (if stated), arrival year, and some links to the passenger record, ship manifest, and the ship's image (if available).

For our example, we type Harry in the Passenger's First Name field, and Houdini in the Passenger's Last Name field. When we click Start Search, we get a list of three results — entries for travel in 1911, 1914, and 1920.

3. Click the ship manifest link for the 1920 record.

When you click the link to see the ship manifest, the Ellis Island site advises that you must be a registered user.

4. **If you're already a member, follow the prompts to sign in, and then go to Step 6. If you're not yet a member, click the Create a Free Account link and go to Step 5.**

    Registration is free and takes only a few minutes.

5. **Complete the online membership registration form, then click Continue.**

    You must provide your first name, last name, email address, password (which has very specific requirements), country, postal code, security question/answer, click the checkbox for the terms and conditions, and enter the captcha code (letter and number combination).

6. **Review the information about this manifest.**

    Figure 5-3 shows the manifest for the ship *Imperator* that sailed from Southampton on July 3, 1920 and arrived on July 11, 1920. If you scroll through the manifest online, you can see that Harry was traveling with his wife.

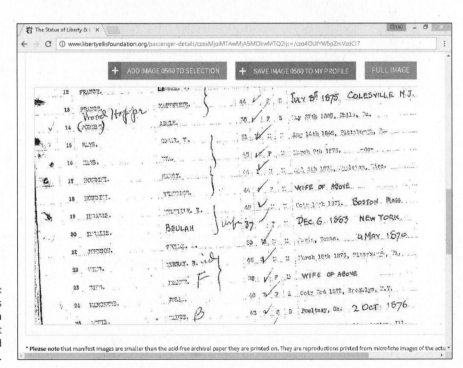

FIGURE 5-3: Harry Houdini's entry in a passenger list at the Ellis Island site.

Naturalization records

The road to citizenship was paved with paper, which is a good thing for researchers. On the Fold3 site (www.fold3.com), you can find naturalization records housed in the National Archives online. Figure 5-4 shows a naturalization record from Fold3.

FIGURE 5-4:
A naturalization petition at Fold3.

Fold3 has more than 7.6 million naturalization records that you can search or browse by location and last name. Some of the collections include

>> Naturalization Petitions for the Southern District of California, 1887–1940

>> Records of the U.S. Circuit Court for the Eastern District of Louisiana, New Orleans Division: Petitions, 1838–1861

>> Petitions and Records of Naturalizations of the U.S. District and Circuit Courts of the District of Massachusetts, 1906–1929

>> Naturalization Petitions of the U.S. District Court for the District of Maryland, 1906–1930

>> Naturalization Petitions for the Eastern District of Pennsylvania, 1795–1930

>> Naturalization Petitions of the U.S. Circuit and District Courts for the Middle District of Pennsylvania, 1906–1930

>> Naturalization Petitions of the U.S. District Court, 1820–1930, and Circuit Court, 1820–1911, for the Western District of Pennsylvania

>> Index to Naturalizations of World War I Soldiers, 1918

For more about Fold3 and all its records, flip back to Chapter 3.

You can also find some database indexes of naturalizations online. Here are some examples:

>> **Arkansas:** Arkansas Naturalization Records Index, 1809–1906, at www. naturalizationrecords.com/usa/ar_natrecind-a.shtml

>> **California:** Index to Naturalization Records in Sonoma County, California, 1841–1906, at www.rootsweb.ancestry.com/~cascgs/nat.htm

>> **California:** Index to Naturalization Records in Sonoma County, California, Volume II, 1906–1930, at www.rootsweb.ancestry.com/~cascgs/nat2.htm

>> **Colorado:** Colorado State Archives Naturalization Records at www.colorado. gov/pacific/archives/naturalization-records

>> **Delaware:** Naturalization Records Database at http://archives. delaware.gov/collections/natrlzndb/nat-index.shtml

>> **Indiana:** Archives and Records Administration's Naturalization Index at www. in.gov/serv/iara_naturalization

>> **Missouri:** Naturalization Records, 1816–1955, at https://s1.sos.mo.gov/ records/archives/archivesdb/naturalization

>> **New York:** Italian Genealogical Group page on New York and New Jersey Naturlizations at www.italiangen.org/records-search/ naturalizations.php

>> **North Dakota:** North Dakota Naturalization Records Index at https:// library.ndsu.edu/db/naturalization

>> **Ohio:** Miami County Naturalization Papers, 1860–1872, at www. thetroyhistoricalsociety.org/m-county/natural.htm

>> **Pennsylvania:** Centre County Naturalization Records, 1802–1929, (includes images of the records) at http://co.centre.pa.us/centreco/hrip/ natrecs/default.asp

>> **Washington:** Digital Archives at www.digitalarchives.wa.gov/default.aspx

Land Ho! Researching Land Records

In the past, an individual's success was often measured by the ownership of land. The more land your ancestors possessed, the more powerful and wealthy they were. This concept encouraged people to migrate to new countries in the quest to obtain land.

In addition to giving you information about the property your ancestor owned, land records may tell you where your ancestor lived before purchasing the land, the spouse's name, and the names of children, grandchildren, parents, or siblings. To use land records effectively, however, you need to have a general idea of where your ancestors lived and possess a little background information on the history of the areas in which they lived. Land records are especially useful for tracking the migration of families in the U.S. before the 1790 census.

Most land records are maintained at the local level — in the town, county, or parish where the property was located. Getting a foundation in the history of land records before conducting a lot of research is a good idea because the practices of land transfers differed by location and time period. A good place to begin your research is at the Land Record Reference page at `www.directlinesoftware.com/landref.htm`. This page contains links to articles on patents and grants, bounty lands, the Homestead Act, property description methods, and how land transactions were conducted. For a more general treatment of land records, see "Land Records," by Sandra Hargreaves Luebking, in *The Source: A Guidebook to American Genealogy,* Third Edition, edited by Loretto Dennis Szucs and Luebking (`https://www.ancestry.com/wiki/index.php?title=Overview_of_Land_Records`).

Surveying land lovers in the U.S.

Land resources are among the most plentiful sources of information on your ancestors in the U.S. Although a census would have occurred only once every ten years on average, land transactions may have taken place multiple times during that decade, depending on how much land your ancestor possessed. These records don't always contain a great deal of demographic information, but they do place your ancestor in a time and location, and sometimes in a historical context as well. For example, you may discover that your ancestors were granted military bounty lands. This discovery may tell you where and when your ancestors acquired the land, as well as what war they fought in. You may also find out how litigious your ancestors were by the number of lawsuits they filed or had filed against them as a result of land claims.

Your ancestors may have received land in the early U.S. in several ways. Knowing more about the ways in which people acquired land historically can aid you in your research.

Your ancestor may have purchased land or received a grant of land in the public domain — often called *bounty lands* — in exchange for military service or some other service for the country. Either way, the process probably started when your ancestor petitioned (or submitted an application) for the land. Your ancestor may have also laid claim to the land, rather than petitioning for it.

If the application was approved, your ancestor was given a *warrant* — a certificate that allowed him or her to receive an amount of land. (Sometimes a warrant was called a *right.*) After your ancestor presented the warrant to a land office, an individual was appointed to make a *survey* — a detailed drawing and legal description of the boundaries — of the land. The land office then recorded your ancestor's name and information from the survey into a *tract book* (a book describing the lots within a township or other geographic area) and on a *plat map* (a map of lots within a tract).

After the land was recorded in the tract book, your ancestors may have been required to meet certain conditions, such as living on the land for a certain period of time or making payments on the land. After they met the requirements, they were eligible for a *patent* — a document that conveyed title of the land to the new owner.

If your ancestors received bounty lands in the U.S., you might be in luck. The Bureau of Land Management (BLM), General Land Office Records (`https://glorecords.blm.gov/default.aspx`) holds more than 5 million federal land title records issued between 1820 and the present, and images of survey plats and field notes from 1810.

Follow these steps to search the records on this site:

1. **Go to the Official Federal Land Records site** (`https://glorecords.blm.gov/default.aspx`).

2. **In the green bar at the top of the page, click Search Documents.**

   This brings you to a search form that you can fill out to search all of the contents at the BLM site. Matthew's interest, for example, is in finding land that one of his ancestors, Jacob Helm, owned in Illinois.

3. **Click the Search Documents by Type tab on the top of the form.**

   The other tabs are Search Document by Location and Search Documents by Identifier.

4. **Click Patents on the left side of the form.**

   The other options are Surveys, LSR (Land Status Records), and CDI (Control Document Index).

5. **In the Locations section of the form, use the drop-down list to select a state and, if desired, a county.**

   For our example, we select Illinois for the State field, and use the default Any County in the County field.

6. In the Names section of the form, type a last name and first name in the appropriate fields.

We type **Helm** in the Last Name field and **Jacob** in the First Name field.

7. If you have other criteria for your search that fits in the Land Description or Miscellaneous sections, you can enter it now.

For our example, we don't know much else than the state and name, so we don't provide any other search criteria.

8. Click the Search Patents button at the bottom of the form.

The results list generates.

9. Scroll through the results and choose one that looks promising. If you want to go directly to the image of the document, click the Image icon. But if you want additional information about the record, click the Accession link.

We want as much information about the record as possible, so we click the Accession link for the single result for Jacob Helm in Illinois. This opens a page with three tabs: Patent Details, Patent Image, and Related Documents.

10. The view defaults to the Patent Details tab. Review the information provided.

Depending on the specific record, this detailed entry provides information such as name on the patent, the land office involved, mineral rights, military rank, document numbers, survey data, and a land description.

11. Click the Patent Image tab to view a digitized copy of the patent.

You can view the document as a PDF within the frame. We can then save the copy of the document on your computer. Figure 5-5 shows the patent for Jacob Helm.

12. If you're interested in learning about your ancestor's neighbors, click the Related Documents tab.

A list of other documents with the same land description — township, range, and section — generates. You can use this list to see who your ancestor's neighbors were and learn more about them.

For secondary land transactions (those made after the original grant of land), you probably need to contact the recorder of deeds for the county in which the land was held. Several online sites contain indexes to land transactions in the U.S. Some of these are free, and other broader collections require a subscription. The easiest way to find these sites is to consult a comprehensive genealogical index site and look under the appropriate geographical area. In a land index, you're likely to encounter the name of the purchaser or warrantee, the name of the buyer (if applicable), the location of the land, the number of acres, and the date of the land transfer. In some cases, you may see the residence of the person who acquired the land.

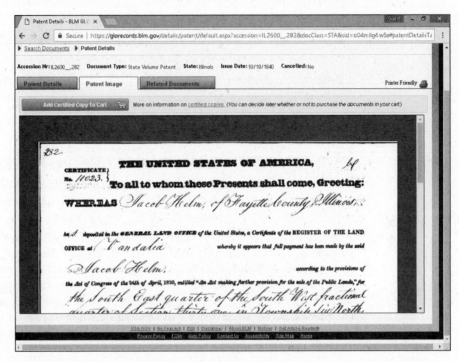

Here are some websites with information on land records:

>> **Legal Land Descriptions in the USA:** http://illinois.outfitters.com/genealogy/land/

>> **Alabama:** Land Records at http://sos.alabama.gov/government-records/land-records

>> **Arkansas:** Land Records at http://searches.rootsweb.ancestry.com/cgi-bin/arkland/arkland.pl

>> **California:** Early Sonoma County, California, Land Grants, 1846–1850, at www.rootsweb.ancestry.com/~cascgs/intro.htm

>> **Illinois:** Illinois Public Domain Land Tract Sales at www.ilsos.gov/isa/landsrch.jsp

>> **Indiana:** Land Records at the State Archives at www.in.gov/iara/2585.htm

>> **Louisiana:** Office of State Lands at www.doa.la.gov/Pages/osl/Index.aspx

» **Maryland:** Land Records in Maryland at `http://guide.mdsa.net/pages/viewer.aspx?page=mdlandrecords`

» **New York:** Ulster County Deed Books 1, 2 & 3 Index at `http://archives.co.ulster.ny.us/deedsearchscreen.htm`

» **North Carolina:** Alamance County Land Grant Recipients at `www.rootsweb.ancestry.com/~ncacgs/ala_nc_land_grants.html`

» **Ohio:** Introduction to Ohio Land History at `www.directlinesoftware.com/ohio.htm`

» **Oregon:** Oregon State Archives Land Records at `http://sos.oregon.gov/archives/Pages/records/aids-land.aspx`

» **Texas:** Texas General Land Office Archives at `www.glo.texas.gov/`

» **Wisconsin:** Wisconsin Public Land Survey Records: Original Field Notes and Plat Maps at `http://digicoll.library.wisc.edu/SurveyNotes`

In addition to the methods we mention in this section, you may want to check out geography-related resources, such as The USGenWeb Project (`www.usgenweb.org`) or the WorldGenWeb Project (`www.worldgenweb.org`). These sites organize their resources by location (country, state, county, or all three, depending on which you use). Of course, if your attempts to find land records and information through comprehensive sites and geography-related sites don't prove as fruitful as you'd like, you can always turn to a search engine such Google (`www.google.com`).

Using HistoryGeo.com to map your ancestor's land

HistoryGeo.com is a subscription site that focuses on land records. It contains two collections. The First Landowners Project allows users to see more than 9 million landowners' names and information on one master map. The project covers 21 states. The antique maps collection contains over 4000 maps and atlases.

The First Landowners Project enables you to search by surname the original owners of public lands in the U.S. You can also restrict the search by state and county, if desired. In examining this site, we search for Matthew's ancestor, Jacob Helm, in Illinois. The results contain numerous Helms, but we know Jacob lived in Fayette County, so we home in on him and his brother rather quickly; see Figure 5-6. Then, by clicking the green person icon, we see details about the land parcel and even connect to an image of the original Bureau of Land Management document.

In addition to being able to see information about the piece of land, you can add markers on the map to indicate events in your ancestors' lives, save people to your list of favorites, and plot migration patterns for multiple ancestors or families at a time.

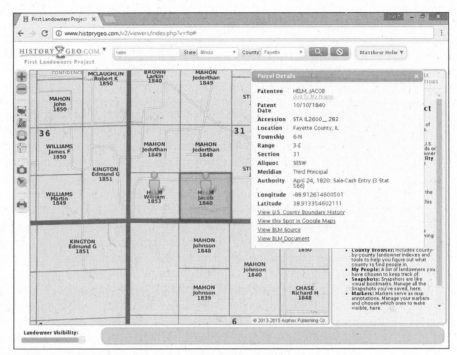

Marching to a Different Drummer: Searching for Military Records

Although your ancestors may not have marched to a different drummer, at least one of them probably kept pace with a military beat at some point. Military records contain a variety of information. The major types of records that you're likely to find are service, pension, and bounty land records. Draft or conscription records may also surface in your exploration.

Service records chronicle the military career of an individual. They often contain details about where your ancestors lived, when they enlisted or were *drafted* (or *conscripted*, enrolled for compulsory service), their ages, their discharge dates, and in some instances, their birthplaces and occupations. You may also find pay records (including muster records that state when your ancestors had to report to military units) and notes on any injuries that they sustained while serving in the military. You can use these records to determine the unit in which your ancestor served and the time periods of their service.

This information can lead you to pension records that can contain significant genealogical information because of the level of detail required to prove service to receive a pension. Service records can give you an appreciation of your ancestor's place within history — especially the dates and places where your ancestor fought or served as a member of the armed forces.

Pensions were often granted to veterans who were disabled or who demonstrated financial need after service in a particular war or campaign; widows or orphans of veterans also may have received benefits. These records are valuable because, to receive pensions, your ancestors had to prove that they served in the military. Proof entailed a discharge certificate or the sworn testimony of the veteran and witnesses. Pieces of information that you can find in pension records include your ancestor's rank, period of service, unit, residence at the time of the pension application, age, marriage date, spouse's name, names of children, and the nature of the veteran's financial need or disability. If a widow submitted a pension application, you may also find records verifying her marriage to the veteran and death records (depending on when the veteran ancestor died).

Bounty lands were lands granted by the government in exchange for military service that occurred between 1775 and 1855. Wars covered during this period include the American Revolution, War of 1812, Old Indian Wars, and the Mexican Wars. To receive bounty lands, soldiers were required to file an application. These applications often contain information useful to genealogical researchers.

If you're new to researching U.S. military records, take a look at the Research in Military Records page at the National Archives site (www.archives.gov/research/military/index.html). It contains information on the types of military records held by the archives, how you can use them in your research, and information on records for specific wars. Also, for the historical context of the time period that your ancestor served, see the U.S. Army Center of Military History Research Material page at www.history.army.mil/html/bookshelves/resmat/index.html. This site contains links to chapters from *American Military History,* which covers military actions from the Colonial period through the war on terrorism.

The largest collections for military records are currently housed in subscription sites. Here we give you a quick rundown on what several subscription sites have within their collections.

Fold3 (https://www.fold3.com) partnered with the National Archives to place digitized images of microfilm (held by the archives) online. As a result, most of the military records on Fold3 are federal. Here are some examples of available record sets:

>> Navy Casualty Reports, 1776–1941

>> Service Records of Volunteers, 1784–1811

>> Revolutionary War Service and Imprisonment Cards

- War of 1812 Pension Files

- War of 1812 Society Applications

- Letters Received by the Adjutant General, 1822–1860

- Mexican War Service Records

- Civil War and Later Veterans Pension Index

- Confederate Amnesty Papers

- Spanish-American War Service Record Index

- Confidential Correspondence of the Navy, 1919–1927

- Foreign Burial of American War Dead

- Naturalization Index — WWI Soldiers

- Military Intelligence Division — Negro Subversion

- Missing Air Crew Reports, WWII

- WWII War Diaries

- Korean War Casualties

- Vietnam Service Awards

- Navy Cruise Books, 1918–2009

Ancestry.com (www.ancestry.com) has more than 1,200 collections of military records. Its collections include records for servicemen from the U.S. and several other countries. These military collections include

- World War I Draft Registration Cards, 1917–1918

- Sons of the American Revolution Membership Applications, 1889–1970

- U.S. Revolutionary War Miscellaneous Records (Manuscript File), 1775–1790s

- U.S. Civil War Soldiers, 1861–1865

- Confederate Service Records, 1861–1865

- Civil War Prisoner of War Records, 1861–1865

- U.S. Colored Troops Military Service Records, 1863–1865

- U.S. Marine Corps Muster Rolls, 1798–1958

- World War I Draft Registration Cards, 1917–1918

- U.S. World War II Army Enlistment Records, 1938–1946

- British Army WWI Service Records, 1914–1920

- British Army WWI Medal Rolls Index Cards, 1914–1920

- British Army WWI Pension Records, 1914–1920

- Germany & Austria Directories of Military and Marine Officers, 1500–1939

- Canada War Graves Registers (Circumstances of Casualty), 1914–1948

- Canada Loyalist Claims, 1776–1835

- New Zealand Army WWII Nominal Rolls, 1939–1948

At WorldVitalRecords.com (http://worldvitalrecords.com), you can find over 1,500 military collections, including:

- List of Officials, Civil, Military, and Ecclesiastical of Connecticut Colony, 1636–1677

- Spanish American War Volunteers — Colorado

- Korean War Casualties

- Army Casualties 1956–2003

- Muster Rolls of the Soldiers of the War of 1812: Detached from the Militia of North Carolina in 1812 and 1814

And, if the big military collections don't quite meet your needs, here is a sampling of the different records that are available on free sites:

- **Muster Rolls and Other Records of Service of Maryland Troops in the American Revolution:** www.msa.md.gov/megafile/msa/speccol/sc2900/sc2908/000001/000018/html/index.html

- **Illinois Black Hawk War Veterans Database:** www.cyberdriveillinois.com/departments/archives/databases/blkhawk.html

- **South Carolina Records of Confederate Veterans 1909–1973:** www.archivesindex.sc.gov

- **National World War II Memorial Registry:** www.wwiimemorial.com/Registry/Default.aspx

Another set of valuable resources for researching an ancestor that participated in a war is information provided by a lineage society. Some examples include:

- **Daughters of the American Revolution** (www.dar.org)

- **Sons of the American Revolution** (www.sar.org)

- >> **Society of the Cincinnati** (www.societyofthecincinnati.org)

- >> **United Empire Loyalists' Association of Canada** (www.uelac.org)

- >> **National Society United States Daughters of 1812** (www.usdaughters1812.org)

- >> **Daughters of Union Veterans of the Civil War** (www.duvcw.org)

- >> **Sons of Confederate Veterans** (www.scv.org)

One collection of military records at a free site is the Civil War Soldiers and Sailors System (CWSS). The CWSS site (https://www.nps.gov/civilwar/soldiers-and-sailors-database.htm) is a joint project of the National Park Service, the Genealogical Society of Utah, and the Federation of Genealogical Societies. The site contains an index of more than 6.3 million soldier records of both Union and Confederate soldiers. Also available at the site are regimental histories and descriptions of 384 battles.

Follow these steps to search the records on this site:

1. **Point your browser to the Civil War Soldier and Sailors System** (https://www.nps.gov/civilwar/soldiers-and-sailors-database.htm).

   On the page are boxes with links to Soldiers, Sailors, Regiments, Cemeteries, Battles, Prisoners, Medals of Honor, and Monuments.

2. **Click the appropriate box for the person you're looking for.**

   We're looking for a soldier who served, so we click the Soldier box.

3. **Type the name of the soldier or sailor in the appropriate field and click Search.**

   If you know additional details, you can select the side on which your ancestor fought, the state they were from, and rank. We typed **Abell** in the Last Name field, **Samuel** in the First Name field, **Kentucky** in the By State field, and **Union** in the By side field. Two search results appeared with that information.

4. **Review your results and click the name of the soldier or sailor to see the Detailed Soldier Record.**

   The soldier details show that Samuel served in Company H, 10th Regiment, Kentucky Infantry; see Figure 5-7. He entered and left the service as a corporal. His information is located on National Archives series M386 microfilm, roll 1.

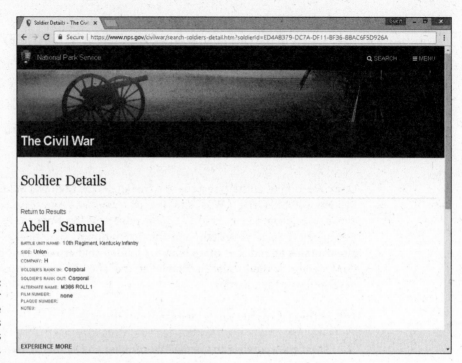

FIGURE 5-7: Detailed soldier record from the Civil War Soldiers and Sailors System.

Taxation with Notation

Some of the oldest records available for research are tax records — including property and inheritance records. Although some local governments have placed tax records online, these records are usually very recent documents rather than historical tax records. Most early tax records you encounter were likely collected locally (that is, at the county level). However, many local tax records have since been turned over to state or county archives — some of which now make tax records available on microfilm, as do Family History Centers. (If you have a Family History Center in your area, you may be able to save yourself a trip, call, or letter to the state archives — check with the Family History Center to see whether it keeps copies of tax records for the area in which you're interested.) And a few maintainers of tax records — including archives and Family History Centers — are starting to make information about their holdings available online. Generally, either indexes or transcriptions of these microfilm records are what you find online. Another source for tax information are newspapers. Localities sometimes published tax assessment information in newspapers annually. We'll look at online sources for newspapers later in this chapter.

Additionally, both Ancestry.com and FamilySearch have some tax records available through their sites. We explore how to use both of these sites in Chapter 3.

Here are just a few examples of the types of resources that you can find pertaining to tax records:

» **Tax List:** 1790 and 1800 County Tax Lists of Virginia at www.binnsgenealogy.com/VirginiaTaxListCensuses

» **Tax List:** Territory of Colorado Tax Assessment Lists, 1862–1866, at http://digital.denverlibrary.org/cdm/ref/collection/p16079coll115/id/1976

» **Land and Poll Tax:** Benton County, Tennessee 1836 Land and Poll Tax List at www.tngenweb.org/benton/databas2.htm

If you're locating records in the U.S., try USGenWeb for the state or county. Here's what to do:

1. **Go to the USGenWeb site (www.usgenweb.org).**

2. **Click a state in the map at the top of the page.**

   We click the Pennsylvania link because we're looking for tax records in Lancaster County.

TIP

   As a shortcut, you can always get to any USGenWeb state page by substituting the two-letter state code for the 'us' in www.usgenweb.org. For example, for Pennsylvania, you could type **www.pagenweb.org.**

3. **From the USGenWeb state page (for the state that you choose), find a link to the county in which you're interested.**

   On the Pennsylvania Counties page, we click the Pensylvania Counties menu item and then the Lancaster link to get to the Lancaster County GenWeb site.

4. **Scroll through the main page for the state you've selected and click any tax-related links that look promising.**

   We clicked the link for Proprietary and State Tax Lists of the County of Lancaster for the Years 1771, 1772, 1773, 1779, and 1782; edited by William Henry Egle, M.D. (1898) under the Documents section.

The state and county websites in the USGenWeb Project vary immensely. Some have more information available than the Pennsylvania and Lancaster County pages, while others have less. The amount of information that's available at a particular USGenWeb site affects the number of links you have to click through to find what you're looking for. Don't be afraid to take a little time to explore and become familiar with the sites for the states and counties in which your ancestors lived.

Trial and Error at the Courthouse

Do you have an ancestor who was on the wrong side of the law? If so, you may find some colorful information at the courthouse in the civil and criminal court records. Even if you don't have an ancestor with a law-breaking past, you can find valuable genealogical records at your local courthouse, given that even upstanding citizens may have civil records on file or may have been called as witnesses. Typical records you can find there include land deeds, birth and death certificates, divorce decrees, wills and probate records, tax records, and some military records (provided the ancestors who were veterans deposited their records locally).

Court cases and trials aren't just a phenomenon of today's world. Your ancestor may have participated in the judicial system as a plaintiff, defendant, or witness. Some court records can provide a glimpse into the character of your ancestors — whether they were frequently on trial for misbehavior or called as character witnesses. You can also find a lot of information on your ancestors if they were involved in land disputes — a common problem in some areas where land transferred hands often. Again, your ancestor may not have been directly involved in a dispute but may have been called as a witness. Another type of court record that may involve your ancestor is a probate case. Often, members of families contested wills or were called upon as executors or witnesses, and the resulting file of testimonies and rulings can be found in a probate record. Court records may also reflect appointments of ancestors to positions of public trust such as sheriff, inspector of tobacco, and justice of the peace.

Finding court records online can be tricky. They can be found using a subscription database service or a general search engine, such as Bing (www.bing.com). Note, however, that good data can also be tucked away inside free databases that are not indexed by search engines. In this case, you will have to search on a general term such as *Berks County wills* or *Berks County court records*. Here is an example:

1. **Go to the Bing search engine site (www.bing.com).**

   The search box is near the top of the page.

2. **Type your search terms in the search box and click the Search icon (magnifying glass) or press Enter.**

   The results page is displayed. We type *Berks County wills* and received 89,700 results. Please note that this number changes often as new sites are added to the database. If the number of results you get is too large to reasonably sort through, you can narrow your search with additional terms, such as specific years or town names.

3. **Click a link that looks relevant to your search.**

We select the link to the Berks County Register of Wills at www.co.berks.pa. us/rwills/site/default.asp. This site contains a database where you can search more than 1 million records covering a variety of areas, including birth, death, marriage, and estate.

Here are some sites to give you an idea of court records that you can find online:

>> **Missouri's Judicial Records:** https://s1.sos.mo.gov/records/archives/ archivesdb/judicialrecords/

>> **Atlantic County Library System's Historic Resources Digitized Wills:** www. atlanticlibrary.org/historical_resources

>> **Earl K. Long Library, The University of New Orleans Historical Archives of the Supreme Court of Louisiana:** http://libweb.uno.edu/jspui/ handle/123456789/1

>> **The Proceedings of the Old Bailey: London's Central Criminal Court, 1674 to 1913:** www.oldbaileyonline.org

Getting the News on Your Ancestors

A friend of ours has a great story — morbid as it is — that illustrates the usefulness of newspapers in family history research. He was looking through newspapers for an obituary about one of his great-uncles. He knew when his great-uncle died but couldn't find mention of it in the obituary section of the newspaper. As he set the newspaper down (probably in despair), he glanced at the front page — only to find a graphic description of how a local man had been killed in a freak elevator accident. And guess who that local man was? That's right! He was our friend's great-uncle. The newspaper not only confirmed for him that his great-uncle lived in that city but also gave our friend a lot more information than he ever expected.

Although newspapers are helpful only if your ancestors did something newsworthy — but you'd be surprised at what was considered newsworthy in the past. Your ancestor didn't necessarily have to be a politician or a criminal to get his or her picture and story in the paper. Just like today, obituaries, birth and marriage announcements, public records of land transactions, advertisements, and gossip sections were all relatively common in newspapers of the past.

Historical newspapers are now finding their way online. Most of these sites contain just partial collections of newspapers, but they may just have the issue that contains information on your ancestor. The following are some of the larger national collections:

- **Chronicling America** (http://chroniclingamerica.loc.gov), a free searchable site containing newspapers from 1789 to 1924

- **GenealogyBank** (www.genealogybank.com), a subscription site containing over 7,000 newspapers

- **Google News Newspapers** (http://news.google.com/newspapers), a free collection of newspapers from the United States and Canada

- **NewspaperArchive.com** (http://newspaperarchive.com), a subscription site with titles from the United States, Canada, Europe, Africa, and Asia.

- **Newspapers.com** (www.newspapers.com), a subscription site containing digitized copies of over 4,900 newspapers from the United States

- **Papers Past** (http://paperspast.natlib.govt.nz), two million pages of New Zealand newspapers from the nineteenth and twentieth centuries

- **Trove** (http://trove.nla.gov.au/newspaper), a free site from the National Library of Australia that has digitized over 205 million pages of newspapers

There are also some state collections, such as the following:

- **Arizona Memory Project,** http://adnp.azlibrary.gov

- **California Digital Newspaper Collection,** http://cdnc.ucr.edu/cgi-bin/cdnc

- **Historic Oregon Newspapers,** http://oregonnews.uoregon.edu

- **Library of Virginia,** http://virginiachronicle.com

- **Missouri Digital Newspaper Project,** http://shsmo.org/newspaper/mdnp

- **New York Heritage Digital Collections,** https://www.nyheritage.org/newspapers

- **North Carolina Newspaper Digitization Project,** http://exhibits.archives.ncdcr.gov/newspaper/

- **Utah Digital Newspapers,** http://digitalnewspapers.org

- **Washington Historic Newspapers,** https://www.sos.wa.gov/library/newspapers/newspapers.aspx

There is even a search engine that you can use to find items in digitized newspapers around the world. Elephind.com (www.elephind.com) indexes over 3,000 newspaper titles from Australia, New Zealand, Singapore, and the United States.

Obituaries can be a key tool for family historians to understand the sequence of events of an ancestor's life. However, it is important to validate the information contained within the obituary and to search for multiple sources for obituaries, in case one was printed in a newspaper in a town the person formally lived in. A good illustration of this is William Henry Abell.

While William Henry Abell died in Hodgenville, Kentucky in 1955, he was buried in Illinois. And he spent a good deal of time living in Illinois prior to his death. He also had a lot of family members still living in Illinois at the time of his death. To see if there were obituaries and funeral notices in Illinois newspapers, we searched the subscription newspaper archive, Newspapers.com.

1. **Go to the Newspapers.com website** (www.newspapers.com).

   If you don't have a subscription to the site, you can click on the Try 7 Days Free offer and fill out the appropriate information. If you do have a subscription, you can log in using the Sign-In link on the right side of the menu bar.

2. **In the search field, type a name and a year of death and click the Search button.**

   We typed **William Abell** and **September 1955**. The results page had 71 matches. We can narrow down the results by altering the date range on the calendar or by selecting a state from the left column.

3. **Select a state from the map to narrow the results.**

   We were interested in Illinois, so we clicked on that state. The results page showed 15 results.

In our case, there were five results that pertained to William Henry Abell — two from the Pantagraph in Bloomington, Illinois; two from the Decatur Daily Review; and one from the Decatur Herald (duplicate of the Decatur Daily Review entry — one is printed in the morning and one in the afternoon). We also changed the state from Illinois to Kentucky and found an additional obituary in the Louisville, Kentucky. Reading carefully, we saw that each entry said different things and may have been written by different people. As a comparison, we also added an obituary copied from microfilm of the Herald News from Hodgenville, Kentucky. Figure 5-8 shows the differences.

Note that each item contains different information and the Decatur Daily Review item from 9 September 1955 misspelled Hodgensville as Hidgenville. The Pantagraph and Decatur Daily Review also mention that the time of death was 6:30 am. The death certificate states that he died at 7:30 am. Although at first glance it might seem to be a discrepancy between the obituary and death certificate, they do match because Hodgenville is on Eastern time and his death at 7:30 Eastern time would have been 6:30 Central time (the time in Decatur and Bloomington, Illinois). The Herald News item appeared a week later and contained a few more details about where William Henry Abell lived while he was in LaRue County, Kentucky.

FIGURE 5-8:
Six items in five different newspapers for William Henry Abell.

» **Locating places on maps and in history**

» **Using maps in your research**

» **Getting information from local sources**

Chapter **6**

Mapping the Past

S ay you dig up an old letter addressed to your great-great-great-grandfather in Winchester, Virginia. But where is Winchester? What was the town like? Where exactly did he live in the town? What was life like when he lived there? To answer these questions, you need to go a little further than just retrieving documents — you need to look at the life of your ancestor within the context of where he lived.

Geography played a major role in the lives of our ancestors. It often determined where they lived, worked, and migrated. (Early settlers typically migrated to lands that were similar to their home state or country.) It can also play a major role in how you research your ancestor. Concentrating on where your ancestor lived can point you to area-specific record sets or offer clues about where to research next.

A number of tools and technologies can assist you in meeting your research goals. These tools include geographic information system applications, geocoding, and geographic applications specific to genealogy. In this chapter, we look at several ways to use geographical resources to provide a boost to your family history research, and to answer some outstanding questions we have about William Henry Abell's family along the way.

For example, we show how we can use geographic-based resources to shed light on why William Henry Abell's wife, Lizzie (Pickerell) Abell, died young, where it happened, and what he was doing between his wife's death and his marriage to Betty a decade later.

Are We There Yet? Researching Where "There" Was to Your Ancestors

What did "there" mean for your ancestors? You have to answer this question to know where to look for genealogical information. These days, a family that lives in the same general area for more than two or three generations is rare. If you're a member of such a family, you may be in luck when it comes to researching. However, if you come from a family that moved around at least every few generations (or a family whose members did not all remain in the same location), you may be in for a challenge.

How do you find out where your ancestors lived? In this section, we look at several resources you can use to establish locations: using known records, interviewing relatives, consulting gazetteers, looking at maps, using GPS devices, and charting locations by using geographical software.

Using documents that you already possess

When you attempt to locate your ancestors geographically, start by using any copies of records or online data that you or someone else has already collected. Read through all those photocopies and original documents from the attic and printouts from online sites — those details can help you determine places to look for additional information about your ancestors. Pay particular attention to any material that provides definite whereabouts during a specific time period. You can use these details as a springboard for your geographical search.

REMEMBER

For example, Matthew's great-grandfather, William Henry Abell, is buried in Sugar Grove Cemetery near Wapella, according to funeral announcements in two local newspapers (for more on these newspaper items, refer to Chapter 5). Because these newspapers were published in Decatur and Bloomington, Illinois, we can assume that Wapella is somewhere close in proximity to the two towns and that William Henry Abell had a connection to that area because his body was transported from Kentucky (where he died) to be buried in Wapella.

One of William Henry Abell's obituaries mentions that Lizzie (Pickerell) Abell died on 12 January 1918, but it doesn't mention where. It appears from the obituary that William Henry Abell was a widower from 1918, until he married Betty Allen in July 1929 in Attilla, Kentucky.

Sifting through the census records that we collected (see Table 4-1 in Chapter 4 for the contents of the Abell census records), we see that William Henry Abell, Lizzie, and four children lived on a rented farm in Tremont Township, Tazewell County, Illinois, in 1910. In 1920, William Henry Abell lived as a wage worker on a farm in Waynesville Township, DeWitt County, Illinois, with his five children.

Because the obituary mentioned that Lizzie died in 1918, we could hypothesize that Lizzie died in one of these two counties. Incidentally, Tremont Township is in the central part of Tazewell County and Waynesville Township is in the upper-west corner of De Witt County. The distance between the two principal towns within the townships (Tremont and Waynesville) is about 40 miles. One county lies in between — McLean County.

We can use these details to launch our search through geographic sites to find some insight on the life of William Henry Abell.

Where is Llandrindod, anyway?

At some point during your research, you're bound to run across something that says an ancestor lived in or was associated with a particular town or county, but your resource contains no details of where that place was — no state or province or other identifiers. How do you find out where that place was located?

A *gazetteer,* or geographical dictionary, provides information about places. By looking up the name of the town, county, or some other kind of place, you can narrow your search for your ancestor. The gazetteer identifies every place by name and provides varying information (depending on the gazetteer) about each. Typically, gazetteers provide at least the name of the principal region where the place is located. Many contemporary gazetteers available online also provide the latitude and longitude of the place.

By adding the information you get from the online gazetteer to the other pieces of your puzzle, you can reduce the list of places with the same name to just those you think are plausible for your ancestors. By pinpointing the location of a place, you can look for more records to prove whether your ancestors really lived there and even visit the location to get pictures of burial plots or old properties.

For research in the United States, a first stop is the U.S. Geological Survey's Geographic Names Information System (GNIS) website. The GNIS site contains information on more than two million places within the United States and its territories (the site also includes data for Antarctica).

REMEMBER

To find the precise location of the cemetery where William Henry Abell is buried, we decided to use the Geographic Names Information System (GNIS) site. Follow these steps:

1. **Start your web browser and head to the U.S. Geological Survey's Geographic Names Information System (GNIS):**

   http://geonames.usgs.gov/pls/gnispublic

   This page contains the search form for the United States and its territories, as shown in Figure 6-1.

2. **Enter any information that you have, tabbing or clicking to move between fields.**

   We're looking for the cemetery in Illinois where we believe William Henry Abell is buried. Remember that we found the name of a cemetery in funeral notice mentioned in the previous section, so we entered *Sugar Grove* in the Feature Name field and selected Illinois from the state drop-down list. To target your search, you can select a Feature Class to the right of the Feature Name field. In our case, we selected Cemetery as the feature class.

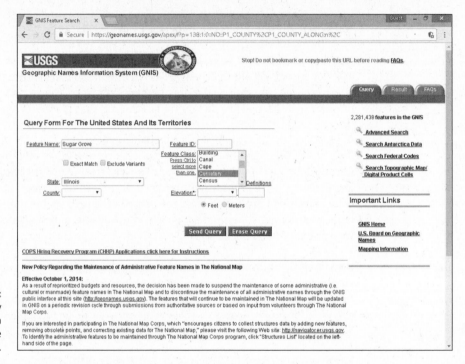

FIGURE 6-1:
Use the query form to search for places in the United States.

TIP

If you're not sure what a particular field asks for but you think you may want to enter something in it, click the title of the field for an explanation.

3. **When you're finished, click Send Query.**

   The search results page appears with nine matches for Sugar Grove Cemetery. Of those results, one Sugar Grove Cemetery is located in De Witt County, Illinois. De Witt County is located between Macon County (where Decatur is located) and McLean County (where Bloomington is located) and Wapella is located in De Witt County (matching the location mentioned in the newspaper articles). The cemetery is located at latitude of 40 degrees, 16 minutes, 5 seconds north and longitude of 88 degrees, 56 minutes, 20 seconds west and is found on the Heyworth map. Next, we can use an online map to plot the longitude and latitude to see the actual location of the cemetery.

TIP

In addition to using the GNIS database, you might want to review some online gazetteers that identify places in other countries as well as places in the United States. One that builds on worldwide data available through Google Maps is Maplandia.com: Google Maps World Gazetteer. To use this gazetteer, follow these steps:

1. **Using your web browser, go to Maplandia.com at `www.maplandia.com`.**

You see the welcome page, which has search fields to look for locations by place-name or region.

2. **In the World Places field, type the name of the place you're trying to locate.**

If you're trying to identify an entire region, you may prefer to use the World Regions field instead.

We entered the *Llandrindod* place-name.

3. **Click Search.**

Figure 6-2 shows the results of the search. The only result for our example was a place called Llandrindod Wells in Powys, Wales, in the United Kingdom. Clicking the result takes us to a page that contains the longitude and latitude of Llandrindod Wells and a map of the town.

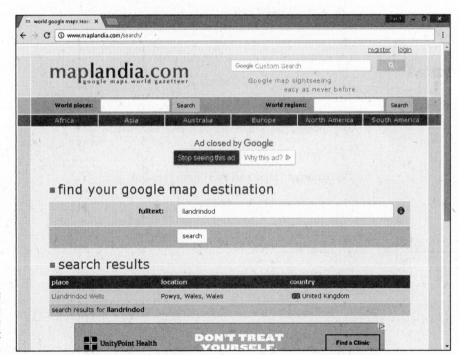

FIGURE 6-2:
Results for a search on Llandrindod at Maplandia.com.

Following are some gazetteer sites for you to check out. You can use some for worldwide searches; others are country specific:

This site has a worldwide focus.

>> **Directory of Cities, Towns, and Regions in Belgium**

www.fallingrain.com/world/BE

>> **Canada's Geographical Names**

www4.rncan.gc.ca/search-place-names/search?lang=en

>> **China Historical GIS**

www.fas.harvard.edu/~chgis

>> **Gazetteer of Australia Place Name Search**

www.ga.gov.au/placename

>> **Gazetteer for Scotland**

www.scottish-places.info

>> **Gazetteer of British Place Names**

www.gazetteer.co.uk

>> **GENUKI Gazetteer**

www.genuki.org.uk/big/Gazetteer

The gazetteer covers England, Ireland, Wales, Scotland, and the Isle of Man.

>> **German Historic Gazetteer**

http://gov.genealogy.net/search/index

>> **Institut Géographique National (in French)**

www.geoportail.gouv.fr/

>> **IreAtlas Townland Data Base (Ireland)**

www.thecore.com/seanruad/

>> **Metatopos.org (in Dutch)**

www.metatopos.org

>> **Land Information New Zealand (LINZ)**

www.linz.govt.nz/regulatory/place-names/find-place-name/
new-zealand-gazetteer-place-names

>> **KNAB, the Place Names Database of EKI (in Estonian and English)**

www.eki.ee/knab/knab.htm

>> **Registro Nacional de Informacion Geografica (in Spanish)**

www.inegi.org.mx/geo/contenidos/rnig/

>> **Kartverk (in Norwegian)**

www.kartverket.no/en/

>> **Swedish Gazetteer**

www.sna.se/gazetteer.html

>> **GPS Data Team: Coordinate Finder**

www.gps-data-team.com/map

Most online gazetteers are organized on a national level and provide information about all the places (towns, cities, counties, landmarks, and so on) within that country. However, you find some exceptions. Some unique gazetteers list information about places within one state or province. One such example is the Kentucky Atlas and Gazetteer (www.kyatlas.com), which has information only about places within — you guessed it — Kentucky.

TIP

If you can't find a location in current gazetteers, you may need to consult a historical gazetteer. Examples of these include A Vision of Britain through Time (British), available at www.visionofbritain.org.uk, and the Digital Gazetteer of the Song Dynasty, at http://songgis.ucmerced.edu. One way to find a historical gazetteer is to visit a general search engine (such as Google, at www.google.com) and search the place-name plus the words *historical gazetteer*. Another option is to visit a thesaurus, such as the Getty Thesaurus of Geographic Names Online at www.getty.edu/research/tools/vocabularies/tgn/index.html. You can type a name into the thesaurus, and it will provide a list of place types that contain the name, including the latitude and longitude and the former names of the place.

There's No Place like Home:
Using Local Resources

A time will come (possibly early in your research) when you need information that's maintained on a local level — like, say, a copy of a record stored in a local courthouse, confirmation that an ancestor is buried in a particular cemetery, or just a photo of the old homestead. How can you find and get what you need?

Finding the needed record is relatively easy if you live in or near the county where the information is maintained — you decide what you need, find out where it's stored, and then go get a copy. Getting locally held information isn't quite as easy, however, if you live in another county, state, or country. Although you can determine what information you need and where it may be stored, finding out whether the information is truly kept where you think it is and then getting a copy is another thing. Of course, if this situation weren't such a common occurrence for genealogists, you could just make a vacation out of it — travel to the location to finish researching there and get the copy you need while sightseeing along the way. But unfortunately, needing records from distant places is a common occurrence, and most of us can't afford to pack our bags and hit the road every time we need a record or item from a faraway place — which is why it's nice to know that resources are available to help.

A lot of resources are available to help you locate local documents and obtain copies, such as these:

>> Geographic-specific websites

>> Local genealogical and historical societies

>> Libraries with research services

>> Individuals who are willing to do lookups in public records

>> Directories and newspapers

>> Localizing searches

Some resources are free, but others may charge you a fee for their time, and still others will bill you only for copying or other direct costs.

Geographic-specific websites

Geographic-specific websites are pages that contain information only about a particular town, county, state, country, or other locality. They typically provide information about local resources, such as genealogical and historical societies, government agencies and courthouses, cemeteries, and civic organizations. Some sites have local histories and biographies of prominent residents online. Often they list and have links to other web pages with resources for the area. Sometimes they even have a place where you can post *queries* (or questions) about the area or families from there in the hope that someone who reads your query will have some answers for you.

You can find several good examples of general geographic-specific websites:

>> **The USGenWeb Project** (www.usgenweb.org) conveys information about the United States. The USGenWeb Project is an all-volunteer, online effort to

provide a central genealogical resource for information (records and reference materials) pertaining to counties within each state.

» **GENUKI: UK + Ireland Genealogy** (www.genuki.org.uk) is an online reference site that contains primary historical and genealogical information in the United Kingdom and Ireland. It links to sites containing indexes, transcriptions, or digitized images of actual records. All the information is categorized by locality — by country, then county, then parish.

» **National Library of Australia** (www.nla.gov.au/research-guides/family-history/other-australasian-resources) has a listing of all sorts of state and territory resources in Australia, including archives, libraries, societies, and cemeteries. It also has links directly to indexes and records at some local levels.

» **WhatWasThere** (www.whatwasthere.com) is a site that ties historical photographs to Google Maps so that you can see how a specific location appeared in the past.

» **The WorldGenWeb Project** (www.worldgenweb.org) attempts the same type of undertaking as USGenWeb, only on a global scale.

REMEMBER

Geographic-specific sites can have a smaller scope. They can be focused on state or local level resources. For example, to find out the cause of Lizzie Abell's death and where it happened, we needed to get her death certificate. The Abells were living in Illinois during census years 1910 and 1920 — but in different counties. We needed to find a local level geographic site that would have information for a death certificate in Illinois.

We typed in the search term *Illinois death records* in Google (for more on searching Google, see Chapter 7). The first result (that wasn't a paid advertisement) was for the Illinois Death Certificates, 1916–1950 Index, hosted by the Illinois Secretary of State (https://www.cyberdriveillinois.com/departments/archives/databases/idphdeathindex.html). As Lizzie died in 1918, she should be covered by the database. We searched the database in the following manner:

1. **Point your web browser to** https://www.cyberdriveillinois.com/departments/archives/databases/idphdeathindex.html.

   The Illinois Death Certificates, 1916–1950 web page appears.

2. **Click the Search button.**

   The search page appears.

3. **Enter the appropriate search criteria and click Submit.**

   We entered *Abell* in the Last Name of Decedent, *Lizzie* in First Name of Decedent, and chose *STATEWIDE* in the Select County box.

Figure 6-3 shows that Lizzie Abell died on 12 January 1919 in Funks Grove Township, McLean County, Illinois.

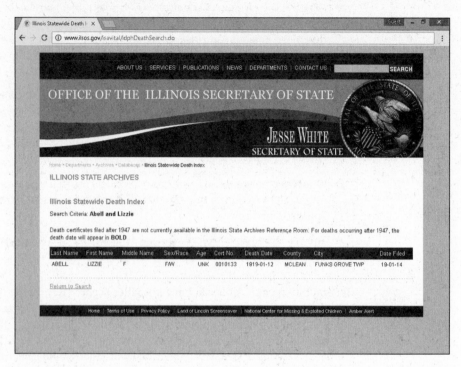

Now we had an inconsistency to resolve. The obituary said she died on 12 January 1918 and the index says she died on 12 January 1919. Only the death certificate (the primary source) could resolve it. Unfortunately, death certificates for the state of Illinois are not online. We had to get the certificate from another source.

Libraries and archives

Often, the holdings in local libraries and archives can be of great value to you — even if you can't physically visit the library or archive to do your research. You can simply go online to determine whether that repository has the book or document you need. (Most libraries and archives have web pages with their card catalogs or another listing of their holdings.) After seeing whether the repository has what you need, you can contact it to borrow the book or document (if it participates in an interlibrary loan program) or to get a copy of what you need. (Most libraries and archives have services to copy information for people at a minimal cost.)

REMEMBER

In our case, we searched and found that the McLean County Clerk's office — which is a type of archive — maintains death certificates. We needed to request the death certificate from the Clerk's office using the information that we discovered in the Secretary of State's index (see the last section for details). We found the contact information for the County Clerk's office using the Google search term *McLean Illinois County Clerk.*

Figure 6-4, shows the copy of the death certificate from the county clerk. Lizzie F. Abell died of influenza and pneumonia after being sick for eight days on 12 January 1919. Contributing to her demise was advanced tuberculosis, which she suffered with for two years.

From the record, we learned two things — the obituary for William Henry Abell (see Chapter 5 for more on the obituaries) was incorrect about her death date and she was a victim of the Spanish flu pandemic that affected thousands of Americans in 1918 and early 1919.

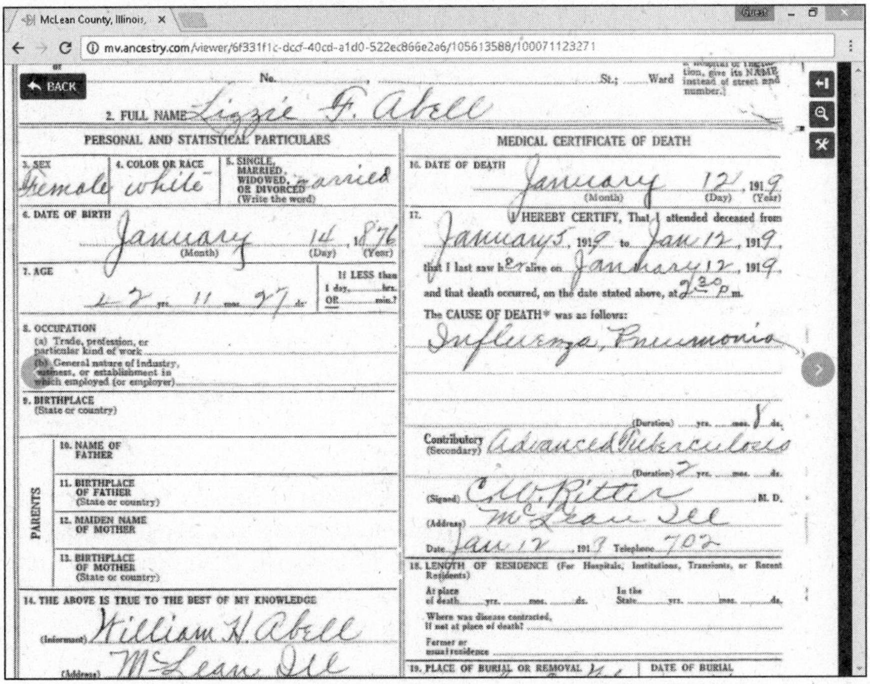
McLean County, Illinois,
mv.ancestry.com/viewer/6f331f1c-dccf-40cd-a1d0-522ec866e2a6/105613588/100071123271
BACK
2. FULL NAME Lizzie F. Abell
PERSONAL AND STATISTICAL PARTICULARS
3. SEX Female
4. COLOR OR RACE white
5. SINGLE, MARRIED, WIDOWED, OR DIVORCED (Write the word) married
6. DATE OF BIRTH January (Month) 14 (Day) 1876 (Year)
7. AGE 42 yrs. 11 mos. 27 ds.
8. OCCUPATION (a) Trade, profession, or particular kind of work (b) General nature of industry, business, or establishment in which employed (or employer)
9. BIRTHPLACE (State or country)
PARENTS
10. NAME OF FATHER
11. BIRTHPLACE OF FATHER (State or country)
12. MAIDEN NAME OF MOTHER
13. BIRTHPLACE OF MOTHER (State or country)
14. THE ABOVE IS TRUE TO THE BEST OF MY KNOWLEDGE
(Informant) William H. Abell
(Address) McLean Ill
MEDICAL CERTIFICATE OF DEATH
16. DATE OF DEATH January (Month) 12 (Day) 1919 (Year)
17. I HEREBY CERTIFY, That I attended deceased from January 5, 1919, to Jan 12, 1919, that I last saw her alive on January 12, 1919, and that death occurred, on the date stated above, at 2:30 p.m.
The CAUSE OF DEATH* was as follows:
Influenza, Pneumonia
(Duration) yrs. mos. 8 ds.
Contributory (Secondary) Advanced Tuberculosis
(Duration) 2 yrs. mos. ds.
(Signed) C.W. Ritter M.D.
(Address) McLean Ill
Date Jan 12 1919 Telephone 702
18. LENGTH OF RESIDENCE (For Hospitals, Institutions, Transients, or Recent Residents)
19. PLACE OF BURIAL OR REMOVAL
DATE OF BURIAL

FIGURE 6-4: Lizzie Abell's (Pickerell) death certificate.

Pulling the obituary

While the death certificate has some facts, we wanted more context to the Abell family's life. A good source for that context can often be an obituary. Newspapers can be a treasure trove of geographic-specific information. Not only do they contain obituaries, but they contain news articles that you can use to develop a picture of the world in which your ancestors lived.

After we determined the actual death date, we searched for an obituary for Lizzie Pickerell at Newspapers.com. We used the search terms *lizzie abell Illinois 1919* in the Newspapers.com search mechanism and received two results. The first result was Lizzie's obituary in the Bloomington, Illinois, *Pantagraph* (see Figure 6-5).

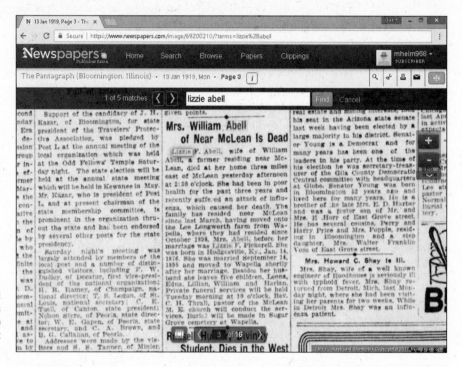

FIGURE 6-5:
Lizzie Abell's (Pickerell) obituary at Newspapers.com.

The obituary contained nice details to help us fill in some gaps. The Abells had moved to Wapella, Illinois, in October 1898, about a month after William Henry Abell married Lizzie Pickerell. In March 1918, they moved to the Lee Longworth farm, three miles east of the town of McLean (where Lizzie died). With the details of the obituary, we can look for resources to approximate where they lived on a map.

Genealogical and historical societies

Most genealogical and historical societies exist on a local level and attempt to preserve documents and history for the area in which they are located. Genealogical societies also have another purpose — to help their members research their ancestors whether they lived in the local area or elsewhere. (Granted, some surname-based genealogical societies, and even a few virtual societies, are exceptions because they aren't specific to one place.) Although historical societies usually don't have a stated purpose of aiding their members in genealogical research, they are helpful to genealogists anyway. Often, if you don't live in the area from which you need a record or information, you can contact a local genealogical or historical society to get help. Help varies from lookup services in books and documents the society maintains in its library to volunteers who locate and obtain copies of records for you. Before you contact a local genealogical or historical society for help, be sure you know the services it offers.

Many local genealogical and historical societies have web pages that identify exactly which services they offer to members and nonmembers online. To find a society in an area you're researching, try a search in a search engine, such as the following:

McLean County Illinois society genealogy OR historical

Or, you can find an index of genealogical and historical societies — such as the FamilySearch United States Societies page (`https://familysearch.org/wiki/en/United_States_Societies`) or the Federation of Genealogical Societies directory (`www.fgs.org/cstm_societyHall.php`).

In our case, we were able to locate the McLean County Museum of History, which houses an archive and the library for the local genealogical society. A directory in that library provided our next piece of valuable information.

Looking at local directories

If you have a general idea of where your family lived at a particular time but no conclusive proof or if you just want to fill in the gaps between censuses, city and county directories may help. Directories can help you confirm whether your ancestors indeed lived in an area and, in some cases, they can provide even more information than you expect.

Like today's telephone books, the directories of yesteryear contained basic information about people who lived in a geographic location, whether the areas were towns, cities, districts, or counties. At a minimum, the directory identified the head of the household and the location of the house. Some directories also included the names and ages of everyone in the household and occupations of any members of the household who were employed.

When looking for a city directory, you can consult a subscription genealogy site, such as Ancestry.com, or look for other sources at the City Directories of the United

States of America at www.uscitydirectories.com. The intent of this site is to identify repositories of city directories online and offline and to guide you to them.

Other sites can lead you to directories for particular geographic areas too. Don's List contains links to directories of a number of states at www.donslist.net/PGHLookups/Dir1Win.shtml. You can find a list of city directories available on microfilm at the Library of Congress for nearly 700 American towns and states through the U.S. City Directories on Microfilm in the Microform Reading Room web page (www.loc.gov/rr/microform/uscity). If you're looking for city directories for England and Wales, look at the Historical Directories site (http://cdm16445.contentdm.oclc.org/cdm/landingpage/collection/p16445coll4). The site contains digitized directories from 1760s to 1910s. You can also often find lists of city directories on the websites of local and state libraries.

Some individuals have posted city directories in their areas. An example of this is the Fredericksburg, Virginia, City Directory 1938 page at http://resources.umwhisp.org/Fredericksburg/1938directory.htm.

For some digitized city directories consult the Internet Archive site at www.archive.org and type "city directories" in the search field for a list of available directories.

TIP

Some genealogical and historical societies and associations have made a commitment to post the contents of directories for their areas or at least an index of what their libraries hold online so that you know before you contact them whether they have something useful to you. Check out the section "Genealogical and historical societies," earlier in this chapter, for more information on how to find these organizations.

Because William Henry Abell was a tenant farmer (meaning he rented the land rather than owning it), it is sometimes difficult to find records showing where he lived (outside of a census year). In this case, we needed to find where he lived in 1918–1919. Because we knew from the death certificate and Lizzie's obituary that they were living in McLean County, we took a trip to the McLean County Museum of History to see if there were resources that could help.

In the museum's library, we found a directory of all farmers for McLean County dated 1917. Not the exact year we needed, but close enough. Lizzie's death certificate said that she died in Funks Grove Township and her obituary mentioned that the Abells lived three miles east of the town of McLean on the Lee Longworth farm. We needed to find an entry in Funks Grove Township for Lee Longworth. Sure enough, in the directory there was an entry for Lester Lee Longworth (with his wife Blanche and son Lyle) who lived on a farm along McLean Route 2. They were tenant farmers on 400 acres belonging to the Wheeler Brothers, located in Section 8 and 9 South in Funks Grove Township. Figure 6-6 shows the entry in the directory found online at the Hathi Trust website (www.hathitrust.org).

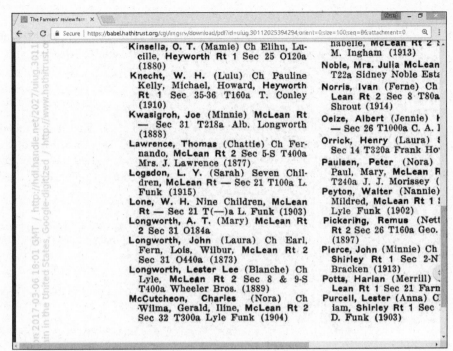

FIGURE 6-6:
Farmer's Review Farm Directory at the Hathi Trust site.

Professional researchers

If we had not been able to find additional information at the McLean County Museum of History ourselves, we might have enlisted the help of others — one option would have been to engage a professional researcher. *Professional researchers* are people who research your genealogy — or certain family lines — for a fee. If you're looking for someone to do all the research necessary to put together a complete family history, some do so. If you're just looking for records in a specific area to substantiate claims in your genealogy, professional researchers can usually locate the records for you and get you copies. Their services, rates, experience, and reputations vary, so be careful when selecting a professional researcher to help you. Look for someone who has quite a bit of experience in the area in which you need help. Asking for references or a list of satisfied customers isn't out of the question. (That way, you know who you're dealing with before you send the researcher money.) To find a researcher in a particular location, you can do a search by geographic specialty on the Association of Professional Genealogists website at www. apgen.org/directory/search.html?type=geo_specialty&new_search=true.

For an introduction on hiring a professional researcher see the FamilySearch Wiki entry at https://familysearch.org/wiki/en/Hiring_a_Professional_ Researcher. Another place to look for help is the genealogyDOTcoach site at https://genealogy.coach. If you just need a boost to your research, you can pay for small amounts of time of a researcher from this website.

Localizing your search

To find a lot of detail about a specific area and what it was like during a specific timeframe, local histories are the answer. Local histories often contain information about when and how a place was settled and may have biographical information on earlier settlers or the principal people within the community who sponsored the creation of the history.

Online local histories can be tucked away in geographically specific websites, historical society pages, library sites, and web-based bookstores. You can also find a few sites that feature local histories:

>> Ancestry.com (www.ancestry.com) features several thousand works in its Stories, Memories, and Histories collection.

>> A collection of Canadian local histories is available at Our Roots/Nos Racines (www.ourroots.ca).

>> You can search by location and find a growing collection of local histories on Google Books (http://books.google.com).

>> FamilySearch Family History Books collection (https://books.familysearch.org) contains over 325,000 genealogy and family history publications including local histories digitized from 12 libraries.

>> The Internet Archive (http://archive.org) contains digitized versions of thousands of local histories. (See Figure 6-7.)

>> The digital library at Hathi Trust (www.hathitrust.org) contains a vast collection of local histories.

To get more details on what was going on in McLean County during the early twentieth century, we read the History of McLean County Illinois published in 1924. The book covered items such as local agriculture (William Henry Abell was a farmer), industrial development, churches, and schools within the county.

Gaining historical perspective

We've mentioned a few times that family history isn't just about names and dates but also about gaining an appreciation of the historical context your ancestors lived within — the things going on in the country or locality they lived in — and how that context might have affected the choices in their lives. One site that

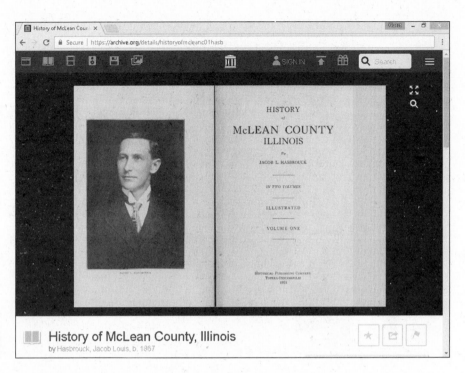

FIGURE 6-7:
A local history at
the Internet
Archive.

attempts to help you sort that out is HistoryLines at `https://historylines.com`. HistoryLines helps you create a sketch of your ancestor's life based upon the time and location that they lived within. Try the following:

1. **Point your web browser to** `https://historylines.com`.

   The HistoryLines web page appears.

2. **Click the Get Started button and complete the sign up process.**

3. **Enter information on the form about an ancestor.**

   We entered *Lizzie F.* in the first name field; *Pickerell* in last name; *14 January 1876* in birth date; *LaRue, Kentucky, United States* in birth place (the field may automatically populate a location while you type); *12 January 1919* in death date; *Funks Grove, McLean, Illinois, United States* in death place; and selected the Female checkbox. You can also opt to import a GEDCOM file or import from a FamilySearch account.

4. **Click the Start a Story button.**

   The historical sketch appears as seen in Figure 6-8.

You can further personalize the sketch by entering your own text and adding photographs.

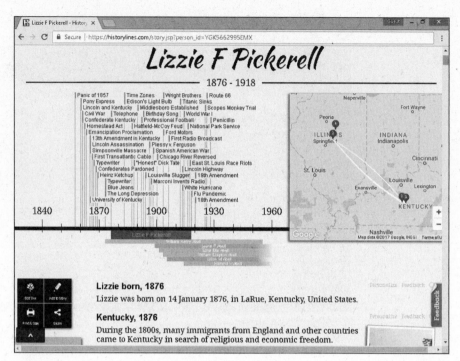

If we had not discovered the death certificate already, the sketch that we produced may have provided a clue as to what happened to Lizzie. Near the bottom of the sketch it mentions that the Spanish flu pandemic of 1918 had a profound effect on the population — killing more than 650,000 Americans.

Mapping Your Ancestor's Way

After you determine where a place is located, it's time to dig out the maps. Maps can be an invaluable resource in your genealogical research. Not only do maps help you track your ancestors' locations at various points in their lives, but they also enhance your published genealogy by illustrating some of your findings.

Different types of online sites have maps that may be useful in your genealogical research.

>> **Historical maps:** Several websites contain scanned or digitized images of historic maps. In a lot of cases, you can download or print copies of these maps. Such sites include the following:

- David Rumsey Map Collection: www.davidrumsey.com

- Perry-Castañeda Library Map Collection, University of Texas at Austin: www.lib.utexas.edu/maps/index.html

- Map Collections of the Library of Congress: www.loc.gov/maps/collections/

You can also find local collections of maps at several university and historical society sites. Here are a few examples:

- Cartography: Historical Maps of New Jersey (Rutgers University): http://mapmaker.rutgers.edu/MAPS.html

- Historical Maps Online (University of Illinois at Urbana-Champaign): http://imagesearchnew.library.illinois.edu/cdm/landingpage/collection/maps

- Massachusetts Maps (The Massachusetts Historical Society): www.masshist.org/online/massmaps

» **Digitized historical atlases:** In addition to map sites, individuals have scanned portions or the entire contents of atlases, particularly those from the nineteenth century. Examples include the following:

- *Countrywide atlases:* Atlas of Historical County Boundaries at http://publications.newberry.org/ahcbp/.

- *County atlases:* The 1904 Maps from the New Century Atlas of Cayuga County, New York www.rootsweb.ancestry.com/~nycayuga/maps/1904/ and Historic Map Works at www.historicmapworks.com.

- *Specialty atlases:* An occupational example is the 1948 U.S. Railroad Atlas at http://trains.rockycrater.org/pfmsig/atlas.php.

» **Interactive map sites:** A few sites have interactive maps that you can use to find and zoom in on areas. When you have the view you want of the location, you can print a copy of the map to keep with your genealogical records. Here are some examples:

- *Google Maps:* https://www.google.com/maps/

- *MapQuest:* https://www.mapquest.com/

- *Bing Maps:* https://www.bing.com/maps

- *National Geographic MapMachine:* http://maps.nationalgeographic.com/maps

- *The U.K. Street Map Page:* www.streetmap.co.uk

Interactive maps are especially helpful when you're trying to pinpoint the location of a cemetery or town you plan to visit for your genealogical research, but they're limited in their historical helpfulness because they typically offer only current information about places.

Earlier in this chapter, we discovered who owned the land that Matthew's ancestor William Henry Abell lived on. Remember, we found the information in a farm directory in this chapter's section on local directories? The directory provided the township section where the farm was located, but we needed a source to tell us exactly where in the township section the land was. A plat map was the solution. Plat maps show the owners of land in map form. So, what we needed to find was a tract of land owned by the Wheeler Brothers in Sections 8 and 9 South in Funks Grove Township.

Fortunately, there was a plat map made in 1914. The McLean County Museum of history had a copy and it is found on line at the Library of Congress Map site. We found it by putting *1914 McLean County Illinois plat map* into the Google search field, which returned the Library of Congress Map site results at `https://www.loc.gov/resource/g4103mm.gct00184/?sp=34`. We looked toward the bottom of the plat map of Funks Grove Township (as the Sections were 8 and 9 *South*) and found the two sections. As seen in Figure 6-9, at the very southern edge of the township sections, on the De Witt county border, was a tract of 400 acres belonging to M.C. W. Wheeler (aka, the Wheeler Brothers).

FIGURE 6-9:
A 1914 plat map from the Library of Congress website.

Zeroing in

We've looked at a few types of maps, but the real promise of mapping technology is the ability to use different maps together to see the whole picture of where your ancestors lived. One of the ways of doing this is by using mapping layers.

Some government agencies and private firms make geographic information systems (GIS) data available on their websites. This data often has a base map and then a variety of layers showing different information that can be placed on top of it. If you want to make your own maps and layers, a good example of mapping layers is the Google Earth technology. Google Earth (www.google.com/earth/index.html) is a downloadable program that combines Google searches with geographic information. Enter a place-name or a longitude and latitude coordinate, and the system maps it for you. Then you can add more map layers to see other information about that particular place.

Several websites make layers that are specifically made to work with Google Earth. For example, you can download historical county boundary data for use on Google Earth (through KMZ files) from the Atlas of Historical County Boundaries maintained by the Newberry Library (http://publications.newberry.org/ahcbp/downloads/united_states.html). With these files you can see what current geographic features might have been in a county in the past.

REMEMBER

We found the farm where William Henry Abell and his family lived on a plat map from 1914 in the previous section. But, where is that land located today? We can see exactly where it is by looking at a layered map. We typed *McLean County Illinois maps* into Google and the first result was the McLean County, IL – Official Website – GIS. From that site, we clicked on the Interactive Maps link that took us to the McLean County Regional Planning Commission website at http://mcgis.org/department/?structureid=3. Here is how we used the map layers to find the location of the land:

1. **Point your web browser to the McLean County Regional Planning Commission page at** http://mcgis.org/department/?structureid=3.

   The Online Mapping page appears.

2. **In the left column, click on the Historic link.**

   The link is located under the In This Section menu about two-thirds of the way down the list of links. The McGIS application appears with a default map. In our case, the default map was from 1856 — too early for our search.

3. **Click the I Want To button in the top-left corner of the page.**

   A drop-down menu appears.

4. **Select Change Visible Map Layers from the menu.**

   A set of layers appears in the left column.

5. **In the left column, deselect the Historic_1856 layer and select the Imagery_2014 layer.**

   A satellite map of McLean County from 2014 appears. We'll use this as our base layer because it is the most current map and because it shows us things as they appear today (well, close enough, anyway).

6. **Click the Historic_1914 layer in the left column.**

The familiar plat map of 1914 is overlaid on top of the 2014 satellite map.

7. **Click on the Plus button near the I Want To button to zoom in on the map.**

We zoomed into the map and then clicked on the map to pull the map up until we saw the bottom of Funks Grove Township.

8. **Locate the appropriate sections and then move the slider to make the historic layer more transparent.**

The slider is located to the right of the Historic_1914 label. Dragging the slider to the left lightens the layer. You should be able to see detail of the satellite map with the outline of the plat map.

9. **Click the Transportation layer in the left column to see current roads.**

With the transportation layer on (in Figure 6-10), we can see which roads to take to get to the actual property.

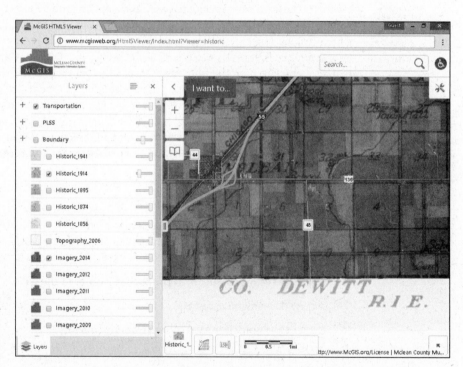

FIGURE 6-10: Layered map of William Henry Abell's residence in 1919.

Although interactive maps are good for getting a general idea of the location of a place, more specific maps are sometimes necessary for feature types such as creeks or ridges. Topographic maps are an especially good set to use for these purposes; they contain not only place-names but also information on features of the terrain (such as watercourses, elevation, vegetation density, and, yes, even cemeteries). At the National Geographic site, you can view a variety of maps, including topographical maps.

To view a topographic map at the National Geographic, follow these steps:

1. **Direct your browser to** `http://www.natgeomaps.com/trail-maps/pdf-quads`.

   A map of the United States appears near the bottom of the page.

2. **In the search box near the middle of the page (on the map of the United States) set the drop-down box to pdf_topo and type in the map name.**

   We typed *Funks Grove* and clicked the Search button. The map zooms into the selected area and a map thumbnail appears.

3. **Click the map thumbnail to see the map.**

   A topographic map appears for McLean, Illinois. There are four areas marked on the map that we can zoom into.

4. **We chose to zoom into section 4 and clicked on the small circle with the number 4 in it.**

   The topographic map appears on the screen. We zoomed into the map to get a better look at the terrain, as shown in Figure 6-11.

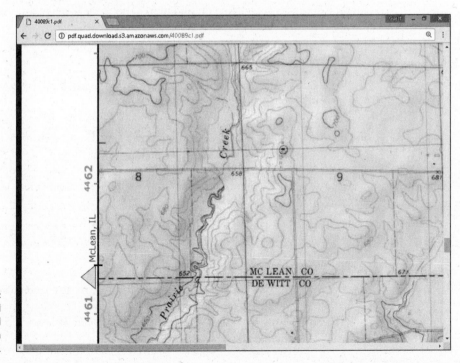

FIGURE 6-11: A topographical map of the land where William Henry Abell lived.

Crossing the line

Just as maps help you track your ancestors' movements and where they lived, they can also help you track when your ancestors *didn't* really move. Boundaries for towns, districts, and even states have changed over time. Additionally, towns and counties sometimes change names. Knowing whether your ancestors really moved or just appeared to move because a boundary or town name changed is important when you try to locate records for them.

To determine whether a town or county changed names at some point, check a gazetteer or historical text on the area. (Gazetteers are discussed earlier in this chapter, in the "Where is Llandrindod, anyway?" section.) Finding boundary changes can be a little more challenging, but resources are available to help you. For example, historical atlases illustrate land and boundary changes. You can also use online sites that have maps for the same areas over time, and a few sites deal specifically with boundary changes in particular locations. Here are a few examples:

>> **Atlas of Historical County Boundaries:** http://publications.newberry.org/ahcbp

>> **The Counties of England, Wales, and Scotland Prior to the 1974 Boundary Changes:** www.genuki.org.uk/big/Britain.html

You can also use software designed to show boundary changes over time. Programs like these can help you find places that have disappeared altogether:

>> **The Centennial Historical Atlas** tracks boundary changes in Europe and the Middle East. Its website is www.clockwk.com.

>> **AniMap Plus** tracks boundary changes in the United States. Its website is www.goldbug.com/AniMap.html.

The following is a quick walkthrough using the Atlas of Historical County Boundaries to see how some counties have changed over time:

1. **Point your web browser to** http://publications.newberry.org/ahcbp.

   The homepage for the atlas appears. You can choose to look at data at a national level or the county level. Continuing with the earlier example, we are interested in finding more information about De Witt County, Illinois.

2. **Click the state that interests you.**

   We clicked on Illinois. A page appears with links to view an interactive map, an index of counties, a chronology of state and county boundaries, individual county chronologies, a bibliography, historical commentary, and downloadable geographic information system (GIS) files.

3. **Click the View Interactive Map heading.**

   A map of the state appears. You can use the toolbar on the left side of the screen to zoom in or out of the map, measure distances, create a query, and print the map.

4. **Under Select Map Date (in the upper-right corner of the screen), type in the date that interests you.**

   We typed in *Feb 26 1845*.

5. **Click the Refresh Map button.**

   The county boundaries change based upon the date that you entered.

6. **Use the Zoom In button on the toolbar to see the county boundaries more clearly.**

   The county boundaries change based upon the date that you entered.

Also, there are a few online resources that can display the movements of your ancestors based upon the contents of your genealogy application or FamilySearch Online Tree, such as Ancestral Atlas (`www.ancestralatlas.com`) and RootsMapper (`https://rootsmapper.com`).

Positioning your family: Using global positioning systems

After discovering the location of the final resting place of great-great-great-grandpa, you just might get the notion to travel to the cemetery. Now, finding the cemetery on the map is one thing, but often finding the cemetery on the ground is a completely different thing. That is where global positioning systems come into play.

A *Global Positioning System* (GPS) is a device that uses satellites to determine the exact location of the user. The technology is sophisticated, but in simple terms, satellites send out radio signals that are collected by the GPS receiver — the device that you use to determine your location. The receiver then calculates the distances between the satellites and the receiver to determine your location. Receivers can come in many forms, ranging from vehicle-mounted receivers to those that fit inside of your smartphone.

While on research trips, we use GPS receivers not only to locate a particular place but also to document the location of a specific object within that place. For example, when we visit a cemetery, we take GPS readings of the gravesites of ancestors and then enter those readings into our genealogical databases. That way, if the marker is ever destroyed, we still have a way to locate the grave. As a final step, we take that information and plot the specific location of the sites on a map, using geographical information systems software. (See the following section for more details on geographical information systems.)

There are several smartphone apps that you can use for GPS readings. For example, although not made specifically for genealogy, the iPhone app MotionX-GPS (gps.motionx.com) contains a variety of tools that are useful for the genealogist in the field. It can show your position on the street, topographic maps, and satellite maps. You can also set the application to track your movements and set waypoints as you go. The application even has a built-in compass and the capability to take a picture and automatically associate it with a latitude and longitude.

Plotting against the family

Although finding the location where your ancestors lived on a map is interesting, it's even more exciting to create maps specific to your family history. One way genealogists produce their own maps is by plotting land records: They take the legal description of the land from a record and place it into land-plotting software, which then creates a map showing the land boundaries. A couple of programs for plotting boundaries are DeedMapper, by Direct Line Software (www.directlinesoftware. com/deedmapper_42), and Metes and Bounds, by Sandy Knoll Software (www. tabberer.com/sandyknoll/more/metesandbounds/metes.html). For an online way to plot a boundary, see Plat Plotter at http://platplotter.appspot.com. And a subscription site called HistoryGeo.com has lands already plotted and searchable for original landowners of public states. For more information on HistoryGeo.com, refer to Chapter 5. You can also find a number of commercial plotting programs by using a search engine such as Google (www.google.com).

Another way to create custom maps is through geographical information systems (GIS) software. GIS software allows you to create maps based on layers of information. For example, you may start with a map that is just an outline of a county. Then you might add a second layer that shows the township sections of the county as they were originally platted. A third layer might show the location of your ancestor's homestead based on the legal description of a land record. A fourth layer might show watercourses or other terrain features within the area. The resulting map can give you a great appreciation of the environment in which your ancestor lived.

To begin using GIS resources, you first must acquire a GIS data viewer. This software comes in many forms, including free software and commercial packages. One popular piece of free software is ArcReader, which is available on the ESRI site at www.esri. com/software/arcgis/arcreader/download.html. Then you download (or create) geographical data to use with the viewer. A number of sites contain data, both free and commercial. Starting points for finding data include ArcGIS Online (www.arcgis. com/home), GIS Data Depot (http://data.geocomm.com), and the geospatial portion of Data.gov (http://catalog.data.gov/dataset?metadata_type=geospatial). For an example of using GIS in genealogy, see the article GIS and Genealogy at esri (www. esri.com/esri-news/arcuser/spring-2014/gis-and-genealogy).

You can also use maps from other sources and integrate them into a GIS map. When visiting cemeteries, we like to use GIS resources to generate an aerial photograph of the cemetery and plot the location of the grave markers on it. When we get back home, we use the aerial photograph as the base template and then overlay the grave locations on it electronically to show their exact positions.

For example, when grave hunting for the Sugar Grove Cemetery (discussed earlier in the chapter), we generated an aerial view of the area at Bing.com (`www.bing.com/maps`). In the search field, we entered the place-name (Bucks Road, Wapella, Illinois) and then clicked on the search icon. When the map appeared, we clicked on the drop-down in the upper-right corner and changed the view from road to Aerial.

Figure 6-12 shows the photograph at its maximum zoom. The cemetery is just to the left of the circle with the address under it. (It's bordered on the north by Bucks Road and on the west by a plowed field.) This view of the cemetery helps a lot when we try to find it on the ground.

From the map, we know that the cemetery is right off the road, among farms, and a house sits directly across from it (although we have to keep in mind that the aerial photograph may have been taken long ago — some things might have changed since then).

After plotting the gravestone locations based on GPS readings at the cemetery, we can store that picture in our genealogical database so that it's easy to find gravestones at that cemetery should we (or anyone else) want to visit it in the future.

FIGURE 6-12:
An aerial map at Bing.com.

Wrapping It Up (with a Surprise)

Just to cover all our bases, we decided to do a search on marriages just to be sure there were no surprises about William Henry Abell. We typed *Kentucky marriage index* into Google and the first result was the Kentucky Marriages, 1785–1979 index at FamilySearch.org. A search of the database yielded one result — the marriage to Lizzie F. Pickerell. Interestingly, the marriage to Betty mentioned in the obituary as occurring in Kentucky in 1929 did not show in the results.

We checked the Illinois, County Marriages, 1810–1940 index at FamilySearch.org to see if the marriage to Betty occurred in Illinois. The search didn't show a marriage to Betty — however, a surprise was lurking. The first result was a marriage of William Henry Abell to Cora Shehan Young in De Witt County, Illinois on 11 February 1922. The father of William Henry Abell was listed as Samuel Abell and mother as Martha S. Beard. Both parents were correct from our sources on William Henry Abell. We ordered the marriage license and marriage record from the Illinois Regional Archives and behold William Henry Abell was married to Cora during the period between Lizzie's death and the marriage to Betty — a fact not mentioned by the family in his obituary (see Figure 6-13).

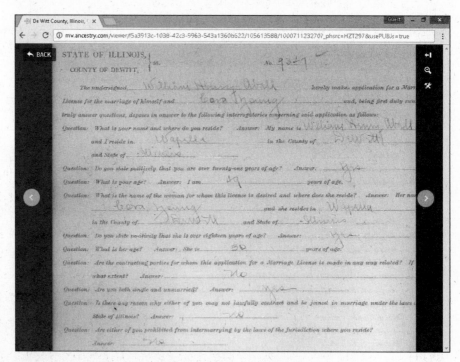

FIGURE 6-13: William Henry Abell and Cora Young's marriage license.

Chapter 7

Searching for That Elusive Ancestor

As a genealogist, you may experience sleepless nights trying to figure out all the important things in life — the maiden name of your great-great-grandmother, whether great-grandpa was really the scoundrel that other relatives say he was, and just how you're related to Daniel Boone. (Well, isn't everyone?) Okay, so you may not have sleepless nights, but you undoubtedly spend a significant amount of time thinking about and trying to find resources that can give you answers to these crucial questions.

In the past, finding information on individual ancestors online was like finding a needle in a haystack. You browsed through long lists of links in hopes of finding a site that contained a nugget of information to aid your search. But looking for your ancestors online has become easier than ever. Instead of merely browsing links, you can use search engines and online databases to pinpoint information on your ancestors.

This chapter covers the basics of searching for an ancestor by name, presents some good surname resource sites, and shows you how to combine several Internet resources to successfully find information on your family.

Letting Your Computer Do the Walking: Using Search Engines

Finding information on an ancestor on the web can be a challenge. In the past, it was sometimes difficult to find any kind of information about a given individual because online collections were just beginning to grow and become accessible. Now, with the myriad resources available, the challenge is sorting through all the non-relevant information to find data that can help progress your research. One of the key online resources that you can use to help locate and filter some of the online data is a search engine.

Search engines are programs that examine huge indexes of information generated by web robots, or simply bots. *Bots* are programs that travel throughout the Internet and collect information on the sites and resources that they find. You can access the information contained in search engines through an interface, usually through a form on a web page.

The real strength of search engines is that they allow you to search the full text of web pages instead of just the title or a brief abstract of the site. This is particularly valuable in a family history because a researcher may be looking for one of thousands of people who descended from a particular individual — for whom the web page may be named. For example, many genealogy websites are named for the progenitor of the family. In Matthew's case, the progenitor for his branch of the Helm family was Georg Helm. A web page for this family might be named something like The Georg and Dorothea Helm Family. If Matthew is looking for one of Georg's great-great-great grandsons, Uriah Helm, he might not know to look under the Georg Helm website to find him. Some genealogy programs create websites with thousands of pages of information, only one of which might pertain to Uriah. If a search engine bot happens to index all the pages of the site, however, Uriah's name becomes visible through the search results.

Although search engines offer a lot of coverage of the web, to find what you're looking for is sometimes more of an art than a science. In the following pages, we look at search strategies as well as the different kinds of search engines that are available to aid your search.

Diving into general Internet search engines

General search engines (such as Google or Bing) send out bots to catalog the Internet as a whole, regardless of the subject(s) of the site's content. Therefore, on any given search, you're likely to receive a lot of hits, perhaps only a few of which hold any genealogical value — that is, unless you refine your search terms to give you a better chance at receiving relevant results.

You can conduct several types of searches with most search engines. Looking at a search engine's Help link to see the most effective way to search is always a good idea. Also, search engines often have two search interfaces — a simple search and an advanced search. With the *simple search*, you normally just type your query and click the Submit button. With an *advanced search*, you can use a variety of options to refine your search. These options can be in the form of checkboxes, or they can be the manner that you format the search terms. The best way to become familiar with using a search engine is to experiment and see what kinds of results you get.

To demonstrate various strategies for using a search engine, we run through some searches using Google for Matthew's ancestor Georg. Before we begin the search, it's a good idea to have some useful facts at hand to help define our search terms. From previous research, Matthew knows that Georg's name is spelled *Georg* on his gravestone — but *George* in land records. He also knows that Georg was born in 1723 and died in 1769 and that he owned land in Winchester, Frederick County, Virginia. He was married to a woman named Dorothea.

Not all search terms are equal

When first using a search engine, a number of people simply type the name of an ancestor, expecting the search engine to take care of the rest. Although search engines do have some default ways of searching, these ways aren't always the best for genealogical searches. The following table lists the number of results that we received with different search criteria.

Search Criteria	Number of Results
Georg Helm	567,000
George Helm	14,800,000
Georg OR George Helm	19,400,000

The first search, using *Georg Helm*, produces hundreds of thousands of results because it looks for any content containing the words *Georg* and *Helm.* The results include not only pages that contain the name Helm but also pages containing the common word *helm.* Some search engines also expand the search to include varia-tions on the spelling of the word. (This practice is common in search engines and is referred to as *stemming.*) The search for *George Helm* yields more results because the addition of the letter *e* in George forms a more popular first name. The third search demonstrates the capability of Google to search for multiple conditions within a single set of search terms. Placing the OR modifier in the search terms allows both Georg and George to be searched and ranked into one set of results. Searching with these dual terms generates a list that includes all the results from the first (*Georg Helm*) and second (*George Helm*) searches.

Although each of these searches produces thousands or millions of results, only a tiny fraction has anything to do with the Georg Helm that we're looking for. So, we need to refine our search method to get a better selection of more appropriate results.

Searching with phrases

Using quotation marks in Google searches helps you specify the exact form of the word to search. Placing *"Georg Helm"* in quotation marks means that you want Google to search words that exactly match *Georg Helm.* Using parentheses indicates the search engine should look for multiple words in conjunction with other words, allowing you to search more efficiently. For example, putting parentheses around both first names with the conjunction OR tells the search engine to look for either of those first names when they appear with that last name.

Even with these modifiers on the first names, you can see that the results for *"Georg" Helm* and *"George" Helm* in the following table still number in the tens of thousands because the search engine is looking for any content that contains both the words *Georg* and *Helm or George and Helm.*

Search Criteria	Number of Results
(Georg OR George) Helm	19,400,000
"(Georg OR George) Helm"	43,500

Performing targeted searches

The search strategies we mention earlier in this chapter are fine for getting a general idea of what's available for a particular name or for searching for a unique name, but they're not necessarily the most efficient for finding information on a specific person. The best strategies involve using specific search terms that include geographic information or other family members associated with the individual.

Using the same example from earlier — searching for information about Georg Helm — we can find more targeted information on Georg Helm by including geographical terms in the search. The following search term yields 955 results:

"(Georg OR George) Helm" (Winchester OR "Frederick County") + Virginia

The search term requires that the online content contain the following:

>> The words *Georg Helm* or *George Helm*

>> The word(s) *Winchester* or *Frederick County*

>> The word *Virginia*

Of these results, less than a quarter of the results have anything to do with the Georg Helm who is the ancestor of Matthew.

Because other George Helms are associated with Frederick County, Virginia, we can further clarify the search terms to include Georg's wife's name — Dorothea. The following search term generates 504 results:

> "(Georg OR George) Helm" (Winchester OR "Frederick County") + Virginia Dorothea

You can also use targeted searches to meet specific research goals. For example, if Matthew is looking for the will of Georg Helm, he could use the following search terms:

> "(Georg OR George) Helm" (Winchester OR "Frederick County") + Virginia Dorothea "will"

A few other Google hints

To get the most relevant content to meet your research goals, you have a few other ways to control the results presented by Google. The first is to exclude certain results by using the – (minus) sign. In the case of Matthew's search for George Helm, several of the results that he received in his previous searches dealt with another George Helm who was born in Frederick County, Virginia, and who is unrelated to Matthew's Georg. This second George was married to Sarah Jackman and later moved to Cumberland County, Kentucky. To avoid seeing results for the second George, we can modify our search terms to the following:

> "(Georg OR George) Helm" (Winchester OR "Frederick County") + Virginia –Jackman –"Cumberland County"

Sometimes searching on a phrase can be too exact. If the person you're researching is listed with a middle name, you might not find the content with a phrase search. One way around this is to use the * wildcard term. A search term such as *Georg * Helm* would pick up content containing the name Georg Smith Helm, as well as content containing Georg and Dorothea Helm.

You can also use number ranges within your search terms to push more relevant search results to the top of your results list. When searching within Google, you can specify number ranges by placing two periods between the range of numbers. So, if you want to search on a range of numbers from 1723 to 1769, place two periods between 1723 and 1769. For example, you could use the following search terms:

> "(Georg OR George) Helm" 1723..1769

This term searches for content with Georg Helm or George Helm with a number between 1723 and 1769. In our example, this search would yield pages related to Georg Helm who died in 1769, as well as his son who was born in 1751.

Google offers a few other useful features for limiting results. If you're searching for a relatively common name, you can try to focus your search on the page titles of content to keep from being overwhelmed by millions of results. To do this, use intitle or allintitle in your search terms. (Yes, you are seeing those correctly — do not put spaces in the phrases intitle [for *in title*] or allintitle [for *all in title*] when using them in the search term. Google knows how to interpret them without the spaces.) For example, the search term *intitle:Georg Helm Dorothea* looks for sites that have Georg, Helm, or Dorothea in the page title. However, the search includes even the sites that don't have all the search terms in the title (although it scores sites that contain all three words higher than those that don't). To search for sites that have all of the search terms in the title, use the allintitle function — *allintitle:Georg Helm Dorothea.*

Similarly, you can use the intext function to limit the results to search terms that appear in the text of the page. By using the search term *intext:Georg Helm Dorothea* (or, if you want all search terms to appear — *allintext:Georg Helm Dorothea*), you can search for sites with those specific words in the text of the web page. If you remember coming across a page with a link that is important to your research but can't remember where you found it, you can use the inanchor function. A search such as *inanchor:Georg Helm* looks for Georg Helm in links within a page. The search modifier allinanchor looks for all the search terms within the link. And finally, if you want to look for search terms within a URL or Uniform Resource Locator (the address where information can be found and the method for retrieving it through the World Wide Web), use the inurl and allinurl search modifiers (such as *inurl:Georg Helm*).

Using the advanced search form

Perhaps you don't want to use the search syntax for the search engine. Fortunately for you, most search engines offer an advanced search form, which makes your search easier. Try the following steps to use the Google advanced search:

1. **Point your web browser to** https://www.google.com/advanced_search.

   The Advanced Search page opens with several fields that you can use to limit the search results.

2. **Type your ancestor's name (or other search term) in one of the fields in the Find pages with section.**

   You can put your search terms in one of the following fields. Here are some hints as to when you might use each field:

   - *All These Words:* When the words can appear in any order or context

- *This Exact Wording or Phrase:* When you're typing a name or location that needs to match the exact order

- *Any of These Words:* When you want Google to look for any site that might have one of many words (such as location names within a state or county)

3. **Enter unwanted search terms into the field marked None of These Words.**

   You might want to enter terms in this field when you want to differentiate your ancestor from someone else with the same name.

4. **Add information into other fields to limit your results in the Narrow Your Results By section.**

   On the first search, you might not want to limit your results, but the fields are there in case you do.

5. **Click the Advanced Search button.**

   A Google results page appears.

Flying with Genealogy Vertical Search Engines

If you have used a general Internet search engine, you know that you can receive a lot of extraneous results that are unrelated to genealogy or local history. Even searching for *Georg Helm* produces hundreds of links about the mathematical theories of the German mathematician, Georg Helm. Although those theories might be interesting, we have only so much time to dedicate to research, and we want to use that time wisely.

One way to maximize your research time is to use a vertical genealogy search engine. A *vertical search engine* is a site that indexes content about a specific topic rather than attempting to index the entire web. So, in theory, the results from a genealogy vertical search engine should contain things that pertain to genealogy and local history. The challenge for the owners of vertical search engines is to ensure that the content that is indexed by the bot is consistent with the topic. That means that the maintainers of the search engine must screen the sites that are included in the index, either through the technology or by indexing only particular sites. A search engine to look at for genealogy and local history is the Genealogy Toolbox (www.genealogytoolbox.com). (In the spirit of full disclosure, we maintain the Genealogy Toolbox search engine.)

The Genealogy Toolbox has been around since 1994. It began as a list of links to genealogy and local-history resources and added a search engine in 1998. Today, the focus of the free site is on the search engine and in preformatted searches.

1. **Navigate to** www.genealogytoolbox.com.

   The Genealogy Toolbox home page appears. Under the section labeled Genealogy Toolbox Full-Text Search is a search box.

2. **Type your search terms in the search box and click the Search button.**

   For hints on search syntax read the information located above the search box. The search results appear, as shown in Figure 7-1.

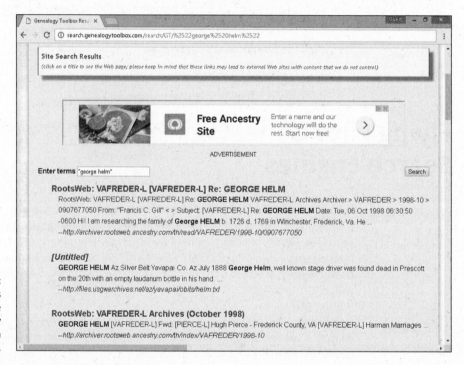

FIGURE 7-1: Search results from the Genealogy Toolbox search engine.

3. **Click on a link that interests you.**

   You can also use the preformatted searches located on the home page to reduce the amount of time spent searching. These preformatted searches appear as links in the Search Categories text box located just below the search form.

Finding the Site That's Best for You

Your dream as an online genealogist is to find a website that contains all the information that you ever wanted to know about your family. Unfortunately, these sites simply don't exist. However, during your search, you may discover a variety of sites that vary greatly in the amount and quality of genealogical information. Before you get too deep into your research, it's a good idea to look at the type of sites that you're likely to encounter.

Personal genealogical sites

The majority of non-subscription pages that you encounter on the web are maintained by an individual who is interested in researching a particular person or family line. These pages usually contain information on the site maintainer's ancestry or on particular branches of several different families rather than on a surname as a whole. That doesn't mean valuable information isn't present on these sites — it's just that they have a more personal focus.

WHAT ABOUT BLOGS?

Since previous editions of this book were published, the Internet has been inundated by blogging. A *blog* is an online, personal journal of sorts — a site where an individual or even a group of people with a common interest can record their daily, weekly, monthly, or whatever-timed-interval thoughts and experiences. The field of genealogy is no exception! Many genealogy blogs are now available, and they can't be categorized under just one of the groupings we've covered so far in this chapter. In other words, they don't all fit into personal genealogical sites, nor do they all fit into family associations or organizations.

One example of a blog that is genealogical and geographic in nature is the Texas History and Genealogy Blog (http://texashistoryblog.blogspot.com). As you might imagine, it covers a variety of topics relating to Texas. At irregular intervals, the host of the blog posts various types of information ranging from cemetery transcriptions, to information about upcoming conferences, to historical markers, to things to see when driving through Texas, to other websites or articles that she thinks will interest readers.

There are also blogs that recount the research pursuits of particular individuals and there are blogs that focus on events in the genealogy world. You can find a list of blogs on the Genealogy Blog Roll page at the GeneaBloggers website (http://geneabloggers.com/genealogy-blogs).

When you're ready to share your knowledge with the world, you might consider setting up your own genealogical blog. We provide the specific steps for doing so in Chapter 14.

You can find a wide variety of information on personal genealogical sites. Some pages list only a few surnames that the maintainer is researching; others contain extensive online genealogical databases and narratives. A site's content depends on the amount of research, time, and computer skills the maintainer possesses. Some common items that you see on most sites include a list of surnames, an online genealogical database, pedigree and descendant charts, family photographs, research blogs, and the obligatory list of the maintainer's favorite genealogical Internet links.

REMEMBER

Personal genealogical sites vary not only in content but also in presentation. Some sites are neatly constructed and use plain backgrounds and aesthetically pleasing colors. Other sites, however, require you to bring out your sunglasses to tone down the fluorescent colors, or they use lots of moving graphics and banner advertisements that take up valuable space and make it difficult to navigate through the site. You should also be aware that the JavaScript, music players, and animated icons that some personal sites use can significantly increase your download times.

An example of a personal genealogical site is the Rubi-Lopez Genealogy Page (http://rubifamilygen.com), shown in Figure 7-2. The Rubi-Lopez page contains articles on different lines of the family, a photo gallery, and links to other family websites.

FIGURE 7-2:
The Rubi-Lopez Genealogy Page is an example of a personal genealogy site.

REMEMBER

After you find a site that contains useful information, write down the maintainer's name and email address and contact him or her *as soon as possible* if you have any questions or want to exchange information. Personal genealogical sites have a way of disappearing without a trace because individuals frequently switch Internet service providers or stop maintaining sites.

One-name study sites

If you're looking for a wide range of information on one particular surname, a one-name study site may be worth your while. These sites usually focus on one surname regardless of the geographic location where the surname appears. In other words, they welcome information about people with the surname worldwide. These sites are quite helpful because they contain all sorts of information about the surname, even if they don't have specific information about your branch of a family with that surname. Frequently they have information on the variations in spelling, origins, history, DNA, and heraldry of the surname. One-name studies have some of the same resources you find in personal genealogical sites, including online genealogy databases and narratives.

Although one-name study sites welcome all surname information regardless of geographic location, the information presented at one-name study sites is often organized around geographic lines. For example, a one-name study site may categorize all the information about people with the surname by continent or country — such as Helms in the United States, England, Canada, Europe, and Africa. Or, the site may be even more specific and categorize information by state, province, county, or parish. You're better off if you have a general idea of where your family originated or migrated from. But if you don't know, browsing through the site may lead to some useful information.

The Rowberry One-Name Study website (`http://www.rowberry.org/`) is a one-name study site with several resources for the Rowberry, Rowbury, Ruberry, Rubery, Rewbury, Robery, Roebury, Rovery, Rowbery, Rowbory, Rowbree, Rowbrey, Rowburrey, Rubbery, Rubbra, Rubra, Rubrey, and Rubury surnames. From the home page (see Figure 7-3), you can choose to view news on recent additions to the site, articles on current discoveries, results of the surname DNA project, research in different countries, and information on how to join a mailing list of the surnames.

TIP

The maintainers of one-name study sites welcome any information you have on the surname. These sites are often a good place to join research groups that can be instrumental in assisting your personal genealogical effort.

To find one-name study sites pertaining to the surnames you're researching, you have to go elsewhere. Where, you ask? One site that can help you is the Guild of One-Name Studies (`www.one-name.org`).

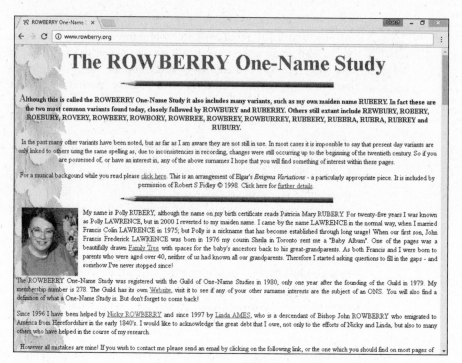

FIGURE 7-3:
The Rowberry
One-Name Study
website.

Gee, we bet you can't figure out what the Guild of One-Name Studies is! It's exactly as it sounds — an online organization of registered sites, each of which focuses on one particular surname. Follow these steps to find out whether any of the Guild's members focus on the surname of the person you're researching:

1. **Open your web browser and go to** www.one-name.org.

   The home page appears with a search field just below the title of the site.

2. **Type the surname you're researching in the field entitled Is Your Surname Registered?**

3. **Click the Search button.**

   If a registered one-name study is available, you see links to the study's website and, if available, DNA website.

Family associations and organizations

Family association sites are similar to one-name study sites in terms of content, but they usually have an organizational structure (such as a formal association, society, or club) backing them. The association may focus on the surname as a whole or just one branch of a family. The goals for the family association site may differ from those for a one-name study. The maintainers may be creating a family history in book form or a database of all individuals descended from a particular person. Some sites may require you to join the association before you can fully participate in their activities, but this is usually at a minimal cost or free.

The Wingfield Family Society site (`www.wingfield.org`), shown in Figure 7-4, has several items that are common to family association sites. The site's contents include a family history, newsletter subscription details, a membership form, queries, mailing list information, results of a DNA project, and a directory of the society's members who are online. Some of the resources at the Wingfield Family Society site require you to be a member of the society to access them.

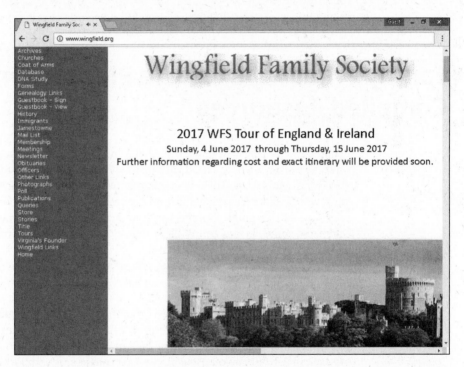

FIGURE 7-4:
The Wingfield
Family Society
site.

To find a family association website, your best bet is to use a search engine. For more on search engines, see the section "Diving into general Internet search engines," earlier in this chapter. Be sure to use search terms that include the surname you're interested in researching and one of these keywords: *society, association, group,* or *organization.*

Surnames connected to events or places

Another place where you may discover surnames is a site that has a collection of names connected with an event or geographic location. The level of information available on these sites varies greatly among sites and among surnames on the same site. Often, the people who maintain such sites include more information about their personal research interests than other surnames, simply because they have more information on their own lines.

Typically, you need to know events that your ancestors were involved in or geographic areas where they lived to use these sites effectively. Also, you benefit from the site simply because you have a general, historical interest in the event or location, even if the website contains nothing on your surname. Finding websites about events is easiest if you use a search engine, a comprehensive website, or a subscription database. Because we devote an entire chapter to researching geographic locations (Chapter 6), we won't delve into that here.

Family Trees Ripe for the Picking: Finding Compiled Resources

Using online databases to pick pieces of genealogical fruit is wonderful. But you want more, right? Not satisfied with just having basic obituary information on his great-grandfather, Matthew is eager to know more — in particular, he'd like to know who William Henry Abell's grandfather was. You have a few research tactics to explore at this point. Perhaps the first is to see whether someone has already completed some research on William Henry Abell and his ancestors.

When someone publishes his or her genealogical findings (whether online or in print), the resulting work is called a *compiled genealogy.*

Compiled genealogies can give you a lot of information about your ancestors in a nice, neat format. When you find one with information relevant to your family, you get an overwhelming feeling of instantaneous gratification. Wait! Don't get too excited yet! When you use compiled genealogies, it's important to remember that you need to verify any information in them that you're adding to your own findings. Even when sources are cited, it's wise to get your own copies of the actual sources to ensure that the author's interpretation of the sources was correct and that no other errors occurred in the publication of the compiled genealogy.

Compiled genealogies take two shapes online. One is the traditional narrative format — the kind of thing that you typically see in a book at the library. The second is in the form of information exported from an individual's genealogical database and posted online in a lineage-linked format (*lineage-linked* means that the database is organized by the relationships between people).

Narrative compiled genealogies

Narrative compiled genealogies usually have more substance than their exported database counterparts. Authors sometimes add color to the narratives by including local history and other text and facts that can help researchers get an idea of the time in which the ancestor lived. An excellent example of a narrative genealogy is found at The Carpenters of Carpenter's Station, Kentucky, at `http://freepages.genealogy.rootsweb.ancestry.com/~carpenter`.

The site maintainer, Kathleen Carpenter, has posted a copy of her mother's historical manuscript on the Carpenter family, as well as some photos and a map of Carpenter's Station. You can view the documents directly through the web or download PDF copies.

To locate narrative genealogies, try using a search engine or comprehensive genealogical index. (For more information on using these resources, see the sections later in this chapter.) Often, compiled genealogies are part of a personal or family association website.

You can also find a collection of family histories at the Family History Books portion of FamilySearch (`https://books.familysearch.org/primo_library/libweb/action/search.do?dscnt=1&vid=FHD_PUBLIC&`). Just type the name that interests you in the search form to see whether a compiled genealogy has been placed online.

Compiled genealogical databases

Although many people don't think of lineage-linked, online genealogical databases as compiled genealogies, these databases serve the same role as narrative compiled genealogies — they show the results of someone's research in a neatly organized, printed format.

For example, the Simpson History site (`http://simpsonhistory.com/_main_page.html`) is a personal site that contains a compiled genealogical database providing information on John "The Scotsman" Simpson and his descendants. You can navigate through descendant charts and family group sheets, clicking particular individuals to access more information about them.

Finding information in compiled genealogical databases can sometimes be tough. There isn't a grand database that indexes all the individual databases available online. Although general Internet search engines have indexed quite a few, some very large collections are still accessible only through a database search — something that general Internet search engines don't normally do.

In the preceding section, we conducted a search on Matthew's great-grandfather, William Henry Abell. Now we want to find out more about his ancestry. We can jump-start our research by using a lineage-linked database in hopes of finding some information compiled from other researchers that can help us discover who his ancestors were (perhaps even several generations' worth). From documents such as his obituary and death certificates, we find out that William Henry Abell's father was named Samuel Abell and his mother was named Martha Susan Baird. And from research, we also know that Samuel Abell was living in Larue County, Kentucky, in the early 1870s. Armed with this information, we can search a compiled genealogical database.

The FamilySearch Internet Genealogy Service (www.familysearch.org) is the official research site for the Church of Jesus Christ of Latter-day Saints (LDS). This free website allows you to search several LDS databases including the Ancestral File, International Genealogical Index, Pedigree Resource File, vital records index, census records, and a collection of abstracted websites — all of which are free. The two resources that function much like lineage-linked databases are the Ancestral File and the Pedigree Resource File. Fortunately, you don't have to search each of these resources separately. A master search is available that allows you to search all of the resources on the site at once. See Chapter 3 for more on how to use the FamilySearch site.

You can find several other lineage-linked collections that may contain useful information. The following list gives you details on some of the better-known collections:

>> **Ancestry Family Tree:** The Ancestry.com site (http://search.ancestry.com/search/db.aspx?dbid=1030) contains a free area where researchers can search through the files of other researchers.

>> **WorldConnect:** The WorldConnect Project (http://wc.rootsweb.ancestry.com/) is part of the RootsWeb.com site. The Project has more than 800 million names in its database.

>> **MyTrees.com:** MyTrees.com (www.mytrees.com) is a site maintained by Kindred Konnections. The site has a lineage-linked database available only by subscription.

>> **OneGreatFamily.com:** OneGreatFamily.com (www.onegreatfamily.com/Home.aspx) hosts a subscription-based, lineage-linked database.

>> **Geni:** Geni (www.geni.com) a site owned by MyHeritage, hosts a free database with subscription-based add-on features.

>> **WikiTree:** WikiTree (www.wikitree.com) is a free site for creating and searching family trees focused on collaboration.

RootsSearch (https://www.rootssearch.io) is a tool for searching through multiple sites using the same search interface. It is available as an extension to the Google Chrome web browser and supports searching of over 20 genealogically focused sites. It does not search all of the sites at the same time; rather, it allows you to enter the information once and then select a site to search (see Figure 7-5).

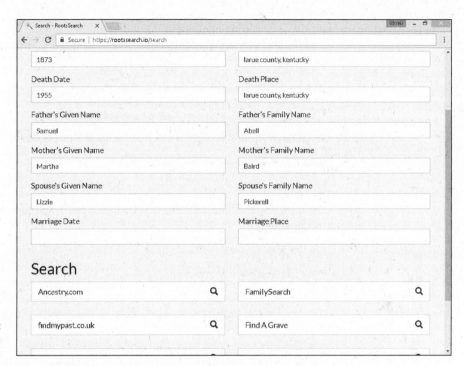

FIGURE 7-5:
The RootsSearch
search form.

Browsing Comprehensive Genealogical Indexes

If you're unable to find information on your ancestor through a search engine or online database, or if you're looking for additional information, another resource to try is a comprehensive genealogical index. A *comprehensive genealogical index* is a site that contains a categorized listing of links to online resources for family history research. Comprehensive genealogical indexes can be organized in a variety of ways, including by subject, alphabetically, or by resource type. No matter how the links are organized, they usually appear hierarchically — you click your way down from category to subcategory until you find the link for which you're looking.

Some examples of comprehensive genealogical indexes include the following:

>> **Cyndi's List of Genealogy Sites on the Internet:** www.cyndislist.com

>> **Linkpendium:** www.linkpendium.com

To give you an idea of how comprehensive genealogical indexes work, try the following example:

1. **Fire up your browser and go to Linkpendium** (www.linkpendium.com).

   This step launches the home page for Linkpendium.

2. **Scroll down to the portion of the main page with the links to surnames.**

3. **Click a link with a letter for your surname.**

   For example, we're looking for Abell, so we click the A surnames link.

4. **Click the link that contains the first three letters of the surname you're researching.**

   We click the link entitled Abe Families.

5. **Click the link to your surname.**

   We click the Abell Family: Surname Genealogy, Family History, Family Tree, Family Crest link. Figure 7-6 shows the links for the Helm surname.

One drawback to comprehensive genealogical indexes is that they can be time-consuming to browse. It sometimes takes several clicks to get down to the area where you believe links that interest you may be located. And, after several clicks, you may find that no relevant links are in that area. This lack may be because the maintainer of the site has not yet indexed a relevant site or the site may be listed somewhere else in the index.

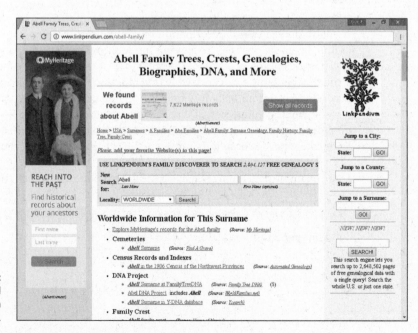

FIGURE 7-6: Looking for Abell resources on Linkpendium.

Chapter **8**

Going Beyond Borders: International and Ethnic Records

At some point in your research, you'll encounter an ancestor who was born outside the United States (or before the U.S. was a country) or who has an ethnic heritage that requires you to use a specific set of sources. These records often have characteristics that make them different from the typical resources found in the U.S. Even if you can't find the actual records online (a lot of international records have been placed online over the past few years), certain sites can help identify what records are available in archives and how to use them to benefit your research. In this chapter, we look at strategies to find these resources online as well as provide links to some key sites to consult.

Fishing for International and Ethnic Sources

You can use a number of strategies when attempting to locate international and ethnic resources online. These strategies range from using genealogical wikis to search engines and comprehensive genealogical indexes.

Wiki-ing for answers

When beginning to research in a new geographical area, we always like to start by seeing what's available in that area at the FamilySearch Research Wiki (`https://familysearch.org/learn/wiki/en/Main_Page`). You can type the country or locality in the search box at the top of the page, or you can browse articles by country by clicking the world map. Some of the topics contained in the articles are Beginning Research, Record Types, Background, and Local Research Resources, as shown in Figure 8-1.

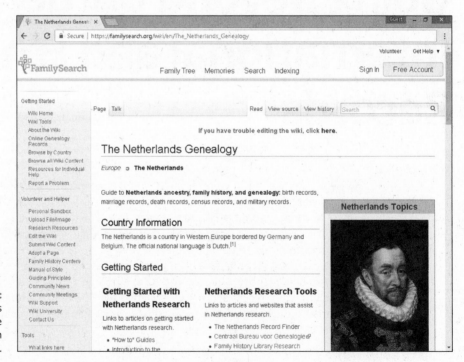

FIGURE 8-1:
The Netherlands topic on the FamilySearch Research Wiki.

You can also search for ethnic entries in the FamilySearch Research Wiki through the search box. Topics on ethnic articles might include Beginning Research, Original Records, Compiled Sources, Background Information, and Finding Aids.

Surveying sites with comprehensive genealogy indexes

To get an idea of what's generally available online, a comprehensive genealogy index is always a good start. These indexes have the benefit of being family-history focused, so you don't have to wade through a lot of links that aren't relevant to genealogy or history. Typically, these sites categorize the links in such a way that you can get to what you're looking for in a few clicks.

For example, if you're interested in researching an ancestor who lived in the Netherlands, you could visit Cyndi's List (www.cyndislist.com), click "N" under Browse Categories, select the Netherlands/Nederland link, and see links organized into 24 groups.

Using search engines

If you haven't found what you're looking for in a comprehensive genealogy index, your next stop should be a general search engine. Similar to searches for information on particular individuals, you need to ensure that your search criteria are fairly specific or you risk receiving too many search results — most of which might be irrelevant to your search. For example, when we type the search term *Belgium genealogy*, we receive 393,000 results in Google and 102,000 results in Bing.

Search engines are a good resource when you're looking for information on records in a specific locality. So, instead of *Belgium genealogy*, if we use the search criteria *Hainaut baptism records*, we receive a fraction of the results.

WorldGenWeb

The WorldGenWeb Project (www.worldgenweb.org) contains links to websites for countries and areas in the world. To find a specific country, follow these steps:

1. **Go to the WorldGenWeb Project site (www.worldgenweb.org).**

   You see a page with a map and a list of resources along the left side of the page.

2. **Click the link to the Country Index under the Main Menu column.**

   For our example, we're looking for information on civil registrations in Jamaica.

3. **Click the link in the WorldGenWeb Region column in the Country Index for your target country.**

   We click the CaribbeanGenWeb link next to the entry for Jamaica. This link takes us to the region project page.

4. **From the region page, find a link to the countries represented in the project.**

   On the CaribbeanGenWeb page, we click the Islands Links link located near the top of the page in the second column. If you didn't choose the same region, you have to find the appropriate link on your particular region page.

5. **Select the link to your country.**

   We click the Jamaica link, which takes us to the Genealogy of Jamaica page.

6. **Choose a link to a resource that interests you.**

   On the Genealogy of Jamaica home page, we find a list of available resources. We click the About Civil Registration (Births, Marriages and Deaths, 1880 - 1930) link, which displays the Civil Registration of Jamaicans page, as shown in Figure 8-2.

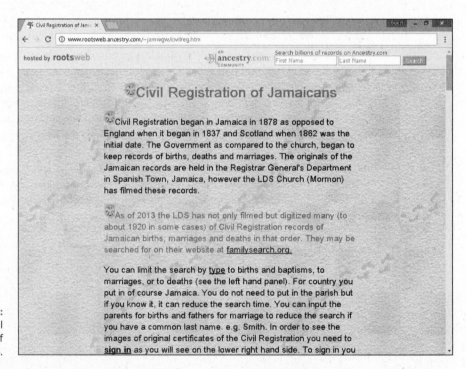

FIGURE 8-2:
Page for Civil Registrations of Jamaicans.

REMEMBER

When researching your European roots, keep in mind that due to the number of European countries, no single European GenWeb Project site exists. Instead, you find the following four European region sites:

» **Ireland & United KingdomGenWeb** (www.iukgenweb.org/) contains projects for British Overseas Territories, Channel Islands, England, Ireland, Isle of Man, Northern Ireland, Scotland, and Wales.

>> **CenEuroGenWeb** (`www.rootsweb.ancestry.com/~ceneurgw/`) lists pages for Belgium, Denmark, Greenland, Germany, Iceland, Latvia, Liechtenstein, Lithuania, Luxembourg, Netherlands, Norway, Poland, Sweden, and Switzerland.

>> **EastEuropeGenWeb** (`https://www.easteuropegenweb.org/`) contains sites for Albania, Austria, Belarus, Bosnia-Herzegovina, Bulgaria, Croatia, Czech Republic, Estonia, Finland, Hungary, Macedonia, Moldova, Montenegro, Romania, Russia, Serbia, Slovak Republic, Slovenia, Ukraine, and Yugoslavia.

>> **MediterraneanGenWeb** (`https://sites.google.com/site/mediterraneangenweb/`) has project pages for Andorra, Azores, France, Gibraltar, Greece, Italy, Madeira, Malta, Monaco, Portugal, San Marino, Spain, and Vatican City.

Translating sites

Within this chapter (and when you search online), you'll encounter sites in languages other than English. Due to advancements in translation websites and web browser translators, the fact that the site is in a different language doesn't mean it's not useful in your research. The translation site Google Translate, at `http://translate.google.com/`, has the capability to translate a block of text, or you can enter a URL to translate an entire web page.

Rather than going to the Google Translate page each time we encounter a site in a foreign language, we prefer to have that functionality built into our browser. The Google Chrome browser (`https://www.google.com/chrome/`) has the Google Translate functionality built in. When you reach a site in a foreign language, the Translate toolbar appears and suggests the language that the site is authored in. It then asks whether you want the site translated. If you say yes, the page is translated — that is, the text that's not part of a graphic is translated. Although the translation isn't perfect, it's usually good enough to give you a good idea of the text's meaning.

Records from the English-Speaking World

Currently, the most prolific number of records available on the web are from countries with English as their native language. In the following sections, we look at records in the United Kingdom, Ireland, Canada, and Australia. For information specifically on census records for these countries, see Chapter 4.

Gathering information from England and Wales

To become familiar with records in England and Wales, visit the National Archives site (www.nationalarchives.gov.uk). By clicking the red circle entitled Menu at the top of the page, you can find a link to Online Collections page (under the Help with Your Research column, about two-thirds of the way down the list), where you find links to their records, including:

>> Aliens' Registration Cards, 1918–1957

>> British Army Medal Index Cards, 1914–1920

>> Country Court Death Duty Registers, 1796–1811

>> Naturalisation Case Papers, 1801–1871

>> Wills, 1384–1858.

Birth, marriage, and death records

A number of online sources are available for transcribed and digitized documents. BMD Registers (www.bmdregisters.co.uk) features images of birth, baptism, marriage, and death records taken from non-parish sources from 1534 to 1865. You can conduct a search of its database; however, you must purchase credits before being able to view an image of the digitized document. The Genealogist (https://www.thegenealogist.co.uk/), a subscription site, has a complete index of birth, marriage, and death records for England and Wales. If you're looking for free birth, marriage, and death records, see the FreeBMD project at www.freebmd.org.uk. This volunteer effort has transcribed more than 260 million records — although the collection is still not complete.

The subscription sites Ancestry.uk (www.ancestry.co.uk or www.ancestry.com), FindMyPast.co.uk (www.findmypast.co.uk), and Genes Reunited (www.genesreunited.co.uk) also have birth, marriage, and death records. For links to subscription and free birth, marriage, and death resources online, see the UK BMD site (www.ukbmd.org.uk).

Other records

There are records (and pointers to records housed in archives) available on both subscription and government sites. These sites include the following:

>> **Discovery** (http://discovery.nationalarchives.gov.uk/) is a consortium of archives in England and Wales. The Access to Archives site features a

database with descriptions of the holdings of 2,500 archives across the country.

>> **British Library — India Office Family History Search** (`http://indiafamily.bl.uk/UI/Home.aspx`) holds records of the government of pre-1949 India. The site features a bibliographical index that contains more than 300,000 entries.

>> **Commonwealth War Graves Commission** (`www.cwgc.org`) is responsible for maintaining the 1.7 million graves of those who died in the two world wars. The CWGC website includes a searchable database under the Find War Dead menu, which provides basic information on those covered by the Commission.

>> **General Register Office** (`https://www.gov.uk/browse/births-deaths-marriages/register-offices`) holds birth, marriage, and death records in England and Wales from July 1, 1837, up to one year ago. The GRO website details how to get copies of certificates and has some basic guides on researching genealogy.

>> **Imperial War Museums** (`www.iwm.org.uk`) chronicles the wars of the twentieth century from 1914. Its website contains fact sheets on tracing ancestors who served in the armed forces and an inventory of war memorials.

>> **National Library of Wales/Llyfrgell Genedlaethol Cymru** (`https://www.llgc.org.uk/`) holds documents such as electoral lists, marriage bonds, probate and estate records, and tithe maps. The library's website contains a list of independent researchers, and you can search databases including an index to the gaol files (*gaol* is the British word for *jail*), applicants for marriage licenses, and descriptions of the library's archival holdings.

FamilySearch

The Historical Records Collections on the FamilySearch site (`https://familysearch.org/search/collection/list#page=1&region=UNITED_KINGDOM_IRELAND`) contains a variety of record sets for the Channel Islands, England, Isle of Man, and Wales. Some examples include

>> Channel Islands, Births and Baptisms, 1820–1907

>> England and Wales censuses

>> English parish registers, probate records, tax assessments, and manorial documents

>> Isle of Man, Marriages, 1606–1911

In the FamilySearch Wiki, you can find a list of England Online Genealogy Records at `https://familysearch.org/wiki/en/England_Online_Genealogy_Records` and Wales Online Genealogy Records at `https://familysearch.org/wiki/en/Wales_Online_Genealogy_Records`.

Ancestry.co.uk

Ancestry.co.uk (`www.ancestry.co.uk`) contains databases related to records for the Channel Islands, England, Isle of Man, and Wales. Records include

>> Census and electoral rolls

>> Birth, marriage, and death, including parish

>> Military

>> Immigration and Travel

>> Newspapers and periodicals

>> Pictures

>> Stories, memories, and histories

>> Maps, atlases, and gazetteers

>> Schools, directories, and church histories

>> Tax, criminal, land, and wills

>> Reference, dictionaries, and almanacs

>> Family trees

Finding help

To contact other genealogists interested in British genealogical research, see the Society of Genealogists (`www.sog.org.uk`). The site includes information on membership, publications, the Society's online library catalog, and it has placed 11 million records online.

For societies at a local level, consult the list of members of the Federation of Family History Societies (`www.ffhs.org.uk`). The Federation's site includes information on its current projects and on upcoming events, as well as a set of subscription databases.

If you're not finding what you're looking for in one of the previously mentioned sites, your next stop should be the GENUKI: United Kingdom and Ireland Genealogy site, at `www.genuki.org.uk`. The GENUKI site is similar to the GenWeb sites (in fact, several of the GenWeb sites point to GENUKI content) in that it contains subsites for the various counties. You can find a variety of guides, transcribed records, and other useful data on the GENUKI sites.

If you need professional help, you can find a list of professional researchers at the Association of Genealogists and Researchers in Archives site at www.agra.org.uk. You can search for researchers by area of expertise, alphabetically, or by region where they are based.

A lot more than haggis — finding Scottish records

The ScotlandsPeople site (www.scotlandspeople.gov.uk) is the official government site for Scottish records. The subscription site contains statutory registers of births (1855–1910), marriages (1855–1937), and deaths (1855–1960); old parish registers of births and baptisms (1553 –1854) and banns and marriages (1553–1854); census records (1841–1911); and wills and testaments (1513–1925).

Other sites that can assist you in tracking down Scottish ancestors follow:

>> **National Records of Scotland** (https://www.nrscotland.gov.uk/) The National Archives of Scotland and the General Register Office for Scotland merged to form the National Records of Scotland site.

>> **Scottish Archive Network** (www.scan.org.uk) is a joint project between the National Archives of Scotland, the Heritage Lottery Fund, and the Genealogical Society of Utah. The project has placed the holdings of 52 Scottish archives into an online catalog and has digitized records.

>> **Scottish Genealogy Society** (www.scotsgenealogy.com) provides assistance for individuals researching their Scottish roots. The website contains information on the society's library, classes, and annual conference.

>> **Scottish Register of Tartans** (www.tartanregister.gov.uk), part of the National Records of Scotland, houses a repository of tartans. On the website, you can search for tartans by name and view an image of the material.

Researching the north o' Ireland

If you're looking for ancestors in Northern Ireland (specifically, the counties of Antrim, Armagh, Down, Fermanagh, Londonderry, and Tyrone), you have a few places to check. The Public Record Office of Northern Ireland, or PRONI (https://www.nidirect.gov.uk/proni), holds items such as estate, church, business, valuation and tithe, school, and wills records. The website includes online data-bases that contain signatories to the Ulster Covenant, freeholders records, street directories, and will calendars. You can also find guides to some of the more popu-lar collections at PRONI on its Your Family Tree Series page at https://www.nidirect.gov.uk/articles/your-family-tree-series.

The General Register Office for Northern Ireland (https://www.nidirect.gov.uk/information-and-services/government-citizens-and-rights/births-deaths-marriages-and-civil-partnerships) maintains registrations of births, stillbirths, adoptions, deaths, marriages, and civil partnerships. The website con-tains summaries of these record types and a family history guide that can assist you with your research in Northern Ireland.

Also, take a look at the North of Ireland Family History Society site (www.nifhs.org). The site contains details on the Society's Research Centre, branches, publi-cations, and meeting calendar. For books on genealogy in Northern Ireland and for research services, see the web page for the Ulster Historical Foundation at www.ancestryireland.com. This site also contains pay-per-view and members-only online databases, including indexes to birth, marriage, and death records for County Antrim and County Down, index to the 1796 Flaxgrowers Bounty List, directories, sporadic census and education records, emigration records, wills, election records, and estate records.

Emerald Ancestors (www.emeraldancestors.com) maintains subscription data-bases on more than 1 million ancestors from Northern Ireland, including birth, marriage, death, and census records. For free resources, see the Northern Ireland-GenWeb site at www.rootsweb.ancestry.com/~nirwgw. The site contains a resource listing and links to a variety of helpful online resources. The Ireland page on GENUKI also contains links to resources in the counties of Northern Ireland at www.genuki.org.uk/big/irl. To find a professional genealogist, consult the Society of Genealogists Northern Ireland website at www.sgni.net.

TIP

Because some of the resources overlap between Northern Ireland and Ireland, you might also look at some of the resources described in the following section.

Traversing the Emerald Isle

As we mention in the previous section, the GENUKI site (www.genuki.org.uk) contains information on a variety of geographic areas in the United Kingdom and Ireland. You see pages for all 32 counties of Ireland, and you can find brief articles on a variety of topics, including cemeteries, censuses, church records, civil registrations, court records, emigration and immigration, land and property, newspapers, probate records, and taxation. You can also find county pages at the Genealogy Projects in Ireland site (http://irelandgenealogyprojects.

rootsweb.ancestry.com) and the Ireland Genealogy Projects and Ireland Genealogy Projects Archives at www.igp-web.com.

To get an overview of Irish genealogy, take a look at the Directory of Irish Genealogy at http://homepage.eircom.net/~seanjmurphy/dir. In particular, look at A Primer in Irish Genealogy, available as a link at the top of the site's home page. You can also find information on genealogy courses and articles on Irish genealogy on this site. On the parent page to this site, the Centre for Irish Genealogical and Historical Studies (http://homepage.tinet.ie/~seanjmurphy), you find guides to the National Archives of Ireland and the General Register Office of Ireland. Ancestry.co.uk also contains some records for Ireland. See the previous section for more on the types of records available on the site. For the latest in Irish genealogy see the Irish Genealogy News site at www.irishgenealogynews.com.

Other Irish genealogy resources

A few sites contain databases and transcriptions of Irish records of interest to genealogists. The Department of Arts, Heritage, Regional, Rural and Gaeltacht Affairs sponsors the Irish Genealogy site (www.irishgenealogy.ie/en/), that features the Indexes of the Civil Registers (GRO) of Births, Marriages, Civil Partnerships, and Deaths and church records of baptism, marriage, and burial from a number of counties.

In addition to census records, the National Archives of Ireland (www.nationalarchives.ie) houses other records of interest to researchers, including Tithe Applotment Books and Griffith's Valuation, wills, estate records, private source records, parish records and marriage licenses, and Crown and Peace records. Tithe Applotment Books for the years 1823 to 1837 are available online at http://titheapplotmentbooks.nationalarchives.ie/search/tab/home.jsp.

If you're looking for maps, check out Irish Townlands (https://www.townlands.ie/), that uses OpenStreetMap to show over 60,000 townlands. The Irish Family History Foundation hosts an online database of 20 million records, including baptism, marriage, and death records, at its RootsIreland.ie site (www.rootsireland.ie). The Foundation also provides research services for a fee. Additional online databases can be found at the Findmypast site (www.findmypast.com). The site includes census, electoral register, marriage, will, burial, military, passenger list, and directory records. Ancestry.com (www.ancestry.com) has over 200 collections of Irish records.

If you need professional assistance, take a look at the Accredited Genealogists Ireland site at http://accreditedgenealogists.ie/. The Association establishes standards for its members to help ensure quality research. The website includes a member directory listing its areas of specialization.

For a topical list of available online resources for Ireland, see the Ireland Online Genealogy Records page on FamilySearch at `https://familysearch.org/wiki/en/Ireland_Online_Genealogy_Records`.

Heading north for Canadian records

So you want to research your ancestors from Canada, eh? Well, a place to start is the Genealogy and Family History page (`www.bac-lac.gc.ca/eng/discover/genealogy/Pages/introduction.aspx`), maintained by Library and Archives Canada. The site contains information for beginners, including what to do first and search strategies for a variety of record types.

To get an idea of what online resources are available for Canadian research, some genealogical link sites specialize in Canada. These include CanGenealogy (`www.cangenealogy.com`) and Canadian Genealogy Resources (`www.canadiangenealogy.net`).

Local resources

For resources on a more local basis, go to the CanadaGenWeb Project site at `www.rootsweb.ancestry.com/~canwgw`. The project site includes links to genealogical sites, research queries, lookups, and a timeline. You also find a branch of the site oriented to kids at `www.rootsweb.ancestry.com/~cangwkid`. The following provinces also have a GenWeb Project page:

>> **Alberta:** `www.rootsweb.ancestry.com/~canab/`

>> **British Columbia:** `www.rootsweb.ancestry.com/~canbc`

>> **Manitoba:** `www.rootsweb.ancestry.com/~canmb/index.htm`

>> **New Brunswick:** `www.rootsweb.ancestry.com/~cannb`

>> **Newfoundland/Labrador:** `www.rootsweb.ancestry.com/~cannf/index.html`

>> **Nova Scotia:** `www.rootsweb.ancestry.com/~canns/index.html`

>> **Northwest Territories and Nunavut:** `www.rootsweb.ancestry.com/~cannt`

>> **Ontario:** `www.geneofun.on.ca/ongenweb`

>> **Prince Edward Island:** `www.islandregister.com/pegenweb.html`

>> **Québec:** `www.quebecgenweb.com/`

>> **Saskatchewan:** `www.rootsweb.ancestry.com/~cansk/`

>> **Yukon:** `www.rootsweb.ancestry.com/~canyk`

Although Acadia is not a province, you can also find an Acadian GenWeb site at `http://acadian-genweb.acadian-home.org/frames.html`.

Other records and resources

The Library and Archives Canada site (`www.bac-lac.gc.ca/eng/discover/genealogy/Pages/access-records.aspx`) not only has images of census records, but also houses images of the following records:

>> Chinese Immigration Registers, 1885–1949

>> Canadians in the South African War, 1899–1902

>> Attestation Papers of Soldiers of the First World War, 1914–1918

>> Upper Canada and Canada West Naturalization Records, 1828–1850

>> Ward Chipman, Muster Master's Office, 1777–1785 (Loyalist registers)

>> Immigrants from the Russian Empire

>> Canadian Patents, 1869–1894

>> Passenger Lists, 1865–1935

The Ancestry.ca or Ancestry.com subscription site maintains a variety of record sets, including census and voter lists; birth, marriage, and death records; military records; newspapers; maps and gazetteers; school and church histories; tax records; and wills. You can also find subscription collections at Findmypast.com and MyHeritage.com.

When it comes time to do some on-site research, you can look at the directory of archives at the Canadian Council of Archives. The website search interface (`www.cdncouncilarchives.ca/directory_adv.html`) allows you to search by an archive name or by province. The information on the site includes an overview of the collections of each archive along with its hours of operation. To get more detailed information on the holdings in various archives across Canada, consult the ArchivesCanada.ca site (`www.archivescanada.ca`) — part of the Canadian Archival Information Network (CAIN). You can use a single search form to search by keyword for descriptions of collections, or you can use a separate form to find online exhibits. For published items held in the Library and Archives Canada and more than 700 other Canadian libraries, you can search the AMICUS national catalog at `http://amicus.collectionscanada.gc.ca/aaweb/aalogine.htm`.

A number of sites contain abstracts of Canadian records. Olive Tree Genealogy (`www.olivetreegenealogy.com`) has free databases of ship and passenger lists, civil registrations, and cemetery records. For pointers to military records, you can search the catalog of the Canadian War Museum at http://catalogue. warmuseum.ca/musvw/Vubis.csp?Profile=Profile. This catalog contains entries (and, in some cases, abstracts) for textual and photographic records.

FamilySearch.org has data extracted from a large number of records available online. You can see a list of resources on FamilySearch.org and other sites at https://familysearch.org/wiki/en/Canada_Online_Genealogy_Records.

If your family immigrated to Canada between 1928 and 1971, take a look at the Pier 21 Immigration Museum site (www.pier21.ca). The site gives a brief overview of the function of Pier 21 and information on the research services available on the site. It also has a ship arrivals database that covers the years 1928 to 1971. From 1869 to 1948, more than 100,000 British children were sent to Canada as laborers until they reached the age of 21. A site dedicated to these children is the Canadian Centre for Home Children, at www.canadianhomechildren.ca. You can also find Home Children resources at the Library and Archives Canada site at http://www. bac-lac.gc.ca/eng/discover/immigration/immigration-records/home- children-1869-1930/Pages/home-children.aspx.

Not able to travel to a distant cemetery in Canada to see the headstone of your ances- tor? Then visit the Canadian Headstone Photo Project (www.canadianheadstones. com) to see whether someone has already snapped a photo or transcribed the head- stone. This site currently boasts more than 1.6 million photos from across Canada.

While searching through records, you may run into a place name that you don't recognize. The Atlas of Canada (www.nrcan.gc.ca/earth-sciences/geography/ atlas-canada) at the Natural Resources Canada site contains a variety of geographical resources including a place-name finder, satellite maps, and topo- graphical maps. For a searchable database of Canadian geographical names, see the Canadian Geographical Names Data Base page at http://www4.rncan.gc.ca/ search-place-names/search?lang=en. If you want a historical perspective on the geography of Canada, look at the Historical Atlas of Canada project at www. historicalatlas.ca/website/hacolp.

Getting help

If you're looking for local genealogical experts, you can turn to genealogical soci- eties in Canada. An example is the Alberta Family Histories Society (www.afhs. ab.ca). The site includes the monthly schedule of meetings, publications for sale, document transcriptions, research aids, queries, and information about the soci- ety library.

Because Canada has a history of immigration for many different ethnicities, you might also check to see whether a site is dedicated to the ethnic group that you're researching. For example, the Chinese-Canadian Genealogy site (`http://guides.vpl.ca/ccg`), maintained by the Vancouver Public Library, contains information on the early Chinese immigrations, Chinese name characteristics, biographic resources, and a survey of the types of record sets associated with the Canadian Chinese population.

Accessing Australian sources

The Australian Family History Compendium (`http://afhc.cohsoft.com.au/`) offers information on societies, archives, and a wider range of record types, as well as maps and a glossary. The National Archives of Australia site is located at www.naa.gov.au/. Also you can find descriptions of resources on the eResources page of the National Library of Australia at `www.nla.gov.au/app/eresources/browse/123`.

A transcription of the convicts on Australia's first three fleets and the Irish convicts that came to New South Wales from 1788 to 1849 is located at `http://members.pcug.org.au/~pdownes`.

The Metropolitan Cemeteries Board of Western Australia has a database of internments in five cemeteries at `http://www2.mcb.wa.gov.au/NameSearch/search.php`. If you are looking for obituaries, check out the Obituaries Australia site at `http://oa.anu.edu.au` and the obits.com.au site (`www.obits.com.au`). For digitized newspaper collections, see the National Library of Australia's Trove site at `http://trove.nla.gov.au/newspaper`. The site also has over 530 million books, images, newspapers, maps, and music items available online.

A searchable index of birth, marriage, and death records for New South Wales is available at `www.bdm.nsw.gov.au/`. Vital records information is also available at the Australasia Births, Deaths, and Marriages Exchange at `www.ausbdm.org`.

The subscription sites Findmypast.com and MyHeritage.com each have collections relating to Australia. Ancestry.com.au (`www.ancestry.com.au`) or Ancestry.com features more than 200 databases of use in Australian research. Examples of databases on the site include

>> Australia, Electoral Rolls, 1903–1980

>> Victoria, Australia, Assisted and Unassisted Passenger Lists, 1839–1923

>> Sands Directories: Sydney and New South Wales, Australia, 1858–1933

>> Rockingham, Western Australia, School Indexes, 1830–1970

Hispanic and Portuguese Roots

A growing number of genealogists are researching their Hispanic and Portuguese roots. If you have these ancestors, you can use several types of records to pursue your genealogy, depending on when your ancestor immigrated.

If your ancestor immigrated in the nineteenth or twentieth century, look for vital records, military records, photographs, passports, church records, passenger lists, naturalization papers, diaries, or other items that can give you an idea of the birthplace of your ancestor. For those ancestors who immigrated before the 19th century, you may want to consult Spanish or Portuguese Colonial records after you exhaust any local records in the region where your ancestor lived.

If you're interested in general conversation on Hispanic genealogy, see the Hispanic Genealogy blog at hispanicgenealogy.blogspot.com.

For more information on researching Hispanic records, see the following:

>> *The Source: A Guidebook to American Genealogy,* Third Edition, edited by Loretto Dennis Szucs and Sandra Hargreaves Luebking (Ancestry, Inc.). In particular, see Chapter 17, "Hispanic Research," written by George R. Ryskamp. You can find this online at www.ancestry.com/wiki/index.php?title=Overview_of_Hispanic_Research.

>> *Hispanic Family History Research in a L.D.S. Family History Center,* written by George R. Ryskamp (Hispanic Family History Research).

Within the United States

Individuals of Hispanic descent have been in the present-day U.S. since St. Augustine was founded in 1565. Consult some of the following helpful resources when conducting research on your Spanish-speaking ancestors:

>> **Hispanic Genealogy Center** (www.hispanicgenealogy.com): Maintained by the Hispanic Genealogical Society of New York, the site contains information on the society's events and publications, including the newsletter *Nuestra Herencia*.

>> **Hispanic Genealogical Society of Houston** (www.hispanicgs.org): The society maintains a list of online resources for Hispanic research.

>> **Hispanic Genealogical Research Center of New Mexico** (www.hgrc-nm.org): The Center maintains the Great New Mexico Pedigree Database and publishes the journal *Herencia*.

- » **Society of Hispanic Historical and Ancestral Research** (`http://shhar.net`): The Society is based in Orange County, California, and publishes the online newsletter *Somos Primos*.

- » **Puerto Rican/Hispanic Genealogical Society** (`www.rootsweb.ancestry.com/~prhgs`): The site contains a transcription of the 1935 Census of Puerto Rico and a query page.

- » **Colorado Society of Hispanic Genealogy** (`www.hispanicgen.org`): The Society hosts a list of links and information in its publication *Colorado Hispanic Genealogist*.

If you are going to Puerto Rico for research, you might consider visiting the websites of the Archivo General de Puerto Rico and the Biblioteca Nacional (`www.puertadetierra.info/edificios/archivo/archivo.htm`) for information on their holdings.

Exploring south of the border: Mexican sources

To get your feet wet with resources from Mexico, check out the FamilySearch Research Wiki at `https://familysearch.org/wiki/en/Mexico_Genealogy`. You can find a primer on tracing your ancestors on the Mexico Genealogy 101 page at the About.com genealogy site (`http://genealogy.about.com/od/mexico/a/records.htm`). A list of collections for Mexican research can be found at the Mexican Genealogy site at `https://mexicangenealogy.info/research/resources-by-state`.

The following are some sites related to genealogy in Mexico:

- » **Baja California:** `www.californiagenealogy.org/labaja`

- » **Durango:** `www.rootsweb.ancestry.com/~mexdur/Durango.html`

- » **Morelos:** `www.rootsweb.ancestry.com/~mexmorel/Morelos.html`

- » **San Luis Potosí:** `www.rootsweb.ancestry.com/~mexsanlu`

- » **Tabasco:** `www.rootsweb.ancestry.com/~mextab`

The Genealogy of Mexico site (`http://garyfelix.tripod.com/index1.htm`) features several sets of transcribed records, including lists of individuals who accompanied Cortez, early entrants into New Spain, surnames contained in literature on Mexico, and a DNA project.

FamilySearch (`https://familysearch.org/search/collection/list#page=1&region=MEXICO`) has also begun placing online records related to Mexico, including the following:

>> Baja California and Baja California Sur, Catholic Church Records, 1750–1984

>> Mexico, Colima, Civil Registration, 1860–1997

>> Mexico, National Census, 1930

>> Mexico, San Luis Potosí, Miscellaneous Records, 1570–1882

Transcribed records are also available on sites that focus on Hispanic ancestors. For example, you can view transcribed records from the 1750 and 1753 censuses of the village of Guerrero at `www.hispanicgs.com/census.html`.

Continental resources

Eventually, your research may take you across the Atlantic, back to the Iberian Peninsula to Spain or Portugal. If you're researching Spain, stop by the Genealogía Española–España GenWeb site at `www.genealogia-es.com`. The site contains an introduction to research, links to surname databases, and links to provincial web pages. The Asociación de Genealogía Hispana (`www.hispagen.es`) also maintains a website dedicated to helping those who are researching their Spanish roots.

For official records, point your web browser to the Portal de Archivos Españoles site at `http://pares.mcu.es`. The portal is designed to point to resources housed in many different national and local archives. A large project housed on the site is the Ibero-American Migratory Movements Portal (`http://pares.mcu.es/MovimientosMigratorios/staticContent.form?viewName=presentacion`). The goal of the project is to provide access to information on individuals who emigrated from Spain to Central America in modern times. The project is a partnership between the Archivo General de la Administración de España, Archivo General de la Nación de México, Archivo General de la Nación de la República Dominicana, and Archivo Nacional de la República de Cuba.

FamilySearch (`https://familysearch.org/search/collection/list#page=1&countryId=1927167`) has placed online over 40 collections of records relating to Spain. Some of these collections include digitized images. Examples from the collection are

>> Catholic Church Records, 1307–1985

>> Consular Records of Emigrants, 1808–1960

>> Province of Cádiz, Passports, 1810–1866

>> Province of León, Municipal Records, 1642–1897

Portuguese official records are housed in a network of national and 16 regional archives coordinated by the Direção Geral de Arquivos (http://antt.dglab.gov. pt/pesquisar-na-torre-do-tombo/genealogia-ou-historia-local//). Another resource to check out is the Biblioteca Nacional de Portugal (www. bnportugal.pt). For a more focused search on genealogy, you may want to search the catalogs on the Biblioteca Genealogica de Lisboa website, at www.biblioteca-genealogica-lisboa.org. For parish records see the Portuguese Parish Records for Genealogy site at http://tombo.pt.

FamilySearch (https://familysearch.org/search/collection/list#page=1& countryId=1927058) contains more than 30 collections of databases and digitized records relating to Portugal. Some sample collections include

>> Aveiro, Passport Registers, 1882–1965

>> Braga, Priest Application Files (Genere et Moribus), 1596–1911

>> Coimbra, Civil Registration, 1893–1980

>> Vila Real, Diocesan Records, 1575–1992

Some Portuguese collections are also available on Ancestry.com and MyHeritage. com.

Those with Basque ancestors may find the resources at the Basque Genealogy page (www.nabasque.org/old_nabo/NABO/genealogy.htm) useful.

Central and South American research

Research in Central and South America has been a rapidly growing area recently. Subscription sites such as Ancestry.com and MyHeritage.com have some resources for individual countries. The following resources, broken down by country, should help you along your way:

>> **Argentina:** The Archivo General de la Nación (www.mininterior.gov.ar/ agn/agn.php) and the Instituto de Estudios Genealógicos y Heráldicos de la Provincia de Buenos Aires (https://www.facebook.com/Instituto-de-Estudios-Geneal%C3%B3gicos-y-Her%C3%A1ldicos-provincia-de-Buenos-Aires-198710254473/) are places to get an idea of records available for Argentina. FamilySearch (https://familysearch.org/search/ collection/list#page=1&countryId=1927135) offers a growing collection

of records from Argentina including Catholic Church records, national censuses, and marriage records.

>> **Brazil:** BrazilGenWeb (`www.rootsweb.ancestry.com/~brawgw`) has a how-to guide and links to individual Brazilian states. To see records available in Brazil, visit the Arquivo Nacional website (`www.arquivonacional.gov.br`). FamilySearch (`https://familysearch.org/search/collection/list#page=1&countryId=1927159`) hosts nearly 30 collections including Catholic Church records, civil registrations, immigration cards, and burial records. You might also find useful resources at the Genealogias.org at `http://buratto.org/gens/`.

>> **Belize:** The BelizeGenWeb page (`www.worldgenweb.org/index.php/96-northamericagenweb/belize/75-belizegenweb?Itemid=115`) has a few links to general resources.

>> **Bolivia:** You can get general information on the national archives at the Archivo y Biblioteca Nacionales site at `www.archivoybibliotecanacionales.org.bo/`. A few collections exist for Bolivia at FamilySearch (`https://familysearch.org/search/collection/list#page=1&countryId=1927158`). Records include baptism, Catholic Church records, deaths, and marriages.

>> **Chile:** A site with several compiled genealogies of Chilean families is the Genealogía de Chile site, at `http://genealog.cl`. See the web page for the Archivos y Museos (`www.dibam.cl`) for Chilean records. A small number of Chilean records are available at FamilySearch (`https://familysearch.org/search/collection/list#page=1&countryId=1927143`) including baptism, civil registration, death, marriage, and cemetery records.

>> **Columbia:** The website for the Columbian Archivo General de la Nación is located at `www.archivogeneral.gov.co`. The site explains the system of archives both at the national and local level and has a catalog of its holdings. Columbian records are available on FamilySearch at `https://familysearch.org/search/collection/list#page=1&countryId=1927162`. The collections include baptism, Catholic Church records, death, marriage, and military records.

>> **Costa Rica:** The GenWeb page for Costa Rica is located at `www.worldgenweb.org/index.php/97-northamericagenweb/costa-rica/76-costa-rica`, and the web page for the Archivo Nacional de Costa Rica is at `www.archivonacional.go.cr`. Costa Rican records are available on FamilySearch at `https://familysearch.org/search/collection/list#page=1&countryId=1927128`.

>> **Cuba:** You can find links to Cuban genealogical resources at the CubaGenWeb.org website (`www.cubagenweb.org`). The site contains a passenger list database and links to personal sites on the web with Cuban

family trees. To find records in Cuba, see the website for the Archivo Nacional de la República de Cuba (www.arnac.cu).

>> **Dominican Republic:** República Dominicana en el proyecto CaribbeanGenWeb (www.rootsweb.ancestry.com/~domwgw/mhhbcgw.htm) contains a few links to resources for the Dominican Republic. Records for the country are held at the Archivo General de la Nación (http://agn.gov.do). FamilySearch (https://familysearch.org/search/collection/list#page=1&countryId=1927011) contains some databases related to the Dominican Republic. The collections include baptism, Catholic Church records, death, marriage, and civil registration records.

>> **Ecuador:** Discover more about records in Archivo Nacional Del Ecuador Ane site, at www.ane.gob.ec/. Records from Ecuador are available on FamilySearch at https://familysearch.org/search/collection/list#page=1&countryId=1927138.

>> **El Salvador:** El Salvadoran records are available on FamilySearch.org at https://familysearch.org/search/collection/list#page=1&countryId=1927124.

>> **Guatemala:** Guatemalan records are available on FamilySearch.org at https://familysearch.org/search/collection/list#page=1&countryId=1927125. In addition to baptism, church, marriage, and death records, you can also find the Guatemala City census of 1877 at the site.

>> **Haiti:** The Généalogie d'Haiti et de Saint-Domingue, at www.rootsweb.ancestry.com/~htiwgw, contains information on the history and geography of the country. It also has links to other Haiti resources. For further information, see L'Association de Généalogie d'Haïti (www.agh.qc.ca). The Archives Nationales d'Haiti is available at http://archivesnationales.gouv.ht. FamilySearch has some digital images of civil registrations available at https://familysearch.org/search/collection/list#page=1&countryId=1927183.

>> **Honduras:** Some basic information is available on the HondurasGenWeb project page at www.worldgenweb.org/index.php/100-northamericagenweb/honduras/77-honduras. You can find baptism and marriage records as well as digital images of civil registrations on the FamilySearch.org site at https://familysearch.org/search/collection/list#page=1&countryId=1927126.

>> **Nicaragua:** The GenWeb page for Nicaragua is at www.rootsweb.ancestry.com/~nicwgw. A brief description of the Archivo General de la Nación can be found at www.inc.gob.ni/bibliotecas-y-archivos/. Nicaraguan records such as civil registrations and digital images of Catholic Church records are available on FamilySearch at https://familysearch.org/search/collection/list#page=1&countryId=1927127.

- » **Panama:** Some brief information on the National Archives is available at the Archivo Nacional de Panamá site, at `www.archivonacional.gob.pa/`. You can find records for baptisms, deaths, marriages, and digital images of Catholic Church records on FamilySearch at `https://familysearch.org/search/collection/list#page=1&countryId=1927175`.

- » **Paraguay:** Information on the holdings of the Archivo Nacional de Asunción is available at www.archivonacionaldeasuncion.org/. Records for baptisms and marriages, plus digital images of cemetery records and Catholic Church records are available on FamilySearch at `https://familysearch.org/search/collection/list#page=1&countryId=1927141`.

- » **Peru:** For records regarding Peru, see the Archivo General de la Nación site, at `www.agn.gob.pe/portal/`. Thirteen Peruvian record collections are available on FamilySearch (`https://familysearch.org/search/collection/list#page=1&countryId=1927168`) including digital images of civil registrations and Catholic Church records.

- » **Uruguay:** You can find an overview of records for Uruguay at the Archivo General de la Nación page (`www.agn.gub.uy`). Baptism and marriage records are available on FamilySearch at `https://familysearch.org/search/collection/list#page=1&countryId=1927142`.

- » **Venezuela:** Information on the Archivo General de la Nación can be found at `http://agn.gob.ve`. FamilySearch contains some digital images of Catholic Church records and civil registrations at `https://familysearch.org/search/collection/list#page=1&countryId=1927137`.

Swimming through Caribbean genealogy

To be successful in researching Caribbean genealogy, you have to be aware of the history of the particular island that you're researching. Some islands have a variety of record sets that may differ significantly depending on what country was in control of the island.

A place to start your research is the CaribbeanGenWeb Project page, at `www.rootsweb.ancestry.com/~caribgw`. The project is an umbrella site for each of the individual islands that have their own project pages. The site contains a list of the transcribed data sets held within the CaribbeanGenWeb Archives portion of the project, along with a global search engine for searching those data sets, descriptions of the mailing lists available for each island, links to surname resources, and some research tips. The individual island pages include

- » **Antigua and Barbuda:** `www.rootsweb.ancestry.com/~atgwgw`

- » **Bahamas:** `www.rootsweb.ancestry.com/~bhswgw`

» **Bermuda:** www.rootsweb.ancestry.com/~bmuwgw/bermuda.htm

» **Jamaica:** www.rootsweb.ancestry.com/~jamwgw/index.htm

» **St. Kitts and Nevis:** www.tc.umn.edu/~terre011/genhome.html

» **Trinidad and Tobago:** www.rootsweb.ancestry.com/~ttowgw

You can also find information on some islands on the GenWeb Project page of the mother country. For example, a resource for the French islands is the Généalogie et Histoire de la Caraïbe (www.ghcaraibe.org). The site contains some transcribed records and articles on the history of the area.

If you have a question about a specific individual, you can post a query on the Caribbean Surname Index (CARSURDEX) at www.candoo.com/surnames/index.php. The site has message boards based on the first letter of the surname and has research specialty boards for the French West Indies, Dutch West Indies, and Spanish West Indies.

Achtung! Using Sites for the German-Speaking World

As German-speaking peoples have migrated to several places in Europe, as well as to the U.S., you could very well encounter an ancestor of German descent. German Roots (www.germanroots.com) contains a variety of information to help you get started in researching your German roots. It contains a directory of websites, a basic research guide, and links to articles on record sets that are useful in completing your research.

To get a bird's-eye view of available German genealogical sites, a good place to start is Genealogy.net (http://compgen.de/). The site includes home pages for German genealogical societies, general information on research, a gazetteer, a ships database, a passenger database, and a list of links to websites. Ahnenforschung.net (http://ahnenforschung.net) is a German-language site containing tips for genealogists and discussion forums on a number of topics.

Along the beautiful Danube: Austrian roots

A place to begin your Austrian journey is the Austrian Genealogy Pages (https://www.austriagenweb.org/). The site contains some general information on Austria as well as links to Austrian resources. From the home page of this site, you can access links to the provinces of Austria. These links are divided into two types — provinces of modern Austria (since 1918) and areas of the Austrian Empire and Austro-Hungarian Empire (until 1918). Areas listed under the second group are covered in other GenWeb projects, such as KüstenlandGenWeb, CzechGenWeb, RomanianGenWeb, UkraineGenWeb, SloveniaGenWeb, CroatiaGenWeb, Polish-GenWeb, ItalianGenWeb, and FranceGenWeb.

If you're looking for help with your Austrian research, check out the Familia Austria website (www.familia-austria.at) maintained by the Österreichische Gesellschaft für Genealogie und Geschichte. The site contains links to a variety of Austrian resources, including maps, cemetery databases, and a wiki covering many topics related to individual provinces. It also has databases developed by the Association, including a family name finder; a birth, marriage, and death index for Wiener Zeitung; a marriage index before 1784; and directories of individuals holding particular occupations.

To get information on records available in the national archives, see the Austrian State Archives page, at www.oesta.gv.at/DesktopDefault.aspx?alias=oestaen&init. Another site to visit is the Österreichische Nationalbibliothek (National Library), at https://www.onb.ac.at/. If you need professional help, you might look at the Historiker Kanzlei research firm (www.historiker.at), which specializes in Austrian research.

FamilySearch (https://familysearch.org/search/collection/list#page=1&countryId=1927070) contains more than a dozen collections centered on Austria. These include digital images of military records, Lutheran Church records, citizen rolls, death certificates, and Jewish registers of births, marriages, and deaths.

Consulting German resources

The Germany GenWeb Project site (www.rootsweb.ancestry.com/~wggerman) has a few resources such as maps and links to other sites. The German Genealogy Group (www.germangenealogygroup.com) was formed to help individuals research their German roots. The website contains descriptions on the various databases that the Group maintains and some presentations on research in Germany.

The German Emigrants Database (www.deutsche-auswanderer-datenbank.de/), maintained by the Historisches Museum Bremerhaven, contains information on emigrants who left Europe for the U.S. from German ports between 1820 and 1897, 1904, and 1907. At the time this book was written, the database contained more than five million emigrants. The site allows users to search an index of individuals and order records for a fee based on the results. For more information on emigrants from the port of Hamburg, see Ballinstadt Hamburg (`www.ballinstadt.de/?lang=en`), a site that describes the emigrant experience at the Hamburg port.

An important group of records in German research are church records. The Archion site (`https://www.archion.de/`) is a collaborative project sponsored by the Evangelical Church in Germany to post detailed inventories of parish registers.

Ancestry.com has a subscription site for German genealogy at `www.ancestry.de` or Ancestry.com. Ancestry.com provides access to more than 1,000 databases, including census records; birth, marriage, and death records; military records; immigration and emigration records; and local and family histories. Examples of databases are the Hamburg Passenger lists (1850–1934), Bremen, Germany Sailors Registry, 1824-1917 and, Bremen, Germany Ships Crew Lists, 1815-1917. For descriptions of records held in archives, see the Bundesarchiv site at `www.bundesarchiv.de/index.html.en`.

FamilySearch `https://familysearch.org/search/collection/list#page=1&countryId=1927074` houses 60 collections of German records, many of them digital images. Examples of collections include

>> Brandenburg, Berlin, Probate Records, 1796–1853

>> Hesse-Nassau, Civil Registers and Church Books, 1701–1875

>> Prussia, East Prussia, Königsberg, Index to Funeral Sermons and Memorials, 1700–1900

You can find resources for other Germanic areas on the Federation of East European Family History Societies site at `http://feefhs.org` and on the following sites:

>> **Liechtenstein:** LiechGenWeb Project (`www.rootsweb.ancestry.com/~liewgw`) and FamilySearch (`https://familysearch.org/search/collection/list#page=1&countryId=1927121`)

>> **Luxembourg:** Luxembourg home page (`www.rootsweb.ancestry.com/~luxwgw`) and FamilySearch (`https://familysearch.org/search/collection/list#page=1&countryId=1927075`)

>> **Swiss:** Swiss Genealogy on the Internet (`www.eye.ch/swissgen/gener-e.htm`), Swiss Roots Genealogy (`www.theswisscenter.org/swiss-roots`), and FamilySearch (`https://familysearch.org/search/collection/list#page=1&countryId=1927039`)

Focusing on French Resources

For an overview of genealogy in French-speaking regions, drop by the Franco-Gene site, at www.francogene.com/genealogy. The site features resources for Quebec, Acadia, the U.S., France, Belgium, Switzerland, and Italy. If you're not familiar with French surnames, you might want to see how common a surname is in France. At Geopatronyme.com (www.geopatronyme.com), you can view the surname distribution of more than 1.3 million names.

GeneaBank (www.geneabank.org) contains transcribed records created by French genealogical societies. To access the information in the site's databases, you must be a member of a society participating in the project. Geneanet (www.geneanet.org) is a site with some fee-based content, such as transcriptions of some civil registers. The Lecture et Informatisation des Sources Archivistiques site (www.lisa90.org) contains a database with more than 360,000 transcribed parish records covering the 18th and 19th centuries, and Migranet (www.francegenweb.org/~migranet/accueil.php) houses a database of more than 95,000 French marriages where one of the participants was listed as a migrant.

Ancestry.fr or Ancestry.com (www.ancestry.fr) has a collection of subscription databases. This collection includes birth, marriage, death, military, and immigration and emigration records as well as maps.

FamilySearch also has a few French digital image record sets at https://familysearch.org/search/collection/list#page=1&countryId=1927089.

Scanning Scandinavian Countries

For a general overview of Scandinavian research, see the Scandinavia portal at the FamilySearch Research Wiki (https://familysearch.org/wiki/en/Scandinavia). The following sections cover available resources for the Scandinavian countries.

Denmark

MyDanishRoots.com (www.mydanishroots.com) contains articles on vital records, census lists, place names, emigration, and Danish history. DIS-Danmark (www.dis-danmark.dk) is a group of genealogists using computing in their research. The website includes information on the districts and parishes of Denmark, data on indexed church books, and a database of Danish online records. The Statens Arkiver is also digitizing church books and placing them online at https://www.sa.dk/brug-arkivet/ao/arkivalieronline.

TIP

Finding another researcher who is researching the same family as you can make your research life a lot easier. Sending a GEDCOM file to the GEDCOMP site, at www.lklundin.dk/gedcomp/english.php, allows it to be compared with other researchers' files to see where overlaps exist. Other members of GEDCOMP can then contact you for further research.

If you're planning a research trip to Denmark, you may want to visit the collection at the Statens Arkiver (State Archives). You can find a list of resources available, as well as descriptions of records that are critical to Danish research, at https://www.sa.dk/en/. FamilySearch houses a few Danish record sets including some digital images at https://familysearch.org/search/collection/list#page=1&countryId=1927025.

Finland

The Finland GenWeb site (www.rootsweb.ancestry.com/~finwgw) has a small number of biographies, some transcribed U.S. census records of individuals of Finnish descent, a few obituaries of people who were born in Finland and died in the U.S., and links to web pages of those interested in Finnish research.

The Genealogical Society of Finland site (www.genealogia.fi/index.php?language_id=1&p=226) contains some advice on getting started in your research, membership information, blogs, and links to member pages.

You can find transcriptions of passport lists for the Åland Islands in Finland at the Transcription of the Borough Administrator's Passport List 1882–1903 (www.genealogia.fi/emi/magistrat/indexe.htm) and Sheriff's Passport List 1863–1916 (www.genealogia.fi/emi/krono/indexe.htm) sites. The database at DISBYT Finland (www.dis.se) contains more than 160,000 individuals who lived in Finland prior to 1913. The Genealogy Society of Finland maintains a list of christenings, marriages, burials, and moves as part of its HisKi project at http://hiski.genealogia.fi/historia/indexe.htm.

TIP

The Institute of Migration/Siirtolaisuusinstituutti (www.migrationinstitute.fi/fi/sukututkimus) maintains a database of more than 550,000 emigrants from Finland.

FamilySearch contains a few collections at https://familysearch.org/search/collection/list#page=1&countryId=1927095.

Keep in mind that up to 1809, Finland was a part of Sweden. So, you may need to consult Swedish records to get a complete picture of your ancestors.

Norway

For help with your Norwegian ancestors, see the article "Basics of Norwegian Research," www.rootsweb.ancestry.com/~wgnorway/list-basics.htm. Another useful guide, "How to Trace Your Ancestors in Norway" (http://digitalarkivet.uib.no/sab/howto.html), is housed on the site for the National Archives of Norway. The Velkommen to Norway Genealogy site (www.rootsweb.ancestry.com/~wgnorway/), part of the WorldGenWeb project, contains a Getting Started article and links to several Norwegian online resources.

The National Archives of Norway hosts a digital archive at http://digitalarkivet.uib.no/cgi-win/WebFront.exe?slag=vis&tekst=meldingar&spraak=e. The site includes digitized parish registers, real estate registers, and probate records. It also has a tutorial on Gothic handwriting, a photo album of farms, and information on the Archive's holdings.

If you're looking for research help, the DIS-Norge site (www.disnorge.no/cms/en/eng/english-pages) has a message board to answer questions, a Nordic dictionary to help with common terms, and a database containing genealogists who are working in a specific geographic area.

FamilySearch has some burial, census, baptism, and marriage records available at https://familysearch.org/search/collection/list#page=1&countryId=1927171.

Sweden

The Federation of Swedish Genealogical Societies/Sveriges Släktforskarförbund hosts the site Finding Your Swedish Roots (www.genealogi.se/index.php?option=com_content&view=article&id=167&Itemid=852) that includes helpful articles on church, legal, and tax records; information on the collection in the Swedish Archives; and a brief history of Sweden.

The Swedish DISBYT database (www.dis.se/) contains 22.2 million Swedes who lived before 1910. Ancestry.se or Ancestry.com (www.ancestry.se) is a subscription site that contains over 40 databases, including emigration lists from 1783 to 1751, passenger and immigration lists from the 1500s to 1900s, and some local histories and published genealogies.

Subscription databases on the Riksarkivet (http://sok.riksarkivet.se/) site include births, convicts, deaths, inventories, marriages, seamen's records, and a village and farm database. The site also contains scanned images of church and tax records.

The Sweden Genealogy site (www.rootsweb.ancestry.com/~wgsweden) contains queries, a list of surnames, and links to other Swedish resources.

FamilySearch includes several digital image collections of Swedish church records at https://familysearch.org/search/collection/list#page=1&countryId=1927041.

Iceland

A few resources are available for Icelandic research. The IcelandGenWeb site (www.rootsweb.ancestry.com/~islwgw) contains a few links to resources for your research.

FamilySearch has a couple of record sets of baptisms and marriages at https://familysearch.org/search/collection/list#page=1&countryId=1927031.

Italian Cooking

A place to begin your Italian research is the Italian Genealogy home page at www.daddezio.com. The site contains useful articles on family history research as well as links to other Italian genealogical resources. The ItalianGenealogy.com home page (www.italiangenealogy.com/) features message boards that cover topics such as genealogy, immigration, geography, and the Italian language.

The Italian Genealogical Group (www.italiangen.org) is based in New York City. Resources on its website include naturalization and vital records databases. Ancestry.it or Ancestry.com (www.ancestry.it) contains more than 100 databases related to Italian genealogy. The bulk of these databases contain birth, marriage, and death records — although some maps and newspapers are available.

FamilySearch (https://familysearch.org/search/collection/list#page=1&countryId=1927178) has more than 100 databases mainly focused on civil registrations and Catholic Church records.

Other European Sites

Several other sites cover European countries and ethnic groups. These include the following:

>> **Armenian:** FamilySearch (https://familysearch.org/search/collection/list#page=1&countryId=1927048)

» **Belarusian:** Belarusian Genealogy (www.belarusguide.com/genealogy1/index.html)

» **Belgium:** Belgium-Roots Project (http://belgium.rootsweb.ancestry.com/) and FamilySearch (https://familysearch.org/search/collection/list#page=1&countryId=1927071)

» **Bosnia-Herzegovina:** Bosnia-Herzegovina Web Genealogy Project (www.rootsweb.ancestry.com/~bihwgw)

» **Bulgarian:** BulgariaGenWeb (www.rootsweb.ancestry.com/~bgrwgw)

» **Croatian:** Croatia GenWeb (www.rootsweb.ancestry.com/~hrvwgw) and FamilySearch (https://familysearch.org/search/collection/list#page=1&countryId=1927181)

» **Czech:** Czech Republic Genealogy (www.rootsweb.ancestry.com/~czewgw) and FamilySearch (https://familysearch.org/search/collection/list#page=1&countryId=1927165)

» **Estonian:** FamilySearch (https://familysearch.org/search/collection/list#page=1&countryId=1927007)

» **Federation of East European Family History Societies (FEEFHS):** If you're looking for research guides for Eastern Europe, start here. The federation's pages (http://feefhs.org) have information on the Albanian, Armenian, Austrian, Belarusian, Bohemian, Bulgarian, Carpatho-Rusyn, Croatian, Czech, Danish, Finnish, Galician, German, Hutterite, Hungarian, Latvian, Lithuanian, Polish, Moravian, Pomeranian, Romanian, Russian, Silesian, Slavic, Slavonian, Slovak, Slovenian, Transylvanian, Ukrainian, and Volhynian ethnic groups.

» **Greek:** GreeceGenWeb (www.rootsweb.ancestry.com/~grcwgw)

» **Hungarian:** HungaryGenWeb (www.rootsweb.ancestry.com/~wghungar) and FamilySearch (https://familysearch.org/search/collection/list#page=1&countryId=1927145)

» **Latvian:** LatvianGenWeb (www.rootsweb.ancestry.com/~lvawgw)

» **Maltese:** MaltaGenWeb (www.rootsweb.ancestry.com/~mltwgw)

» **Moldovian:** MoldovaGenWeb (www.rootsweb.ancestry.com/~mdawgw) and FamilySearch (https://familysearch.org/search/collection/list#page=1&countryId=1927051)

» **Polish:** PolandGenWeb (www.rootsweb.ancestry.com/~polwgw) and FamilySearch (https://familysearch.org/search/collection/list#page=1&countryId=1927187)

» **Romanian:** RomaniaGenWeb (www.rootsweb.ancestry.com/~romwgw)

>> **Russian:** RussiaGenWeb (www.rootsweb.ancestry.com/~ruswgw) and FamilySearch (https://familysearch.org/search/collection/list#page=1&countryId=1927021)

>> **Serbian:** Serbia GenWeb (www.rootsweb.ancestry.com/~serwgw)

>> **Slovak:** Slovak Republic Genealogy (https://wgwslovakia.wordpress.com/) and FamilySearch (https://familysearch.org/search/collection/list#page=1&countryId=1927146)

>> **Slovenian:** SloveniaGenWeb (www.rootsweb.ancestry.com/~svnwgw) and FamilySearch (https://familysearch.org/search/collection/list#page=1&countryId=1927180)

>> **Ukrainian:** Ukraine GenWeb (www.rootsweb.ancestry.com/~ukrwgw) and FamilySearch (https://familysearch.org/search/collection/list#page=1&countryId=1927132)

Asian Resources

If your ancestors came from Asia or the Pacific Rim, your success at finding records greatly depends on the history of the ancestor's ethnic group and its record-keeping procedures. Currently, you don't find much online genealogical information that pertains to these areas and peoples. Here's a sampling of Asian and Pacific Rim resources:

>> **Bangladesh:** Bangla Desh Genealogy (www.rootsweb.ancestry.com/~bgdwgw)

>> **Bhutan:** BhutanGenWeb (www.rootsweb.ancestry.com/~btnwgw)

>> **China:** ChinaGenWeb (www.rootsweb.ancestry.com/~chnwgw),FamilySearch (https://familysearch.org/search/collection/list#page=1&countryId=1927073), House of Chinn (http://houseofchinn.com/ChineseGenealogy.html), and My China Roots (www.mychinaroots.com/)

>> **India:** FamilySearch (https://familysearch.org/search/collection/list#page=1&countryId=1927063)

>> **Indonesia:** FamilySearch (https://familysearch.org/search/collection/list#page=1&countryId=1927029)

>> **Japan:** JapanGenWeb (www.rootsweb.ancestry.com/~jpnwgw) and FamilySearch (https://familysearch.org/search/collection/list#page=1&countryId=1927172)

- » **Korea:** FamilySearch (https://familysearch.org/search/collection/list#page=1&countryId=6118214)

- » **Lebanon:** Lebanon GenWeb (www.rootsweb.ancestry.com/~lbnwgw)

- » **Melanesia:** MelanesiaGenWeb (www.rootsweb.ancestry.com/~melwgw)

- » **Philippines:** FamilySearch (https://familysearch.org/search/collection/list#page=1&countryId=1927042)

- » **Polynesia:** PolynesiaGenWeb (www.rootsweb.ancestry.com/~pyfwgw)

- » **Saudi Arabia:** Saudi Arabia GenWeb (www.angelfire.com/tn/BattlePride/Saudi.html)

- » **South Korea:** SouthKoreaGenWeb (www.rootsweb.ancestry.com/~korwgw-s)

- » **Syria:** Syria Genealogy Web (www.rootsweb.ancestry.com/~syrwgw)

- » **Sri Lanka:** Sri Lanka Genealogy (www.rootsweb.ancestry.com/~lkawgw) and FamilySearch (https://familysearch.org/search/collection/list#page=1&countryId=1927054)

- » **Taiwan:** TaiwanGenWeb (www.rootsweb.ancestry.com/~twnwgw)

- » **Tibet:** TibetGenWeb (www.rootsweb.ancestry.com/~tibetwgw)

- » **Turkey:** Turkey Genealogy Web (www.rootsweb.ancestry.com/~turwgw)

- » **Vietnam:** VietnamGenWeb (www.rootsweb.ancestry.com/~vnmwgw)

Researching African Ancestry

It's a common misconception that tracing African ancestry is impossible. In the past decade or so, much has been done to dispel that perception. If your ancestors lived in the U.S., you can use many of the same research techniques and records (census schedules, vital records, and other primary resources) that genealogists of other ethnic groups consult, back to 1870. Prior to 1870, your research resources become more limited, depending on whether your ancestor was a freedman or a slave. To make that determination, you may want to interview some of your relatives. They often possess oral traditions that can point you in the right direction.

If your ancestor was a slave, try consulting the slave owners' probate records (which you can usually find in local courthouses), deed books (slave transactions were often recorded in deed books — which you can also find in local courthouses), tax records, plantation records, Freedman's Bureau records, and runaway-slave records. These types of records can be helpful because they identify persons by name.

Although your first inclination may be to turn to a slave schedule in the U.S. Census (slave schedules show the owner's name and the age, sex, and color of slaves), such schedules are not as useful as other sources in your research because the *enumerators* who collected the census information didn't record the names of all slaves, nor did the government require them to do so. This fact doesn't mean that looking at slave schedules is a total waste of time; the schedules simply don't identify your ancestor by name. You need to find other resources that name your ancestor specifically.

If your ancestors served in the American Civil War, they may have service and pension records. You can begin a search for service records in an index to Civil War records of the United States Colored Troops or, if your ancestor joined a state regiment, in an Adjutant General's report. (An *Adjutant General's report* is a published account of the actions of military units from a particular state during a war; these reports are usually available at libraries or archives.) A good place to begin your search for Civil War records is the Civil War Soldiers and Sailors System at https://www.nps.gov/civilwar/soldiers-and-sailors-database.htm.

Two other sources of records to keep in mind are the Freedmen's Bureau and the Freedman's Savings and Trust. Following are a few sites that contain information from these two organizations:

>> **The Freedmen's Bureau** (its full name was the Bureau of Refugees, Freedmen, and Abandoned Lands) was established in 1865 to assist ex-slaves after the American Civil War. For more on the Bureau, see the article by Elaine C. Everly at https://www.archives.gov/publications/prologue/1997/summer/freedmens-bureau-records.html.

>> **The Freedmen's Bureau Online** offers examples of Freedmen's Bureau records at www.freedmensbureau.com.

>> **The Freedman's Savings and Trust Company** was also established in 1865 as a bank for ex-slaves. For more information, see the article by Reginald Washington at www.archives.gov/publications/prologue/1997/summer/freedmans-savings-and-trust.html. Several of the bank's contributors were members of the United States Colored Troops during the American Civil War. The company failed in 1874; its records are now kept at the National Archives and Records Administration along with the records for the Freedmen's Bureau.

>> **The National Archives and Records Administration** provides information about Freedman's Savings records (and their availability on microfilm) at www.archives.gov/research/guide-fed-records/groups/105.html.

Ancestry.com (www.ancestry.com) contains records from the Freedmen's Bureau Field Offices (1863–1878), marriages recorded by the Freedmen's Bureau (1815–1866), and Freedman's Bank records (1865–1871).

For more information on using records to research your African ancestry, try the resources that follow:

>> *The Source: A Guidebook to American Genealogy,* Third Edition, edited by Loretto Dennis Szucs and Sandra Hargreaves Luebking (Ancestry, Inc.). In particular, see Chapter 14, "African American Research," written by Tony Burroughs. This is available online at www.ancestry.com/wiki/index.php?title= Overview_of_African_American_Research.

>> *Black Roots: A Beginner's Guide to Tracing the African American Family Tree,* written by Tony Burroughs (Touchstone).

>> *Black Family Research: Records of Post-Civil War Federal Agencies at the National Archives,* available online at www.archives.gov/publications/ref-info-papers/rip108.pdf.

>> *Slave Genealogy: A Research Guide with Case Studies,* written by David H. Streets (Heritage Books).

Genealogical resource pages on the web

To find out more about research resources, the AfriGeneas website (www. afrigeneas.com/) is a good place to start. (See Figure 8-3.) At the site you can find:

>> A beginner's guide to researching genealogy

>> Links to census schedules and slave data on the Internet

>> A digital library of transcribed resources

>> A link to a database of African-American surnames and their corresponding researchers

You can find a high-level overview of the subject at African American Lives 2 (www.pbs.org/wnet/aalives). The site is the companion to the PBS show that originally aired in early 2006. Items on the site include

>> Profiles of individuals featured on the show

>> Tips on how to effectively use documentation in researching African ancestral roots

>> A brief primer on DNA testing

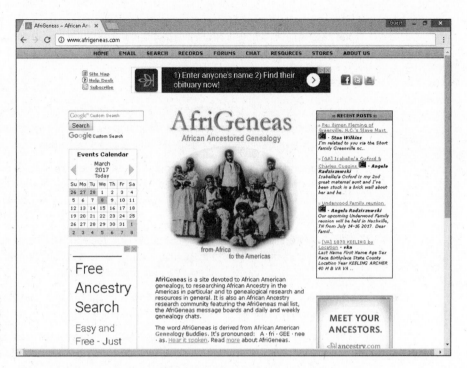

FIGURE 8-3: The AfriGeneas site aids in finding your African ancestors.

>> An introduction to some of the issues and pitfalls surrounding research

>> A list of stories from other researchers

For a brief list of resources that you can use for research, see the University of Pennsylvania African Studies Center bibliography page, at `www.africa.upenn.edu/Bibliography/menu_Biblio.html`.

Other sites with helpful content include

>> Sankofa-gen Wiki (`http://sankofagen.pbworks.com/w/page/14230533/FrontPage`)

>> Slave Archival Collection Database (`http://rootsweb.ancestry.com/~ilissdsa/text_files/database_intro2.htm`)

Transcribed records pertaining to ancestors with African roots

Many genealogists recognize the benefits of making transcribed and digitized records available for other researchers. More and more of these websites are popping up every day. A few websites have transcribed records that are unique to the study of African ancestry online. Some examples are

» **Cemetery records:** For a transcribed list of cemeteries, see African American Cemeteries Online at http://africanamericancemeteries.com.

» **Freedmen's Bureau records:** You can find transcribed Freedmen's Bureau records at the Freedmen's Bureau Online at www.freedmensbureau.com.

» **Manumission papers:** For examples of *manumission papers* — documents reflecting that a slave was granted freedom — see the Bourbon County Deeds of Manumission Abstracts site at www.rootsweb.ancestry.com/~kyafamer/Bourbon/manumissions.htm.

» **Registers:** At The Valley of the Shadow site, you can view transcribed Registers of Free Blacks in Augusta County and Staunton, Virginia at http://valley.lib.virginia.edu/VoS/govdoc/free.html.

» **Slave schedules:** You can find digitized versions of slave schedules at Ancestry.com's subscription site (www.ancestry.com).

» **Slave Ships:** The Trans-Atlantic Slave Trade Database (www.slavevoyages.org) contains information on nearly 36,000 slaving voyages and names of over 90,000 Africans who were enslaved.

» **Wills and probate records:** Slaves were often mentioned in the disposition of wills. A list of slaves mentioned in probate records of Noxubee County, Mississippi, can be found at http://earphoto.tripod.com/SlaveNames.html.

TIP

The preceding sites are a few examples of transcribed records that you can find on the Internet. To see whether online records exist that pertain specifically to your research, visit a comprehensive genealogical site and look under the appropriate category.

Special ethnic pages about African ancestry

Many websites include information on a subset of individuals of African ancestry. Here are some you may want to visit:

» The African-Native American Genealogy Homepage provides details on blended families in Oklahoma (www.african-nativeamerican.com).

» You can find information on French Creoles on the French Creoles Free People of Color website (www.frenchcreoles.com/CreoleCulture/freepeopleofcolor/freepeopleofcolor.htm).

Original records

You can find digitized original records online at some subscription sites. For example, Fold3.com (`www.fold3.com`) has the federal and Supreme Court case files for the case involving the seizure of the Amistad, a ship carrying slaves seized by the U.S. Navy in 1839.

American Indian Resources

Tracing your American Indian heritage can be challenging. Your ancestor may have moved frequently, and most likely, few written records were kept. However, your task isn't impossible. With a good research strategy, you may be able to narrow your search area and find primary resources to unlock some of the mysteries of your ancestors.

One key to your research is old family stories that have been passed down from generation to generation. Interviewing your family members is a good way to find out what tribe your ancestor belonged to and the geographic area in which that ancestor lived. After you have this information, a trip to your local library is well worth the effort to find a history of the tribe and where it migrated throughout time. From this research, you can then concentrate your search on a specific geographic area and gain a much better chance of finding records of genealogical value.

Fortunately, the U.S. government did compile some records on American Indians. For example, you can find annual census lists of American Indians, dating from 1885 to 1940, in the National Archives — as well as digitized copies of the censuses on Ancestry.com, as shown in Figure 8-4. You can also find probate and land records at the federal level, especially for transactions occurring on reservations. In federal repositories, you can also find school records for those who attended schools on reservations. Additionally, the Bureau of Indian Affairs has a vast collection of records on American Indians. For more information about American Indian resources that are available from the National Archives and Records Administration, visit `www.archives.gov/research/alic/reference/native-americans.html`.

You may also be able to find records on your ancestor in one of the many tribal associations in existence. To find out how to contact tribes recognized in the U.S., go to the American Indian Tribal Directory, at `http://tribaldirectory.com/`.

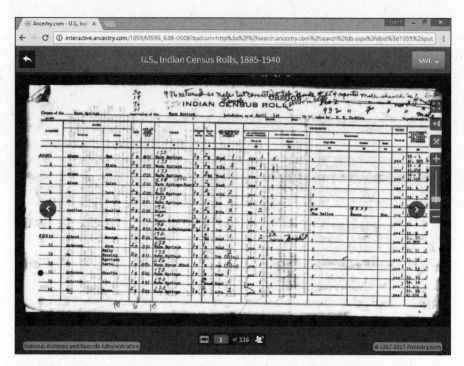

FIGURE 8-4:
Image of an
American Indian
census record at
Ancestry.com.

For more information about researching American Indian records, see the following resources:

>> *The Source: A Guidebook to American Genealogy,* Third Edition, edited by Loretto
   Dennis Szucs and Sandra Hargreaves Luebking (Ancestry, Inc.). In particular,
   see Chapter 19, "Native American Research," written by Curt B. Witcher and
   George J. Nixon. You can find this online at www.ancestry.com/wiki/index.
   php?title=Overview_of_Native_American_Research.

>> *Native American Genealogical Sourcebook,* edited by Paula K. Byers and
   published by Gale Group.

>> *Guide to Records in the National Archives of the United States Relating to American
   Indians,* published by the National Archives and Records Services
   Administration.

Where to begin looking for information about American Indians

For a general look at what Internet resources are available on American Indians,
see NativeWeb (www.nativeweb.org). NativeWeb includes a resource center with
hundreds of links to other Internet sites on native peoples around the world.

Another resource worth exploring is the National Archives and Records Administration's Catalog, at https://www.archives.gov/research/catalog. The catalog contains indexes to a small portion of the archive's holdings. Among the Native American collections in the catalog are

» Images of the Index to the Final Rolls of the Citizens and Freedmen of the Five Civilized Tribes in Indian Territory

» Images of the Index to Applications Submitted for the Eastern Cherokee Roll of 1909 (Guion Miller Roll)

» Records of the Bureau of Indian Affairs Truxton Canon Agency

» Record of Applications under the Act of 1896 (1896 Citizenship Applications) received by the Dawes Commission

» Descriptions for records of the Cherokee Indian Agency and the Seminole Indian Agency

» Descriptions for records of the Navajo Area Office, the Navajo Agency, and the Window Rock Area Office of the Bureau of Indian Affairs

» Some images of Cherokee, Chickasaw, Creek, and Seminole Applications for Enrollment to the Five Civilized Tribes (Dawes Commission)

» Images of the Kern-Clifton Roll of Cherokee Freedmen

» Images of the Wallace Roll of Cherokee Freedmen in Indian Territory

» Surveys of Indian Industry, 1922

» Classified Files of the Extension and Credit Office, 1931–1946

» Selected Documents from the Records of the Bureau of Indian Affairs, 1793–1989

» American Indians, 1881–1885

To search the catalog, try this:

1. **Go to** https://research.archives.gov/search.

2. **Place a term into the search field and click the search icon.**

We type Annie Abbott in the box.

3. **Click a link to content that interests you.**

We click the link for the Enrollment for Cherokee Census Card M1394 that shows more information about the record.

REMEMBER

At this point, the catalog contains descriptions of only a portion of the Archives' total holdings. So, if you don't find something, it doesn't mean it doesn't exist.

You can find a brief outline of how to trace American Indian ancestry at the U.S. Department of the Interior site (`https://www.doi.gov/tribes/trace-ancestry`).

American Indian resource pages on the web

Researching American Indian roots would be much easier if some sites were dedicated to the genealogical research of specific tribes. If your ancestor's tribe passed through the state of Oklahoma, you may be in luck. Volunteers with the Oklahoma USGenWeb project developed the Twin Territories site, at `http://okgenweb.net/~itgenweb/`.

Some links to various tribes available on the web are

» Cherokee Nation, Indian Territory (`www.rootsweb.ancestry.com/~itcherok`)

» Cherokee Archival Project (`www.rootsweb.ancestry.com/~cherokee`)

» NC Cherokee Reservation Genealogy (`www.ncgenweb.us/cherokeereservation`)

» Cheyenne-Arapaho Lands of Oklahoma Genealogy (`www.rootsweb.ancestry.com/~itcheyen`)

» Chickasaw Nation, Indian Territory, 1837–1907 (`www.rootsweb.ancestry.com/~itchicka`)

» Researching Your Choctaw Ancestry (`https://www.choctawnation.com/tribal-services/membership/genealogy`)

» Kiowa-Comanche-Apache Indian Lands (`www.genealogynation.com/kiowa`)

» Muscogee Nation of Oklahoma (`www.genealogynation.com/creek`)

» Native Genealogy People of the Three Fires: Chippewa, Ottawa, and Potawatomi (`www.rootsweb.ancestry.com/~minatam`)

» Quapaw Agency Lands of Indian Territory (`www.rootsweb.ancestry.com/~itquapaw`)

» Seminole Nation in Indian Territory (`www.seminolenation-indianterritory.org`)

Transcribed American Indian records

Some websites have transcribed records that are unique to researching American Indian roots. Two examples are

>> **Chickasaw History and Culture:** This page contains transcriptions of a few records, such as guardianship records and land sales, at www. chickasawhistory.com.

>> **1851 Census of Cherokees East of the Mississippi:** This site provides a transcription of the census, including names, family numbers, ages, and relationships to head of household, all at http://freepages.genealogy.rootsweb.ancestry.com/~gilmercountyrecords/1851silerrollforgilmercounty.htm.

REMEMBER

Many families have legends that they are descended from famous American Indians. These claims should always be researched carefully and backed up with appropriate proof. One of the most prolific legends is descent from Pocahontas. If that legend runs through your family, you may want to visit the Pocahontas Descendants page for resources that can help you prove your heritage. You can find it at http://pocahontas.morenus.org/poca_gen.html.

Chapter **9**

Specializing in Your Family History

Many people who are familiar with genealogy know to use vital records, census returns, tax lists, and wills to find information about their ancestors. These records offer historical snapshots of an individual's life at specific points in time. But as a family historian, you want to know more than just when your ancestors paid their taxes — you want to know something about them as people.

For example, April once came across a photograph of her great-great-grandfather while she was looking through an old box full of pictures and letters. He was dressed in a uniform with a sash and sword, and he was holding a plumed hat. As far as April knew, her great-great-grandfather hadn't been in the military, so she decided to dig for some information about the uniform. Although part of the picture was blurry, she could make out three crosses on the uniform. One was on his sleeve, the second was on the buckle of his belt, and the third was a different kind of cross that was attached to his sash. April suspected that the symbols were Masonic. She visited a few Masonic sites on the web and found that the crosses indicated that her great-great-grandfather had been a member of the Order of the Temple in the Masonic organization. She may not have discovered that he was a member of that organization had she depended solely upon the usual group of records used by genealogists.

This chapter looks at some examples of unique or hard-to-find records that can be useful in family history research, including records kept by religious groups and fraternal orders, photographs, and adoption records.

Researching Religious Group Records

In the past, several countries required attendance at church services or the payment of taxes to an ecclesiastical authority. Although your ancestors may not have appreciated those laws at the time, the records that were kept to ensure their compliance can benefit you as a genealogist. In fact, before governments started recording births, marriages, and deaths, churches kept the official records of these and other events (such as baptisms and lists of vestrymen). You can use a variety of records kept by church authorities or congregations to develop a sketch of the everyday life of your ancestor.

Some common records that you may encounter include baptismal records, parish registers, lists of people holding positions in the church (vestrymen, deacons, elders, lay ministers), marriage records, death or burial records, tithes, welfare rolls, meeting minutes, and congregation photographs. Each type of record may include several different bits of information. For example, a baptismal record may include the date of birth, date of baptism, parents' names, and where the parents lived. Parish registers may have names of household members and addresses, and possibly an accounting of their tithes to the church. The amount of data present on the records depends on the church.

Several sites provide general information and links to all sorts of resources that pertain to specific religions and sects. Here are a few examples:

>> **Anabaptist:** The Global Anabaptist Mennonite Encyclopedia Online (GAMEO) site (www.gameo.org) has an extensive collection of articles related to Amish, Mennonite, Hutterite, and Brethren in Christ congregations, as well as confessions and faith statements from some church members. It also has links to other resources for Anabaptist-Mennonite research. Additionally, you can find genealogical databases of Anabaptists at the Swiss Anabaptist Genealogical Association site (www.saga-omii.org/index.html).

>> **Baptist:** The Baptist History & Heritage Society site (www.baptisthistory.org) contains an overview of the Society and information about Baptists in the American Civil War.

» **Catholic:** The Local Catholic Church and Family History & Genealogy Research Guide (`http://localcatholic.webs.com`) includes links to information on diocese and genealogy, categorized by location.

» **Church of the Brethren:** The Fellowship of Brethren Genealogists website (`www.cob-net.org/fobg`) contains information on the organization and the current projects sponsored by the Fellowship.

» **Church of Scotland:** The National Records of Scotland site (`www.scotlandspeople.gov.uk`) features searchable indexes of births, baptisms, banns, marriages, deaths, and burials from the Old Parish Registers dating from 1553 to 1854. For a description of church registers, see `www.scotlandspeople.gov.uk/guides/church-registers`.

» **Huguenot:** The Huguenots of France and Elsewhere site (`http://huguenots-france.org/english.htm`) contains genealogies of several Huguenot families. Also, you find a surname index at the Australian Family Tree Connections site (`www.aftc.com.au/Huguenot/Hug.html`).

» **Hutterite:** The Hutterite Genealogy Home Page (`http://feefhs.org/erg/hutterites`) gives an introduction and links to resources for this denomination found in Austria, Bohemia, Moravia, Slovakia, Hungary, Romania, Canada, the United States, and the Ukraine.

» **Jewish:** The JewishGen site (`www.jewishgen.org`) has information about the JewishGen organization and FAQs about Jewish genealogy, as well as indexes of other Internet resources, including searchable databases, special interest groups, and JewishGen family home pages.

» **Lutheran:** The Concordia Historical Institute site has a page on Researching Your Lutheran Ancestor at `www.lutheranhistory.org/ancestor.htm`.

» **Mennonite:** The PA and Mennonite Research Corner (`www.ristenbatt.com/genealogy/mennonit.htm`) features general information about Mennonites and a collection of online resources for researchers. For a Canadian perspective, visit the Mennonite Genealogy Data Index at `http://mgdi.mennonitehistory.org`.

» **Methodist:** The Genealogy and Family Research page (`www.gcah.org/research/genealogy-and-family-research`) contains general advice on getting started with your research and links to online resources.

» **Moravian Church:** The Moravian Church Genealogy Links page (`https://sites.google.com/site/moravianchurchgenealogylinks`) features links to articles on the history of the church, as well as links to genealogical resources.

>> **Quaker:** The Quaker Corner (www.rootsweb.com/~quakers) contains a query board, a list of research resources, and links to other Quaker pages on the web.

>> **Seventh-day Adventist:** The Center for Adventist Research at Andrews University site (www.centerforadventistresearch.org/) contains information on the university's archives and research center and databases including a periodical index, obituary index, bibliographies, and photographs.

A few church organizations have online descriptions of their archives' holdings:

>> **Brethren in Christ Archives:** www.messiah.edu/archives

>> **Catholic Archives of Texas:** https://www.catholicarchivesoftx.org

>> **Fresno Pacific University's Mennonite Library and Archives:** http://fresno.libguides.com/mla

>> **Concordia Historical Institute Department of Archives and History (Lutheran Church — Missouri Synod):** www.lutheranhistory.org

>> **General Commission on Archives and History for the United Methodist Church:** www.gcah.org/

>> **Greek Orthodox Archdiocese of America Department of Archives & Resource Center:** www.goarch.org/archdiocese/departments/archives

>> **Moravian Archives:** www.moravianchurcharchives.org

>> **United Church of Canada Archives:** www.united-church.ca/local/archives/on

The following sites can give you a better idea of the types of information available on the Internet for religious groups:

>> **Baptism records:** You can find a list of those baptized in the Wesleyan Methodist Baptismal Register at http://freepages.genealogy.rootsweb.ancestry.com/~wjmartin/wm-index.htm.

>> **Cemetery records:** The Quaker Burying Ground Cemetery, Galesville, Anne Arundel County, Maryland, site is www.interment.net/data/us/md/anne_arundel/quaker.htm. This web page is part of the Interment.net: Cemetery Records Online site, which provides transcribed burial information, including the person's name and dates of birth and death, as well as some other information, as shown in Figure 9-1.

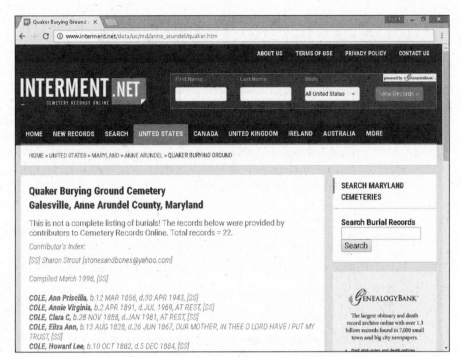

FIGURE 9-1:
A cemetery transcription from Interment.net.

>> **Marriage records:** The Moravian Church, Lititz Marriages 1742–1800 page (`http://files.usgwarchives.net/pa/lancaster/church/moravianlititz.txt`) contains a list of marriage dates along with the names of the bride and groom married in the church located in Lancaster County, Pennsylvania.

>> **Parish directories:** The Holy Trinity Church, Boston, Massachusetts site (`http://homepages.rootsweb.com/~mvreid/bgrc/htc.html`) has a searchable 1895 parish directory, an ongoing project to identify and post information about church members who served in the Civil War, and a list of church members who served in World War I.

Ancestry.com (`www.ancestry.com`) and MyHeritage has various collections of church records on their subscription sites. Findmypast (`www.findmypast.com`) has launched the Catholic Heritage Archive, that currently contains records from the Archdiocese of New York, Archdiocese of Philadelphia, and Archdiocese of Baltimore.

FamilySearch (`www.familysearch.org`) also has a growing number of church records, especially Catholic Church records in countries outside the U.S.

Finding Fraternal Orders and Service Clubs

Were any of your ancestors members of fraternal orders or service clubs? These groups are organized around a feature or attribute (such as a religion, military service, occupation, and so forth) and generally work toward a common good. Many such organizations exist and, chances are, you have at least one ancestor who was a member of an order or club. Although most of the better-known organizations are for men, affiliated organizations for women exist, too. A few general-information sites on fraternal orders and service clubs (where you might find contact information) are

>> **The American Legion:** www.legion.org

>> **Ancient Mystical Order Rosae Crucis:** www.amorc.org

>> **Ancient Order of Hibernians in America:** www.aoh.com

>> **DeMolayInternational:** https://demolay.org/

>> **Eagles (Fraternal Order of Eagles):** https://www.foe.com/

>> **Elks (Benevolent and Protective Order of Elks):** www.elks.org

>> **Freemasonry:** The Philalethes Society (www.freemasonry.org) and A Page About Freemasonry (http://web.mit.edu/dryfoo/www/Masons/index.html)

>> **Improved Order of Red Men:** www.redmen.org

>> **Job's Daughters International:** www.jobsdaughtersinternational.org

>> **Kiwanis International:** www.kiwanis.org

>> **Knights of Columbus:** www.kofc.org/un/en/index.html

>> **Lions Clubs'LionNet:** www.lionnet.com

>> **Military Order of the Loyal Legion of the United States:** www.suvcw.org/mollus/mollus.htm

>> **Modern Woodmen of America:** www.modern-woodmen.org/Pages/HomePage.aspx

>> **MooseInternational:** www.mooseintl.org/public/default.asp

>> **Odd Fellows (Independent Order of Odd Fellows):** www.ioof.org

>> **Optimist International:** www.optimist.org

>> **Order of the Eastern Star (Grand Chapter Order of the Eastern Star):** www.easternstar.org

- » **Orioles (Fraternal Order of Orioles):** http://fraternalorderorioles.homestead.com/

- » **Rainbow for Girls (International Order of the Rainbow for Girls):** www.iorg.org

- » **Rebekahs:** www.ioof.org/IOOF/About_Us/Whats_an_Odd_Fellow/Rebekah/IOOF/Rebekah.aspx?hkey=b56bd9ab-9e56-4eec-a8bc-8faeee1420e3

- » **Rotary International:** https://www.rotary.org

- » **Shriners International:** www.shrinersinternational.org

- » **Veterans of Foreign Wars of the United States:** www.vfw.org

Most sites related to fraternal orders provide historical information about the clubs and current membership rules. Although the sites may not provide you with actual records (membership lists and meeting minutes), they do give you an overview of what the club is about and an idea of what your ancestor did as a member. The sites also provide you with the names and addresses of local chapters — you can contact them to see whether they have original resources available for public use or whether they can send you copies of anything pertaining to your ancestor.

REMEMBER

Having information about a fraternal order doesn't necessarily make a site the organization's *official* site. This is particularly true for international organizations. You may find web pages for different chapters of a club in several different countries, and although each site may have some general club information in common, they are likely to have varying types of information specific to that chapter of the organization.

If you're looking for sites that contain information on fraternal organizations, you may want to try some of the comprehensive genealogy sites. If you can't find sufficient information there, try one of the general Internet search engines.

TIP

You might notice a unique marker on your ancestor's gravestone when visiting the cemetery or looking at photos. The marker may indicate your ancestor's membership in one of these fraternal orders or service clubs. The Pennsylvania USGenWeb Archives has a resource that may be helpful in just such a situation. The Guide to Identifying Grave Markers in Pennsylvania Social and Fraternal Organizations (www.usgwarchives.net/pa/1pa/tscarvers/veteran-markers/social-fraternal/social-fraternal-organizations.htm) contains information and illustrations that pertain to more than just Pennsylvania.

A Photo Is Worth a Thousand Words

In Chapter 2, we discuss the value of photographs in your genealogical research. But a lot of us don't have photographs of our family beyond two or three generations, though it sure would be great to find at least an electronic copy of a picture of your great-great-grandfathers. Such pictures may exist. Another researcher may have posted them on a personal site, or the photographs may be part of a collection belonging to a certain organization. You may also be interested in pictures of places where your ancestors lived. Being able to describe how a certain town, estate, or farm looked at the time your ancestor lived there adds color to your family history.

You can find various types of photographic sites on the Internet that can assist you with your research. Some of these sites explain the photographic process and the many types of photographs that have been used throughout history. Some sites contain collections of photographs from a certain geographic area or time period in history, and some sites contain photographs of the ancestors of a particular family. Here are some examples:

>> **General information:** City Gallery's Learning page (`www.city-gallery.com/learning`) has a brief explanation of the types of photography used during the 19th century (see Figure 9-2), a photography query page, and a gallery of photographs from one studio of the period.

>> **Photograph collections:** You can find general collections of images online at sites such as American Memory Collections: Original Format: Photos and Prints at `http://memory.loc.gov/cgi-bin/query/S?ammem/collections:@field(FLD003+@band(origf+Photograph)):heading=Original+Format%3a+Photos+&+Prints`. You can find pictures also at sites that have a specific focus, such as the Civil War (`https://www.flickr.com/photos/usnationalarchives/collections/72157622495226723/`), or images of people and places in Florida (`www.floridamemory.com/PhotographicCollection`).

>> **Photograph identification:** The DeadFred Genealogy Photo Archive contains more than 100,000 photographs at `www.deadfred.com`. Each photograph includes descriptive information, including where the photograph was taken, the names of the subjects, and an approximate time frame; see Figure 9-3.

>> **Personal photographs:** The Harrison Genealogy Repository site is an example of a personal website with a photo gallery: `http://freepages.genealogy.rootsweb.com/~harrisonrep/Photos/harrphot.htm`. The gallery includes the likenesses of several famous Harrisons, including Benjamin Harrison V, President William Henry Harrison, and President Benjamin Harrison.

FIGURE 9-2:
Find out about photographic methods of the past at City Gallery.

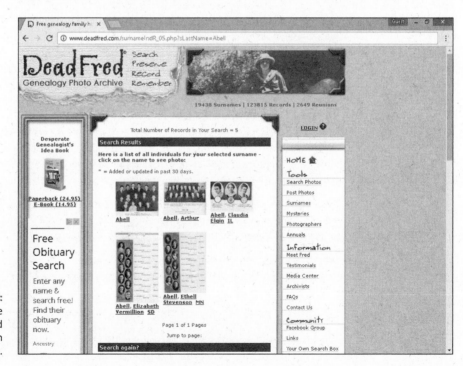

FIGURE 9-3:
An entry on the DeadFred photograph archive site.

DIGGING UP INFORMATION FROM THE GRAVE

Most genealogists recognize what a valuable resource a cemetery can be when researching family history. Your ancestors' gravestones (or tombstones) may contain an abundance of clues for you to use in further research. But traveling to visit all the cemeteries where your ancestors' are buried may not be possible because of financial, health, or physical constraints. Luckily, there is an online resource designed to help!

Billion Graves (`http://billiongraves.com`) is an effort to collect photos of gravestones, transcribe and index the information on them, and post the photo and transcription online for all to use.

The basic search interface is easy to use. Follow these steps:

1. Go to Billion Graves at `http://billiongraves.com`.

2. In the Find Their Graves Search box, enter first name and last name.

3. Click the Start Your Search button.

4. Sort through any results and click on any that look promising.

   If you want to specify a location, you can refine your search using the Advanced Search functionality.

Not all gravestones in all cemeteries are included at the site. And even those that are photographed may not yet be transcribed and indexed. Much of the content relies on volunteers. There are several ways to get involved with Billion Graves. Volunteers can:

- Take and upload photos of gravestones near where they live or travel using an iPhone or Android smart-phone camera application. The application can be downloaded from the iPhone AppStore or the Google Play site. The application maps the photo to the cemetery (provides the global positioning information embedded in the photo's code).

- Transcribe the information contained in the photos of the gravestones. This makes the information easily indexed for searching, which helps others who are looking for family history information on the site.

- Offer to photograph cemeteries or specific gravestones that other users are looking for. The website has a Request Board where people can post "look-up" needs.

While you can search for headstones without registering at the site, you will need to register if you want to volunteer in any way. Registration is fast and free. Just fill out the Register box on the home page for Billion Graves, then click Register. You can also opt for the Billion Graves Plus service that lists nearby graves and sends notifications of new records matching your searches.

For tips on using photographs in your research take a look at Maureen Taylor's blog at https://maureentaylor.com/blog/.

Accessing Adoption Records

Adoption records are of interest to a lot of genealogists, including those who were adopted themselves, those who gave up children for adoption, and those who have ancestors who were adopted. With the advent of DNA testing as a genealogy tool, even those who are not adopted may become interested in researching a person who is a match with them who was adopted and may not have much information on how they fit into the family. For example, Matthew is an administrator of a surname DNA project. During the course of testing, he found two individuals who were adopted that are a close match in DNA. So, for them, participation in the surname DNA project became a project to find how the two individuals fit into the family lines.

If you fall into the first two groups (you were adopted or gave up a child for adoption), some online resources may help you find members of your birth family. The online resources include registries, reference materials, advice and discussion groups, and information on legislation pertaining to adoption. Registries enable you to post information about yourself and your adoption, with the hope that a member of your birth family may see the posting and contact you. (Likewise, if you're the birth parent of an adoptee, you can post a message with the hope that the adoptee sees it and responds.)

It is also worthwhile to look for information on how to use DNA testing to jump-start your research. For example, the International Society of Genetic Genealogy has published the brief article Utilizing DNA Testing to Break Through Adoption Roadblocks at www.isogg.org/adoption.htm. The article points to a few other sites that can help in your research and contains some success stories. The Mixed Roots Foundation has launched a DNA effort under the Global Adoptee Genealogy Project page at http://discovergagp.org.

Unfortunately, you won't find online sites that contain actual adoption records — for legal reasons, generally. Instead, you need to rely on registries and other resources that point you toward more substantial information about adoption. If you have a successful reunion with your birth parent(s) by registering with an online site, you can, with any luck, obtain information about their parents, grandparents, and so on — so that you know where to begin your genealogical pursuit of that family line.

Here are some online sites that have adoption registries, reference materials, advice and discussions, or legislative information:

>> **Child Welfare Information Gateway: Access to Adoption Records:** https://www.childwelfare.gov/systemwide/laws_policies/ statutes/infoaccessap.cfm

>> **Adoption.org:** www.adoption.org

>> **Adoption Registry Connect: Worldwide Adoptee and Birth Parent Search Database:** www.adopteeconnect.com/index.htm

>> **Adoption Search - How to Find Your Birth Family:** https://www. thoughtco.com/how-to-find-your-birth-family-1420433

If you're interested in adoption records because you have ancestors who were adopted, finding information may be more difficult. Although some article- and blog-type sites exist that give general research information relating to adoption, we have yet to discover any sites specifically designed to aid in research for adopted ancestors. Most likely, you'll have to rely on the regular genealogical resources — particularly query pages and discussion groups — and the kindness and knowledge of other researchers to find information about your adopted ancestors.

Preparing to Be Schooled

Relatively few readily available records chronicle the early years of an individual. Educational records can help fill in the gaps. These records can take a number of forms, including enrollment records, transcripts, yearbooks, directories, and fraternity and sorority records.

The first step is to find out what educational institution your ancestor attended. If you're looking for an elementary or secondary school, you might visit the USGen-Web page (www.usgenweb.org) for the county where your ancestor lived to see whether information is available on the location of schools. If the USGenWeb page doesn't have the information, try to find the website of the local historical or genealogical society.

You might also discover this information by finding a reference to your ancestor and a school in a newspaper article available on a subscription newspaper site. For example, on a routine search on a subscription site, Matthew found a brief article in a local newspaper that listed the participants in a play in a school. From that, he was able to gather the school name, teacher's name, and the names of classmates.

After you discover the name of the institution, find out who has the records for that school. Some schools — such as colleges and universities — have their own archives. For primary and secondary schools, you may need to contact the school district or the overarching parish. Or, if the school no longer exists, you need to find out where the records for that school were transferred.

If you're not sure where the records are located, you can use WorldCat, at www.worldcat.org, by following these steps:

1. **Use your web browser to pull up** www.worldcat.org.

2. **In the search field, enter your criteria and then click Search Everything.**

We search for Harvard enrollment records.

3. **Select a result that looks promising.**

Figure 9-4 shows the results of our WorldCat search.

FIGURE 9-4:
Results from the WorldCat search for Harvard enrollment records.

Another set of resources that you might find online are school yearbooks. Some subscriptions sites, such as Ancestry.com have digitized high school and college yearbooks and placed them online. E-Yearbook.com (www.e-yearbook.com) contains collections of yearbooks for middle schools, high schools, colleges, and military organizations.

Turning to Bible Records

Bible records are a great source of birth, death, and marriage information for time periods before vital records were required. Because most Bible records are held by private individuals, it's sometimes difficult to locate them. Recognizing the importance of these records, groups have created websites to share the information contained in the Bibles. A few sites worth visiting are

- **» Ancestor Hunt Family Bible Records:** www.ancestorhunt.com/family_bible_records.htm
- **» Bible Records Online:** www.biblerecords.com
- **» Family Bible Records in Onondaga County:** www.rootsweb.ancestry.com/~nyononda/BIBLE.HTM
- **» DAR Bible Records and Transcriptions:** http://services.dar.org/Public/DAR_Research/search_bible
- **» Maine Family Bible Archives:** www.rootsweb.com/~meandrhs/taylor/bible/maine.html

Similar to looking for educational records, you can also find Bible records in some archives. You can use WorldCat (www.worldcat.org) to see what is available in different institutions. For details on how to use WorldCat, see the preceding section. Some subscription sites might also have Bible records. For example, Ancestry.com (www.ancestry.com) has Bible records from New York, Tennessee, Missouri, and Virginia, as well as a collection called Old Southern Bible Records.

Snooping through Great-Grandma's Diary

Another excellent source of information that can add color to your family history is a diary, journal, or memoir kept by your ancestor. Diaries and journals are books in which a person writes his or her thoughts and experiences, typically within a short time of events occurring. Memoirs are written reflections on one's life. Like Bibles and photos online, finding these personal memory keepers on the Internet is somewhat hit-and-miss. Individuals and organizations tend to place online digital images or transcriptions from these resources for their own family members or people from whom an organization has inherited the document. You can search for such records in the same way that you look for Bibles and photos: Look by location or surname using a site such as USGenWeb (www.usgenweb.org) or a search engine such as Google (www.google.com). Some example sites to check out, which may give you an idea of what you can expect from these types of records, are

>> **Diaries, Memoirs, Letters, and Reports Along the Trails West:** www.over-land.com/diaries.html

>> **Historical Journals and Diaries Online:** www.aisling.net/journaling/old-diaries-online.htm

>> **The Civil War: Women and the Homefront: Primary Sources Online:** http://guides.library.duke.edu/c.php?g=289364&p=1929646

Nosing through Newspaper Records

A lot of the day-to-day details of your ancestor's life can be filled in by reading local newspapers. You can find obituaries, marriage announcements, social activities, and tax assessments information. Also, you can find background information on the locality that he or she lived in so that you gain a better perspective of your ancestor's life.

A lot of effort has been expended to digitize newspapers over the last few years. Newspapers.com offers a collection of more than 4,900 newspaper databases online. The newspapers featured in the collection are digitized images that have been indexed by *optical character recognition (OCR)* — a software method in which letters in an image are translated into characters (typically letters of the alphabet) that a computer can read. Each page of the newspaper is searchable. When a search result is found, the text is highlighted on the page. The optical character recognition system doesn't always know the context of the words on the page — so the system sometimes generates false-positive search results. Figure 9-5 shows the interface for the newspaper collection at Newspapers.com.

Several large newspapers have also begun to place their back issues online — often with a subscription service. For example, you can find the *Los Angeles Times* back to 1881 online at http://pqasb.pqarchiver.com/latimes/advancedsearch.html, the *Washington Post* from 1877 at http://pqasb.pqarchiver.com/washingtonpost/search.html, and the *Chicago Tribune* from 1852 at http://pqasb.pqarchiver.com/chicagotribune/advancedsearch.html.

You can find more about using newspapers in your research in Chapter 6.

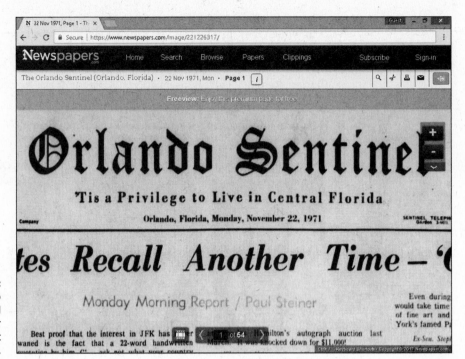

FIGURE 9-5:
The Orlando
Sentinel
newspaper
image at
Newspapers.com.

3

Putting Your Family History to the Test

Learn how to use DNA tests to assist researching your direct male and female lines.

Discover the probability of your ethnicity with DNA tests.

Find distant cousins with Automsomal DNA and X-DNA.

Chapter **10**

Fitting into Your Genes: Genetic Genealogy

t sounds like something right out of a crime scene investigation: You swab your cheek or spit in a tube, send the sample to a lab, the results are analyzed, and presto! You find the identity of someone super-important. However, instead of identifying some master-minded criminal, you find the identity of that long-lost ancestor for whom you've been searching. Although the science behind molecular genealogy traces its roots to identifying individuals from crime scenes, it hasn't advanced to the point where you can simply take the test and watch your entire genealogy unfold. But it can provide valuable evidence that you're related to a particular family line.

Although *deoxyribonucleic acid* (DNA) testing is just one of many tools to use in documenting your research, it holds great potential for the future of genealogy. You may be familiar with the use of DNA testing in identifying the remains of Nicholas, the last Czar of Russia, and his family; in debating the last resting place of Christopher Columbus; or in determining the true fate of Jesse James. The methods used in these investigations are the same methods you can use to complement your documentary research.

In this chapter, we provide an overview of how DNA testing works and where you can order tests.

Ask What DNA Can Do for You

You probably have seen the commercials on television. A quick DNA test and now you are ready to go out and buy a kilt or lederhosen or schedule that trip to West Africa. Well, DNA testing can do a whole lot more for your family history research than estimate your ethnicity. Think of DNA testing as another type of record you can use as evidence for your family history— much like a census, vital, or tax record.

Some of the things that DNA testing can accomplish include:

>> Determining whether two people are related when one or both were adopted

>> Identifying whether two people are descended from the same ancestor

>> Discovering whether a person is related to others with the same surname

>> Providing evidence for family tree research

>> Providing clues about ethnic origin

>> Finding out about inherited traits from your family

Four types of DNA testing are currently used with frequency by family historians. As is the case with traditional record types, each type of test is used to gather a specific piece of information. For example, a vital record tells you the birth date of an ancestor. If you want to know how much tax an ancestor paid in a certain location, consult a tax record. In the genetic family history world, the same specialization applies: If you want to know something about a direct-line male relative, you might use a Y-chromosome test. If you want to compare the results of anyone related to you, you might use an autosomal test.

As in any pursuit, individuals who test their DNA can have a variety of objectives. Understanding this can explain why some testers will respond to a message and why some won't. Here are a few of the common objectives of DNA testers:

>> **Ethnicity estimation:** Some testers just want to know their ethnicity/ancestral origins and may never log into the testing website again. Unfortunately, this can be frustrating for family historians who find a match on a site, only to see that the person who matches hasn't logged in for two years. Hopefully, the tester will become interested in learning more at some point down the road.

>> **Family history research:** These testers are interested in finding related researchers to provide evidence for their family trees and to discover new sources of documents, family photographs, and stories. Sometimes family

historians slide in and out of genetic genealogy tools as they research other record types.

>> **Mapping ancestors to specific regions on the tester's chromosome:** These testers want to know which ancestor was responsible for contributing genetic material at a certain location on a chromosome. This may be to determine the ethnicity of an ancestor or might be used to determine where an inherited trait or condition came from.

>> **Reconstructing an ancestor's DNA:** Some testers would like to know what their ancestor's DNA looked like for ethnicity, inherited traits, or to use a pseudo-result to compare to other current DNA samples to find more descendants of that ancestor. Testers that are conducting this type of research will have to find as many descendants as they can to create as complete a sample as possible.

>> **Adoption discovery:** Adopted testers may be looking for genetic clues to their adoptive parents' ethnicity or inherited traits, or may be trying to locate biological family members.

>> **Inherited traits/conditions:** Some testers are concerned with the medical aspects of DNA testing. They are interested in the probability that they might eventually develop a particular medical condition.

And, of course, there are those of us that fit into more than one category of the above — that jump from one to another as time allows or when prompted by another researcher.

A Friendly Word of Caution

WARNING

Before you embark into the world of genetic genealogy, consider a few things: First, by taking a DNA test, you may discover something you would rather not know. For example, some people have discovered that they're not biologically related to the family from which they've always claimed descent. Sometimes this occurs due to a *non-paternal (or paternity) event (NPE)*, also known as misattributed paternity, where the biological father was not the person listed on the birth record. (This may have occurred in the immediate family or in a past generation.) Others have discovered they do not have the racial or ethnic composition that they've always identified with. Also, some testing services provide probabilities that a particular disease or medical condition might occur. If you prefer not to know the medical part, you can skip that portion of the results, or take an ancestry-only test.

The second thing to remember is that genetic genealogy is a science, but not an absolute one. DNA test results show the probability that something is true.

(*Probability* is the likelihood that a specific fact or outcome will occur.) Nothing is ever a hundred percent certain. In addition, sometimes (but rarely) mistakes are made by the testing facility, or new research is discovered that changes the way a test result is viewed. This is especially true in the realm of ethnicity estimates. DNA testing for genealogy is still undergoing development and being refined. As long as you can adapt to change and accept new technology, you'll be just fine in the world of DNA genealogy.

Lastly, it is important to understand that genetics is a sensitive subject and care should be used when using genetic information. You should use the same standards for disclosing information as you would for other records that contain sensitive information. In fact, a group of genealogists and scientists gathered together to draft genetic genealogy standards. The standards can be found at www. geneticgenealogystandards.com. Some of these standards include:

>> **Consent for a DNA test:** This sounds reasonable enough, but there was a case where someone attempted to take a DNA sample from a used coffee cup when an individual refused to test. Also, consent should be given by a parent or legal guardian for minor testers and from a legal representative in the case of a deceased individual.

>> **Raw data and results:** Testers have the right to their test results and raw data, even if someone else paid for the test.

>> **Terms of service of testing companies:** Genealogists and testers should ensure that they understand the terms and conditions of the testing company when purchasing a DNA test.

>> **Privacy:** Genealogists should only test with companies that respect and protect the privacy of testers. Also, it is understood that complete anonymity of testing results can't be guaranteed.

>> **Access by third parties:** Genealogists and testers should recognize that if results are posted to public sites, then those results can be accessed, copied, and analyzed by a third party without permission.

>> **Sharing results:** Genealogists should respect the tester's wishes when sharing test results.

Delving into DNA

Some people might think we're attempting the impossible — explaining how DNA works in only one part of this book. After all, genetic testing is so complex that the information on it can fill many books. However, we feel it is our duty to give you at least a basic introduction to genetic research so that you can use all the technological means available to you when digging for information on your ancestors.

You need an understanding of the terminology and the way the testing process works in order to interpret your test results. If you find that our elementary explanations merely whet your appetite, you can get a healthy dose on the subject with *Genetics For Dummies, 2nd Edition*, by Tara Rodden Robinson.

Getting down to bases

There's no doubt about it: DNA is hard to explain. We do our best to keep it simple but informative here. Being a family historian, most likely you've taken a research trip to a particular town to find the burial location for an ancestor. When you reached that town, your first stop was probably the local library. Entering the library, you quickly made your way to the reference room. You leafed through the reference room collection, looking for a cemetery index for that area. Finding an index, you located the chapter that contained a list of gravestones for the cemetery where your ancestor is buried. Thumbing through the chapter, you found your ancestor's name, which is typed with some combination of 26 letters (assuming it contains no special characters and the book is in English).

You can think about the components of DNA like the preceding library. (Figure 10-1 shows a model of the components of DNA.) The basic building blocks of humans are *cells* that function like little towns. Within each cell is a *nucleus,* which is the structure that contains all the DNA. This nucleus acts as the library for the cell. Within the nucleus is the *genome* (the complete set of instructions defining how the cell will operate). You can think of the genome as the reference book collection of the library.

The human genome contains 23 pairs of chromosomes (a total of 46 chromosomes). A *chromosome* is the container that holds the strands of DNA. Each type of chromosome has a different set of instructions and serves a different purpose. Sticking with our analogy, like a library's reference collection has several types of reference books, the genome has several types of chromosomes. One pair of chromosomes is referred to as the sex chromosomes. Males have one Y chromosome and one X chromosome in the pair. Females have two X chromosomes in the pair. The remaining 22 pairs of chromosomes (44 chromosomes) are called autosomal chromosomes. Particular sections of a chromosome are called genes. *Genes* contain specific sequences of information that determine an inheritable characteristic of a human. If a chromosome is a reference book, genes are the chapters in the book.

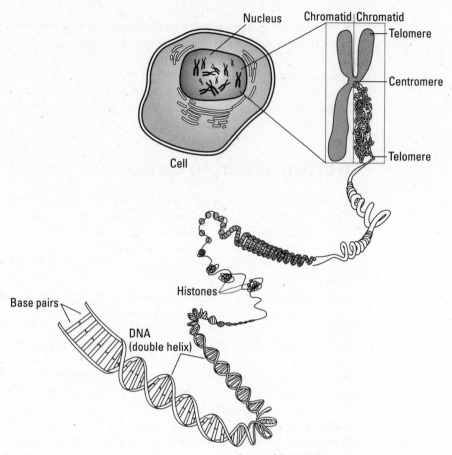

FIGURE 10-1:
A model of a cell nucleus, chromosome, and deoxyribo-nucleic acid.

Courtesy of the National Human Genome Research Institute

A particular gene can come in different forms called *alleles.* For example, the gene for eye color might come in a blue eye allele or a brown eye allele. To use our book analogy, a specific chapter of a book can be laid out in different ways. Alleles would be different layouts that the chapter could have.

Genes are composed of *bases,* also called *nucleotides,* which form the rungs of the DNA ladder that hold the DNA molecule together. You find four types of bases: adenine (A), guanine (G), cytosine (C), and thymine (T). When forming the rungs of the DNA molecule, bases attach in only one way. Adenine always pairs with thymine on the opposite strand, and guanine always pairs with cytosine. The attachment of bases is called *base pairing.* The bases are the language of DNA. You read the sequence of the base pairs to determine the coding of the allele — just like reading the sequence of letters in a book forms a recognizable sentence (see Figure 10-2).

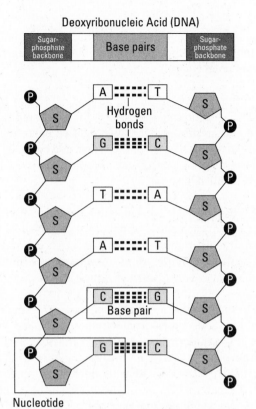

Deoxyribonucleic Acid (DNA)

Hydrogen bonds

Base pair

Nucleotide

FIGURE 10-2:
The structure
of base pairs
or nucleotides.

Courtesy of the National Human Genome Research Institute

Please understand that our DNA-library analogy is a very simplistic explanation of the molecular parts that are considered in genetic testing. DNA plays a much more complicated role in genetics than what we just covered. However, for the purpose of this chapter, our basic presentation on genetic structure should be sufficient for understanding the broader implications in DNA testing for molecular genealogy. We add further clarification in the upcoming chapters on the DNA testing types so that you get a good idea of what function the test is performing.

Variations in DNA

To help you understand how DNA is passed from one generation to another, we have to take a little trip back to high-school science or health. Our description here oversimplifies the process, but it's designed to point out things relevant to genetic genealogy. Yes, you guessed it — we are going to have "the talk" about the birds and the bees.

Sexual reproduction is the combining of genetic information from two individuals of different sexes. In humans, this is done by combining the genetic material from a sperm cell with that of an egg cell.

As we mentioned in the previous section, a human cell has 23 pairs of chromosomes for a total of 46 chromosomes. However, for sexual reproduction to work, the total number of chromosomes contributed by each parent needs to be cut in half — 23 chromosomes — so that when the sperm and egg cells unite, there is a total of 46 chromosomes to create the 23 chromosome pairs in the resulting zygote. This process is called *meiosis*.

Just before meiosis begins, a cell is created with a random collection of half of the chromosomes — one from each pair — from one donor. Also included in the cell is a random set of half the chromosomes from the other donor. For example, for chromosome 1, the contributed chromosome may have come from the mother. For chromosome 2, it may have come from your father, and so on.

The chromosomes in the new cell are then duplicated. The single paternal chromosome 1 is copied into a second paternal chromosome 1, and so forth for all 23 chromosomes. The single maternal chromosome 1 is also copied. The two copies of the paternal chromosome 1 are then attached together with a centromere to form a single paternal chromosome 1 (having double the genetic material). The same happens with the maternal chromosome. By the end of the process, you have two chromosome 1s, one supplied from paternal genetic material and one from the maternal genetic material.

During the first phase of the first stage of meiosis the paternal and maternal chromosome 1s may overlap each other and go through a process of recombination. During recombination, genetic material (alleles) from a portion of the paternal chromosome 1 may be exchanged (or cross over) with the genetic material of the maternal chromosome 1 at the point of overlap.

In later phases of the first stage of meiosis, the paternal and maternal chromosome 1s are pulled to opposite ends of the cell and unravel; the cell divides into two cells. During the second stage of meiosis the cells further divide into four cells. These gamete cells are now ready to be merged with the gamete cells of another sex (see Figure 10-3).

This process of the selection of particular portions of a chromosome pair, in conjunction with recombination, accounts for the variation seen in children from the same parents. As this occurs, during each successive generation, more variation occurs and at some point genetic material from a particular ancestor disappears among all of the selection and recombination.

We come back to this subject in our discussion of how these selections and recombinations affect interpretation of DNA results in Chapter 12 when we focus on autosomal DNA testing.

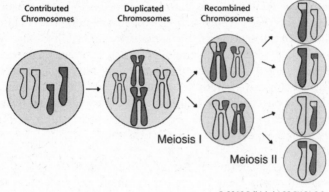

FIGURE 10-3: Recombination of chromosomes during meiosis.

Family History: Documentation versus Genetics

In the first parts of this book, we talk about ways to create a documented family history. The documentation on a birth record can indicate the father and mother of a particular individual. Census records can map the family relationships of several individuals from a single entry (father, mother, children, in-laws, and so forth). A documented family tree might look like the one in Figure 10-4.

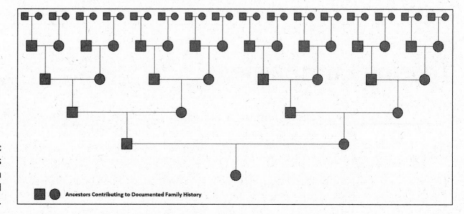

FIGURE 10-4: The individuals involved in a documented family tree.

Ancestors Contributing to Documented Family History

However, when you are looking at a genetic family tree, the individuals involved are a subset of the documented family tree. Everyone in your genetic family tree should be part of your documented family tree. But, not everyone in your documented family tree will be in your genetic family tree (see Figure 10-5).

The reason for this is the chromosome selections and recombinations that we discussed in the previous section. This means unless two siblings were identical twins, they did not inherit the same DNA. One sibling may have inherited DNA from a great-great-great grandfather and another sibling may have not (this means that none of the second sibling's offspring will ever inherit DNA from that great-great-great grandfather — unless they inherit it from an ancestor of that sibling's spouse, one who happened to be descended from the same great-great-great grandfather). However, a cousin to the siblings may have inherited the same DNA from the great-great-great grandfather.

We talk more about this in Chapter 12 in our discussion of autosomal DNA, but we thought it was a good idea to let you know this upfront. That way, when you encounter this in your research, you won't be disappointed.

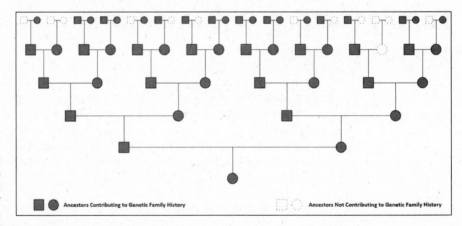

FIGURE 10-5: The individuals involved in a genetic family tree.

Testing Companies

These days, a number of companies offer DNA testing. However, for the purposes of this book, we look at the three main companies used by family historians — Family Tree DNA, 23andMe, and AncestryDNA.

Family Tree DNA (www.familytreedna.com) has been offering direct to consumer DNA testing since 2000. The company offers Y-chromosome (Y-DNA), mitochondrial (mtDNA), and autosomal (atDNA) services. The company's website is home to a variety of surname and location-based DNA projects. Family Tree DNA uses cheek swabs to collect the DNA for analysis.

23andMe (www.23andme.com) was founded in 2006. The company offers an ancestry-only test or a test with health information. Through the test, you can get information on Y-DNA, mitochondrial DNA, and autosomal DNA (along with X-chromosome DNA). The 23andMe test is conducted with a saliva sample.

AncestryDNA (www.ancestry.com/dna) has been offering DNA testing since 2012. The test provides information on autosomal DNA. AncestryDNA offers shared ances-tor hints, DNA Circles (uses public family trees to identify cousins), and Genetic Communities (identifies groups of testers that may have descended from a popula-tion of common ancestors). The AncestryDNA test is done with a saliva sample.

Selecting the Right Test for You

After you gain a basic understanding of genetics, you may find your curiosity piqued — are you ready to jump right in and gather DNA samples willy-nilly? Slow down! You have more to discover so that you don't lose time and momentum by submitting your swabs for the wrong types of tests.

Four types of tests are commonly available from DNA testing companies:

>> **Y-chromosome DNA testing:** Humans have 23 pairs of chromosomes. Of these 23, males and females have 22 pairs in common and one pair not in common. In that one pair, males have one X and one Y chromosome, whereas females have two X chromosomes. The Y-chromosome DNA test explores the Y chromosome in this uncommon pair of chromosomes. As you might suspect at this point, this particular test is available only for men because females do not carry the Y chromosome. However, just because you — the reader — might be female, don't fail to read the following section on Y-chromosome DNA testing. You can always have a male relative (such as your father, brother, uncle, or cousin) take this test for you to discover the hidden secrets in your familial Y-DNA.

>> **Mitochondrial DNA testing:** The mitochondrion is considered by some to be the "power plant" of the cell. (Remember, the cell is the basic building block of the human body.) It sits outside the nucleus of the cell, and it contains its own distinct genome — that means its genome is separate from the genome found in the nucleus of the cell. This distinct genome is known as mtDNA in genetic testing. The mtDNA is inherited only from the female parent, is passed to all offspring (male and female), and mutates (or changes) at a slow rate

over generations. All of these aspects of the mtDNA make it good for identifying genetic relationships over hundreds of generations.

>> **Autosomal DNA testing:** Autosomal DNA consists of 22 pairs of non–sex-specific chromosomes that are found in the cell nucleus — this means that they don't contain the X or Y chromosome. Autosomal DNA is found in males and females and is the part of the DNA responsible for characteristics such as height and eye color. This DNA is inherited from both parents. Autosomal testing, also called admixture or biogeographical testing, is used to determine paternity, indicate ethnicity, and diagnose potential health problems.

>> **X-chromosome DNA testing:** As we mention earlier, males have one X and one Y chromosome, whereas females have two X chromosomes. This test looks at the mixture of the X chromosomes inherited over several generations.

Given the complexity of genetic research, we expect the tests to be complicated as well. Hence, each test warrants its own attention. In the next two chapters, we explore them in a little more depth.

Finding Helpful DNA Sites

Within this chapter, we were able to cover only the tip of the iceberg in using DNA testing for genealogical purposes. Some websites can provide additional information to help you decide whether DNA testing is useful for your research or to keep abreast of the current developments in DNA research.

If you're looking for some basic information on using DNA testing in genealogy, see the International Society of Genetic Genealogy Beginners Guides to Genetic Genealogy page at https://isogg.org/wiki/Beginners%27_guides_to_genetic_genealogy. There is a lot of other information on genetic genealogy on the website, so you might want to check out their Wiki pages.

Because DNA testing methods and capabilities change on a frequent basis, it's a good idea to consult some sites that provide updates on the technology and issues related to using the technology. A few sites to consult include

>> **Genealogy-DNA mailing list archives:** http://lists5.rootsweb.ancestry.com/index/other/DNA/GENEALOGY-DNA.html (You can also subscribe to the mailing list from this page.)

>> **Genetic Genealogist blog:** www.thegeneticgenealogist.com

>> **segment-ology:** https://segmentology.org/

Chapter **11**

Direct-Line Genetic Tests

H ave you hit a brick wall with researching either your father's or mother's direct-line ancestors? Before you give up all hope of finding those elusive ancestors, why not try a direct-line ancestor DNA test? This chapter focuses on genetic testing of the Y chromosome (used for direct-line male ancestors) and mitochondrial DNA testing (used for direct-line female ancestors). We take you through the process of analyzing the results of both types of tests and point you to some sites that can help you find others with similar results.

Upfront we have to ask you to keep in mind that both tests are very limited in their scope. They are designed to provide evidence on a specific line of ancestors. For tests that apply to a broader set of ancestors, see Chapter 12.

Y chromosome (Y-DNA) testing

The Y chromosome is part of the one chromosomal pair that is not common between males and females; in males, the pair has an X and a Y chromosome, whereas in females, the pair has two X chromosomes. Because the Y chromosome isn't paired with another Y chromosome, it doesn't go through recombination in the same way that autosomal chromosomes do. For a quick refresher on recombination, flip back to Chapter 10. As it doesn't go through recombination with another Y chromosome, it changes little over time as it is passed from father to son, unless a mutation occurs. Having said that, there are small areas where the

Y chromosome can recombine with the X chromosome. However, these areas are not used in the Y chromosome DNA tests discussed in this book.

The Y-DNA test is available only for men (as only they carry the Y chromosome) — although women can participate in Y chromosome projects by using a father, brother, or male cousin as a proxy. (Figure 11-1 shows how the Y chromosome is passed from one male to another.) Now it's time to get into the details of the test.

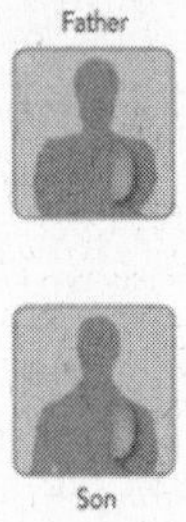

Father

Son

FIGURE 11-1:
A Y chromosome is passed from father to son relatively unchanged.

Courtesy of the Sorenson Molecular Genealogy Foundation, the scientific backbone of GeneTree.com

"Junk" DNA is worth something

When scientists began studying chromosomes, they discovered that not all the base pairs were used as instructions for the cell. These *noncoding regions,* sometimes referred to as "junk" DNA because they seem to just be hanging around without helping guide the cell to fulfill its larger purpose, contain alleles that differ from person to person. This means that the junk DNA has characteristics that distinguish individuals from each other. Scientists soon began to use these alleles to identify individuals, especially in criminal investigations.

As more research was performed on the Y chromosome, scientists found that the noncoding regions could be used to define not only individual characteristics but also characteristics of larger populations into which individuals with these characteristics fit. In essence, these scientists discovered how to determine what population a particular human was a member of by using the noncoding regions of the DNA. They also discovered that the Y chromosome changes (or mutates) very little or not at all between fathers and sons. Because the Y chromosome is passed only from father to son, it is useful for tracing the direct paternal line of an individual's ancestry (as illustrated in Figure 11-2).

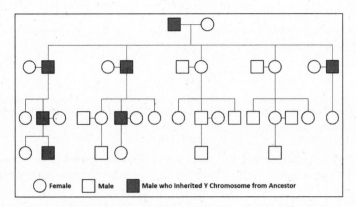

FIGURE 11-2:
The path of the Y chromosome through a family.

Female ○ Male □ ■ Male who Inherited Y Chromosome from Ancestor

The testing process

If you are interested in testing only testing Y-DNA, Family Tree DNA (www.family treedna.com) may be your best bet. There are two methods of testing the Y chromosome — Y-STR and Y-SNP. Both tests can be conducted using the same sample.

The process of testing the Y chromosome starts with a man swabbing the inside of his cheek with a sample collection device that usually looks something like a Q-Tip cotton swab. The swab collects cheek cells, which serve as the source for the DNA. After the laboratory receives the swab, the DNA is extracted using a process called *polymerase chain reaction* (PCR). This process makes thousands of copies of the DNA so that it can be analyzed.

In Y-STR (Y-short tandem repeat) testing, after copies of the DNA are made, short segments of DNA along the Y chromosome are analyzed. These sequences are called *markers,* and the location of the markers on the chromosome is called the *locus* (or plural *loci*). The markers are read by the sequence of the bases. (Remember, as we mention in Chapter 10, the bases are abbreviated A, G, C, and T.)

Each marker is given a name that usually begins with *DYS* — short for *DNA Y-chromosome segment*. When analyzing the markers, laboratory technicians look for the number of times that a segment of bases (usually three to five bases long) repeats. These segments of repeating bases are called *short tandem repeat polymorphisms* (STRPs).

Is your head spinning yet from all the definitions? Try using the book analogy again: Think of this book as the Y chromosome and this chapter as a gene on the chromosome. This page would be the locus where the segment is located — that is easily found by using the page number. The DNA Y-chromosome segment is the following sentence:

I like this book VERY VERY VERY much.

The short tandem repeat is the phrase *VERY VERY VERY* in the sentence — a set of letters that repeat.

Now see whether you can make sense of a real sequence of bases for the marker DYS393, keeping in mind that you can refer to the book example if needed:

gtggtcttctacttgtgtcaatac AGAT AGAT AGAT AGAT AGAT AGAT AGAT AGAT AGAT AGAT AGAT AGAT AGAT AGAT AGAT atgtatgtcttttctatgagacatac ctcatttttttggacttgagttc

To make it easier for you to see, we capitalized the letters and inserted spaces between the base segments composing the STR (which are AGAT). If you count the number of times the bases AGAT repeat, you find that the number of repeats for DYS393 for this individual is 15.

Comparing the results

After the number of repeats within a marker is calculated, we can compare the results of that marker plus a few other markers to see whether two or more individuals are related. We recommend testing at least 37 markers, so that you can differentiate your results from other individuals, especially if you have a common haplotype. (We discuss haplotypes in more detail in a minute). Family Tree DNA currently tests up to 111 markers. Table 11-1 shows a comparison between the markers of four individuals.

If you compare the results between Individuals A and B in Table 11-1, you can see that they have the same number of repeats in 11 of the 12 markers. Only at DYS439 is there a difference in the number of repeats, commonly called a *mutation*. Based on this information, we would say that a genetic distance of 1 exists between these two individuals. At 37 markers, a genetic distance of 1 would indicate that these two individuals are probably related; however, testing more markers would certainly give a better indication of how closely they may be related. A higher probability exists that Individuals B, C, and D are related because they match on all 12 markers — however, testing more markers would provide more conclusive evidence.

The result of a set of markers for an individual is called a *haplotype*. So, in the preceding chart, the haplotype for Individual A is DYS393 – 13, DYS390 – 25, DYS19/394 – 14, DYS391 – 11, DYS385a – 11, DYS395b – 11, DYS426 – 12, DYS388 – 12, DYS439 – 13, DYS389-1 – 13, DYS392 – 13, DYS 389-2 – 29.

TABLE 11-1   **A Comparison of 12 Markers for 4 Individuals**

ID	DYS393	DYS390	DYS19/394	DYS391	DYS385a	DYS385b	DYS426	DYS388	DYS439	DYS389-1	DYS392	DYS389-2
A	13	25	14	11	11	11	12	12	13	13	13	29
B	13	25	14	11	11	11	12	12	12	13	13	29
C	13	25	14	11	11	11	12	12	12	13	13	29
D	13	25	14	11	11	11	12	12	12	13	13	29
Modal	13	25	14	11	11	11	12	12	12	13	13	29

After you have haplotype results for an individual, it's important to get results from relatives of that individual. More specifically, it's important to get the haplotype results for relatives whose relationships can be documented by primary sources, including those in the extended family. These results help confirm the results of Individual A and establish an overall specific haplotype for the family. For example, say that all the individuals in Table 11-1 are related, and the fact is well documented with primary sources. After analyzing the results, a *modal haplotype* can be calculated by looking at the number of repeats that have the highest occurrence for each marker. Because all the results are the same for 11 out of 12 markers, the modal values for these are the same as the number of repeats for that marker. That leaves only one marker to calculate — DYS439. The results for DYS439 include one 13 and four 12s. That makes the modal value for that marker 12 — because it appears the most. So, the row marked *Modal* in Table 11-1 shows the haplotype for Individual A's family.

The modal haplotype for a family can be used to compare that family to other families with the same surname to determine the probability that the two families are related. A good way to see these relationships is to join a surname DNA project — we talk about how to find these projects later in this chapter.

Assessing the probability of a relationship

After the test is taken and the results compared, it's time to figure out the probability that two individuals are related. This probability is calculated by determining how often a change might occur to a marker over time. Fortunately, the testing companies calculate this for you and typically give you a tool (in the form of an online chart or written instructions) to compare two results.

Reviewing the data in Table 11-1, say that you want to determine how closely related Individual A may be to Individual B. To do this, you need to identify the *Time to Most Recent Common Ancestor* (TMRCA) for the two individuals. The TMRCA is pretty much what it sounds like — a calculation to determine when two individuals may have shared the same ancestor. As you'll see from this example, the calculation is not extremely precise, but it is close enough to point you in the right direction as you begin looking for supporting documentation.

The easiest way to determine the TMRCA between two individuals is to use an online utility. If you used Family Tree DNA, you can use the Time Predictor (TiP) tool that accompanies your results. The TiP tells you the probability that you matched another individual within a particular set of generations. If your testing company doesn't have one — or you're comparing results from more than one testing company — you can use the Y-Utility: Y-DNA Comparison Utility at www.mymcgee.com/tools/yutility.html. You have a lot of options with this utility, so we take it a step at a time.

1. **Point your web browser to the Y-Utility website at** `www.mymcgee.com/tools/yutility.html`**.**

   The page has a number of options and ways of displaying the data. We adjust some of these to make it easier to see the results.

2. **Ensure that the Marker table includes those markers necessary for the calculation.**

   In the table at the top of the screen, you can see 100 markers. In this example, you work with the first 13 markers from the left. Make sure that the following markers are selected for Exists and Enable: DYS393, DYS390, DYS19/394, DYS391, DYS385a, DYS385b, DYS426, DYS388, DYS439, DYS389-1, DYS392, and DYS 389-2. Be sure that DYS19b is not selected. You can leave the rest of the markers selected.

3. **Select the options that provide the appropriate calculation.**

   You are looking only for the TMRCA, so deselect the check boxes next to Ysearch, SMGF, Ybase, Yhrd, and Genetic Distance. Under the General Setup column, deselect the Create Modal Haplotype checkbox.

4. **Enter the marker values into the Paste Haplotype Rows Here field.**

   Make sure that you separate the values with a space, as shown here:

   ```
   A 13 25 14 11 11 11 12 12 13 13 13 29
   B 13 25 14 11 11 11 12 12 12 13 13 29
   ```

5. **Click Execute.**

   A new browser window appears with the calculation. In this example, the time to most recent common ancestor between Individuals A and B is estimated at 1,110 years. (The box with the TMRCA contains a blue background.)

Figure 11-3 shows the estimated TMRCA for Individuals A and B. Essentially, the results show a 50 percent probability that Individuals A and B shared a common ancestor within the past 1,110 years. So, as you can see, just testing on 12 markers doesn't give you conclusive evidence of how closely two people are related. However, it can certainly indicate that two individuals are not related — especially if more than 2 markers out of 12 don't match.

Haplogroups

We mention earlier in this chapter that haplotypes are a set of results of markers for an individual. When several similar haplotypes are categorized together, they compose a *haplogroup*. Haplogroups are useful for deep ancestry research (that is, research that is further back than the advent of surnames) and for placing a geographical context around the possible origin of the individuals in the haplogroup.

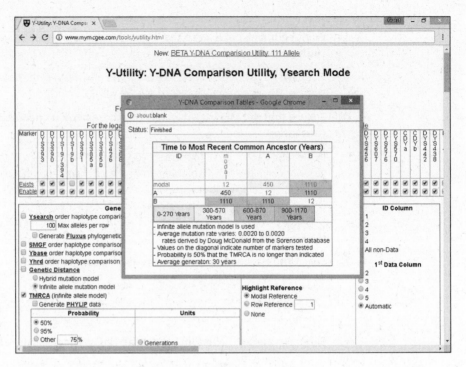

FIGURE 11-3:
Estimated TMRCA from the Y-Utility website.

Y chromosome haplogroups are categorized by the letters A through T. You can find the current Haplogroup Tree at `www.isogg.org/tree/`. These letter designations are based on mutations of certain locations of the Y chromosome. For instance, if an individual has a mutation at the M89 locus, that individual falls into a haplogroup between F and J. If the individual has a mutation at both the M89 and M170 loci, the individual is classified in the I haplogroup.

Haplogroups can also be used to show the genetic distribution of individuals in a geographic area. For example, Doug McDonald maintains a map of the distribution of haplogroups at `www.scs.uiuc.edu/~mcdonald/WorldHaplogroupsMaps.pdf`. So, if you're interested in finding out the distribution of Haplogroup I in Europe, you can match the color (pink) on the pie charts to determine how prevalent the haplogroup is in a particular area. From this chart, you can see that Haplogroup I has a strong concentration in Scandinavia and Northwest Europe.

Because haplogroups are large collections of haplotypes, it is useful to break down haplogroups into subgroups that have common traits. These subgroups are referred to as *subclades*. Subclades can help genealogists get a clearer picture of the geographical setting of that portion of the haplogroup.

Although the typical Y chromosome test can suggest a haplogroup and perhaps a high-level subclade, it normally takes additional testing to refine the subclade. In these additional tests, specific positions of the Y chromosome are examined for differences called *single nucleotide polymorphisms* (SNPs, or *"snips"*). Some SNPs are common and apply to a large population of people within a haplogroup. Other SNPs can be unique to an individual or a family — referred to as private SNPs. New SNPs are constantly being discovered, and that sometimes results in changes to the labels of subclades or the discovery of new subclades. To find the most up-to-date list of subclades, take a look at the International Society of Genetic Genealogy (ISOGG) Y-DNA Haplogroup Tree at `www.isogg.org/tree/`.

To illustrate how subclades work, look at the Haplogroup I example. Haplogroup I has a concentration in Northern Europe and a concentration in the Balkans. If you're in that haplogroup, you might be curious about which region your direct male ancestor came from. To find this out, SNP tests would be conducted on several areas of the Y chromosome and compared with the Y-DNA Haplogroup I and Its Subclades chart at `www.isogg.org/tree/ISOGG_HapgrpI.html`. (See Figure 11-4.) If the individual had mutations at the positions L41/PF3787, M170/PF3715, M258, P19_1, P19_2, P19_3, P19_4, P19_5, P38, P212, U179, that individual would be in the Haplogroup I (also referred to as I-M170). If further mutations were found at locations L64, L75, L80, L81, L118, L121/S62, L123, L124/S64, L125/S65, L157.1, L186, L187, L840, M253, M307.2/P203.2, M450/S109, P30, P40, S63, S66, S107, S108, S110, S111, the individual would be classified in the subclade I1 (or I-M253). Discovery of a mutation at DF29/S438 would put the individual in the subclade I1a (or I-DF29), and so on.

With the subclade in hand, you can consult a haplogroup distribution map to see where the subclade has the highest distribution. Figure 11-5 shows the distribution of Haplogroup I from a map on Family Tree DNA (`https://www.familytreedna.com/public/I1d/default.aspx?section=results`). Note that subclade I1 is listed as M253 on the map and that its greatest concentration of the subclade is found in Norway, Sweden, and Denmark, with lesser concentrations in eastern England and Normandy. This information can give you a hint as to where your ancestors may have originated.

After you discover the haplogroup of your results, you can join a Y-chromosome project for a particular haplogroup. Through a haplogroup project, you might be able to find out more about the origins of the haplogroup or the subclade within the haplogroup and communicate with others who are studying the same genetic group. To find a project for your haplogroup, see whether your DNA testing company already has a project for it or do a search using a general Internet search engine, such as Google, for something like *"Y-DNA Haplogroup I project"* or look for a haplogroup project hosted by the company that conducted your testing.

FIGURE 11-4:
The subclades of Haplogroup I from the ISOGG website.

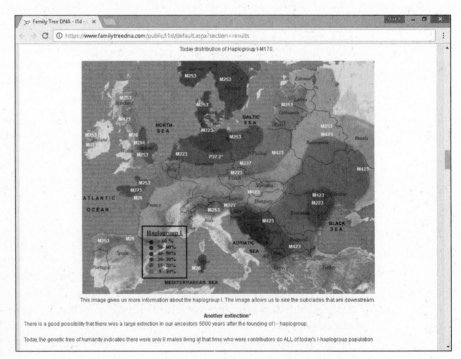

FIGURE 11-5:
Haplogroup I distribution map on Wikipedia.

Locating others with the same results

Spending the money to perform a Y-chromosome test doesn't do you much good unless you have something to compare the results with. The first place to look is your testing company. A list of matches will show you the test results of those who matched you exactly or were close matches. For example, Figure 11-6 shows a match list from Family Tree DNA. The table lists the genetic distance, name of the individual (we've blurred that column for privacy), the tests the person has taken, the most distant ancestor, Y-DNA haplogroup, terminal SNP, and match date.

To find others who have tested and received results that may match your results, you should look for a surname project currently under way for your direct male line. Some of the testing companies have established mechanisms for people to set up the projects that are housed on the testing companies' servers. For example, you can find a list of projects at the Family Tree DNA site at https://www.familytreedna.com/projects.aspx.

Even if you're a member of a surname project, you may want to distribute your results to a wider audience in the hopes of locating others with matching results. Ysearch (www.ysearch.org) allows you to enter your results, which can be then searched by other researchers.

If you don't want your results to be publicly accessible, you can use these sites to search for others with your same haplotype and contact them directly. Say that you want to see whether any matches exist for the surname Abell in Ysearch. Follow these steps:

1. **Open your web browser and go to** www.ysearch.org.

   At the top of the page are blue tabs with labels such as Create a New User, Edit an Existing User, Alphabetical List of Last Names, Search by Last Name, Search for Genetic Matches, Search by Haplogroup, Research Tools, and Statistics.

2. **Click the Search by Last Name tab.**

   The resulting page contains two ways to search. You can search by entering a surname or by using a user ID. Also, you can limit the search to a specific geographic area.

3. **In the Type Last Names to Search For field, type the surname you're researching, type the two words in the Captcha box, and click Search.**

   Note that you can search for multiple names at the same time using commas to separate them. It's a good idea to do this if the last name has some common derivations. For the purposes of this example, type **Abell, Abel, Able.**

4. **Click the numeral in the Name or Variants results box.**

5. **Choose a match by clicking a link in the results table.**

   In our example, the results page shows seven results. When we click the Abell result, the screen shows us brief information on each name, including an Abell from Maryland in Haplogroup I1.

6. **Click the User ID link to see the DNA results for this individual.**

   Figure 11-7 shows the test results for this individual. You also find a link on the page where you can email the individual who submitted the result to Ysearch.

A general reference database is also available. The Y Chromosome Haplotype Reference Database, at www.yhrd.org, allows you to see the distribution of a particular haplotype. However, it is a scientific database geared toward DNA researchers, so it doesn't contain a lot of information useful to genealogists. Oxford Ancestors (www.oxfordancestors.com) also allows you to search its database if you log in as a guest.

Mitochondrial (mtDNA) testing

In the preceding section, you look at Y-chromosome DNA testing that assists in the genetic identification of the direct male line of a family. In this section, you look at mitochondrial DNA testing, which allows the identification of the genetic information of the direct female line of a family.

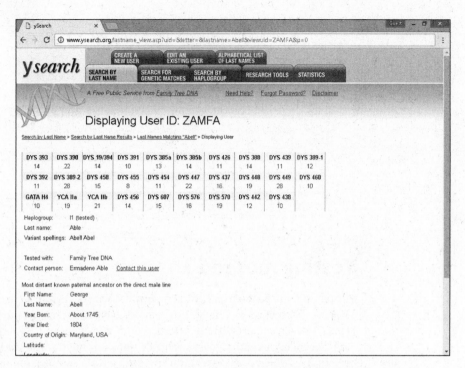

FIGURE 11-7:
Results from
Ysearch.org for
the surname *Abel*.

The mitochondrion is the power plant of the cell. It's outside the nucleus and has its own distinct genome, called mtDNA, which is inherited from the female parent by both male and female children. (Figure 11-8 shows the inheritance.) Because it also mutates at a very slow rate, the mtDNA is good for identifying genetic relationships over many, many years and generations, as shown in Figure 11-9.

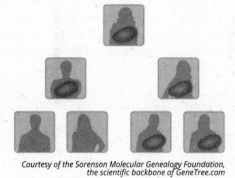

FIGURE 11-8:
Mitochondrial
DNA is passed
from the mother
to her children.

*Courtesy of the Sorenson Molecular Genealogy Foundation,
the scientific backbone of GeneTree.com*

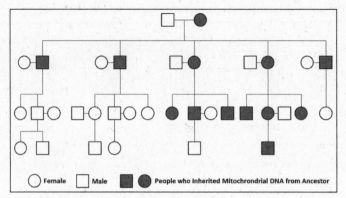

FIGURE 11-9:
The path of the
mitochondrial
DNA through a
family.

Testing method

For testing, mitochondrial DNA is divided into three regions — a coding region, a
Hypervariable Region One (HVR1), and a Hypervariable Region Two (HVR2).
Genealogical tests are usually conducted on a sequence of Hypervariable Region
One, a sequence of both Hypervariable Regions One and Two, or the full mtDNA. The
results from these sequences are compared with a sample from either the Cambridge Reference Sequence (CRS), revised Cambridge Reference Sequence (rCRS),
or the Reconstructed Sapiens Reference Sequence (RSRS). The CRS is the mitochondrial sequence of the first individual to have her mitochondrial DNA
sequenced. The differences between the sample and the CRS are considered mutations for the purposes of assigning a haplogroup to the sample.

How is this accomplished in practical terms? At the beginning of the previous
chapter, we mention that DNA testing was used to identify the remains of the
family of the last Czar of Russia. The results of the remains thought to be Czarina
Alexandra were compared with Prince Philip, and the results matched. (Prince
Philip and Czarina Alexandra were both descended from Queen Victoria.) The
results were listed as the following:

```
HVR1: 16111T, 16357C HVR2: 263G, 315.1C
```

In Chapter 10, we talk about how DNA is coded. In that section, we mention that a
DNA sequence contains four bases: adenine (A), guanine (G), cytosine (C), and
thymine (T). These same bases are used in sequencing mitochondrial DNA.

The first result for Czarina Alexandra was 16111T. This result is interpreted as the
substitution of thymine in the location 16111 of the Hypervariable One region.
The second result translates as the substitution of cytosine at location 16357 of the

same region. The next result, 263G, shows a substitution of guanine at location 263 in the Hypervariable Two region. The fourth result is a bit different in that it contains a .1, indicating that an extra base was found at that location. This means that the fourth result shows that an extra cytosine is found at the 315 location in the Hypervariable Two region. Based on the changes between Czarina Alexandra's sequence and the Cambridge Reference Sequence, her sample was classified in mitochondrial Haplogroup H.

TIP

Keep in mind that although they're named in the same manner, Y chromosome haplogroups and mitochondrial haplogroups are two different entities.

It is worth noting that 23andMe (www.23andme.com) tests mitochondrial DNA using SNP sequencing. However, it doesn't publish the results as differences with the reference sequence. If you want to know the difference, you need to download the mitochondrial result from 23andMe and compare it to a reference sequence yourself.

Making sense of the results

Mitochondrial DNA changes (or mutates) at a slow rate. This makes its uses for genealogical purposes very different than the uses for Y chromosomes, which change at a faster rate and can link family members together at closer intervals. However, mtDNA is useful for determining long-term relationships, as in the case of the Romanov family.

When two individuals have the same mutations within the Hypervariable One region, it is considered a *low-resolution match*. If the individuals have a low-resolution match and are classified in the same haplogroup, there is about a 50 percent chance that they shared a common ancestor within the past 52 generations (or about 1,300 years). If they have a low-resolution match and the haplogroups are not the same, it is considered a coincidence, and the probability is that the two individuals did not share a common ancestor within a measurable time frame. Depending on your result set, you might get a lot of low-resolution matches. To see whether a connection really exists, it is useful to test both the Hypervariable One and Hypervariable Two regions.

A *high-resolution match* occurs when two individuals match exactly at both Hypervariable One and Hypervariable Two regions. Individuals having high-resolution matches are more likely to be related within a genealogically provable time frame. With a high-resolution match, there is about a 50 percent probability of sharing a common ancestor within the past 28 generations (about 700 years).

Finding others with the same results

Similar to Y chromosome testing, you might want to post your mitochondrial DNA results to some public databases. One place to post results is at www.mitosearch.org, shown in Figure 11-10. To find more information on mitochondrial DNA scientific databases, check out MITOMAP at www.mitomap.org.

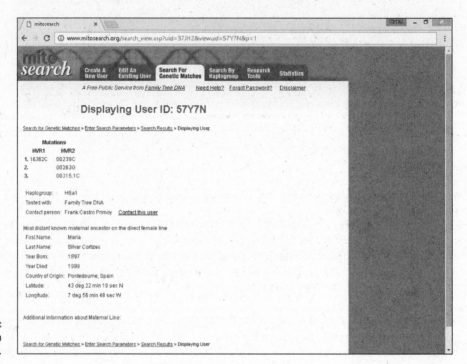

FIGURE 11-10:
An entry from
MitoSearch.org.

» **Finding cousins with autosomal DNA**

» **Using utilities for autosomal DNA results**

Chapter **12**

Autosomal DNA (atDNA) Testing

Wouldn't it be great if you could take a single DNA test and then immediately see your genetic connection to all your ancestors? That day isn't here quite yet, but testing your autosomal DNA is a step in the right direction. Over the course of this chapter, we look at the various uses of autosomal DNA (atDNA) and check out some of the utilities that can help you sort out the pieces of the puzzle that is autosomal DNA.

But First a Quick Review

You might remember from Chapter 10 (if not, feel free to flip back there for a quick look), that humans have 23 pairs of chromosomes. One pair of those chromosomes are the sex chromosomes (X and Y chromosomes). The remaining 22 pairs are referred to as autosomal chromosomes. Autosomal chromosomes are inherited from your parents — one chromosome in each pair from your father and one from your mother. As you are inheriting only one chromosome in each pair from each parent, you are inheriting about half of your parent's DNA. As you go back further in time, each successive generation is only inheriting half of the previous generation.

Your parents inherited about half of their DNA from each of their parents, therefore you inherit about one-quarter of each of your grandparent's autosomal DNA, 12.5 percent of each great-grandparent's DNA, and so forth. We use the term "about" because it isn't an exact number, and it varies from person to person. For example, Figure 12-1 shows the results of autosomal DNA inheritance of two girls who are sisters. Notice that Daughter 2 received far less DNA from her paternal grandmother than Daughter 1. Conversely, Daughter 1 received almost exactly a half split of her maternal DNA.

	Paternal		Maternal	
	Grandfather	Grandmother	Grandfather	Grandmother
Daughter 1	23.03948	26.96052	24.906165	25.0938335
Daughter 2	31.532865	18.467135	22.204345	27.795655

Not only did each girl receive a different percentage of DNA, they also did not receive contribution of DNA from the grandparents on exactly the same locations on the chromosome. Figure 12-2 shows the amount and location of the inherited DNA from each grandparent on each chromosome. Notice that for any given chromosome, the location and length of the segments (a segment is the DNA contained between two points on a chromosome) are different. And, on Chromosome 20, notice that Daughter 2 did not inherit any DNA from her paternal grandmother, whereas Daughter 1 has a good amount of DNA from each paternal grandparent. We think it is interesting that there is a strong tendency for Daughter 2 to inherit all or almost all of the DNA from a single grandparent on Chromosomes 20, 21, and 22, where Daughter 1 tends to be a mix.

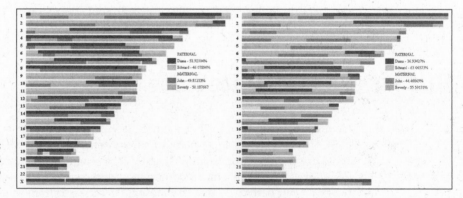

FIGURE 12-2:
Locations of DNA
inherited by two
girls.

It is important to keep in mind that, except for identical twins, autosomal DNA is different in every individual. You might recall this is because of the process of recombination (for quick review on recombination, refer to Chapter 10). Two sisters won't match as a result of recombination; neither will cousins, aunts, uncles, and so on. Nor will each person inherit DNA from the same set of distant ancestors — this becomes important in analyzing autosomal DNA results, as we discuss later in this chapter. Just because your sibling matches a distant ancestor and you don't doesn't mean that you aren't related to the ancestor — just not through genetic family history.

Testing Process

You might be asking, "How does DNA testing work?" After you submit a saliva sample, the testing company inspects the sample to ensure it is useable. Then DNA is extracted from the sample and several copies are made. The copies are then examined to determine the nucleotide (or base) value at certain locations — or single nucleotide polymorphisms (SNPs). These values are either A, T, C, or G. For a quick recap on SNPs, revisit Chapter 11. And for a review of nucleotides and bases, check back in Chapter 10. Figure 12-3 shows what the raw output looks like from the testing service 23andMe.

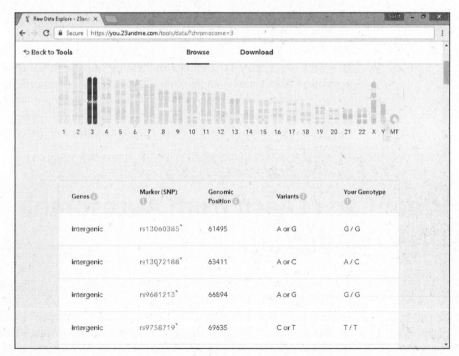

FIGURE 12-3:
The raw data view of a chromosome at 23andMe.

Genes	Marker (SNP)	Genomic Position	Variants	Your Genotype
intergenic	rs13060385	61495	A or G	G / G
intergenic	rs13072188	63411	A or C	A / C
intergenic	rs9681213	66894	A or G	G / G
intergenic	rs9758719	69635	C or T	T / T

The Marker (SNP) column shows the name of the marker and contains a link to the National Center for Biotechnology Information (NCBI) page for that SNP (containing a lot of scientific details). The Genomic Position column contains the location of the marker on the chromosome. The variants column lists the nucleotide value that can be contained in that position — it will be two of the four nucleotides. The final column shows the nucleotides that are present in the tester's DNA sample.

As autosomal DNA is composed of more chromosomes than Y-DNA or mitochondrial DNA, a lot more SNPs are tested — numbering in the hundreds of thousands. Now, you are probably thinking that you don't have the time to compare the values of hundreds of thousands of SNPs. And, you're absolutely right. Fortunately, you don't have to because the testing company does it for you.

To establish whether someone is related, the testing company looks at how many SNPs are the same along an area of the chromosome. This is different than how it's done when testing for Y-DNA or mitochondrial DNA, which both compare the individual values of SNPs. In other words, when comparing autosomal DNA, the testing company looks to see how long a segment of like-DNA is between two individuals. The longer the segment on a chromosome and the more shared segments across all chromosomes, the more DNA is shared and therefore, the greater the probability is that two individuals are related. We show a practical example of this later in the chapter.

When the sequencing is complete, the testing company then runs an algorithm to determine what samples in its database match your sample. The algorithm varies between testing companies, so you can have two samples that are exactly the same, but yield a slightly different degree of relatedness between companies. The tester can then look at results from the database in the matches section of their reports.

What Can I Learn from Autosomal DNA Testing?

The two major uses for autosomal DNA in terms of family history are ethnicity estimation and "cousin matching." Ethnicity estimation is what you likely have seen on television commercials for DNA testing companies — "I found out that I am x percent Scottish." Cousin matching is using autosomal DNA to find people who are related to you genetically. By finding a third or fourth cousin, sometimes you can learn a great deal about a part of the family you may not even know existed.

Other uses for autosomal DNA testing are to map the DNA of your ancestors, once you find enough cousins who share DNA, and to look at inherited traits and health conditions.

Ethnicity Estimation

When forensic scientists began looking at DNA, they recognized that certain genetic markers were common to particular ethnicities. After enough markers were identified with ethnicities, they could begin to assess what percentage of ethnicity a person might possess. Family historians picked up on this and believed the same types of tests might be able to shed some light on the ethnicities of their ancestors — especially in the areas of identifying Native American, Jewish, and African ancestry.

The first important thing to notice is that we use the term ethnicity *estimate*. This is because it is just an estimate; not a comprehensive examination of the ethnicity of all of your ancestors. It is simply an estimate based upon the sample that you provided. And, keep in mind, you may not match the ethnicity estimate of your sibling. Remember, we all recombine differently leading to different results.

So, how do testing companies create the ethnicity estimates, you ask? They test the DNA of *reference populations,* then compare that DNA to your DNA. A reference population can be created when a testing company surveys a group of people in a specific location. They may ask questions about how long the family has lived in the location that they currently live, and so forth. After the testing company determines that the person is a good candidate for a reference population, their DNA results are added to others in the same area or with the same ethnicity to create a reference sample (much like the reference sample that we talked about with mitochondrial DNA in Chapter 11).

When you take an autosomal DNA test, your results are compared to the sample from reference populations. If you share enough of the segment of a reference population, then that reference population is included in your ethnicity estimate. Figure 12-4 shows ethnicity estimates overlaid on the chromosomes of a tester — what 23andMe calls *chromosome painting*. As you can see, there are different ethnicities estimated on each pair of chromosomes. Notice that one of the pairs of Chromosome 3 has a lot of mixture of ethnicities, including British and Irish, Native American, West African, broadly Northwestern European, and Southern European. The other pair on that chromosome is all British and Irish.

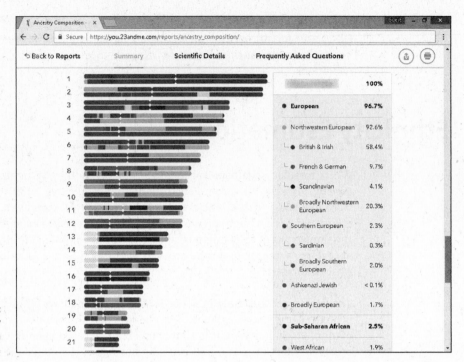

FIGURE 12-4:
Ethnicity
estimates shown
at 23andMe.

If you take an ethnicity test, you can expect to receive a copy of the sequences examined and an interpretation of the results. The interpretation usually comes in the form of a percentage of a certain ethnicity. For example, Figure 12-5 shows a view of a person's ethnicity at Family Tree DNA. In this case, it shows the following general ethnic percentages:

European: 95%

West Africa: <2%

Central Asia: 2%

South America: <2%

REMEMBER

The controversy with autosomal testing is that the DNA in each individual recombines differently. This means two children born from the same two parents could measure with different ethnicities because their DNA does not recombine the exact same way. Also, the percentages quoted by testing companies can often have a significant error rate or change over time as new research comes to light. And, the estimates are heavily dependent upon the reference population that it is compared against. Things such as migration patterns can have a large effect on the reference population. As a result, you could get different findings from different companies. For example, Figure 12-6 shows the findings of the same person tested at Family Tree DNA, 23andMe, and AncestryDNA.

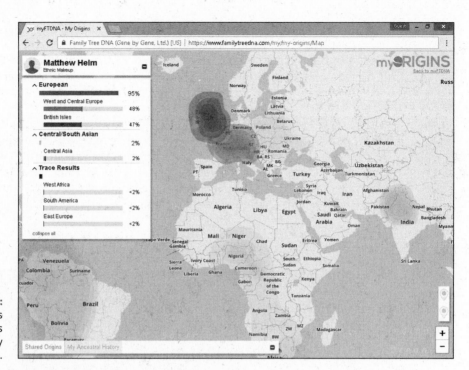

FIGURE 12-5:
myOrigins
ethnicity results
from Family
Tree DNA.

FIGURE 12-6:
Comparison of
ethnicity
estimates at
three testing
companies.

	Family Tree DNA	23andMe	AncestryDNA
European	95	98.7	--
--Northwestern European	--	94.4	--
---British & Irish	47	58.5	86
---French & German	--	12.2	--
---Scandinavian	0	5.3	1.0
---Broadly Northwestern European	--	18.4	--
--Southern European	--	2.2	--
---Sardinian	--	0.3	--
---Italian	--	0.2	3.0
---Iberian Peninsula	0	--	1.0
---Broadly Southern European	--	1.7	--
--Ashkenazi Jewish	0	<0.1	--
--Broadly European	--	1.9	<1.0
--West and Central Europe	48	--	--
East Europe	<2.0	--	<1.0
Subsaharan African/Africa	0	1.0	<1.0
--West African	<2.0	1.0	<1.0
East Asian & Native American	0	0.3	--
--Native American	0	0.2	--
--Broadly East Asian & Native American	--	<0.1	--
South America	<2.0	--	--
Asia South	--	--	<1.0
West Asia	--	--	4.0
--Caucasus	--	--	4.0
Unassigned	--	<0.1	--

Another testing company, Living DNA (`https://www.livingdna.com/en-us`) is focusing on creating reference populations on a more localized level. Currently, they have defined 80 world regions, including 21 in Britain and Ireland. They recently announced an effort to create local level populations in Germany.

A slight twist on ethnicity estimates is Genetic Communities at AncestryDNA. Genetic Communities are defined by Ancestry DNA as groups of testers who are connected through DNA because they descend from a population of common ancestors. A lot of these communities are based on geographic locations or migration paths of the population. An example of a Genetic Community — Early Settlers of the Lower Midwest and Virginia — is shown in Figure 12-7.

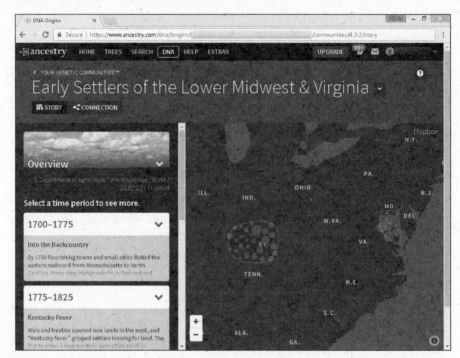

FIGURE 12-7:
A Genetic Community at AncestryDNA.

Relationship Testing

As we mention earlier, Y chromosome testing is useful for tracing the direct male line. Mitochondrial testing is good for tracing a direct female line. Autosomal testing is useful for tracing ancestors anywhere in your pedigree, as shown in Figure 12-8.

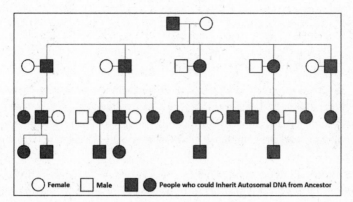

FIGURE 12-8:
Individuals who can potentially inherit autosomal DNA.

However, before autosomal DNA testing can find a match between two testers and an ancestor, important things need to be in place:

» Tester 1 must have inherited DNA from Ancestor A.

» Tester 2 must have inherited DNA from Ancestor A.

» Tester 1 and Tester 2 must have inherited DNA from Ancestor A at the same location on the same chromosome (a matching segment).

» The length of the matching segment between Tester 1 and Tester 2 must meet or exceed the matching criteria of the testing company.

As we mentioned before, there are reasons why someone who is descended from a specific ancestor did not receive DNA from that ancestor — recombination being a principal reason. Each time a new generation is born, the likelihood of recombination reducing inherited segments to a length beneath the matching criteria increases.

Having said that, it is almost a "guarantee" that second cousins and closer will share DNA. If they don't, a non-paternity event (such as adoption or misattributed paternity) should be investigated. However, after second cousins, the chance of matching starts decreasing rapidly. By the time you get to a sixth cousin, you have a probability measuring in the single digits of matching their autosomal DNA with enough length to show as a match. Before we get started on how to analyze autosomal DNA results, there are a few terms that you need to know.

» A segment of DNA is considered *identical by state* (IBS) if two individuals possess segments containing identical nucleotides. For a review of nucleotides, see Chapter 10.

» If the IBS segment can be shown to come from a common ancestor of the two individuals unchanged by recombination, then it is considered *identical by descent* (IBD). All IBD segments are IBS, but not all IBS segments are IBD.

>> A method to help figure out whether a segment is IBD is called *phasing*. Phasing consists of identifying whether a particular DNA segment came from the mother or father of the tester.

>> When three or more testers share a matching DNA segment (same location on the same chromosome) and have documented descent from an ancestor(s) it is called *triangulation*. The more individuals that can triangulate a segment, increases the confidence in the assignment of that segment to the ancestor.

We know all these definitions can be confusing. To reduce a little of the confusion, going forward we will refer to two types of segments — *identical by descent (IBD)* or *non-identical by descent (non-IBD)*. Either the segment can be matched to an ancestor through triangulation (IBD segment) or it can't be matched (non-IBD segment). We won't refer to IBS anymore, but we gave you the definition earlier in this chapter in case you see it in the future.

Back to a familiar family

REMEMBER

You probably thought you had heard the last of William Henry Abell and Elizabeth "Lizzie" Pickerell (our faithful example ancestors from earlier in this book). Well, they're back! To give you real world examples of how to interpret autosomal DNA results, we'll use results from testing descendants of William Henry and Lizzie, as well as descendants of Lizzie's sister Mary and her husband William. To orient you to the family tree and the descendants, take a look at Figure 12-9.

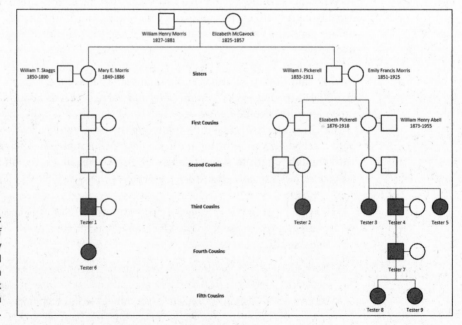

FIGURE 12-9: Family tree of William Henry Morris and Elizabeth McGavock annotated with DNA testers.

You probably already realized that William as a first name was popular with this family, so we'll do our best to add last names to clarify who we are talking about. At the top of the family tree are Lizzie's grandparents, William Henry Morris and Elizabeth McGavock. William Henry Morris and Elizabeth McGavock had more than two children, but to simplify things we only included those that were relevant to our analysis. Two of their daughters were Mary E. Morris who married William T. Skaggs and Emily Francis Morris who married William J. Pickerell. William J. Pickerell and Emily Morris were the parents of our Lizzie Pickerell.

There are nine testers involved in this analysis. They are indicated as shaded shapes on the above chart. They come from three different family lines and represent three generations. We included descriptions down the middle so you can see at a glance the relationships between the family in the left column and the family in the right column. In this example, Tester 1 and Tester 2 are third cousins. In truth, only three testers were needed for triangulation, however; we show you as we go along why using more testers provides more opportunities for discovery.

Objectives of the test

We want to accomplish a few things with this analysis. First, we want to provide evidence of Matthew's descent from William Henry Morris and Elizabeth McGavock. Although we have census records, marriage records, and birth records to substantiate this, we want another piece of evidence to help confirm the relationship.

Second, as Lizzie Pickerell died early in her life, Matthew's family lost touch with the Pickerell side. We don't know much about the family and want to find distant cousins who might know more information about the family that wouldn't be found in the records that we already have.

Third, in their "spare" time, Matthew and his daughter are working on a project to estimate what the genome of his grandparents looked like. Matthew's grandparents passed away before DNA testing became an "in" thing. Thus we need to test his father, aunts, and uncles, as well as, members of the extended family to help recreate the genomes as best we can. As his family has double cousins, it is difficult to sort out what DNA segments belong to what family. By comparing the results of extended family members, we can begin to sort out the genomes.

Fourth, we want to begin constructing the genomes of Matthew's distant ancestors — Emily Francis Morris and Elizabeth Pickerell. By identifying what segments are from these ancestors, we can identify other researchers who have DNA matches, but don't know how they are related.

Playing the match game

To launch the analysis, we identified individuals who were related along the Pickerrel and Morris family lines using match lists on two different websites. We found Tester 2 using the match list at 23andMe and found Tester 6 at the GEDmatch site (we discuss GEDmatch later in the chapter).

Each of the three major testing companies maintains a database of results. They use algorithms to compare the results between two individuals and determine whether they are related in a genealogically relevant time period (that is, a time period where the relationship could be confirmed through historical records). When testers decide to find relatives, they consult *match lists*. Figure 12-10 shows the match list on the AncestryDNA (https://www.ancestry.com/dna) website.

FIGURE 12-10: AncestryDNA match list.

The AncestryDNA match list contains the username of the individual, a calculation of the relationship, a confidence level of the match, and a link to a family tree of the individual if they maintain one. If you see the shaky leaf, then AncestryDNA has calculated who it thinks is the most recent common ancestor(s). Clicking on the username gives you additional information such as the date last logged in (very useful to see if the person is an active researcher), pedigree and surnames (if the individual has posted a public family tree you can reach it from here), shared matches, map and locations (shows birth locations that are in common in both the individual's and your family trees) and a button to send the individual a message. To see the amount of shared DNA between you and the individual, click on the information (i) button next to the confidence level. It will show you the number of centimorgans and shared segments. This can be a little misleading depending on the length of the segments. We talk more about segment length in a minute. AncestryDNA shows a person as being a match if they share at least one segment of 5 cM. Unfortunately, at that level, you may see some false positives.

The Family Tree DNA FamilyFinder match mechanism works in a similar way. The match list contains the name of the tester, a link to a pedigree (if they have posted one), a link to email the tester directly, match date, relationship calculation, amount of shared centimorgans, longest shared block, an indicator of whether there is a match on the X chromosome, a link to add the individual to the family tree stored on the Family Tree DNAWeb site, and a list of ancestral surnames (if the tester has designated those). Clicking on the plus sign on the right side of the match will show the tests that have been taken by the tester, and the mitochondrial and Y-DNA haplogroups of the tester. The FamilyFinder will show a match if the largest segment of matching DNA is at least 5.5 cM. The site cautions that it is rare to be able to show genealogical relationships in a match where the largest segment is less than 7 cM.

23andMe's match list is in the DNA Relatives section. Here you can see the individual's name, sex, relationship calculation, the side of the match (this appears if a parent has tested and you have connected them with your results) and the sharing status (if the person is not sharing Ancestry Reports, there is limited information that you can view). If you are sharing Ancestry Reports with the tester, clicking on the match will show you how much DNA you share with the individual, which segments you share DNA on, ancestor locations (available if the tester submitted them), ethnicity estimates shared with the tester, haplogroups of the tester, and a list of names shared in common with the tester. If you are not sharing reports, you will see how much DNA you share with the individual, a button to request sharing, ancestor locations (available if the tester submitted them), ethnicity estimates shared with the tester, haplogroups of the tester, and a list of names shared in common with the tester. 23andMe DNA Relatives will show matches where at least one segment is 7 cM or greater, plus matches on 700 single nucleotide polymorphisms (SNPs).

Set your phasing to stun

In Chapter 10, we discussed that you receive one chromosome from your father and one from your mother. When testing companies look at your DNA, they record the nucleotides and their position on the chromosome, but they don't know which parent contributed the DNA. To figure that out, a process called *phasing* can be done by the testing company or by the tester themselves.

Phasing is the process of attributing your DNA as being inherited from your father or your mother. This becomes critical for assigning things like ethnicity estimates to a parent or for figuring out whether a segment match is on the DNA contributed by your father or mother (or both).

Two things that phased results can do for you include reducing the number of false positive (non-IBD) results among your matches and helping to assign segments to specific ancestors (chromosome mapping).

There are a few ways to phase your DNA:

» **Trio phasing:** This is phasing that can be done when both parents and a child have been tested (hence the trio). To increase confidence of the phasing, you can also include siblings in the phasing process.

» **Family phasing:** If both parents are not available for testing, you can test one parent and all of the children of those parents. Also, testing grandchildren and the parents' first cousins can help fill in the gaps.

» **Statistical phasing:** Testing companies sometimes use statistical phasing based upon the frequency of alleles in reference populations. Statistical phasing is most accurate for longer segments.

For more on phasing, see the International Society of Genetic Genealogy Wiki entry on Phasing at https://isogg.org/wiki/Phasing. You can also find a list of phasing utilities towards the end of the article.

As we had DNA test results from a father, mother, and son, we could do trio phasing for this project (the mother isn't listed on the diagram as being a tester but we had her results for phasing purposes).

We have something In Common With you

One of the ways to reduce the amount of time spent assessing how a match is related to you is to use the *In Common With* functionality on the testing company's website. As you might have guessed, In Common With functionality indicates other testers who share DNA with the same individual that you match.

If your parents have tested and they show up as having DNA in common with another individual, then you know which side (or potentially, sides) the tester matches. If results from your parents are not available, you can use another person (aunt, uncle, cousin, etc.) for whom you know the ancestry to determine whether the match is on the maternal or paternal side.

In the case of 23andMe, after selecting the individual from the DNA Relatives list, you will see the relatives in common section at the bottom of the page. The table lists the relative in common, how they are related to you, the calculated relationship between the tester and the relative in common, and a link to show the shared DNA segments in the chromosome browser (if sharing is enabled).

There are two ways to use the In Common With functionality in Family Tree DNA. The first way is to check the box next to a match on the Family Finder matches page and then click the In Common With button at the top of the page. The page will refresh showing all the matches that share DNA between you and the selected tester. A second and more targeted way is to use the Family Finder Matrix tool. You can find a link to the Matrix Tool on the Family Tree DNA dashboard page in the Family Finder section, just under the myOrigins button. Within the Matrix tool, you can select a group of up to ten people and it will show you a grid of the relationships between each individual (see Figure 12-11).

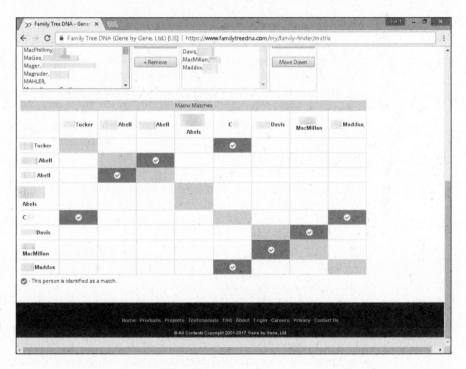

FIGURE 12-11:
Family Finder
Matrix showing
matches with
DNA in common.

In AncestryDNA, you can use the Shared Matches tab. When you click on a username in your match list, you are taken to the tester's page. In the middle of the page are three buttons, Pedigree and Surnames, Shared Matches, and Map and Locations. Click on the Shared Matches button and you are shown a list of shared matches sorted by the relationship calculation.

REMEMBER

Just because a person shows up with the In Common With tool doesn't mean all three people share a common ancestor. It is possible that Tester A shares Ancestor 1 with Tester B. However, Tester B shares Ancestor 2 with Tester C. Tester C will still show up in the In Common With results because they indeed share DNA with both — just not the same DNA with both.

In our case, we knew we were on the right trail with Tester 2, when we used the In Common With section of the 23andMe site. Testers 3, 4, 5, 8, and 9 were listed as sharing DNA with Tester 2. So, we knew that it was probable that Tester 2 was on the paternal side of the family

Sticking with tradition

Before getting too far down the road, it's important to establish the paper trail, so that we were sure we were investigating the correct family line. We needed to make sure that we could document that Tester 2 and Tester 6 were descended from William Henry Morris and Elizabeth McGavock.

Tester 2 had posted four surnames in the relatives section of her page on 23andMe. One of these names was Pickerrell, a variant spelling of Pickerell. Pickerell is not a common name, so we thought this was a promising lead — knowing that Matthew was descended from William Henry Morris and Elizabeth McGavock through Lizzie Pickerell. Matthew used 23andMe's internal message system to contact Tester 2. Tester 2 confirmed that their common ancestors was William J. Pickerell and Emily Francis Morris.

It was a little bit easier to find the link with Tester 6. Tester 6 had posted her family tree on the GEDmatch site. Matthew just had to identify the common ancestor in the tree. In this case, the common ancestors were William Henry Morris and Elizabeth McGavock.

A quick check of supporting documentation showed the descent of both individuals, so we were off and running.

Browsing through the chromosomes

After we located suitable candidates with evidence of descent, it was time to analyze the chromosomes to determine the location and length of all the shared segments. We could do this through a chromosome browser.

Unfortunately, only Family Tree DNA and 23andMe have chromosome browsers. The lack of a chromosome browser on AncestryDNA is a big hurdle to overcome when trying to triangulate results. To get around this limitation, if you find a match on AncestryDNA and wish to triangulate the results, you will have to ask the tester on AncestryDNA to submit their results to a third-party utility site (see the section on utilities at the end of the chapter for more information).

You can find a button for the Family Tree DNA Family Finder chromosome browser on the myDashboard page. Once on the chromosome browser page you can select up to five matches to see where and how much DNA testers share.

On 23andMe you first must be sharing Ancestry Reports to use the chromosome browser to compare results with another tester. Once you are sharing Ancestry Reports, you can click on a tester from the DNA Relatives page. A static version of the chromosome browser is available showing the number of overlapping segments and their locations. For a more interactive chromosome browser, click on the DNA link at the top of the DNA Relatives page. From this page, you can select six testers to compare. Figure 12-12 shows the comparison of Tester 2 and Tester 7 using the 23andMe chromosome browser.

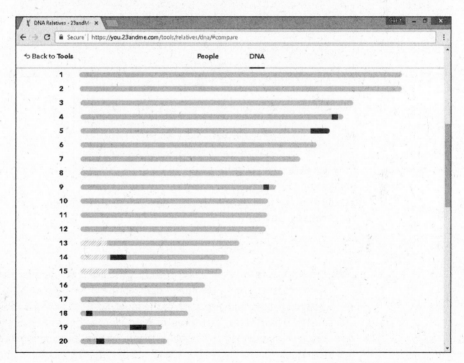

FIGURE 12-12: The 23andMe chromosome browser.

In the case of Tester 6, we were able to use the chromosome browser on GEDmatch to compare our results. GEDmatch allows testers to import the results from the major testing services into their website for comparison. AncestryDNA results are accepted on the site — the workaround for the lack of a chromosome browser on the AncestryDNA site.

Triangulating the data

Now that we could view the data of the testers through chromosome browsers we could analyze the data. When two or more testers share a matching DNA segment and have documented descent from an ancestor(s) it is called *triangulation*. Triangulation is the objective in an autosomal DNA test. So, we want know the location of the triangulated segments for each tester. We used Kitty Munson's segment mapper utility (www.kittymunson.com/dna/SegmentMapper.php) to generate Figure 12-13. The figure shows the locations of some of the shared segments of the testers. These are not all the shared segments. To keep things simple we only included the locations on five chromosomes in the figure. Also, the segments that are mapped are not to scale. The length of the lines representing the segments are in proportion to the overall size of the chromosome. So, a small line on one chromosome may actually be a segment that is longer than a segment with a longer line on another chromosome. We analyze each of the five chromosomes to show you how triangulation works.

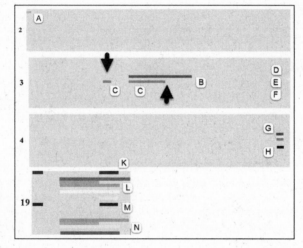

FIGURE 12-13: Locations of shared segments on five chromosomes.

>> **Chromosome 2:** Tester 1 and Tester 3, who are third cousins, matched with a segment length of 8.1 cM (marked as segment A on Figure 12-13). As neither Tester 2 (from another branch of the family) or Testers 4 or 5 (siblings of Tester 3) matched at that same location, we wouldn't immediately say that the result is triangulated. It is possible that it is a non-IBD segment (a segment that does not match through descent, but rather by recombination). Consulting Tim Janzen's probability table (https://isogg.org/wiki/Identical_by_descent#Ranges_of_total_centiMorgans_of_IBD_segments_based_on_family_relationship), there is a five percent chance that Tester 1 and 3 share a common ancestor in the last six generations with a segment match of this length. We could triangulate this segment in the future, if we found more testers with proven descent that matched at this location.

» **Chromosome 3:** Tester 2 and Tester 5, who are second cousins, matched on two segments — one segment with a length of 9.3 cM and the other 8.6 cM (segment C). Tester 2 and Tester 3, also second cousins (Testers 3 and 5 are siblings), matched with a segment length of 26.2 cM (segment B). The overlap of segment B and the second segment C of 8.6 cM is a definite triangulation. However, it is quite probable that the first part of segment C and the last un-overlapped portion of segment B are IBD, as well. Probably what we see here is that a recombination occurred with Tester 3 that eliminated the first segment that would have matched Tester 5's first segment C. Also, Tester 5 seems to have had a recombination at the end of segment C, otherwise it would have been as long as Tester 3's segment B. Because Tester 3 and Tester 5 are siblings segments B and C should have been the same length — except that recombinations (where the black arrows are located) occurred changing the DNA that was inherited from their mother. And Tester 4 (Tester 3 and 5's brother) recombined the entire segment out of his DNA. If we were only testing Tester 4 and his descendants, we wouldn't have found this shared segment. This is a good example of why it is useful to test more than one person from a family group. Tester 4 did match Tester 2 near the end of the chromosome (segment D) at 8.7 cM. Segment E is Tester 4's son, Tester 7 who matched at 8.4 cM. Tester 7 lost some of the DNA, perhaps to recombination. Tester 7's daughter (Tester 9) shares the same amount at 8.4 cM, so no recombination occurred. But what about Tester 8, Tester 7's other daughter? Due to recombination, she no longer has DNA that matches Tester 2 at that position in the chromosome. We mentioned there was a triangulation on this chromosome. However, we can't triangulate this to William Henry Morris and Elizabeth McGavock. As no one from the Mary E. Morris line triangulated, the best we can do is triangulate these segments to the nearest common ancestor to Testers 2, 3, 4, and 5 — William J. Pickerell and Emily Francis Morris. In the future, it may be possible to triangulate this to a more distant ancestor with test results from someone outside of the Pickerell-Morris line. But for right now, we don't know whether the segments are from the Pickerell or Morris line (or both).

» **Chromosome 4:** Tester 2 matches segment G with Testers 3, 4, and 5. But again, it can only be traced back to William J. Pickerell and Emily Francis Morris. In this case, all of Tester 4's descendants match on the segment, so this part of the DNA was handed down relatively unchanged.

» **Chromosome 19:** Tester 1 matched Tester 2 on a 13.8 cM segment K. Tester 1 also matched Tester 4 on a 66.1 cM segment L that encompassed segment K. Tester 5 (Tester 4's sister) matched on a segment that was only one-third of the size of Tester 4. Tester 7 (Tester 4's son) inherited only about half of the DNA segment at 34 cM. Tester 7's daughter (Tester 9) inherited the same DNA unchanged at 34 cM. The segments labled N are those matches between Tester 1's daughter Tester 6 and the rest of those matching Tester 1. From this, we can triangulate most of the segment shared by Testers 1 and 4 as belonging to William Henry Morris or Elizabeth McGavock. We can't tell whether the segment comes from the Morris or McGavock side, or both. We would need additional testers to reach a more distant ancestor.

Meeting the objectives

We know triangulation is enough to make your head spin. But the question is did we meet our objectives? Here is how we fared.

The first objective was to provide evidence of Matthew's descent from William Henry Morris and Elizabeth McGavock. By triangulating with the descendant of Mary E. Morris we had two documentary paths to William Henry Morris and Elizabeth McGavock, plus the DNA evidence of a relationship between the lines. Finding additional testers among descendants of the other children of William Henry Morris and Elizabeth McGavock will help solidify the evidence.

Second was to find cousins that might know more information about the family. Through DNA testing, three new relatives were found (Testers 1, 2, and 6), all of whom had information about the family.

Third was to recreate the genome of the grandparents. A lot more work will have to be done to accomplish this, but we did get a start on identifying DNA from the Pickerell and Morris families. So, we can reasonably say that the grandparent descended from the Pickerell and Morris families possessed the segments shown in Figure 12-14.

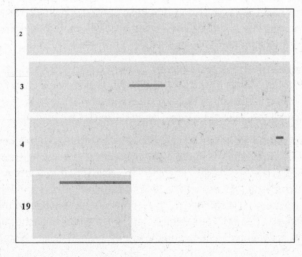

FIGURE 12-14:
Segments mapped to a grandparent.

Fourth was to construct the genomes of Emily Francis Morris and Elizabeth Pickerell. Similar to the grandparent, Elizabeth Pickerell would also have possessed the DNA in Figure 12-14. Emily Francis Morris would have at least had the DNA segment pictured in Figure 12-15. By finding a segment at a time, in theory we could construct enough of the genome for testing purposes, if we found enough other testers — although we wouldn't be able to reconstruct the entire genome.

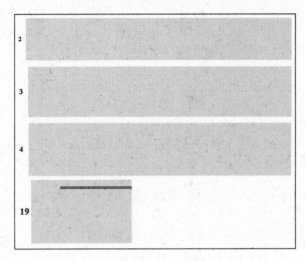

FIGURE 12-15:
Segment mapped
to Lizzie Pickerell.

X-Chromosome DNA Testing

X-chromosome testing can fill in some of the gaps between what Y-chromosome and mitochondrial testing can show. But, it can only do so for a portion of the family tree. The test is usually part of autosomal testing, so you normally don't need to run a separate test.

As we mention earlier, females have two X chromosomes and males have one X and one Y chromosome. The mother's X chromosomes act like autosomes in that the two X chromosomes can recombine, and one X chromosome is passed from the mother to each child, regardless of sex. The mother can pass on an X chromosome that is identical to her mother's X chromosome, identical to her father's X chromosome, or a recombined X chromosome. Figure 12-16 shows the possible inheritance of the X chromosome from a female ancestor.

The father passes a copy of his X chromosome only to his daughters. Because he has only the one X chromosome, no recombination takes place. Figure 12-17 shows the possible inheritance of the X chromosome from a male ancestor.

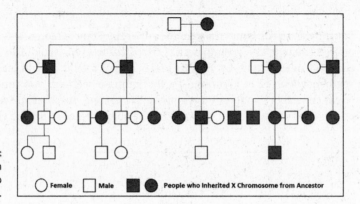

FIGURE 12-16:
Mothers pass an X chromosome to all their children.

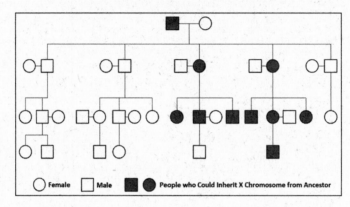

FIGURE 12-17:
Fathers pass a non-recombined X chromosome only to their daughters.

The methods of analysis of X chromosome results are the same as the autosomal methods that we discussed in the last section. The difference being that possible matches are smaller than the potential autosomal matches. You can view the matched segments using the chromosome browsers at 23andMe and Family Tree DNA.

The criteria for X chromosome matching from the testing companies is also different than the threshold for autosomal tests. 23andMe compares the X chromosome for each person meaning that you may find X-chromosome-only matches. The criteria for matching depends upon who is being tested. If two males are compared, a match needs to be a segment of 1 cM in length and 200 single nucleotide polymorphisms (SNPs). If a male and female are compared, a match is 6 cM and 600 SNPs. If two females are compared there are two possible thresholds. If the two females share DNA on just one copy of the chromosome (half-IBD), they must match at least 6 cM and 1200 SNPs. If they match at the same location on both chromosomes (full-IBD), they must match at least 5 cM and 500 SNPs.

Family Tree DNA reports matches on the X chromosome, only if there is also a match in autosomal DNA. For the match to be apparent, autosomal DNA must match at 7.7 cM and 500 SNPs and the X chromosome must be 1 cM with 500 SNPs.

AncestryDNA does not use X chromosome when creating its match lists.

Utilities to the Rescue

At some point in your genetic research, you will encounter the need to examine DNA kits from multiple testing companies or to see results in a different manner than the testing companies allow. Genetic genealogists have constructed utilities to help you with analysis and with keeping track of all the results that you discover along the way.

GEDmatch (www.gedmatch.com) is a website with several useful utilities. Testers can upload the results from their testing company and run analyses on multiple kits, run triangulation reports, and view results through chromosome browsers. The site has some free utilities and you can pay to upgrade to the Tier 1 utilities. It accepts uploads of AncestryDNA kits so it can compensate for the lack of a chromosome browser at the testing company. We used this site to compare kits from both AncestryDNA and 23andMe for the earlier portions of this chapter.

DNAGedcom (https://dnagedcom.com) also contains valuable utilities including KWorks, which creates a spreadsheet of possible triangulations. And GWorks that compares family tree information to identify ancestors who are shared between individuals.

Another utility worth exploring is Genome Mate Pro (www.genomemate.org). Genome Mate Pro is a tool that you install on your computer to track your genetic research. You can import data from 23andMe, Family Tree DNA, and GEDmatch. We will warn you that it is a complex program and before using it, we highly recommend you watch the series of YouTube video tutorials that explain the features of the tool. We use it to keep track of our research, including correspondence from other researchers and view overlapping segments of other testers. Also, we find the segment map utility particularly handy (see Figure 12-18).

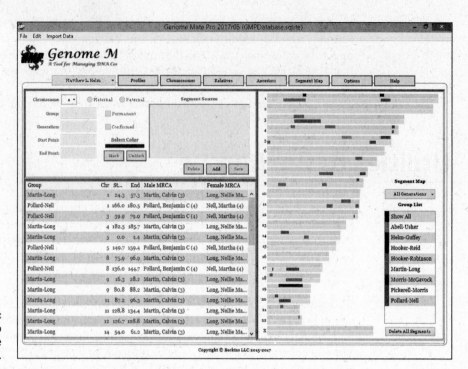

FIGURE 12-18:
Segment map
tab in Genome
Mate Pro.

4

Casting Your Nets in the Genealogy Sea

Chapter **13**

Finding Your Research Path

Talking about the methods for working on genealogy or family history research isn't very exciting. However, we would be doing an injustice to you if we sent you out into the jungle that is family history research without giving you some advice from the traditional world of research.

This chapter is designed to provide a research foundation that helps you spend your time as efficiently as possible. In the following pages, we look at how to develop a plan to research your ancestors and cover the phases of research. In the latter parts of the chapter, we go through some gentle reminders that can help you keep your research as relevant as possible.

Introducing the Helm Online Family Tree Research Cycle

Your question at this point is probably, what is the *Helm Online Family Tree Research Cycle*? All great projects start with a plan, and starting a genealogical project is no exception. A well-thought-out plan can help you make efficient use of your time and keep you focused on the goals that you've set for a particular research session. Now, we realize that not everyone enjoys coming up with a plan. Finding your ancestors is the fun part — not the planning. So, to help speed things along, we've come up with a basic process that we hope helps you make the most of your research time. We call this plan the *Helm Online Family Tree Research Cycle.* Most of our plan is common sense. Figure 13-1 shows the six phases of the cycle: planning, collecting, researching, consolidating, validating, and distilling.

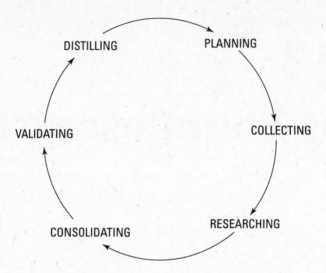

FIGURE 13-1:
The Helm Online
Family Tree
Research Cycle.

Sticking with the *family tree* motif here, we liken the cycle to the steps you take to plant and sustain a tree:

>> **Planning:** The first step in planting a tree is figuring out what kind of tree you want and then finding a good place in your yard for the tree to grow. This step in the cycle is the *planning* phase. In genealogy, the planning phase consists of selecting a family that you know enough about to begin a search and thinking about the resources that can provide the information that you're looking for.

>> **Collecting:** After you plan for the tree, you go to a nursery and pick a suitable sapling and other necessary materials to ensure that the tree's roots take hold. The second phase of the cycle, *collecting,* is the same — you collect information on the family that you're researching by conducting interviews in person, on the phone, or through email, and by finding documents in attics, basements, and other home-front repositories.

>> **Researching:** The next step is to actually plant the tree. You dig a hole, place the tree in it, and then cover the roots. Similarly, you spend the *researching* phase of the cycle digging for clues, finding information that can support your

family tree, and obtaining documentation. You can use traditional and technological tools to dig — tools such as libraries, courthouses, your computer, and the web.

» **Consolidating:** You planted the tree and covered its roots. However, to make sure that the tree grows, you put mulch around it and provide the nourishment that the tree needs to survive. The *consolidating* phase of the cycle is similar in that you take information you find and place it into your computer-based genealogical database or your filing system. These systems protect your findings by keeping them in a centralized location and provide an environment in which you can see the fruits of your labor.

» **Validating:** To ensure that you're providing your tree with all the nutrition and care that it needs, you might pick up a book or watch a gardening show to confirm that your actions will nurture the tree. The *validating* phase in genealogy allows you to do the same with your research. By using additional research tools and by finding multiple sources, you can feel more confident that your discoveries are placing your research on the right track.

» **Distilling:** After your tree takes root and begins to grow, you need to prune the old growth, allowing new growth to appear. Similarly, the *distilling* phase is where you use your computer-based genealogical database to generate reports showing the current state of your research. You can use these reports to prune from your database those individuals you've proven don't fit into your family lines — and perhaps find room for new genealogical growth by finding clues to other lines with which you want to follow up.

We think that using our research model makes looking for genealogical information a lot easier and more fulfilling. However, this model is merely a guide. Feel free to use whatever methods work best for you — as long as those methods make it possible for someone else to verify your research (through sources you cite and so on).

Planning your research

Your computer puts the world at your fingertips. Discovering all the wonderful online resources that exist makes you feel like a kid in a candy store. You click around from site to site with wide eyes, amazed by what you see, tempted to record everything for your genealogy — whether it relates to one of your family lines or not.

Because of the immense wealth of information available to you, putting together a research plan before going online is very important — it can save you a lot of time and frustration by keeping you focused. Millions of pages with genealogical content exist on the Internet. If you don't have a good idea of exactly what you're looking for to fill in the blanks in your family history, you can get lost online. Getting lost is even easier when you see a name that looks familiar and start following its links, only to discover hours later (when you finally get around to pulling out the notes you already had) that you've been tracking the wrong person and family line.

Now that we've convinced you that you need a research plan (at least we hope we've convinced you), you're probably wondering exactly what a research plan is. Basically, a *research plan* is a commonsense approach to looking for information about your ancestors online. A research plan entails knowing what you're looking for and what your priorities are for finding information.

If you're the kind of person who likes detailed organization (such as lists and steps), you can map out your research plan in a spreadsheet or word processor on your computer, write it on paper, or use a genealogical software tool. If you're the kind of person who knows exactly what you want and need at all times, and you have an excellent memory of where you leave off when doing projects, your research plan can exist solely in your mind. In other words, your research plan can be as formal or informal as you like — as long as it helps you plot what you're looking for.

For example, say that you're interested in finding some information on your great-grandmother. Here are some steps you can take to form a research plan:

1. **Write down what you already know about the person you want to research — in this case, your great-grandmother.**

    Include details such as the dates and places of birth, marriage, and death; spouse's name; children's names; and any other details you think may help you distinguish your ancestor from other individuals. Of course, it's possible that all you know at this time is Great-grandma's name.

2. **Survey a comprehensive genealogical index to get an overview of what's available.**

    Visit a site such as Linkpendium (www.linkpendium.com) to browse for information by name and location. Using Great-grandma's name and the names of some of the locations where she lived will allow you to see what kinds of resources are available. (Chapter 7 goes into more detail about online tips and searching for this type of information.) Make sure that you make a list of the sites that you find in a word processor document, in a spreadsheet, or on a piece of paper; bookmark them on your web browser; or record them in your genealogical application. Also, given that websites come and go frequently, you may want to consider downloading the web page for future offline browsing. Most web browsers allow you to download a web page by selecting Save As from the File menu at the top, and then providing the path to the file where you want to save a copy.

3. **Prioritize the resources that you want to use.**

Browsing a comprehensive genealogical index may turn up several types of resources, such as sites featuring digitized copies of original records, transcriptions of records, online genealogy databases, or an online message board with many posts about people with the same last name. We recommend that you prioritize which resources you plan to use first. You may want to visit a website that contains specific information on your grandmother's family first — rather than spending a lot of time on a website that just contains generic information on her surname. You may also want to visit a site with digitized original records first and leave a site with transcribed records or a database for later use.

4. **Schedule time to use the various resources that you identify.**

Family history is truly a lifelong pursuit — you can't download every bit of information and documentation that you need all at once. Because researching your genealogy requires time and effort, we recommend that you schedule time to work on specific parts of your research. If you have a particular evening open every week, you can pencil in a research night on your calendar, setting aside 15–30 minutes at the beginning to review what you have and assess your goals, then spending a couple of hours researching, and ending your evening with another 15–30 minutes of review in which you organize what you found.

Here are a few resources that can help you sharpen your planning skills:

>> **Crafting a Genealogy Research Plan:** www.youtube.com/watch?v=iZEJC7oruT0

>> **Sample Family History Research Plan:** www.familytreemagazine.com/article/sample-research-plan

>> **Basic Genealogical Research Plans (National Institute):** https://familysearch.org/wiki/en/Basic_Genealogical_Research_Plans_(National_Institute)

Collecting useful information

After you generate a research plan (see the preceding section), you may need to fill in a few details such as dates and locations of births, marriages, and deaths. You can collect this information by interviewing family members and by looking through family documents and photographs. (See Chapter 2 for tips on interviewing and using family documents and photographs.) You may also need to look up a few places in an atlas or a *gazetteer* (a geographical dictionary) if you aren't sure of certain locations. (Chapter 6 provides more information on online gazetteers.)

It's useful to jot down peripheral information such as the names of siblings, other family members, and the names of neighbors, if they're available. This extra information might be enough to determine whether the record you're looking at pertains to your ancestor. For example, if you're looking for a pension record for your ancestor, and you run across several pension records for people with the same name, then knowing the names of others with ties to your ancestor can help you determine which of the pension records is the right one. One detail to help confirm that the record relates to your ancestor may be the name of a witness. Sometimes the applicant would use neighbors or extended family members as witnesses. Recognizing the name of the witness might help speed up your search.

For a list of things that may be useful to collect, see Chapter 2. In the meantime, here are a few online resources that can help you get started with your family history:

> **National Genealogical Society, Getting Started page:** www.ngsgenealogy. org/cs/videos_online/janet_a_alpert/getting_started

> **5 First Steps to Finding Your Roots:** https://www.thoughtco.com/ first-steps-to-finding-your-roots-1421674

> **Getting Started in Genealogy and Family History:** www.genuki.org.uk/gs

Researching: Through the brick wall and beyond

A time will undoubtedly come when you run into what genealogists affectionately call the *brick wall syndrome* — when you think you've exhausted every possible way of finding an ancestor. The most important thing you can do is to keep the faith — don't give up!

Websites are known to change frequently (especially as more records are digitized, indexed, and placed online). Although you may not find exactly what you need today, you may find it next week at a site you've visited several times before or at a new site altogether. The lesson here is to check back at sites that you've visited before.

Another way to get past the brick wall is to ask for help. Don't be afraid to post a message on a mailing list or email other researchers you've corresponded with in the past to see whether they have answers or suggestions for finding answers. Also, you may be able to use the expertise of members of a genealogical or historical society who can point you to specific resources that you may not have known existed. We talk more about genealogical and historical societies in Chapter 6.

Fortunately, you can also find suggestions posted online on how to get through that brick wall when you run up against it. Check out these sites:

>> **Brick Wall Strategies for Dead-End Family Trees:** `https://www.thoughtco.com/brick-wall-dead-end-family-trees-1421671`

>> **50 Best Genealogy Brick Wall Solutions:** `www.genealogyintime.com/GenealogyResources/Articles/50_best_genealogy_brick_wall_solutions_part1_page_01.html`

>> **Breaking Through Your Genealogy Brick Walls:** `https://www.youtube.com/watch?v=zQLhtzYx7Bk`

Consolidating information in a database

After you get rolling on your research, you often find so much information that it feels like you don't have enough time to put it all into your genealogical application.

A *genealogical application* is a software program or online application that allows you to enter, organize, store, and use all sorts of genealogical information on your computer. You can find more information on using a genealogical application in Chapter 1.

When possible, try to set aside some time to update your database with information you recently gathered. This process of putting your information together in one central place, which we call *consolidating*, helps you gain a perspective on the work that you've completed and provides a place for you to store all those nuggets you'll need when you begin researching again. By storing your information in a database, you can always refer to it for a quick answer the next time you try to remember something specific, such as where you found a reference to a marriage certificate for your great-great-grandparents, or where your great-grandfather lived during a particular time frame. Placing your information in a genealogical database has a bonus — you can take your research with you when you travel. You can carry your database on your laptop's hard drive, or you can even find smartphone and tablet applications that can display the contents of genealogical databases.

Validating your findings

After discovering information on your ancestor, it's critical that you take the time to validate your findings. Just because something is printed online doesn't mean that it's correct. Even primary sources can contain incorrect data, either because of a clerical error or because the individual who was the source of the record intentionally misled the recorder. For example, you've probably heard stories of underage relatives who lied about their age to enlist in the army. So, you might find that the birthdate in a recruitment record is different than the birthdate in a pension record. To ensure that you have the best evidence possible, we recommend that you find three sources to triangulate any key piece of information on your ancestor. We understand that this isn't always possible, but it is a good practice to validate any evidence that you can find.

Beyond just finding additional records to validate ancestry, we also recommend using other available tools, such as DNA testing, to validate records. Non-paternal events did happen in the past and it's possible that the father listed on a birth record was not the biological father. DNA testing can also be used when there is not enough evidence to be certain about a particular conclusion but there is some circumstantial evidence that you would like to test. For example, Matthew's progenitor, George Helm, was located in the same county at the same time as another Helm family. A few authors asserted that George may have been a disowned son of the family. However, after DNA testing several individuals, including Matthew and some descendants from that Helm family, it's clear that those assertions were not true. The two families are in different haplogroups, which allows us to conclude that they were definitely two different families with the same surname. For more on DNA testing, see Chapter 10.

For more on validating your research, check out the following sites:

>> **Validation of Genealogical Lineages Using DNA:** http://ggdna. blogspot.com/2012/11/validation-of-genealogical-lineages.html

>> **Learn to Validate Your Online Research:** www.familytree.com/learn/ learn-to-validate-your-online-research/

Distilling the information that you gather

The final step in the cycle is distilling the information that you gather into a report, a chart, an organized database, or a detailed research log that you can use to find additional genealogical leads. Frequently, you can complete the distillation process by producing a report from your genealogical application. Most genealogical applications allow you to generate reports in a variety of formats. For example, you can pull up a pedigree chart (a chart showing a primary person with lines representing the relationships to his or her parents, then lines connecting them to their parents, and so on) or an outline of descendants from information that you entered in the database about each ancestor. You can use these reports to see what holes still exist in your research, and you can add these missing pieces to the planning phase for your next research effort — starting the entire cycle over.

Another advantage to genealogical reports is having the information readily available so that you can *toggle* back to look at the report while researching online, which can help you stay focused. (*Toggling* is flipping back and forth between open programs on your computer. For example, in Windows, you press Alt+Tab to toggle, or you can click the appropriate item on the taskbar at the bottom of the screen. On a Macintosh, you can use ⌘+Tab or the Application Switcher in the upper-right corner of the screen.) If you prefer, printing copies of the reports and keeping them next to the computer while you're researching online serves the same purpose.

Too Many Ancestor Irons in the Research Fire

When you begin your research, take your time and don't get in a big hurry. Keep things simple and look for one piece of information at a time. If you try to do too much too fast, you risk getting confused, having no online success, and getting frustrated with online research. This result isn't encouraging and certainly doesn't make you feel like jumping back into your research, which would be a shame because you can find a lot of valuable information and research help online.

TIP

A good strategy is to focus on one person or immediate family unit at a time. With the advances in search technology on genealogical sites, it's often tempting to conduct a search to find information on a variety of family members in a single search. However, try to resist jumping from one family member to another. Although you can accumulate records on several individuals, you might miss opportunities to systematically find records on your ancestor.

Verifying Your Information

A piece of advice for you when you're researching:

REMEMBER

Don't believe everything you read.

Well, actually, a genealogy purist might say, "Don't believe *anything* you read." Either way, the point is the same: Always verify any information that you find online — or, for that matter, in print — with primary records. (For more on primary records, see Chapter 2.) If you can't prove it through a vital record, census record, or some other authoritative record, the information simply may not be as valuable as you think. However, don't discount something just because you can't *immediately* prove it. You might want to hold on to the information and continue to try to prove or disprove it with a primary document. At some time in the future, you may run across a record that does indeed prove the accuracy of the information; in the meantime, it might give you some leads for where to look for more about that person.

You've probably seen courtroom dramas on television where the lawyer must prove his case before a jury. In family history, researchers go through a similar process to prove that a particular event occurred in the lives of their ancestors. At times, you won't be able to find a record that verifies that your ancestor was born on a certain date. Perhaps the birth record was destroyed in a courthouse fire or the birth was never properly recorded. Or worse yet, you may find two records that contain conflicting information about the same event.

So, how do genealogists and family historians know when they have sufficiently proved something? Well, for the longest time, no published guidelines existed on what constituted sufficient proof. To assist professional genealogists figure out the appropriate level of proof for their clients, the Board for Certification of Genealogists (BCG) created the *Genealogical Proof Standard* as part of the BCG Genealogical Standards Manual (published in 2000 by Ancestry).

The Genealogical Proof Standard contains five steps. If these five steps are completed, sufficient proof exists for a professional genealogist to create a research report stating that a certain event happened. We paraphrase the steps a bit to make them a little easier to understand:

1. Conduct a reasonably exhaustive search for all information related to a particular event.

2. Include a complete and accurate citation of the information that you use for your research.

3. Analyze the quality of the information. (For example, is the information from a primary source or is it from a reliable source?)

4. Resolve conflicts between two sources of information (such as two resources stating two different birth dates for the same person).

5. Arrive at a sound conclusion based on the information related to an event.

Although these steps were established for professional genealogists, they are good steps for you to follow to make sure that any person reading your research can follow your conclusions. Following these steps does not ensure that your conclusions are accurate 100 percent of the time. You always have the chance that a new piece of evidence will surface that may disprove your conclusions.

Chapter **14**

Share and Share Alike

Your genealogical database is growing with information about your relatives and ancestors. You're excited about new findings and leads, and you want to share the news! Or maybe you've gone as far as you can on one bloodline and you need a boost. All of these are valid indicators that it's time to start sharing the valuable information you discovered.

Sharing information is one foundation of a solid genealogical community. When you share information, you often get a lot in return from other researchers. For example, shortly after we began the Helm/Helms Family Research web page, several other Helm researchers throughout the world contacted us. We discovered several Helm lines existed that we didn't even know about. Plus, we received valuable information on our own line from other researchers, not to mention we connected with some really nice folks we probably wouldn't have met otherwise.

There is a vast number of resources online for sharing information about all sorts of subjects — including family history! In the early days of Internet-based gene-alogy, our advice to readers was to create from scratch and post your own home page (website) where you could open the doors to guests, inviting others to come to you for information and advice. But those days are long gone. There are much easier and friendlier options than mastering HyperText Markup Language (HTML) and other coding programs.

In this chapter, we focus on methods you can use to share information and con-nect with people via social networking sites and blogs. Also, we review how to use genealogical utility programs to help put content in specific formats for sharing.

Why Would Anyone Want Your Stuff?

Why would anyone want my stuff? seems like a logical first question when you stop and think about making the many tidbits and treasures you collected available to others. Who would want a copy of an old, ratty-looking photograph of Great-grandpa as a dirty-faced toddler in what appears to be a dress? Nobody else wanted it in the first place, and that's probably how you ended up with it, right? The picture has sentimental value only to you. Wrong! Some of Great-grandpa's other descendants may be looking for information about him. They, too, would love to see a picture of him when he was a little boy — even better, they'd love to have their own electronic copy of that picture!

As you develop more online contact with other genealogists, you may find a lot of people who are interested in exchanging information. Some may be interested in your research findings because you share common ancestors, and others may be interested because they're researching in the same geographical area where your ancestors were from. Aren't these the same reasons that you're interested in seeing other researchers' stuff? Sharing your information is likely to encourage others to share theirs with you. Exchanging information with others may enable you to fill in some gaps in your own research efforts. Even if the research findings you receive from others doesn't directly answer questions about your ancestors, they may give you clues about where to find more information to fill in the blanks.

Also, just because you haven't traced your genealogy back to the Middle Ages doesn't mean that your information isn't valuable. Although you should not share information on living persons without their explicit permission, feel free to share any facts you know about deceased ancestors. Just as you may not know your genealogy any further than your great-grandfather, someone else may be in the same boat — and with the same person! Meeting with that fellow researcher can lead to a mutual research relationship that can produce a lot more information in a shorter amount of time.

Making Friends on Facebook

Whether you're an avid computer user or new to the game, chances are you've heard of social networking sites. In particular, you've likely heard of Facebook (www.facebook.com). In the couple of decades, Facebook has become a household name. Facebook touts itself as a social utility meant to connect people with a common strand in their lives, whether that's working together, attending the same school, or living in the same or nearby communities. Facebook lends itself well to genealogists connecting with relatives and other researchers. Let's explore how to use this general social networking site for our family history purposes.

Jumping on the Facebook bandwagon

Before we can explore how to use Facebook for genealogy-related connections, you need to register for a free Facebook account. It's easy. Just follow these steps:

1. **Open your favorite web browser and go to** www.facebook.com.

2. **In the Sign Up section on the right side of the screen (see Figure 14-1), type your First Name and Last Name in the appropriate fields.**

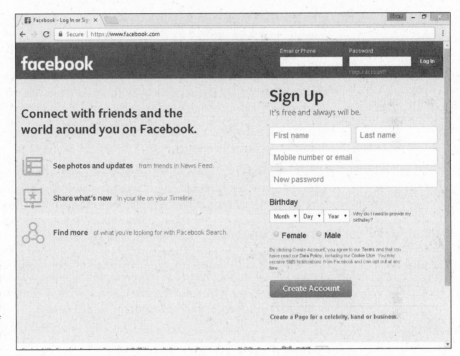

FIGURE 14-1:
Complete the
Facebook signup
form to start the
process of
registering for an
account.

3. **Provide your email address in both the Your Email and Re-enter Email fields.**

4. **Select a password and type it in the New Password field.**

   As with any site, your password should consist of characters that you can remember but that someone else cannot easily figure out. A combination of upper- and lowercase letters, numbers, and special characters make a strong password.

5. **Using the drop-down lists, select the month, day, and year of your birthday.**

6. **Click the appropriate radio button next to your gender.**

7. **Click the Sign Up button.**

If you have pop-up notifications blocked by your web browser, a window generates to ask if Facebook can Show Notifications. If you want to receive pop-up notifications from Facebook when online, click Allow. Otherwise, click Block.

This takes you to the Find Your Friends form. You'll have the chance to look for Facebook friends later, so we'll skip this step for now.

8. **Click the Next button at the bottom-right. If you get a Find Your Friends pop-up, click Skip Step.**

This takes you to the Welcome to Facebook form, where you can authorize Facebook to scan through your email to look for friends who have Facebook accounts, take a privacy tour, add a profile photo of yourself, or choose to proceed with finding friends.

At the top of the page are instructions to check your email account to complete the sign-up process. Follow the steps in the email from Facebook to confirm your account.

You're taken to your Facebook page. Depending on your web browser, you may see a box at the top of the page offering to Remember Password. Below that will be your Newsfeed, although it likely won't have any messages yet unless you chose to search for friends in an earlier step.

Down the right side of the page, you'll see navigation links to different parts of Facebook. Click on your name to set up your profile — this is where you can add a photo of yourself, describe yourself, and provide information about where you live, as well as your work, education, and family.

Making Facebook friends

The main purpose of Facebook is to connect with people — old and new friends, relatives, and acquaintances. Finding friends is relatively easy. If you're using a computer to sign up, follow these steps anytime you sign in to Facebook:

1. **If you're not already signed in to Facebook, fire up your computer, open a web browser, and head over to www.facebook.com.**

2. **Click your name in the top navigation bar to get to your main profile page.**

This takes you to the page with your timeline and profile information. This is where you can select any interests you want to share on Facebook, as well as set up other profile information, upload photos, and lots more.

3. **Scroll down and click the Friends link on the right.**

4. **Click the Find Friends button near the top of the Friends view.**

   This opens a page that displays any new Friends requests that are sent to you, as well as has a search form where you can enter information to guide your search for friends on Facebook.

5. **Use the Search for Friends fields to search by names, identify locations, educational institutions, or employers with which you have ties.** Facebook immediately starts identifying other users who match your search criteria.

6. **Scroll through the list of matches to see if you recognize anyone.**

   You can click the person's name to see her Facebook page to learn more about her.

7. **If you find someone you know who you want to add to your friends list, click the Add Friend button by the person's name.**

After you've friended a few people, Facebook continues to look for other users that have experiences, interests, and locations in common with you. It displays them in a box in your Newsfeed labelled People You May Know. When you're reading through your Newsfeed, periodically, look through the list to see if there's anyone new that you'd like to extend a Friend invite to.

Sorting your Facebook friends

After you've connected with a few friends, you may find that you want to categorize them. This makes it easier to post genealogical triumphs and questions to only those friends with whom you share a research interest. It also makes it easier to restrict posts to only family members, if you so desire. To set up specific lists in Facebook, follow these steps:

1. **If you're not already signed in to Facebook, fire up your computer, open a web browser, and head over to** www.facebook.com.

2. **Click the Home link in the top navigation menu (upper-right).**

3. **Click the Friend Lists link on the left side of the screen.**

   This takes you to a page displaying the default and existing lists for categorizing your friends. The defaults are Close Friends, Family, and Restricted.

4. **Click the Create List button at the top of the screen.**

   The Create New List dialog box pops up.

5. **Type the name of your list in the List Name field.**

   For example, we might type the word Genealogy in the List Name field if we want a category of genealogy friends, or we might type a surname if we want to track our friends who share a family line or research interest.

6. **Start typing a friend's name in the Members section.**

   Facebook starts anticipating the name you're typing and offers suggestions. Click your friend's name if it comes up.

7. **Repeat Step 6 as many times as you want, adding all of your friends who you want to include in this list.**

8. **After you've added everyone you want, click the Create button.**

   The page for your new list opens and offers you the opportunity to post a status to the friends in this list, or add photos to share with this group.

Return to this page anytime you want to post messages restricted to these specific friends who share your genealogical interests, or to add more friends to the list.

Posting statuses on Facebook

When you're ready to announce a research triumph, or pose a question to your friends with the same research interests, you can post your status on Facebook. A *status* is a quick update on your Facebook page that tells the world what you're doing, thinking, or celebrating. When you post a status, Facebook sends out a notice to your friends — all of your friends unless you've restricted the list of recipients using the steps in the previous section of this chapter — and it appears in their Newsfeeds. Likewise, when your friends post statuses, some of them may appear in your Newsfeed, which is typically on the first page that you access in Facebook.

You can post a status to multiple places. Just look for the What's On Your Mind? field.

Sharing photos via Facebook

Facebook is an easy way to share photos with your family and fellow researchers.

You might wish to share current photos from reunions and research trips, or you might want to share digitized copies of treasured family photos of ancestors. Here's how to upload photos to Facebook:

1. **If you're not already signed in to Facebook, fire up your computer, open a web browser, and head over to www.facebook.com.**

   If you prefer to create an entire album of ancestral photos, you may click the Photo Album button in the top of the Create a Post box instead. Then follow the steps to set up an album before clicking the Photo/Video button and selecting photos to upload. You might want to categorize your photos in collections by surname, or ancestor, or specific research trip.

2. **Click the Photo/Video link in the Create a Post box.**

   If you're on your Newsfeed, the Create a Post box with the Photo/Video link is near the top-center of the page. This opens a file manager window where you can browse and pick the photo(s) you want to upload.

3. **Type the filename for the location on your computer where the photos you want to upload are stored. Or you can use the navigation bar at the top to click through the directory tree to find the location.**

   For our example, we click the appropriate links in the left navigation menu until we get to the directory that stores the photos that we want to share with our Facebook friends. See Figure 14-2.

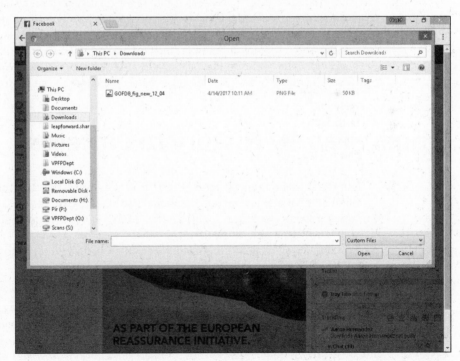

FIGURE 14-2: Navigate to the directory on your computer where you store photos in order to pick those that you want to upload.

4. **Highlight the pictures you want to upload.**

To select all of the pictures in the directory, highlight the first one, then hold the Shift key and click the last photo in the set. This should highlight all of the pictures between the first and the last. Or if you want to upload only certain photos, highlight one, and then hold the Control key while clicking the others that you wish to select.

5. **Click the Open button.**

This begins the upload process and takes you to the album setup page.

6. **If you wish to provide a narrative about the photo, type your comment in the Say Something about This Photo field.**

7. **If you want to name someone in the photo or acknowledge who was with you, type the name in the With (Who Were You With) field.**

You may also choose to Check In to provide the location for the photo, add an emoticon showing your emotional reaction to the photo, or Tag Friends so they get notification you've posted the photo.

If you decide to create a photo album to house multiple pictures, you can allow your friends to contribute. This is handy for relatives who may have attended the same reunion or fellow genealogists who are researching the same family lines. When you're in the Photo Album window, you can click the Make Shared Album button at the top and follow the steps for adding the names of those friends who can contribute to the album. The album also becomes visible through their time-lines and gives them credit anytime they add a photo to the album.

Pinning Family History to Pinterest

Pinterest is both a social networking site (where you can connect with others with similar interests) and an organizational site of sorts (where you can "pin" links to other web pages, articles, photos, ideas, pretty much anything online to review or reference again at a future date).

To use Pinterest, you must set up a free account. Here's how:

1. **Open your browser and go to** `https://www.pinterest.com/`

This results in the Welcome to Pinterest, the world's catalog of ideas page. If you prefer to link your Pinterest account with an existing Facebook account, click the Continue with Facebook button instead and follow the instructions online. Otherwise, continue with the following steps.

2. Enter your email address in the Email field.

3. Type a password for your account in the Create a Password field.

4. Click the Continue button.

This brings up the Welcome to Pinterest window, where you can enter more information about yourself.

5. Enter your first and last name in the Full Name field.

6. Enter your age in the Age field.

7. Select your gender by clicking the appropriate radio button next to Male, Female, or Custom.

If you select Custom, a new pop-up box asks you to identify your Custom Gender, then click Save.

8. Click the Sign Up button.

9. In the Like 5 Topics box, scroll through the list to click on (like) five topics or type a topic in the Search For Any Topic field.

For example, if you type "genealogy" in the Search field, and hit Enter, four topics appear — Genealogy, Genealogy Chart, Genealogy Organization, and Genealogy Humor. You can select all four, but you'll still need to pick one more to get to five. Search for another topic of interest to select it.

10. A window pops up asking if you want to Get the Pinterest Browser Button. Click Get It Now if you want the button on your browser page so you can easily click it to save information for Pinterest. Otherwise, click the Skip link.

If you get a box asking if you want to Add Pinterest Save Button? Click Add Extension.

A box appears indicating you are all set to start. A new tab within your browser opens with a tutorial on how to use Pinterest. We recommend you take a few minutes and go through the tutorial so you'll be better prepared to use Pinterest.

11. When you're done with the tutorial, close the tab and return to the tab where your Pinterest account is displaying, with links to resources related to the five topics you selected.

Next to the Search field at the top of the page are three icons: a circle with a diamond in it takes you to an Explore Pinterest page; a person icon takes you to your Pinterest page; and a dialogue bubble opens chat functionality where you can communicate with people who follow you. To view things you've saved to your Pinterest account, click the person icon.

As you're researching online and see something you want to remember or revisit, use the Pinterest button you authorized earlier (which now appears next to the URL field of your browser) to mark the item (photo or article) or page to "save" it to your Pinterest account. You can choose to save it to an existing board in your account, or to create a new board related to the item.

For example, if you find a treasure of photos for a county where several of your ancestors lived, you might want to save the site or the individual photos to your Pinterest, and to file them on a new board with the name of the county and state, or you might want to file them to an existing board with the surname of the family that lived there.

You can also visit and/or follow other peoples' Pinterest pages. Use the Search functionality to locate others with similar interests, then browse through their boards or choose to follow the person. If you click on an item on their Pinterest page, it will give you more information — at a minimum, it will tell you who posted the item. Some items have descriptions as well.

Realizing Instant Gratification with Instagram

Instagram is an application you can use on your smartphone to share photos with people who follow you. More and more genealogists are finding this to be a handy tool for sharing their research victories, as well as distributing beloved family treasures to others with the same family lines. In addition to allowing a user to send a picture to a multitude of interested parties at the same time, Instagram allows the user to attach a hashtag (#). The hashtag enables others to find the posting via search engines. This leads others who may have the same research interests to find and connect with you.

Networking Genealogy-Style

Like the number of networking sites in general, the number of genealogical-networking sites has grown at an incredible pace over the past few years. There are some significant differences between general networking or social sites and genealogical networking sites. Most genealogy-based networking sites have you start by sharing information from your Pedigree chart (also called a family tree) and research findings, rather than beginning with your profile of personal information about you. And the most interesting feature of some of these sites is that they use mathematical algorithms to link your tree(s) with trees that other people have submitted. In essence, this means they're trying to help connect you to others with the same family lines. The drawback to some of these sites is that they charge subscription fees for some of their functionality or for value-added services such as access to online records.

You might have heard of some of these:

>> Geni (www.geni.com)

>> Familyrelatives.com (www.familyrelatives.com)

>> OneGreatFamily (www.onegreatfamily.com)

>> FamilyLink.com (www.familylink.com)

Sharing your history on Geni.com

If you're looking to set up a genealogy-networking site where others can discover your family lines and contribute information directly to you in a public forum, Geni is one place to start.

Geni.com has space where you can initiate public discussions about research, ancestors, or just about anything genealogy-related you can think of. Much like other social networking sites, it has areas within your profile where you can upload photos and videos, and maintain a timeline. Unlike typical social networking sites though, it has a section where you can cite sources of your research findings and share DNA results.

Here's what to do to get started:

1. **Using your web browser, go to** www.geni.com.

2. **In the Start My Family Tree box, begin by selecting the option for your gender.**

3. **In the First Name field, enter your first name.**

4. **In the Last Name field, enter your last name.**

5. **In the Email Address field, type your preferred email address.**

6. **Click the Start My Family Tree button.**

   The registration opens to a page where you can activate your family tree by adding relatives.

7. Click the parent whose information you are ready to add; see Figure 14-3.

For this example, to enter information about your father, click the left parental box above your box on the family tree. A dialog box appears where you can enter information.

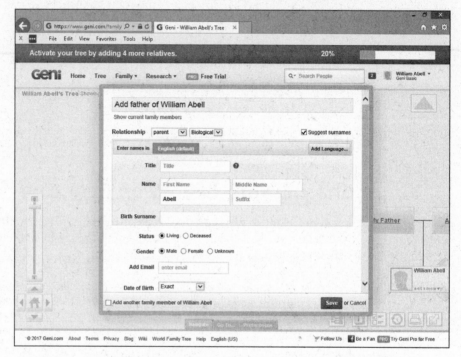

FIGURE 14-3:
You can navigate to other ancestors through the Geni. com family tree to add information about your family.

8. Using the drop-down menus at the top of the box, pick the appropriate Relationship.

The choices include parent, spouse, ex-spouse, partner, ex-partner, fiancé, sibling, or child in the first drop-down, and Biological, Adoptive, or Foster in the second drop-down.

9. In the First Name field, enter your father's first name.

10. If your father's last name is different from the one that automatically populates, fix it in the Last Name field.

11. Select the appropriate option for Status to indicate whether your father is living or deceased.

12. Select the appropriate Gender for your father.

13. **If you like (and you have your dad's permission), type your father's email address in the Email (Optional) field.**

Geni.com will use this email address to send this person an invitation to join Geni.com. Some relatives may consider these uninvited invitations to be spam, so be careful about entering other people's email addresses at networking websites. For more information about protecting your relatives' privacy, be sure to read the section "Earning a Good Citizenship Award," later in this chapter.

14. **Select a parameter from the drop-down next to Date of Birth — your choices are Exact, Before, After, and Between. The type your dad's date of birth. If the date is approximate and not known for sure, you can click the Circa button next to Date.**

If you did not enter an email address, Geni.com presents you with a pop-up box offering to welcome your relative to the family tree by giving you another opportunity to add his or her email address. If you don't want to see these pop-up boxes every time you enter a relative, select the Do Not Show This Message Again checkbox in the lower left, then click the Skip button.

15. **Provide the place name where your father was born in the Place of Birth field.**

16. **If you wish, you can enter a Current Location and Occupation in the last two fields in the box.**

17. **If you have other relatives to add, you can check the box labeled Add another family member of [focus person's name].**

On saving this person's data, this opens another box where you can enter information about another relative immediately.

18. **Click the Save button.**

After you add information about a person using one of the boxes in the family tree, the box becomes activated, and little yellow arrows surround it. You can click these arrows to navigate to that person's parents, spouse(s), and children to add more individuals to your tree.

The Geni.com site is impressive in the ways it helps you share your family tree research with others. Here's a quick overview of the various parts of the site:

» **Tree:** On this tab, you can view information about the family members included in the tree as a family tree (pedigree chart) or a list. You can navigate in the standard Geni.com format by clicking the yellow arrows and name boxes, or you can search by name in the Go To section.

>> **Family:** Several handy functions are accessible on the Family menu including Lists, Photos, Videos, Calendar, Map, Statistics, Timeline, and a Last Names Index. This is also where you can find links to share your tree and to generate the Family Tree Chart. The Lists, Photos, and Videos sections are places for you to add items to your file to enhance the content. If you enter birth dates and anniversaries for your family members, the Calendar gives you a consolidated list that helps you remember special events. The Family Map shows you where your family members currently live and were born, if you include locations in the individualized data you record on the site. The Statistics section is very interesting if you like to look for overall patterns within the family, such as average life expectancy or number of children. The Timeline gives you a quick glance of all your Geni.com activities since registering. And the Last Name Index is just that — a list of last names in your records. Share Your Tree enables you to extend invitations to other users to view and/or contribute information. It also has a GEDCOM Export functionality so you can convert your tree for sharing. Lastly, the Family Tree Chart option builds an attractive family tree that you can then download for printing and sharing.

>> **Research:** The Research menu offers services to help you connect with others to share research. It includes a Merge Center where you can see matches between people in your tree and other members' trees and online records. There are also sections for discussions with other members, projects where you can create and administer joint research with others, and documents you can upload to support your research. Additionally, there's a list of surnames in Geni.com to explore and a list of popular profiles for famous people that you can view. And if you want to order a DNA testing kit, the Research menu has information about services offered by their partner, MyHeritage DNA.

>> **PRO Free Trial:** The PRO Free Trial tab allows you to register to try the PRO Geni.com membership for free for 14 days. The PRO membership enables access to enhanced service features and allows you to store unlimited photos, videos, and documents. It also offers a premium level of support if you have questions or need help. Be aware that you are required to provide a credit card when you sign up for the free trial. At the end of the trial period, you will automatically be charged the one-year membership fee to continue the service if you do not notify Geni.com to end your free trial before the 14 days are over.

>> **Profile:** The menu to the Profile section appears under your name, to the right of the Search field in Geni.com. This Profile section is where you can store data specifically about you — everything from your birth date and age, to educational information, to your work experience, to personal narratives about your life, aspirations, and research interests, or whatever you'd like to say about yourself in the free-form text boxes. This is also where you can track

who you've invited to view and participate in your Geni tree. The data is sorted into seven tabs: Basics, Relationships, About, Personal, Contact, Work, and Schools. Depending on which setting you choose, various aspects of your profile may or may not be visible.

Discovering contacts through Member Connect

If you have a paid subscription to Ancestry.com, it gives you an additional feature of the online family tree that is worth mentioning — Member Connect. The Member Connect feature actively looks for other people who are posting information about your ancestor on their online family trees. After finding a potential match, Member Connect lists the member's name on the tab.

To find members who are researching one of your ancestors, follow these steps:

1. **Go to Ancestry.com and log in.**

2. **Near the top of the landing page, you will see a box titled Recent Member Connect Activity (see Figure 14-4). If Ancestry.com found any recent activity on your family lines, the results will appear in this box.**

3. **Click the appropriate link for the action you wish to take.**

The links in the results will vary. If someone posted an article or document related to a person you're researching or matching a surname in your list, you can click the link to see the item. If a person posted a general interest or listed a surname that matches one of yours, the link will lead to that person's profile. There may be other links present next to a person-based entry too, such as View Family Tree or Send a Message. These links help eliminate a few steps in the process if you're only interested in his family tree or messaging him.

TIP

Ancestry.com subscribers see links to the family trees containing the related information about the ancestor. Nonsubscribers see only the number of records, sources, and photos available on that family tree.

Showing context in LifeStory

A social networking type benefit of a paid subscription to Ancestry.com is the LifeStory feature. LifeStory in Ancestry Family Tree allows you to create an online timeline and retelling of your ancestor's life, giving color and context to it. Using records and information you've collected, in conjunction with information about historical events and areas, LifeStory builds a narrative for the ancestor.

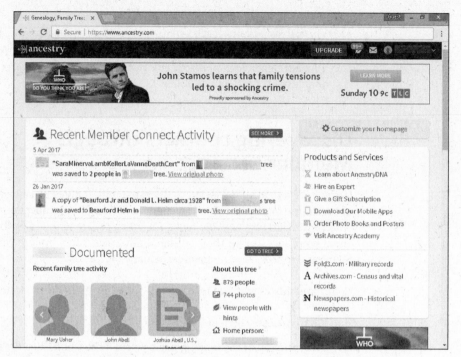

Interested in adding a LifeStory for one of your ancestors? Here's how:

1. **Go to Ancestry.com and log in.**

2. **Select the Trees menu at the top of the page, and click on the family tree that contains the ancestor for whom you want to create a LifeStory.**

   For example, if we want to create a LifeStory for William Henry Abell, we select the Abell tree from our drop-down.

3. **Click on the box in the tree for the ancestor, then select Profile.**

   We clicked on William Henry Abell's box. As he is currently the main focal point of this tree, his box is in the center of the page.

   Near the top of the page, there is a menu bar with options for Lifestory, Facts, Gallery, and Hints. The page defaults to the Facts view.

4. **Click on the LifeStory feature in the menu bar.**

   The LifeStory generates in the form of a timeline. On the timeline are events about which you've entered information. There are maps of locations found in records for the ancestor, and historical facts that add color.

   In our example (see Figure 14-5), the LifeStory for William Henry Abell has basic information about his birth, death, parents, and marriages, as well as general information and maps on the locations where he lived. The LifeStory also includes general information on the First Kentucky Derby, as William Henry Abell lived nearby in Kentucky at the time of the first derby. There is also an entry for the Great Lakes Storm in 1913 because William Henry Abell was living in Illinois when that weather system took its toll on the Midwest, so he may have been affected.

5. **Choose which content to keep in the LifeStory.**

If you see wrong information about your ancestor or wish to update something, you can choose to Edit the entries that come from facts you've entered in Ancestry.com.

If there are general historical entries that you don't want to include in your ancestor's LifeStory, simply click on the Ignore button next to the entry. It will disappear.

Use the Add drop down at the top-right of the screen if you wish to add photos or videos to the LifeStory. This allows you to select media that is already attached to the profile record for the ancestor.

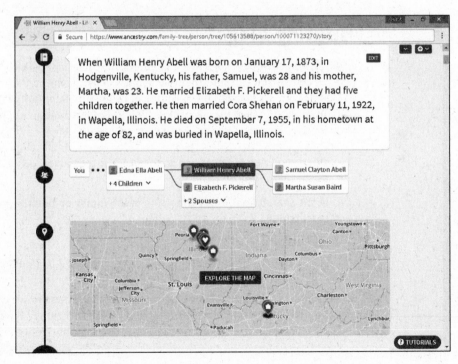

FIGURE 14-5:
William Henry Abell's LifeStory at Ancestry.com.

Blogging for Attention

Blog is a common term around the Internet. But what exactly is a blog? *Blog* is an abbreviated name for a *web log*, and it's just what it sounds like: an online journal or log. Typically blogs include narratives on whatever topic the blogger (the person who maintains the blog) feels like writing about. Therefore, genealogy blogs typically contain narratives on family history research. These narratives are much like the web boards of years past, where people could go and post information about their research findings or needs, and others would post replies. The main difference is that the blogger typically updates the blog on a regular and frequent basis, anywhere from daily to weekly to monthly, and the blogger is the one who initiates the topics of discussion that are welcome on that blog. Some blogs even contain photos, video or audio clips, and links to other sites — all depending on the blogger's interests and abilities to include these things.

Blogs are available about all aspects of genealogy, including how-tos, news, ethnic-based research, surnames, conferences, technology, and document preservation.

Hunting blogs

Looking for genealogy blogs to aid in your family history research? A lot are available. Of course you can find them by using a general Internet search engine such as Google.com. Or you can use a couple of other simple options for finding blogs. The first is to visit the Genealogy Blog Finder search engine at `http://blogfinder.genealogue.com`. Here's how to use it:

1. **Open your web browser and go to `http://blogfinder.genealogue.com`, as shown in Figure 14-6.**

2. **In the Search field, enter the name of the family or location you're researching.**

3. **Click Search.**

   You see a list of results with links to each. Click any that interest you.

If you're not sure of a spelling or if you just want to browse to see what's available, you can also use the menu system to navigate the Genealogy Blog Finder. All the topics under which the blogs are organized are accessible from the main web page.

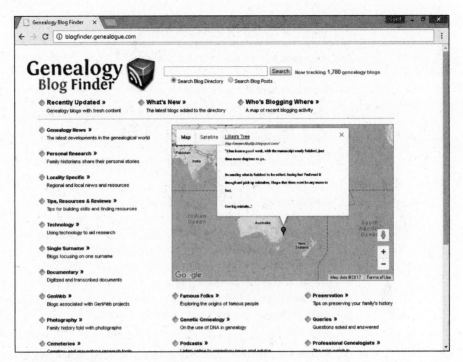

FIGURE 14-6:
Genealogy Blog
Finder helps you
locate blogs of
interest.

Getting a blog of your own

If you're ready to start your own blog where you can share information about your research pursuits and genealogical interests, you have some options available. One is to use the blogging functionality at one of the popular networking sites — check out the section "Making Friends on Facebook," earlier in this chapter, for more information. Another option is to use a site specifically designed to host your personal blog. A couple that come to mind are Google Blogger (www.blogger.com) and WordPress.com (www.wordpress.com).

These sites offer easy-to-use instructions for creating your blog. You can choose from templates for the overall design at each site and privacy controls so that you can determine who has access to your blog and what levels of permission the user has (whether the user can just read your narratives or post replies, as well as whether he or she can contribute original narratives initiating online discussions). They also offer the ability to post photos and files.

Here's a walk-through on how to set up your own blog at Google Blogger:

1. Open your web browser and go to www.blogger.com.

This opens the Google Blogger site. In the middle of the page is a box with sign-in fields. Under the box is a Create an Account link.

2. **Click the Create Your Blog button.**

If you already have an account with Google, it will prompt you to log in. If you do not yet have an account with Google, this brings you to the Create Your Google Account page. Setting up an account is the first step in the process.

3. **Enter your first and last names in the appropriate fields.**

4. **Type the username you'd like to have for your account.**

5. **Complete the Create a Password field, typing a password that's at least eight characters long.**

TIP

Remember that when setting up a password, you want to choose a combination of letters, numbers, or characters that won't be easy for others to decipher. Don't use your pet's name or your mother's maiden name. Instead, choose something that's not common knowledge about you — such as the name of your favorite book character with your favorite number on the end or a special text character such as $, #, or %. Click the Password Strength link, if you want Google Blogger–specific information about selecting a password. Google Blogger provides some excellent hints on making your password as safe as possible.

6. **In the Confirm Your Password field, provide the same password again.**

7. **In the Birthday fields, enter your date of birth.**

8. **Select your gender from the drop-down list.**

9. **Type your mobile phone number in the appropriate field.**

10. **In the Your Current Email Address field, type your current or preferred email address.**

11. **In the Type the Text box, retype the words or numbers that you see above the field.**

The letters and numbers are usually presented in a wavy, distorted way.

12. **Select your location.**

13. **Click the Terms of Service and read through them. If you agree to Blogger's terms, select the I Accept the Google Terms of Service and Privacy Policy check box.**

14. **Click Next Step.**

Google shows you how your profile name will appear and then takes you to the Welcome page.

15. **Click the Back to Blogger button.**

This brings up the Welcome to Blogger page.

16. Scroll down and click the Continue to Blogger button.

17. Select the type of Profile you would like to use for your Blog: Google+ or Blogger.

The profile you select affects how your blog will work and who can find it. The Google+ profile allows any blog created under your login to be publicly searched and indexed by search engines. It has the potential to reach a larger audience. The Blogger profile has the potential to afford you anonymity, should you need or want it. With a Blogger profile, you can use pseudonyms (other name versions for yourself, such as nicknames or aliases).

For our example, we choose a Blogger profile.

18. Type the name you want to be displayed on your blog in the Display Name field.

19. Click the Continue to Blogger button.

20. Click the New Blog button in the upper left.

The Create a New Blog page opens.

21. In the Title field, enter a name for your blog.

22. In the Address (URL) field, type part of a web address for your blog.

When choosing what to use for the section of the web address that you get to designate, think about using something that fits with the title of your blog. For example, if your blog will be called Gerty's Genealogical Adventures, you might try using GenAdventure or GGAdventure in the URL.

As you type the name of your choice, the system automatically checks to see if that selection is available.

23. Scroll through the list of templates and select the one that you like best.

24. Click Create Blog.

Congratulations! You've just created your blog. You get a message confirming that you have completed the blog-creation process, and you're now ready to begin posting to your blog.

You may get a box titled Google Domains offering to find a domain name for your blog and connect it instantly. Click No Thanks.

The Google Blogger template is easy to use for posting your blog content. You'll probably want to spend a little time exploring how it works and available options.

Building Your Own Home

When we wrote the first couple of editions of *Genealogy Online For Dummies*, the web was a very different place. Networking sites and blogs were not commonplace. Back then, we were quick to recommend designing your own home page (or website, if you will) from scratch. These days, we recommend coding your own site in HTML (HyperText Markup Language) only if you are a die-hard fan of writing code.

If you are the type of person who lives for creating things personally, fear not. You don't need to be sufficiently versed in coding HTML. There are web hosting sites that have templates enabling you to create a professional-looking page without being an expert computer programmer.

Free web-hosting services

Some websites give you free space for your home page, provided you agree to their rules and restrictions. We can safely bet that you won't have any problems using one of these freebies because the terms (such as no pornography, nudity, or explicit language allowed) are genealogist-friendly.

If you decide to take advantage of web space, remember that the companies providing the space must pay their bills. They often make space available free to individuals by charging advertisers for banners and other advertisements. In such cases, the web host reserves the right to require that you leave these advertisements on your home page. If you don't like the idea of an advertisement on your home page, or if you have strong objections to one of the companies being advertised on the site that gives you free space, you should find a fee-based web space for your home page.

Here are a few free web-hosting services:

>> Google sites (www.google.com/sites)

>> Tripod (www.tripod.lycos.com)

>> Wix (www.wix.com)

>> RootsWeb.com (http://www.rootsweb.com)

Most of these hosting services allow you to pick templates that make setting up your web page a breeze. You point and click to pick the look you like. Typically you can adjust colors if you'd like. And then you create and upload the content (or create it directly in the template), add photos or other media, and . . . *voilà!* Your page is ready to share.

GEDCOM: THE GENEALOGIST'S STANDARD

As you probably have already discovered, genealogy is full of acronyms. One such acronym that you'll hear and see repeatedly is GEDCOM (GEnealogical Data COMmunication). GEDCOM is the standard for individuals and software manufacturers for exporting information to and importing information from genealogical databases. Simply put, GEDCOM is a file format intended to make data transferable among different software programs so that people can share their family information easily.

The Church of Jesus Christ of Latter-day Saints developed and introduced GEDCOM in 1987. The first two versions of GEDCOM were released for public discussion only and were not meant to serve as the standard. With the introduction of version 5.x and later, however, GEDCOM was accepted as the standard.

Having a standard for formatting files is beneficial because you can share the information that you collect with others who are interested in some (or all) of your ancestors. It also enables you to import GEDCOM files from other researchers who have information about family lines and ancestors in whom you're interested. And you don't even have to use the same software as the other researchers! Having GEDCOM as the standard in software programs enables you to create and exchange GEDCOM files with other researchers who use different programs. Similarly, GEDCOM enables you to transfer data from your smartphone genealogical application to your home computer.

To convert the data in your genealogical database to a GEDCOM file, follow the instructions provided in your software's manual or Help menu. You can create the GEDCOM file relatively easily; most software programs guide you through the process with a series of dialog boxes.

In addition to creating GEDCOM files to exchange with other researchers, you can generate GEDCOM files to submit to larger cooperatives that make the data from many GEDCOM files available to thousands of researchers worldwide. You can also convert your GEDCOM file to HTML so you can place the data directly on the web for others to access.

Although GEDCOM has been around for a while, efforts are underway to engineer the future of the standard. GEDCOM X (www.gedcomx.org) is a project to develop a new model to improve the capability of genealogical software and websites to share data.

Do you speak HTML?

HyperText Markup Language (or HTML) is the language of the web. HTML is a code in which text documents are written so that web browsers can read and interpret those documents, converting them into graphical images and text that you can see with a browser. HTML is a relatively easy language to learn, and many genealogists who post web pages are self-taught. If you prefer not to read about it and teach yourself by experimenting instead, you can surely find classes as well as other resources in your area that could teach you the basics of HTML. Check with a local community college for structured classes, local genealogical societies for any workshops focusing on designing and posting web pages, or the web itself for online courses. Or, check out *HTML, XHTML & CSS For Dummies,* 7th Edition, by Ed Tittel and Jeff Noble.

Deciding which treasures to include

Although the content of genealogical web pages with lots of textual information about ancestors or geographic areas may be very helpful, all-text pages won't attract the attention of your visitors. Even we get tired of sorting through and reading endless narratives on websites. We like to see things that personalize a website and are fun to look at. Graphics, icons, and photographs are ideal for this purpose. A couple of nice-looking, strategically placed photos of ancestors make a site feel more like a home.

If you have some photographs that have been scanned and saved as `.jpg` or `.gif` images or some media clips (such as video or audio files) in a format that meets the compatibility requirements for your web-hosting service, you can post them on your website.

WARNING

Just as you should be careful about posting facts about living relatives, be careful about posting photos or recordings of them. If you want to use an image that has living relatives in it, get their permission before doing so. Some people are sensitive about having their pictures posted on the web. Also, use common sense and good taste in selecting pictures for your page. Although a photo of little Susie at age 3 wearing a lampshade and dancing around in a tutu may be cute, a photo of Uncle Ed at age 63 doing the same thing may not be so endearing!

Including Your GEDCOM

Suppose that you contact others who are interested in your research findings. What's the best way to share your information with them? Certainly, you can type everything, print it, and send it to them. Or, you can export a copy of your genealogy database file — which the recipients can then import into their databases and create as many reports as they want — and save a tree in the process.

Most genealogical databases subscribe to a common standard for exporting their information called *GEenealogical Data COMmunication,* or *GEDCOM.* Beware that some genealogical databases deviate from the standard a little — making things somewhat confusing.

A *GEDCOM file* is a text file that contains your genealogical information with a set of tags that tells the genealogical database importing the information where to place it within its structure.

You may be asking, "Why is GEDCOM important?" It can save you time and energy in the process of sharing information. The next time someone asks you to send your data, you can export your genealogy data into a GEDCOM file and send it to him or her instead of typing it or saving a copy of your entire database.

WARNING

If you plan to share the contents of your genealogical database online by generating and exporting a GEDCOM file, make sure that your file is ready to share with others. By this we mean be sure that it's free from any information that could land you in the doghouse with any of your relatives — close or distant!

Some genealogical software programs enable you to indicate whether you want information on each relative included in reports and GEDCOM files. Other programs don't allow you to do this. This may mean that you need to manually scrub your GEDCOM file to remove information about all living persons.

Generating GEDCOM files

Making a GEDCOM file using most software programs is quite easy. This is true for RootsMagic Essentials, too. If you have not yet downloaded and installed RootsMagic Essentials, flip back to Chapter 1. After you have the program ready to go, try this:

1. **Open RootsMagic Essentials.**

   Usually, you can open your software by double-clicking the icon for that program or by choosing Start ➪ Programs (or Start ➪ All Programs) and selecting the particular program.

2. **Use the default database that appears, or choose File ➪ Open to open another database.**

3. **After you open the database for which you want to create a GEDCOM file, choose File ➪ Export.**

   The GEDCOM Export dialog box appears.

4. **Choose whether you want to include everyone in your database in your GEDCOM file or only selected people. You can also choose the output format and what types of information to include. Then click OK.**

   If you choose to include only selected people in your GEDCOM file, you need to complete another dialog box marking those people to include. Highlight the individual's name and then select Mark People ➪ Person to include him or her. After you select all the people you want to include, click OK.

5. **In the File Name field, type the new name for your GEDCOM file and then click Save.**

   Your GEDCOM file is created.

After a GEDCOM file is created on your hard drive, you can open it in a word processor (such as WordPad or Notepad) and review it to ensure that the information is formatted the way you want it. See Figure 14-7 for an example. Also, reviewing the file in a word processor is a good idea so you can be sure that you did not include information on living persons. After you're satisfied with the file, you can cut and paste it into an email message or send it as an attachment using your email program.

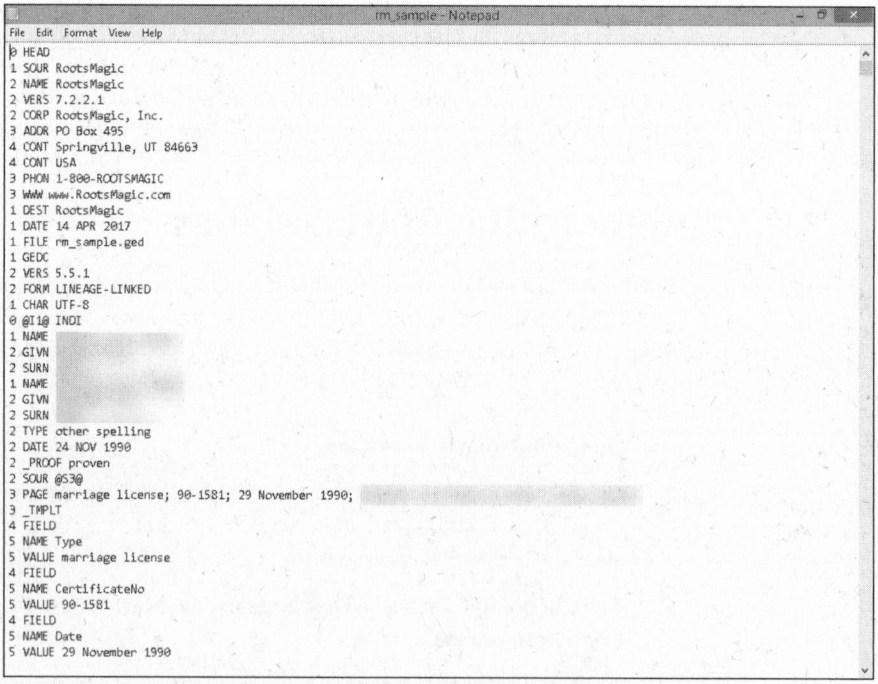

```
rm_sample - Notepad
File Edit Format View Help
0 HEAD
1 SOUR RootsMagic
2 NAME RootsMagic
2 VERS 7.2.2.1
2 CORP RootsMagic, Inc.
3 ADDR PO Box 495
4 CONT Springville, UT 84663
4 CONT USA
3 PHON 1-800-ROOTSMAGIC
3 WWW www.RootsMagic.com
1 DEST RootsMagic
1 DATE 14 APR 2017
1 FILE rm_sample.ged
1 GEDC
2 VERS 5.5.1
2 FORM LINEAGE-LINKED
1 CHAR UTF-8
0 @I1@ INDI
1 NAME
2 GIVN
2 SURN
1 NAME
2 GIVN
2 SURN
2 TYPE other spelling
2 DATE 24 NOV 1990
2 _PROOF proven
2 SOUR @S3@
3 PAGE marriage license; 90-1581; 29 November 1990;
3 _TMPLT
4 FIELD
5 NAME Type
5 VALUE marriage license
4 FIELD
5 NAME CertificateNo
5 VALUE 90-1581
4 FIELD
5 NAME Date
5 VALUE 29 November 1990
```

FIGURE 14-7: An example of a GEDCOM file opened in Notepad.

Checking a GEDCOM for possible errors

We've talked a lot about sharing your GEDCOM with others, but there are a few things you need to know about receiving GEDCOM files too. Just as you would be careful about trusting information written out in a report or chart, you need to be careful before importing someone else's GEDCOM file into your genealogical database. If they have wrong information about an ancestor you share, you could corrupt your whole database and set you back in your efforts.

Lucky for you, there's an application that can help you identify inconsistencies in a GEDCOM file. This helps you find information that may need to be corrected before or shortly after you import the file into your database. It's called gedantic (http://gedantic.org/). Here's how to use it:

1. Open a web browser and head over to http://gedantic.org/.

2. Click the Select File button.

3. Search in your computer directory for the GEDCOM file you saved earlier in this chapter. Select the file and click Open.

The gedantic program runs against the file and generates a report of potential problems. Across the top of the report are categories that will help you restrict the types of inconsistencies into a manageable number. The categories are All, Problem, Families, Missing Data, Individuals, and Sources.

4. Click on a blue box identifying a potential type of problem in the file.

This generates a list of things to review or double-check in the file to determine whether you need to fix or clean up something. For example, you can see a list of Children of Young Parents for one of Matthew's Helm-Proven GEDCOM files (see Figure 14-8). We want to review the people identified on this list to see if there might have been an error on the parent's or child's date of birth to ensure they are correct.

Creating traditional trees and reports

The process for generating a family tree or report should be similar for most genealogical software. Because we explain in earlier parts of this book how to download and install RootsMagic Essentials, that's the software we use to demonstrate the process of creating reports. If you've not yet installed it or entered or imported some data into it, you might want to check out Chapter 1. It gives step-by-step instructions for entering all your detailed family information into RootsMagic Essentials.

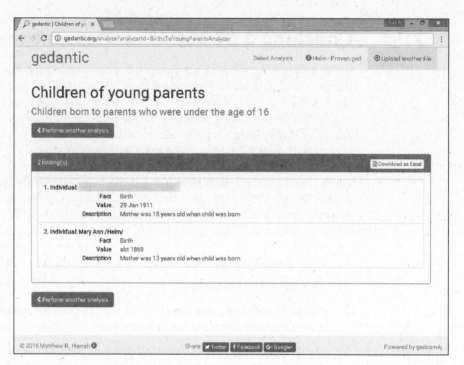

FIGURE 14-8:
A gedantic
analysis of
Children of Young
Parents in a
GEDCOM file.

Before you can generate a report, you have to find the person who will be the focus of that report. Here's a quick refresher on how to get to the appropriate person's record:

1. **Open RootsMagic Essentials and select the family file for which you want to generate a chart or report by highlighting the filename and clicking Open.**

   Usually, you can open your software by double-clicking the icon for that program or by choosing Start ⇨ Programs (or Start ⇨ All Programs) and selecting the particular program.

2. **Highlight the name of the person who will serve as the focus for your report.**

   On the Pedigree tab, highlight the name of the focal person of the family you select. For example, if Matthew wants to generate a report for his ancestor Samuel Clayton Abell, he highlights the Samuel Abell file.

3. **On the Reports menu, select a chart or report.**

   Some report types are not available in the RootsMagic Essentials version. You have to purchase the full product to generate them.

344 PART 4 Casting Your Nets in the Genealogy Sea

4. **Select the content to include in the report.**

   You can choose whether to generate the report on the current family or only selected people. You can also choose what information to include (such as spouses and children, photos, and notes) in the output. And you can manipulate some formatting options, such as layout, title, fonts, and sources.

5. **Click Generate Reports.**

   RootsMagic Essentials generates the report and displays it on your screen.

Earning a Good Citizenship Award

To be a good genealogical citizen, you should keep a few things in mind, such as maintaining privacy, respecting copyrights, and including adequate citations. In this section, we discuss these key topics.

Mandatory lecture on privacy

Sometimes, we genealogists get so caught up in dealing with the records of deceased persons that we forget one basic fact: Much of the information we've collected and put in our databases pertains to living individuals and thus is considered private. In our haste to share our information with others online, we often create our GEDCOM files and reports, and then ship them off to recipients without thinking twice about whether we may offend someone or invade his or her privacy by including personal information. The same thing goes for posting information directly to websites and in our blogs — we sometimes write the data into the family tree or include anecdotal information in our blog narratives without thinking about the consequences to living individuals. We need to be more careful.

WARNING

Why worry about privacy? Ah, allow us to enlighten you:

>> **You may invade someone's right to privacy.** We've heard horror stories about Social Security numbers of living individuals ending up in GEDCOM files that are available on the Internet. We've also heard of people who didn't know that their biological parents weren't married (to each other, anyway) and found out through an online database. Your relatives may not want you to share personal information about them with others, and they may not have given you permission to do so. The same is true for photos and video clips. Just because you're gung-ho to show the world the group photo from your family reunion does not mean that every one of your parents, siblings, aunts,

uncles, and cousins feels the same way. So don't share the information or the image without the permission of everyone involved.

» **Genealogists aren't the only people who visit genealogical Internet sites.** Private detectives and other people who search for information on living persons frequently use genealogical databases to track people. They are known to lurk about, watching for information that may help their cases. Estranged spouses may visit sites looking for a way to track down their former partners. Also, people with less-than-honorable intentions may visit a genealogical website looking for potential scam or abuse victims. And some information, such as your mother's maiden name, may help the unscrupulous carry out fraud. For these reasons, it is illegal in some states and countries to share information about living persons on the Internet without first getting each person's written permission.

When sharing genealogical information, your safest bet is to clean out (exclude) any information on living individuals from your GEDCOM file or report when sharing it with others and include only the data that pertains to people who have long been deceased — unless you've obtained written consent from living persons to share information about them. By *long been deceased*, we mean deceased for more than ten years — although the time frame could be longer depending on the sensitivity of the information. You may also want to keep in mind that the U.S. Government standard dictates that no record covered under the Privacy Act is released until it's at least 72 years old.

Respecting copyrights

Copyright is the controlling right that a person or corporation owns over the duplication and distribution of a work that the person or corporation created. Although facts themselves can't be copyrighted, *works in which facts are contained* can be. Although the fact that your grandma was born on January 1, 1900, can't be copyrighted by anyone, a report that contains this information and was created by Aunt Velma may be. If you intend to include a significant portion of Aunt Velma's report in your own document, you need to secure permission from her to use the information.

With regard to copyright and the Internet, remember that just because you found some information on a website (or other Internet resource) does not mean that it's not copyrighted. If the website contains original material along with facts, it is copyrighted to the person who created it — regardless of whether the site has a copyright notice on it!

To protect yourself from infringing on someone's copyright and possibly ending up in a legal battle, you should do the following:

>> Never copy another person's web page, email, blog, or other Internet creation (such as graphics) without his or her written consent.

>> Never print an article, a story, a report, or other material to share with your family, friends, genealogical or historical society, class, or anyone else without the creator's written consent.

>> Always assume that a resource is copyrighted.

>> Always cite sources of the information in your genealogy and on your web pages. (See the next section in this chapter for more information.)

>> Always *link* to other web pages rather than copying their content on your own website.

If you don't understand what copyright is or if you have questions about it, be sure to check out the U.S. Copyright Office's home page at www.copyright.gov. Two U.S. Copyright Office pages of particular interest at the site are Copyright Basics and Frequently Asked Questions (FAQs).

Citing your sources

We can't stress enough the importance of citing your sources when sharing information — online or through traditional means. Be sure to include references that reflect where you obtained your information; that's just as important when you share your information as it is when you research it. Not only does referencing provide the other person with leads to possible additional information, but it also gives you a place to double-check your facts if someone challenges them. Sometimes, after exchanging information with another researcher, you both notice that you have conflicting data about an ancestor. Knowing where to turn to double-check the facts (and, with any luck, find out who has the correct information) can save you time and embarrassment.

Here are some examples of ways to cite online sources of information:

>> **Email messages:** Matthew Helm, [< ezgenealogy@aol.com > or 111 Main Street, Anyplace, Anystate 11111]. "Looking for George Helm," Message to April Helm, 12 October 2009. [Message cites vital records in Helm's possession.]

>> **Newsgroups:** Matthew Helm, [< ezgenealogy@aol.com > or 111 Main Street, Anyplace, Anystate 11111]. "Computing in Genealogy" in soc.genealogy.computing, 05 June 2006.

>> **Websites:** Matthew Helm, [< ezgenealogy@aol.com > or 111 Main Street, Anyplace, Anystate 11111]. "Helm's Genealogy Toolbox." <genealogy.tbox.com> January 2004. [This site contains numerous links to other genealogical resources on the Internet. On July 12, 2010, located and checked links on Abell family; found two that were promising.]

With a note like the preceding one in brackets, you expect that your next two citations are the two websites that looked promising. For each site, you should provide notes stating exactly what you did or did not find.

TIP

Although most genealogical software programs now enable you to store source information and citations along with your data, many still don't export the source information automatically. For that reason, double-check any reports or GEDCOM files you generate to see whether your source information is included before sharing them with other researchers. If the information isn't included, create a new GEDCOM file that includes sources.

IN THIS CHAPTER

» Sharing the workload

» Joining research groups and societies

» Mining family reunions

» Locating professional researchers

» Pursuing online education

Chapter **15**

Help Wanted!

You can think of genealogical research as a journey. You may begin the journey by yourself and know exactly where you're going. After a while, you discover that the trip would go a lot faster if you had someone along for the ride or you find you need directions. In your genealogical journey, travel partners and help can take various forms — books and classrooms, others researching the same family, a research group interested in one of your family lines, or a genealogical society that coordinates the efforts of many people researching different families in a specific location.

This chapter explores ways to find (and keep) research partners, as well as ways that research groups and genealogical societies can help you meet your research goals.

Getting Out of Your Comfort Zone

We think it's only natural to want to do all your own research. After all, that way you have control over how the research is conducted, whether it's documented correctly, and what piece of information you get next. For you, it may even be comfortable to be alone in your quest. We understand that you may feel this way, but we're here to tell you that it's time to step outside your comfort zone. Although researching alone some of the time is great, don't try to do all the research yourself. As you'll discover, an awful lot of people out there are digging for answers, and it would be a shame for you not to take advantage of their work and vice versa.

By knowing the family lines and regions that other researchers are pursuing, you can coordinate your efforts with theirs — not only sharing information you've already collected but also working together toward your common goal. Maybe you live closer to a courthouse that holds records relating to your ancestor than does a distant cousin with whom you're communicating online. Maybe the cousin lives near a family gravesite that you'd like to have a photo of. Rather than duplicating efforts to collect the court records and photographs, you can arrange for each of you to get the desired items that are closest to you and then exchange copies of them over the Internet or through traditional mail.

The Shotgun Approach

WARNING

You're probably wondering how to find others with whom to share your information. Well, you could start by going through telephone books and calling everyone with the surname that you're researching. However, given how some people feel about telemarketers, we don't recommend this as a strategy.

Sending mass emails to anyone you find with your surname through one of the online white-pages sites, networking sites, or online social circles is similar to the telemarketing strategy we've just warned you against. We refer to this mass email strategy as the *shotgun approach,* and many people refer to it as spamming. You shoot out a bunch of email messages aimed in various directions, with hopes of successfully hitting one or two targets. Although you may find one or two people who answer you in a positive way, a lot of people may find such unsolicited email irritating. And, quite honestly, gleaning email addresses from online white pages is not as easy as it was even just a few years ago. Most of the online directories that allow you to search for email addresses no longer give the precise address to you. Rather, they either enable you to send an email from their sites to the individuals, leaving it up to the recipient to respond to you, or they require you to purchase the specific information about the person from them or one of their sponsors. This is their way of protecting that person's online privacy, and for some it's a means to earn money.

Instead of spending hours trying to find email addresses through online directories and following a three- or four-step process to send an initial message to someone, go to a site that focuses on genealogy to find the names of and contact information for researchers who are interested in your surname. This is a much gentler, better way to go about finding others with the same interests as you.

Also, note that we aren't saying that email directories are completely useless in genealogy. Email directories can be a good means for getting in contact with a relative whose email address you've lost or one you know is interested in your email.

Making Friends (and Keeping Them) Online

You may be wondering where to find fellow researchers. You can find them by searching query pages on the web, forums, mailing lists, and social networking sites.

If you decide to use email to contact other researchers, send them an email message introducing yourself and briefly explaining your purpose for contacting them. Be sure to include a listing of the ancestors you're researching in your message.

Before you rush out and start contacting people, however, we must offer the following sage advice:

>> **Before sending messages to a website maintainer, look around the site to see whether that person is the appropriate one to approach.** Often the person who maintains a website is indeed the one who is researching the surnames you find on that website. However, it's not unusual for site maintainers to host information on their sites for other people. If they do, they typically have separate contact addresses for those individuals and an explanation that they're not personally researching those surnames. Some even go so far as to post notices on their sites stating that they don't entertain research questions. When you see a list of surnames on a site, don't automatically assume that the website maintainer is the person to contact. Look around a little to ensure that you're addressing the most appropriate person.

>> **Make your messages brief and to the point.** Email messages that run five or six pages long can overwhelm some people. If the person you send the message to is interested in your information and responds positively to you, you can send one or more detailed messages at a future date.

>> **Ensure that your message is detailed enough for the recipients to decide whether your info relates to their research and whether they can help you.** Include names, dates, and places as appropriate.

>> **Use net etiquette, or** *netiquette,* **when you create your messages.** Remember, email can be an impersonal medium. Although you may mean one thing, someone who doesn't know you may mistakenly misinterpret your message. (For more on netiquette, see the nearby sidebar, "Netiquette: Using your manners online.")

NETIQUETTE: USING YOUR MANNERS ONLINE

Part of being a fine, upstanding member of the online genealogy community is communicating effectively and politely on the Internet. Online communication is often hampered by the fact that you can't see the people with whom you're corresponding, and you can't hear the intonation of their voices to determine what emotions they're expressing. To avoid misunderstandings, follow some simple guidelines — called *netiquette* — when writing messages:

- Don't send a message that you wouldn't want posted on a bulletin board at work or the library or that you wouldn't want printed in a newsletter. You should expect that every email you send is potentially public.

- Make sure that you don't violate any copyright laws by sending large portions of written works through email.

- If you receive a *flame* (a heated message usually sent to provoke a response), try to ignore it. Usually, no good comes from responding to a flame.

- Be careful when you respond to messages. Instead of replying to an individual, you may be replying to an entire group of people. Checking the To line before you click the Send button is always a good idea.

- Use sentence case when you write email messages. USING ALL UPPERCASE LETTERS INDICATES SHOUTING! The exception to this guideline is when you send a query and place your surnames in all-uppercase letters (for example, George HELM).

- If you participate in a mailing list and you reply with a message that is most likely of interest to only one person, consider sending that person a message individually rather than emailing the list as a whole.

- When you're joking, use smileys or type <grins> or <g>, but use these symbols sparingly to increase their effectiveness. A *smiley* is an emoticon that looks like :-). (Turn the book on its right side if you can't see the face.) *Emoticons* are graphics created by combinations of keys to express an emotion in an email. Here are a few emoticons that you may run into:

  :-) Happy, smiling

  ;-) Wink, ironic

  :-> Sarcastic

  8-) Wearing glasses

  :-(Sad, unhappy

  :-< Disappointed

  :-o Frightened, surprised

  :-() Mustache

>> **Don't disclose personal information that could violate a person's privacy.**
Information such as addresses, birth dates, and Social Security numbers for
living persons is considered private and should not be freely shared with
other researchers. Also, we don't recommend that you send much personal
information about yourself until you know the recipient a lot better. When
first introducing yourself, your name and email address should suffice, along
with the information about the deceased ancestors you're researching.

>> **Get permission before forwarding messages from other researchers.**
Sometimes researchers may provide information that they don't want made
available to the general public. Asking permission before forwarding a
message to a third party eliminates any potential problems with violating the
trust of your fellow researchers.

Joining a Herd: Research Groups

If your relatives are tired of hearing about your genealogy research trips or the
information that you found on Great-Uncle Beauford, but you'd like to share your
triumphs with someone, you may be ready to join a research group.

Research groups consist of any number of people who coordinate their research and
share resources to achieve success. These groups may start conducting research
because they share a surname, family branch, or geographic location. Individuals
who live geographically close to each other may make up a research group, or the
group may consist of people who have never personally met each other but are
interested in descendants of one particular person. Research groups may have a
variety of goals and may have a formal or an informal structure.

A good example of a research group is one that Matthew discovered shortly after
he posted his first web page many years back. An individual who was researching
one of his surnames on the East Coast of the United States contacted him. After
exchanging a few emails, Matthew discovered that this individual was part of a
small research group studying the origins of several branches of the Helm surname. Each member of the group contributes the results of his or her personal
research and provides any information that he or she finds, which may be of use
to other members of the group. Over the years, the group has continued to work
together and expanded their efforts. The group as a whole has sponsored research
by professional genealogists in other countries to discover more about their
ancestors there, and they've spun off a more formal research group that focuses
solely on molecular research (DNA-based) of the Helm bloodlines. The vast majority of the communication for these two research groups is through email.

Becoming a solid member of geographical societies

Genealogical societies can be great places to discover research methods and to coordinate your research. Several types of societies exist. They range from the more traditional geographical or surname-based societies to *cybersocieties* (societies that exist only on the Internet) that are redefining the way people think about genealogical societies.

Chapter 6 introduces geography-based genealogical societies as groups that can help you discover resources in a specific area in which your ancestors lived, or as groups in your hometown that can help you discover how to research effectively. However, local genealogical societies can provide another service to their members. These societies often coordinate local research efforts of the members in the form of projects.

These projects can take many forms. For example, the Illinois State Genealogical Society (www.ilgensoc.org) is working on several projects, including creating a database of county marriage records, updating a list of Illinois pioneers, forming a list of all cemeteries in the state (see Figure 15-1), and compiling indexes of Civil War, World War I, and World War II certificates issued.

Smaller groups of members sometimes work on projects in addition to the society's official projects. For example, you may belong to a county genealogical society and decide to join with a few members to write a history of the pioneers who settled a particular township in the county.

To locate geographical societies, follow our advice in Chapter 6 or check out the site of a genealogical-society federation such as one of these:

>> **Federation of Genealogical Societies, Society Hall page:** www.fgs.org/cstm_societyHall.php

>> **Federation of Family History Societies:** www.ffhs.org.uk

Rooting for family and surname associations

In addition to geographically based associations, you can find groups tied to names or family groups. Typically, they're referred to as — you've probably already guessed — surname or family associations or research groups.

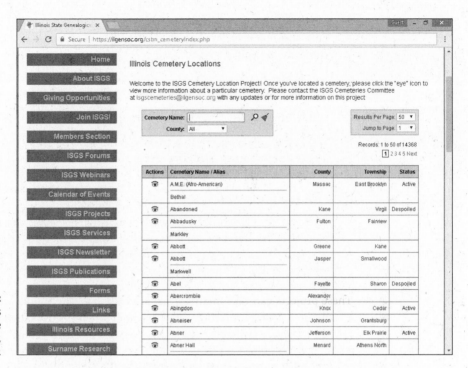

Family associations also frequently sponsor projects that coordinate the efforts of several researchers. These projects may focus on the family or surname in a specific geographic area or point in time, or they may attempt to collect information about every individual possessing the surname throughout time and then place the information in a shared database.

To find family and surname associations, your best bet is to visit a comprehensive genealogical website, a search engine, or a site that specializes in surnames, such as SurnameWeb at `www.surnameweb.org`.

The following steps show you how to find groups pertaining to a surname on the site:

1. **Launch your web browser and go to the SurnameWeb site at**
   `www.surnameweb.org`.

   After the page loads, you see a search field and the letters of the alphabet near the top center of the page.

2. **Click the letter of the alphabet that's the first letter of the surname that you're researching.**

   For example, say that the surname you're researching begins with the letter *P*. Find the link to the letter *P* and click it. This action brings up a web page with the *P* index.

3. **Click the next level link corresponding to the first and second letter of the surname you're researching.**

   We selected the link labeled Po. You see a list of surname links that begin with the letters *Po.*

4. **Scroll through the list and click a surname link.**

   We wanted to find sites relating to the surname *Pollard,* so we clicked the link for the Pollard surname, which displayed a Results page entitled Pollard Surname Resource Center.

5. **Choose a site to visit.**

   Scroll down past all the links to search other commercial websites until you reach the links you're most interested in. We wanted to see the links that would take us directly to personal and group web pages containing information about people named Pollard, so we selected the link titled Pollard Genealogy Web Pages under Pollard Surname Search.

In addition to using comprehensive genealogy sites and specialized surname sites, you can use other strategies to identify possible research groups. One way to find research groups pertaining to surnames is to visit a one-name studies index. You can find a list of one-name studies sites at the Guild of One-Name Studies page (www.one-name.org).

Joining the crowd — Crowd Sourced Indexing, that is

You can use steps in the preceding sections for finding research groups in the form of genealogical societies and surname studies, and many of the groups you find have projects on which you can become a contributor. But there is another, newer way to find indexing projects, and it may save you time.

Crowd Source Indexing (http://csi.idogenealogy.com/), which is in beta testing, is a collective of genealogical projects to index a variety of resources. This effort enables individuals across the globe to help with indexing projects for all types of records and in several locations. Volunteers who sign up to help are assigned a page at a time for the project in which they are interested. After indexing the page, they can choose whether to continue helping index records that are included in the Crowd Source Indexing site.

Gathering Kinfolk: Using the Family Reunion for Research

You may have noticed that throughout this book, we strongly recommend that you interview relatives to gather information about your ancestors both to use as leads in finding records and to enhance your genealogy. Well, what better way to gather information from relatives than by attending a family reunion?

Family reunions can add a lot to your research because you find many relatives all in one place, and typically most are eager to visit. A reunion is an efficient way to collect stories, photographs, databases (if others in the family research and keep their records in their computers), and even copies of records. You might even find some people interested in researching the family along with you. A family reunion can be great fun, too.

When you attend your next family reunion, be sure to take along your notebook, list of interview questions (refer to Chapter 2 if you haven't developed your list yet), and camera. You can take some printed charts from your genealogical database, too — we bet that lots of your relatives will be interested in seeing them.

Rent-a-Researcher

A time may come when you've exhausted all the research avenues directly available to you and need help that family, friends, and society members can't provide. Maybe all the records you need to get past a research brick wall are in a distant place, or maybe you have too many other obligations and not enough time to research personally. You needn't fret. Professional researchers are happy to help you.

Professional researchers are people to whom you pay a fee to dig around and find information for you. They can retrieve specific records that you identify, or they can prepare an entire report on a family line by using all the resources available. And, as you might expect, the amount that you pay depends on the level of service that you require. Professional researchers are especially helpful when you need records from locations to which you cannot travel conveniently.

When looking for a professional researcher, you want to find someone who is reputable and experienced in the area in which you need help. Here's a list of questions you may want to ask when shopping around for a professional researcher:

>> **Is the researcher certified or accredited and, if so, by what organization?**
In the genealogy field, certifications function a bit differently than in other

fields. Rather than receiving a certification based on coursework, genealogical certifications are based on demonstrated research skills. You find two main certifying bodies in the field: the Board for Certification of Genealogists (www.bcgcertification.org) and the International Commission for the Accreditation of Professional Genealogists (www.icapgen.org).

The Board for Certification of Genealogists (BCG) awards two credentials: Certified Genealogist and Certified Genealogical Lecturer. The credentials are awarded based on a peer-review process — meaning that a group of individuals possessing the credentials evaluate a research project of an applicant.

You might also run into some old certifications such as Certified Lineage Specialist (CLS), Certified American Indian Lineage Specialist (CAILS), Certified Genealogical Records Specialist (CGRS), and Certified Genealogical Instructor (CGI), which are no longer used by the organization.

The International Commission for the Accreditation of Professional Genealogists (ICAPGen) awards the Accredited Genealogist (AG) credential. The accreditation program originally was established by the Family History Department of the Church of Jesus Christ of Latter-day Saints. In 2000, the program was launched as an independent organization called ICAPGen. To become accredited, an applicant must submit a research project and take an examination. Accredited Genealogists are certified in a geographical or subject-matter area. So, you want to make sure that the accreditation that the researcher possesses matches your research question.

Some professional researchers do not hold either of these credentials but might hold a professional degree such as a Masters in Library and Information Science or advanced history degree from an accredited college or university. Depending on the research area, they could be just as proficient as a credentialed genealogist.

>> **How many years of experience does the researcher have researching?** In general, we tend to think of a person as improving in knowledge and efficiency as he or she has more years of experience researching. But the answer to this question needs to be considered in context of some other questions. The researcher might have only a little time researching genealogies for others but might have an educational degree that required historical research experience.

>> **What is the researcher's educational background?** The methods for researching and the type of reports that you can get from an individual can be directly influenced by his or her educational background. If the researcher has a degree in history, you may get more anecdotal material relating to the times and places in which your ancestor lived. If the researcher attended the school of hard knocks (and doesn't have a formal education per se but has lots of experience researching), you may get specific, bare-bones facts about your ancestor.

» **Does the researcher have any professional affiliations?** In other words, does he or she belong to any professional genealogical organizations and, if so, which ones? Much like the question dealing with certification or accreditation, a researcher's willingness to belong to a professional organization shows a serious commitment. One organization to look for is membership in the Association of Professional Genealogists (www.apgen.org). The APG is an umbrella organization of all types of researchers and those providing professional services. It includes researchers credentialed under both BCG and ICAPGen, as well as other noncredentialed researchers. All members of the APG agree to be bound by a code of ethics and meet certain research standards.

» **What foreign languages does the researcher speak fluently?** This is an important question if you need research conducted in another country. Some research firms send employees to other countries to gather information, but you need the reassurance that the employee has the qualifications necessary to obtain accurate information.

» **What records and resources does the researcher have access to?** Again, you want the reassurance that the researcher can obtain accurate information and from reliable sources. You probably don't want to pay a researcher to simply read the same documents that you have access to at your local library and put together a summary.

» **What is the professional researcher's experience in the area where you need help?** For example, if you need help interviewing distant relatives in a foreign country, has he or she conducted interviews in the past? Or, if you need records pertaining to an ethnic or religious group, does the researcher have experience researching those types of records?

» **How does the researcher charge?** You need to know how you're going to be charged — by the record, by the hour, or by the project. Is there a downpayment due before researching begins? And it's helpful to know up front what methods of payment the researcher accepts so that you're prepared when payment time comes. And you should ask what you can do if you're dissatisfied with the researcher's services (although we hope you never need to know this).

» **Is the researcher currently working on other projects and, if so, how many and what kinds?** It's perfectly reasonable to ask how much time the researcher can devote to your research project and when you can get results. If the researcher tells you that it's going to take a year to get a copy of a single birth certificate from an agency in the town where he or she lives, you might want to rethink hiring that person.

» **Does the researcher have references you can contact?** We think that a researcher's willingness to provide references speaks to his or her ethics. And we recommend that you contact one or two of the references to find out what exactly they like about this researcher and whether they see the researcher as having any pitfalls of which you should be aware.

One way to find professional researchers is to look for them on comprehensive genealogy sites. Another is to consult an online directory of researchers, such as the Association of Professional Genealogists (`www.apgen.org/directory/index.html`) directory. Follow these steps to check the APG directory:

1. **Using your web browser, go to the APG site at `www.apgen.org`.**

2. **Click the link from the list in the left column of the page under the Find a Specialist heading.**

   For example, we looked for a researcher who specializes in adoption.

3. **Click the link for a researcher who, based on the description posted, looks promising.**

   Figure 15-2 shows the researchers specializing in adoption.

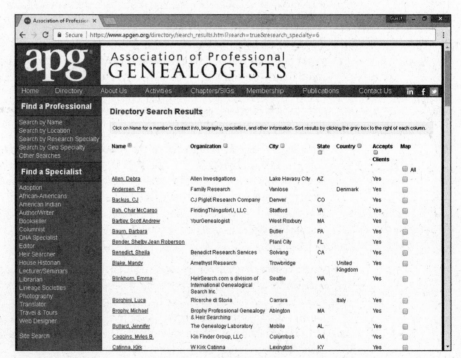

FIGURE 15-2: Researchers specializing in adoption at the Association of Professional Genealogists site.

When you find a professional researcher, make your initial contact. Be as specific as possible about your needs. That helps the researcher pinpoint exactly what he or she needs to do and makes it easier to calculate how much it will cost you.

DNA Consulting

In addition to generalized genealogical researchers, some paid researchers specialize in helping you understand your DNA tests. If you've taken one or more DNA tests and you just don't understand what it all means, you might consider hiring one of these DNA consultants. Some have built companies that will create a report that interprets your DNA results after they've been processed by a lab. The International Society of Genetic Genealogy maintains a list of DNA consultants at www.isogg.org/consult.htm.

Be sure to get answers to the following questions before engaging a consultant:

>> What are the academic qualifications of the consultant? Does the consultant have a degree in genetics, biology, or a related field?

>> How long has the consultant been involved in genetic genealogy?

>> What is the assistance that you require? Some consultants specialize in a particular type of DNA analysis.

>> Does the consultant have a relationship with a specific testing company?

>> As DNA research changes over time, will the consultant update the research as new information becomes available, and how much will the consultant charge for that service?

Helping Yourself

Earlier sections of this chapter dealt with finding research assistance in the form of others — finding contributors via societies and projects, and hiring researchers. But research assistance can come in the form of self-help, too. Self-help allows you to discover new or different ways to research, or new perspectives on existing resources that might help you over a research hump.

Reading up on genealogical things

In the past couple of decades, there has been an explosion in the number of online books available. You no longer have to go to a physical library to read up on research and documentation methods, or to dig for information on a geographic location or specific set of people. There's everything from instructional guides to history books to human interest non-fiction that might contribute to your genealogical research. There are a couple of online reading resources worth mentioning: Kindle Unlimited and Google Books.

Kindle Unlimited (`https://www.amazon.com/kindle-dbs/hz/signup?_encoding=UTF8&*entries*=0&*Version*=1`) is a service offered by Amazon.com. For a monthly subscription fee, you can read or listen to as many online books as your heart desires. The collection has over one million book titles in print, and thousands of audio books. Also, it has a substantial collection of magazines. If you don't have a Kindle device per se, don't fret. You can download the free Kindle application to another variety of tablet, smartphone, or computer.

Google Books (`https://books.google.com/`) is a combination digital library and searching service available from — you guessed it — Google. You can go directly to Google Books and enter a search term, then scan the results. Or you can log into your Google account (associated with your gmail account if you have one), then start the search process. When you enter the search terms and a list of results generates, it will include out-of-print books that are available for viewing on Google, as well as books that you can purchase or check-out/borrow printed copies.

Getting educated online

Digital libraries and accessing printed materials isn't the only form of self-help. There are online courses available too. You might consider the resources available at two sites that deliver instructional material over the web: the Family History Guide and Ancestry Academy.

The Family History Guide (`www.thefhguide.com`) is a free resource from FamilySearch.com. The learning content at this site is divided into nine projects: Family Tree, Memories, Descendancy, Discover, Indexing, Help, Technology, DNA, and Countries and Ethnic Groups. From there, you can drill down to more specific topics, each of which has a training plan with links to research projects, tips, videos, and records.

Let's explore how to use the Family History Guide. Say we need assistance in learning how to research Native American ancestors. Follow these steps to see what the Family History Guide offers:

1. **Using your web browser, go to Family History Guide (www.thefhguide.com)**

2. **Click the link Countries and Ethnic about mid-way down the main page.**

3. **Scroll down and click on the link for Native American in the Ethnic section at the bottom of the Countries/Ethnic page.**

The resulting page, Project 9: Native American, is divided into four sections, or Goals: Get Started (Learn About Native American Research), Special Topics, Search Records, and Get Help. Read through the guide and follow any links to additional resources and records that look useful.

Figure 15-3 shows Goal 1: Learn About Native American Research in the Family History Guide.

FIGURE 15-3: The Get Started section of the Native American research project at the Family History Guide.

Similar to FamilySearch.com, Ancestry.com also offers online instructions for researching. Ancestry Academy (https://www.ancestry.com/academy/courses/recommended) offers video courses online for a variety of topics, including getting started, documenting findings in Ancestry family trees, how to use specific types of records, and DNA research.

5

The Part of Tens

IN THIS PART . . .

Discover genealogical sites that you'll want to visit time and again.

Find useful mobile applications for family history.

Chapter **16**

Ten Sites Worth a Visit

There are a lot of unique sites on the Web that could be useful to your research, or are interesting to check out, at the very least. The following sections describe just a few that might give you a new perspective on doing your family history research.

rootsfinder

www.rootsfinder.com

There are more and more sites for creating your online family tree. Each has different functionality that sets it apart from the rest. rootsfinder is such a site. One of the drawbacks of the FamilySearch online family tree is your lack of control over it. If someone adds or deletes something, it affects your tree whether you like it or not. Fortunately, rootsfinder can integrate with your FamilySearch online family tree, but it also allows you to control what comes in from FamilySearch and, more importantly, what does not.

Some other key features of rootsfinder include hints from other online sites, a "Web Clipper" that copies data from genealogy sites directly into your tree (reducing transcription errors), and a nifty evidence analysis report that helps identify conflicting information. The online tree also has a Pinterest-like media wall and a video maker, allowing you to tell your family's story with narration and music.

FamilySearch Help Center

```
https://familysearch.org/ask/
```

The FamilySearch Help Center contains several resources to help with your research. The Center covers support for FamilySearch products, live research assistance from individuals with expertise in particular areas, getting started tutorials, a learning center with online courses, and the FamilySearch Research Wiki. With more than 85,000 articles related to genealogical research, the Family-Search Research Wiki is an invaluable guide to assist you with your research. Whether you're looking for guidance on a specific locality, a type of record, or an ethnic group, or if you need general help with research, you should be able to find an applicable article. The site is set up like a typical wiki and is maintained by the genealogical community at large.

WeRelate

```
www.werelate.org/wiki/Main_Page
```

WeRelate started as a wiki developed jointly by the Foundation for On-Line Genealogy and the Allen County Public Library. It accepts contributions from the user community, mostly in the form of pages on specific ancestors. It claims to be the largest genealogy wiki with ancestor pages numbering more than 2,800,000.

kindex

```
https://app.kindex.org/
```

The objective of kindex is to create a searchable archive of source material. You can add sources to kindex in two ways — through the kindex Add a Record screen or by adding a Memory from FamilySearch.org. After a record is added, you can transcribe the contents of the record using the index screen. After transcription, you can tag key pieces of information such as name, place, and date. When it's indexed, the record can be shared (if you desire) with a link or through social media. You can even print the record with a QR-code PDF for quick access.

One-Step Webpages by Stephen P. Morse

```
http://stevemorse.org
```

Key resources available online can often be confusing to use. Stephen Morse's one-step tools offer time-saving shortcuts for getting the most out of these sites. Resources at the site include one-steps for:

>> Ellis Island and Castle Garden

>> U.S. censuses

>> Canadian and British censuses

>> New York census

>> Birth, death, and other vital records

>> Calendar, sunrise/sunset, maps

>> Dealing with characters in foreign alphabets

>> Holocaust and Eastern Europe

>> Genetic genealogy

>> Creating your own Search Applications and Viewers

Photogrammar

```
http://photogrammar.yale.edu/
```

Looking for photographs from 1935 to 1945? The Yale University Photogrammar site simplifies the search for photographs taken by the United States Farm Security Administration and the Office of War Information. The photographs chronicle life during the Great Depression and World War II. A searchable interactive map shows the geographic location for 90,000 photographs.

Story Corps

```
https://storycorps.org
```

Story Corps is a collection of interviews of over 250,000 Americans who wanted to leave a legacy to the next generation. Projects included on the website focus on individuals with serious illnesses, youth with experience in the juvenile and adult justice system, stories of the lesbian, gay, bisexual, transgender, and queer (LGBTQ) community, and September 11th initiative.

American Battle Monuments Commission

```
https://www.abmc.gov/
```

The American Battle Monuments Commission is responsible for the care of overseas cemeteries and memorials honoring the United States Armed Forces. The website has information on the individual cemeteries and monuments and hosts a database of burials with the names of over 218,000 individuals buried at those sites. The database is a good place to check if you have an ancestor who "disappears" around the time of World War I or II. For the stateside equivalent, see the National Cemetery Administration Nationwide Gravesite Locator at http://gravelocator.cem.va.gov/index.html.

Atlas of the Historical Geography of the United States

```
http://dsl.richmond.edu/historicalatlas/
```

A historical atlas can be a good tool to use to get context of the life of your ancestor. The Atlas of the Historical Geography of the United States displays nearly 700 maps from the atlas, first published in 1932. The maps are georectified — that is, they are warped so that they can be layered on top of a digital map. The site contains a variety of maps touching on topics such as:

>> The natural environment

>> Cartography, 1492–1867

>> Indians, 1567–1930

>> Explorations in the West and Southwest, 1535-1852

>> Settlement, population, and towns, 1650–1790

>> States, territories, and cities, 1790–1930

>> Population, 1790–1930

- » Colleges, universities, and churches, 1775–1890
- » Boundaries, 1607–1927
- » Political parties and opinions, 1788–1930
- » Distribution of wealth, 1799–1928
- » Military history, 1689–1919

ArchiveGrid

```
https://beta.worldcat.org/archivegrid/
```

Sometimes primary source information can be hard to find if it is housed in non-government archive. ArchiveGrid contains over 4,000,000 records of historical documents, personal papers, and family histories housed at over 1,000 institutions. Also, on the site is a searchable map so that you can see what archives are physically close to an area that you are visiting.

» Saving family interviews and photos using a smart device

» Carrying your reference library in a handy way

Chapter **17**

Ten Mobile Applications for Genealogy Research

Perhaps you are one of those people so addicted to genealogy that you need to constantly be in a state of research. If so, you don't want to have to lug a computer around with you everywhere you go. However, if you have a smart phone, here are some apps that might help you satisfy your genealogy craving while you are on the go.

Ancestry

If you have an online family tree at Ancestry.com then this app is a must. It syncs with your online family trees and you can add new family members, upload source documents, and research Ancestry.com hints.

There are three sections to the app — Hints, Tree, and DNA. The Hints view contains a listing of available tips or clues that you can scroll through and review when you have the time. The Tree view is similar to the online Family Tree view, and you can select an individual to see the LifeStory page, Family page, or Gallery. The DNA section shows information on your genetic ancestry, DNA matches, and DNA circles (if you have tested with AncestryDNA).

Within the Tree view, there are some features that provide the ability to search records directly from the app (especially useful if you have a subscription to Ancestry.com). The app's search interface also allows you to filter the results to cut down on the number of items to review. In the app's settings, you can choose the default family tree displayed by the app, and you can elect to create a new family tree. Figure 17-1 shows the Family page for William Henry Abell. Ancestry also has a few other apps including:

>> **Ancestry Academy:** The app provides training videos on genealogical research and how to use Ancestry.com.

>> **AncestryDNA:** If you have tested your DNA with Ancestry, the app will provide the ethnicity estimate and show you your matches.

>> **Find a Grave:** The companion app to the online cemetery website.

>> **Shoebox:** The app is for taking pictures with your phone and adding it to individuals in your online family tree.

>> **We're Related:** Purely for entertainment purposes, the app hypothesizes how you are related to celebrities based upon online trees (which may or may not be substantiated through sources).

FIGURE 17-1:
Ancestry app
Family Page.

FamilySearch Tree

FamilySearch Tree is the companion app to the FamilySearch Family Tree website. The app provides a pedigree view of your ancestors and you can build your family tree directly from the app. You can view your ancestors with tasks associated with them and search the collection of historical records and attach them to your tree through the app. The app has a memories screen that allows you to upload photos, audio files, stories, or documents. Also, you can view Adobe PDF versions of pedigree, family, family with sources, fan and portrait pedigree charts. Figure 17-2 shows the Pedigree view within the app. FamilySearch also produces the Memories app that allows you to save photographs, stories, documents, and audio files.

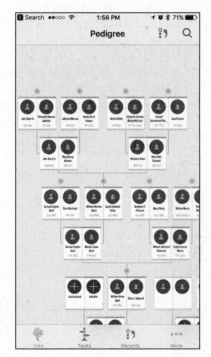

FIGURE 17-2: The FamilySearch Tree Pedigree View.

RootsMagic

The RootsMagic app is a companion to the RootsMagic software available on personal computers. Rather than syncing with a web application, like Ancestry and FamilySearch Tree, RootsMagic uses the actual RootsMagic file.

You can place the file on your smart phone/tablet by uploading the RootsMagic file on your computer to Dropbox (www.dropbox.com) or by transferring it through iTunes (for Apple devices). As it is a copy of your RootsMagic file, you won't be able to change items on the device. Along with information about your ancestors, you can also find lists of sources, things to-do, research, addresses, repositories, and places. There are also nifty tools in the app including date calculator, relationship calculator, soundex calculator, and a perpetual calendar.

BillionGraves

The BillionGraves app serves two purposes. The first is a way to photograph cemeteries and enter the information into the BillionGraves database — if you have registered at the site. The second is a search mechanism for cemeteries already documented in the database. As for the latter, you can search for individuals or you can pull up a cemetery. There is even a clever function to route you to the location of a cemetery using the mapping application on your phone once you have found an individual grave you are interested in visiting. Figure 17-3 shows the location of William Henry Abell's grave in Sugar Grove Cemetery.

FIGURE 17-3: Map of William Henry Abell's grave in the BillionGraves app.

Evernote

If you want easy access to your research notes and documents, consider using Evernote and its companion app. With the app, you can create notes and embed photographs or audio from your phone. You can add tags to the notes to make them easier to locate the next time that you need them and you can add a location to the notes to georeferenced them. After the notes are synced, you can access them with any device (including computers) that supports Evernote.

The Family Nexus

While researching on the road, we sometimes forget all of the people who are associated with the particular place that we are researching. We might be somewhere researching the Abell family, forgetting that someone from the Helm family also lived in the area. That is where The Family Nexus app is useful. If you have an account on FamilySearch tree, you can hook the app up to your online family tree and it will plot on the map where specific events occurred. For example, Figure 17-4 shows a map of the area around Wapella, Illinois, where four events noted in the family tree occurred.

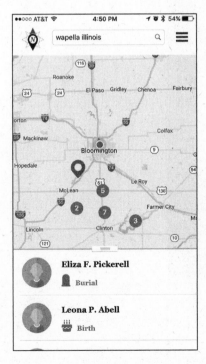

FIGURE 17-4: Events around Wapella, Illinois through The Family Nexus.

Saving Memories Forever

In Chapter 2, we talk about interviewing your relatives to get nuggets of information that will power your family history research. Saving Memories Forever is an app and website that together assist you in asking specific questions and saving the recordings. There is a free version of the app/site that limits the number of storytellers to two. The fee-based version provides additional tools, including expanded search capabilities, the ability to add photos and Word documents to stories, unlimited storytellers, and backup for your recordings.

The app contains categories such as Childhood, Teenage Years, Celebrations, Religion, and Jokes. Within each category are specific questions that you can ask. The recording interface, shown in Figure 17-5, is simple and easy to navigate. After you have recorded the interview, it is uploaded to the Saving Memories Forever website. The app also provides the opportunity for you to upload the interview to Facebook. After the interview is posted to the website, you can create tags to make recordings easier to find.

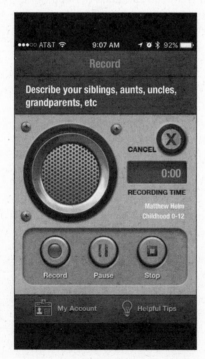

FIGURE 17-5:
The easy recording interface for Saving Memories Forever.

OldNews USA

The OldNews USA app for Andriod helps you locate newspaper articles within the Library of Congress "Chronicling America" collection. This collection contains more than 11 million newspaper pages from 1789 to 1922. You simply put in a person's name, date range, and location and the app suggests newspapers that are the most likely have articles about your ancestor. The app then creates a search suggestion that you use to query the Library of Congress site. A similar app on iPhone is American Chronicle.

QromaTag

Have you scanned hundreds of photographs only to not be able to find the one that you want when you need it? The solution may be QromaTag — an app that allows you to say indexing terms such as name, location, and date while you scan with your device. It then turns the items into industry standard metadata that is stored with the scan. You can import your GEDCOM or contact list to tag individuals in your photographs. QromaTag also allows you to embed up to 2,000 characters per story within your image.

Kindle

A handy app to have on hand while researching in the field is the Kindle app. (See Figure 17-6.) We like to have our favorite research "books" handy, just in case they are needed for a quick reference. One of the Kindle books that we use a lot is *Evidence Explained: Citing History Sources from Artifacts to Cyberspace* by Elizabeth Shown Mills. Using this work ensures that we cite our sources in the best way while we are researching, saving time in correcting sources later.

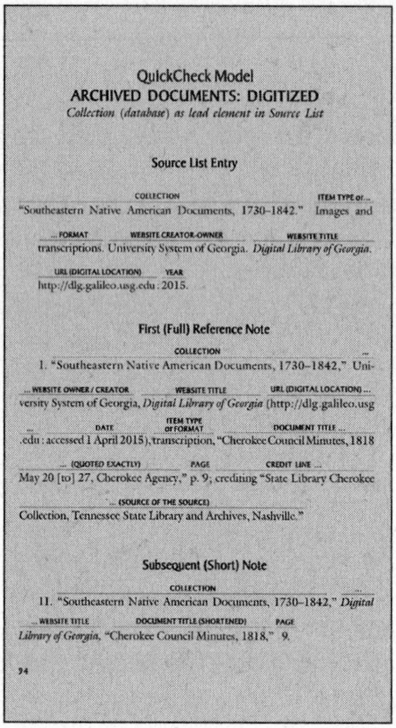

QuickCheck Model
ARCHIVED DOCUMENTS: DIGITIZED
Collection (database) as lead element in Source List

Source List Entry

COLLECTION   ITEM TYPE or...
"Southeastern Native American Documents, 1730–1842."   Images and

...FORMAT   WEBSITE CREATOR-OWNER   WEBSITE TITLE
transcriptions. University System of Georgia. *Digital Library of Georgia.*

URL (DIGITAL LOCATION)   YEAR
http://dlg.galileo.usg.edu : 2015.

First (Full) Reference Note

COLLECTION
1. "Southeastern Native American Documents, 1730–1842," Uni-

...WEBSITE OWNER / CREATOR   WEBSITE TITLE   URL (DIGITAL LOCATION) ...
versity System of Georgia, *Digital Library of Georgia* [http://dlg.galileo.usg

...   DATE   ITEM TYPE   DOCUMENT TITLE ...
                                    or FORMAT
.edu : accessed 1 April 2015), transcription, "Cherokee Council Minutes, 1818

... (QUOTED EXACTLY)   PAGE   CREDIT LINE ...
May 20 [to] 27, Cherokee Agency," p. 9, crediting "State Library Cherokee

... (SOURCE OF THE SOURCE)
Collection, Tennessee State Library and Archives, Nashville."

Subsequent (Short) Note

COLLECTION
11. "Southeastern Native American Documents, 1730–1842," *Digital*

WEBSITE TITLE   DOCUMENT TITLE (SHORTENED)   PAGE
Library of Georgia, "Cherokee Council Minutes, 1818," 9.

94

FIGURE 17-6:
A quick citation
check using the
Kindle app.

Index

Symbols and Numerics

A

About the Authors

Matthew L. Helm is the chief executive officer of Boneyard Creek Heritage, Inc., a family and local history services company. He is the creator and maintainer of the award-winning Helm's Genealogy Toolbox, the Helm/Helms Family Research Page, and a variety of other websites. Matthew speaks at national genealogical conventions and lectures to genealogical and historical societies. He holds an A.B. in history and an M.S. in library and information science from the University of Illinois at Urbana-Champaign.

April Leigh Helm is the president of Boneyard Creek Heritage, Inc. She also works as a systems analyst for a Fortune 500 company. April lectures on genealogy and other topics for various conferences and groups. She holds a B.S. in journalism and an Ed.M. in higher education administration from the University of Illinois at Urbana-Champaign.

Together, the Helms have coauthored several books in addition to the eight editions of *Genealogy Online For Dummies*. These books include *Family Tree Maker For Dummies*, *Your Official America Online Guide to Genealogy Online*, *AARP Genealogy Online: Tech to Connect*, and *Get Your Degree Online*.

Dedication

For Kyleakin and Cambrian: Our future in genealogy.

Author's Acknowledgments

We want to acknowledge Katie Mohr, Christopher Morris, and Sharon Mealka. They've been a great team to work with, and without them this edition would not exist.

Publisher's Acknowledgments

Executive Editor: Katie Mohr

Project Editor: Christopher Morris

Copy Editor: Christopher Morris

Technical Editor: Sharon Mealka

Editorial Assistant: Susan Simmons

Production Editor: Antony Sami

Sr. Editorial Assistant: Cherie Case

Cover Image: © MishaKaminsky/Getty Images